HISTORY OF AMERICAN
PHYSICAL EDUCATION AND SPORT

ABOUT THE AUTHOR

Paula D. Welch is a professor of Exercise and Sport Sciences at the University of Florida. She completed degrees at the Florida State University, George Peabody College of Vanderbilt University, and the University of North Carolina at Greensboro. Her postdoctoral courses have been taken at the Institute of Irish Studies at Trinity College in Dublin, Ireland and the History Department at the University of Florida. Her research focuses upon the history of women in sport, the Olympic Games, and sport governance. In addition to numerous articles and research presentations, she serves as Vice-Chair of the Education Committee of the United States Olympic Committee. She has also served as Chair of the History of Sport and Physical Education Academy of the National Association of Sport and Physical Education.

HISTORY OF AMERICAN PHYSICAL EDUCATION AND SPORT

Second Edition

By

PAULA D. WELCH, ED.D.

College of Health and Human Performance
University of Florida
Gainesville, Florida

CHARLES C THOMAS • PUBLISHER
Springfield • Illinois • U.S.A.

...ibuted Throughout the World by

CHARLES C THOMAS • PUBLISHER
2600 South First Street
Springfield, Illinois 62794-9265

© *1996 by* CHARLES C THOMAS • PUBLISHER

ISBN 0-398-06565-9 (cloth)
ISBN 0-398-06566-7 (paper)

Library of Congress Catalog Card Number: 95-25845
First Edition, 1981
Second Edition, 1996

With **THOMAS BOOKS** *careful attention is given to all details of manufacturing
and design. It is the Publisher's desire to present books that are satisfactory as to
their physical qualities and artistic possibilities and appropriate for their particular
use.* THOMAS BOOKS *will be true to those laws of quality that assure a good
name and good will.*

Printed in the United States of America
SC-R-3

Library of Congress Cataloging-in-Publication Data

Welch, Paula D.
    History of American physical education and sport / by Paula D.
    Welch. — 2nd ed.
        p.   cm.
    Includes bibliographical references and index.
    ISBN 0-398-06565-9. — ISBN 0-398-06566-7 (pbk.)
    1. Physical education and training—United States—History.
2. Sports—United States—History.   I. Title.
GV429.W44   1996
796'.0973—dc20
                                                                95-25845
                                                                CIP

TO MY FAMILY

ACKNOWLEDGMENTS

The author wishes to express her gratitude for the major contributions made by Dr. Harold A. Lerch as co-author of the first edition of this project. The opportunity to revise and add to a second edition of *American Physical Education and Sport* would not have been possible without the interest of the Charles C Thomas Publisher. Although history does not change, opportunities to seek previously unknown primary sources can provide a better view of the past. Since the first edition, I have learned significantly more about the first generation of women Olympians, changes in the Olympic movement, the impact of legislation on sport, and trends in the physical education profession.

The dedicated staff of the University of Florida libraries has provided invaluable service. Their genuine interest in my research is greatly appreciated. I am especially indebted to Sherman Butler, Dolores Jenkins, James Liversidge, Richard Saltzburg, Jo Talbird, and Dr. John Van Hook of the Department of Humanities and Social Science Services. In addition, Mary Wisnieski, Archivist in the Documents Department assisted with the project.

Dr. David Young, Professor, in the Classics Department, at the University of Florida added valuable insight into the origins of the modern Olympic Games. Young's meticulous research of earlier Greek and English versions of competitive sport have clarified the genesis of the modern Olympic Games. Retired Director of Communications of the United States Olympic Committee, C. Robert Paul, Jr., who is currently Special Consultant to the United States Olympic Committee, rendered a most valuable contribution by reading and commenting on the Olympic Games chapters. Shirley Luckhardt, the National Secretary of the American Turners, contributed materials pertaining to the current status of the Turners in the United States.

Special appreciation is extended to Dr. Ruth H. Alexander for her meticulous reading of and suggestions for the manuscript. In addition, Dr. Peggy Stanaland's encouragement and suggestions were especially helpful. Finally, I would like to thank the many friends, family members, colleagues, and students for their interest and encouragement expressed throughout the revision of this book.

PAULA WELCH

CONTENTS

HISTORY OF AMERICAN
PHYSICAL EDUCATION AND SPORT

Chapter 1

A PRELUDE TO AMERICAN
PHYSICAL EDUCATION AND SPORT

During the latter years of the nineteenth century physical education was known as gymnastics, physical training, and physical culture. Early physical activity experiences in school settings were limited in scope and not accessible to a large portion of the populace. In contrast, twentieth century physical educators apply the dynamics of human movement to games, sport, and dance. Students in kindergarten through grades 12 and those in post-secondary institutions benefit from varied activities.

Athletic programs in the United States involve varsity competition between schools, with most contests occurring at the secondary and college or university levels. Athletic programs were the invention of male college students in the 1850s and became securely ingrained in institutions of higher learning. As the turn of the century approached, female students were briefly introduced to athletics, but it was not until three quarters of the twentieth century had passed that women's athletics were a visible entity in society.

Physical activity as characterized in games, sports, and dance has been an integral part of American culture since its beginnings. The nation's exercise heritage has assumed diverse forms with origins from native Americans and immigrants who came to the New World. Early exercise as a part of human expression was influenced by the will to survive in a hostile environment which once tamed, gave way to less utilitarian and more pleasure-seeking forms of amusement. As with any social institution in a highly complex society, games, sports, and dance have been directly influenced by other institutions such as religion, education, government, and industry. To more fully comprehend the scope of contemporary programs and practices, one must be familiar with their origins and development. Possessing a working knowledge of the history of physical education and sport can enhance one's understanding of current trends in society and provide a proper perspective as a guide for present and future program direction. An overview of sport and physical activity in the United States completes the remainder of Chapter 1 with subsequent chapters containing specific topical material.

CHANGES IN SPORTING INTERESTS AND STYLES OF PLAY

The Indians or native Americans who first settled in what is presently the United States viewed physical activity as an inherent part of their life-style. Their games had deep religious overtones which were neither understood nor fully appreciated by early Caucasian observers. The game of lacrosse has remained one lasting contribution to the nation's sports scene provided by native Americans. The colonists who later settled in America ushered in the colonial era beginning in 1607. In spite of severe hardships they found time for their own unique forms of expression through games and dances of European ancestry. Hunting skills were at first used out of necessity and later became a source of enjoyment. Contests such as hammering a nail by firing a rifle provided both entertainment and practice of hunting skills for frontier pioneers. As hunting became less pertinent for both urban and western dwellers other activities were substituted. The interaction between people of geographic settings produced differing styles of play and rules often varied from region to region. In general, the sports that became the rage in the east spread west and south.

AMERICANS BECOME ENAMORED WITH SPORT

Horseracing was the most organized sport before the Civil War, but its growth did not proceed without criticism. It appealed to all classes of people and to both men and women. Other sports which attracted a large segment of the citizenry after the war between the states included boxing and baseball. Some sports became professional enterprises. Both amateur and professional sports consumed the interest of Americans and they became enamored with them as evidenced by early newspaper accounts of their spectatorship and participation. *The National Police Gazette,* first published in 1845, recounted crimes and devoted space to numerous sports events. A writer for the *Gazette* described the prevailing feeling toward sports in 1867:

> The powerful impetus which Out Door Sports of every kind have received within the past few years in this country, and their rapid extension, evinces the deep interest which the American people feel in all those manly and athletic exercises which conduce so materially to physical and mental development. Athletic amusements are coeval with the world's earliest days. Leading to health, and promotive of cheerfulness, they supply to friendly intercourse a generous warmth and manly spirit they have often ennobled the social attributes of a people. They are important, viewed merely as a medium of pleasure; but to appreciate them in all their effects, is to give them a still higher position. They have formed the characteristics of nations, and they share with literature and art the classical pages of history. It is a plain axiom of experience that the just blending of labor and recreation produces the highest order of longevity.[1]

The American public has spent large sums of money on sport which encompasses both amateur and professional competition. Although professional sports helped to establish America as a "sporting nation," the text does not extend the coverage of professional sports into the twentieth century. It is the intent of the author to use them only to show how they contributed to America's enthrallment with sports.

ETHNIC INFLUENCE

Some of the immigrants who arrived in America continued to cultivate their own language, religion, recreational activities, and political beliefs, while others more readily took on the mores of their new homeland. Contributions were made by these new Americans, whether or not they continued to practice their familiar customs or more readily blended into what became known as the American way of life. Those who came from Germany preserved much of their culture and introduced a system of gymnastics and physical education to the cities. The Scots continued their interest in sports and initiated the Caledonian Games. The first club was founded in 1853 and demonstrates by way of one example how early practices influenced sport development. A description of the Brooklyn club's activities in 1867 illustrates several unique features of the clubs. The Brooklyn Caledonian Club organized March 9, 1866, and had attracted a membership of 200 a year later. Its purpose was "to foster fellowship and to perpetuate in memory the old customs, legends, and glory of 'auld Scotia.'"[2] Club members planned to construct a library, reading room, and gymnasium. During the summer of 1867 the Brooklyn club invited other Caledonian groups from New York, New Jersey, Massachusetts, and Pennsylvania to participate in their Scottish Games. The events were held at Jones' Woods which was a site for many New York City amusements. The participants in full Highland dress marched to the accompaniment of pipers. A Scottish reel preceded the program which was also interspersed with dancing. The twenty-one-event program consisted of:

1. Putting the heavy stone (24 pounds)
2. Putting the light stone (18 pounds)
3. The standing jump
4. Throwing the heavy hammer (21 pounds)
5. Throwing the light hammer (16 pounds)
6. The running jump
7. The Highland fling
8. The short race
9. The running high leap
10. The boys' race
11. The three-legged race
    Intermission
    Scottish reel
12. Vaulting with pole

13. The long race
14. Tossing the caber
15. The broadsword dance
16. The sack race
17. The standing high leap
18. The egg race
19. The hurdle race
20. Hop, step, and jump
21. Wheelbarrow race

Prizes were awarded for first through third place finishes in the various events. These included medals, a picture of Mary Queen of Scots, Scotch bonnet, tartan hose, and silver shoe buckles. A silver medal valued at $12.00 was awarded to the neatest dressed participant. Because of rain the participants adjourned to the dancing pavilion where they enjoyed more Scottish dances. The uncontested athletic events were postponed until September.[3] The Caledonian Games promoted interest in track and field in the United States.

Dance forms in America have undergone marked changes due to the influences of those peoples who have encouraged the development of dance. African dances, for example, were brought to America by slaves who eventually developed other unique expressions, such as jazz. Additionally, Europeans have had a distinct impact on the shaping of American dance.

BASEBALL: AMERICA'S TRADITIONAL NATIONAL GAME

Games resembling baseball had been played since colonial days. These bat and ball games were variations of the same general theme called base ball, two old cat, rounders, town ball, and goal ball. Some authorities suggest that the game was played by collegians in the 1820s.

Alexander J. Cartwright played a decisive role in organizing the first baseball club. Although a group of men had been gathering for practice games in Manhattan since 1842, it was in the spring of 1845 that Cartwright proposed the formation of a club.[4] His proposal was approved and the Knickerbocker Base Ball Club of New York was organized September 23, 1845. The club maintained its amateur status for more than thirty years. Social amenities were important to the Knickerbockers. Several rules in the 1866 regulations substantiate the enforcement of proper player behavior:

Members using profane or improper language on the field, shall be fined ten cents for each offense.

Any member disputing the decision of an umpire during the time of exercise, shall be fined twenty-five cents for each offense.

Any member who shall audibly express his opinion before the decision of the umpire is given, (unless called upon him to do so) shall pay a fine of twenty-five cents for each offense.

Figure 1.1. Putting the stone.

Figure 1.2. Throwing the hammer.

Figure 1.3. A sack race at the Caledonian games.

Any member refusing obedience to his Captain in the exercise of lawful authority, shall pay a fine of fifty cents.[5]

Baseball experienced rapid growth during the decade of the 1850s. In 1859 the first contest between colleges was played making it the second sport after rowing to achieve intercollegiate status. Further activation of the game occurred during and after the Civil War when soldiers who had played the game continued their involvement with baseball when they returned to their home towns. The game was played in cities, villages, and hamlets across the nation and attracted large crowds. Players of the professional game became the idols of thousands. Albert G. Spalding, who established a sporting goods firm, became convinced that baseball was firmly established as America's national game. In 1911 he wrote:

> the day has come when nearly every man and boy in the land is versed in all the intricacies of the pastime; thousands of young women have learned it well enough to keep score, and the number of matrons who know the difference between the short-stop and the back-stop is daily increasing.[6]

Although promoted as America's national game, the popular belief that baseball was invented by Abner Doubleday at Cooperstown, New York, in 1839 is questionable. Many historians agree that the game was not invented by a particular person at this time but rather it evolved from earlier games. The Knickerbocker Club is credited with developing rules which served as the foundation for the modern version of the game.

THE SHAPING OF SPORT AND PHYSICAL EDUCATION

America's social, political, religious, sport, and physical education heritage has been shaped by countless events that have occurred since the civilization of the country. The immigration and industrialization of America spawned the growth of large, populated cities. Sports clubs were formed that offered those individuals having fewer work hours opportunities to engage in leisure activities. The physical education profession was initially directed by medical doctors and other people interested in the effects of exercise upon the health and well-being of the general population. From this impetus arose recognized programs of study, or teacher training institutions, to prepare and certify teachers of physical education. The tragedy of wars, poor health of the nation's citizens, and economic depression have had both positive and negative effects on sport, physical education, and leisure pursuits. War curtailed physical activities when certain materials were in demand and were not readily available for the production of sports equipment. It also brought service personnel together and exposed them to recreational activities which they continued after the cessation of conflict in diverse parts of the nation. The low health status of Americans focused attention on the need for physical activity and physical educators rallied to improve the physical fitness of the nation's youth. The physical education profession has been cognizant of the necessity to influence Americans to continue physical activity after leaving the school setting. The Great Depression, as might be expected, had an adverse impact on some sports. For example, private golf clubs affiliated with the United States Golf Association (USGA) numbered as many as 1,000 in 1930 and by 1936 the number plunged to 743.[7] Thousands failed to renew their memberships in spite of special summer rates. Conversely, municipal golf courses increased between 1930 and 1936, while numerous courses, probably most of which were privately owned, declared bankruptcy.[8]

SPORTS READILY ACCEPTABLE
FOR ONLY THE MALE MEMBERS OF SOCIETY

At first, sport was solely a male dominated bastion. Before the advent of intercollegiate athletics large numbers of men were enjoying sports events and reaping their many benefits. It was not only acceptable but expected that men would pursue sports endeavors. Women were slow to gain acceptance as sports participants let alone as serious sportswomen. They were small in number but women did engage in what was referred to as socially sanctioned activities of a physical nature. Early recognized women's activities included horseback riding, bathing, and archery. An account of a "girls' regatta" occurred in 1878:

> Excitement ran high on the 19th, in Fair Haven, New Jersey, on the beautiful
> Shrewsbury. The white skirts of Jersey belles fluttered in the breeze. . . . The
> sails of yachts sparkled in the sunshine, and rowboats flitted . . . to and fro. The

occasion was a regatta for the fair sex, and bevies of pretty girls danced along the . . . shore. . . . Prior to the races there was quite a debate in the parlors of Van Fine's Hotel on the subject of coaching. The Fair Haven contestants did not want coaching, but the other fair contestants did. It was put to a vote, and . . . it was decided not to have coaches on the water, so the coaches stayed ashore.[9]

There were three races and the course for senior sculls was three-quarters of a mile straight away. The starters were Misses Sarah Bennett; her sister, Annie; and Emily Snyder. Sarah Bennet accented her dress with a white straw hat, black trimmings, and white feather. Her sister wore a navy blue costume, while Miss Snyder dressed in white wore a straw sailor hat with red trimmings. Sarah Bennett won the race in 7 minutes, 35 seconds. "Isn't she just splendid?" queried one of Miss Bennett's admirers while she pocketed gloves and bonbons, and "Ain't it just too awfully mean for anything?" retorted one of Miss Snyder's followers as she forfeited her wager. The second race was over a half-mile course for junior sculls, and perhaps because of the fever of the first race betting ran high. Caramels and cotton candy were wagered. There were three contestants two of whom were 13 years of age and the other 16 years of age. The closing race over a quarter of a mile was between two eleven-year-olds.[10] *The National Police Gazette* did not identify the prizes which were awarded the winners. Lemonade and ice cream were served after the contests.

Large numbers of spectators were attracted to tournaments where, in some cases, men and women competed together. Oftentimes these tournaments were held on festive occasions such as holidays. Men and women competed in archery competition together in the National Archery Association's 1881 tournament which began July 12 at the Prospect Park Parade Ground in Brooklyn. The archers competed before 500 spectators.

The first day of the tournament started at 11:00 A.M. and continued until sundown. The program consisted of the National Round* for women and the New York Round† for men. There were 20 women and 40 men archers. The contestants marched to the beat of a drum when they crossed the range to determine the scores.[11] On the final day of the three-day tournament a crowd of 1,000 had gathered when the bugle sounded to signal the commencement of the competition. The women's team championship was won by the Newark Topopholites, and the men's championship was won by the College Hill Club of Cincinnati. There was also individual competition, and a total of 96 prizes valued at over $2,000 were awarded. On the final day of competition a "press match" for newspaper reporters was held. Mrs. Gibbs of Newark was presented with the "championness medal" and chose a

---

*The National Round consisted of shooting 48 arrows from a distance of 60 yards and 24 arrows from 50 yards.

†The York Round consisted of shooting 72 arrows from 100 yards, 48 arrows from 80 yards, and 24 arrows from 60 yards.

Figure 1.4. A rowing contest.

diamond pin and a dozen arrows. Mrs. Morton, who placed second, was given the next opportunity to choose her prize and selected a set of table-spoons and forks with a moracco case. Frank Walworth won the men's champion medal and chose three Horseman bows, one dozen arrows, and a high silk hat.[12] In time, social mores were to change bringing about a redefinition of what were considered to be "proper" activities in which a woman could participate without fear of social criticism.

RAGES AND RACES

Since the beginning of recorded sport history, rages and races have attracted devotees to numerous competitive events. As sportsmen and sportswomen became more sophisticated, participants dressed in their sport attire, thereby producing a multimillion dollar clothing industry. It became fashionable to appear in sporting apparel even if one had no intention of engaging in physical activity.

During the latter half of the twentieth century, tennis became the rage. Beginning in the 1970s, the sport was visible across the country. By the end of the decade racquetball had gained converts. Running, by the end of the 1970s, acquired millions of participants who had taken to the streets, parks, roads, and specially designed running trails. Road races from one to 26 miles and 385 yards became numerous and well attended. Ultramarathons of 50 to 100 miles attracted a surprising number of participants who tested themselves against unique and challenging terrain. One event indicative of the running boom is Atlanta's Peachtree Road Race traditionally held on the Fourth of July. In 1970, 100 people ran the 10,000 meter event in blistering heat and with little fanfare.[13] Ten years later this race attracted 25,000 runners ranging from elementary school children to senior citizens. On July 4, 1994, under overcast skies and drizzling rain, 50,000 runners celebrated the 25th anniversary of the Peachtree Road Race.[14]

The Boston Marathon also illustrates America's phenomenal interest in running. The first race held in 1897 attracted only a handful of participants, whereas by 1970 nearly 10,000 official and unofficial runners entered the country's oldest marathon with the largest number of competitors representing the 40 to 44 age group. Since the first race, runners have had to meet designated time standards established for age groups. A classic Boston marathon features nearly 10,000 runners who have met the time standards. An exception was made for the centennial running of the world's oldest annual marathon when Boston Athletic Association (BAA) officials decided to admit 15,000 additional runners for the "100th Open Division" in the 1996 race.

A myriad of reasons exist as to why this activity has become so widely accepted. Television coverage of the marathon at the 1972 Munich Olympics and media exposure about the benefits of running to a health conscious public are two motivating factors. Large corporations also became involved by staging road races. One of the more profound influences which has encouraged millions of Americans to run on a regular basis is found in the work of Dr. Kenneth Cooper. In his book, *Aerobics,*[15] as with subsequent works throughout the 1970s and 1990s, he extolled the virtues of running as well as other forms of regular vigorous exercise. He also provided readers with a practical guide to establishing a sound program of regular exercise through running or related forms of activity. The public dissemination of knowledge concerning the values of running, combined with media exposure, has influenced millions of Americans to actively seek improvement in their overall health and fitness.

THE OLYMPIC MOVEMENT

The Olympic Games of the modern era have become an extravagant spectacle attracting global attention and excitement. The quadrennial competition which brings contingents of athletes from all over the world is the most prestigious international sporting event of all. The Olympic movement is an all-encompassing concept open to individual interpretation and meaning for those who are attracted by the spirit of the Olympic Games. The magnetism of the Olympic ideals draws from the beginning athlete to the highly skilled performer. Athletes, coaches, physical educators, media representatives, members of national and international sport governing bodies, officials, trainers, spectators, and those who study the medical, social, psychological, philosophical, and historical aspects of the Olympic Games constitute those who influence and are influenced by the Olympic movement. The Olympic movement brings together peoples of diverse culture, language, religious, and political beliefs. Nearly 200 nations, commonwealths, and geographical areas have National Olympic Committees recognized by the International Olympic Committee (IOC).

Dramatic changes have occurred within the Olympic movement during the 1980s and 1990s. In his 1990 lecture at the XIV United States Olympic Academy at Emory University in Atlanta, Georgia, Richard Pound of Canada addressed transformations in the Olympic movement. Pound, then Vice President of the IOC, staunchly supported open competition, limiting the number of Olympic athletes at the Olympic Games, and commercialization.[16] Open competition or the admission of professional athletes represents a drastic change from the once strict amateur requirement which did not permit athletes to benefit monetarily from their sports participation. Pound emphasized that the Olympic Games should be "accessible to the best athletes in the world, regardless of their social, economic, or political backgrounds."[17] Uncontrolled increase in the number of athletes has the potential to inflict greater financial and logistical problems on organizing committees. In a realistic summary of the financial status of sport, Pound explained to his audience, "Governments have made it . . . clear that they are unable, or unwilling, to assume the entire financial burden of sport, not only at the domestic level, but also at the international."[18] Commercialization of sport has become a necessity to ensure the continuation of the Olympic Games and other sport programs such as intercollegiate athletics.

REFERENCES

1. "Sporting," *National Police Gazette.* May 11, 1867, p. 3.
2. "Scottish Games," *National Police Gazette.* August 24, 1867, p. 3.
3. "Scottish Games," *National Police Gazette.* August 24, 1867, p. 3.
4. Albert G. Spalding. *America's National Game.* New York: American Sports Publishing Co., 1911, pp. 51–52.
5. *By-Laws, Regulations and Rules of the Knickerbocker Base Ball Club of New York.* New York: F.F. Taylor, Stationer and Printers, 1866, p. 10.
6. Spalding, *America's National Game,* op. cit., p. 10.
7. "Associations and Societies," *The 1930 World Almanac and Book*
8. "Associations and Societies," *The 1936 Almanac and Book of Facts.* New York: *The New York World,* p. 408.
9. "The Girls' Regatta," *National Police Gazette.* October 5, 1878, p. 3.
10. "The Girls' Regatta," *National Police Gazette.* October 5, 1878, p. 3.
11. "The Archery Tournament," *The New York Times,* July 13, 1881, p. 5.
12. "End of the Tournament," *The New York Times,* July 15, 1881, p. 5.

13. Official Program, "Tenth Annual Peachtree Road Race," *Atlanta Magazine,* July 4, 1979, p. 10.
14. Matt Winkeljohn, "Home Crowd Spurs Women's Winner," *The Atlanta Constitution,* July 5, 1994, p. 1, E.
15. Kenneth H. Cooper. *Aerobics.* New York: Bantam Books, 1968.
16. Richard Pound, "Without Laurel, There Is No Gold," *Proceedings United States Olympic Academy XIV,* Emory University, Atlanta, Georgia, June 13–17, 1990, pp. 21–24.
17. Ibid, p. 21.
18. Ibid, p. 23.

Chapter 2

NATIVE AMERICANS

Scholars are in general agreement that the Mound Builders were the first natives to live within the borders of the present United States. Remnants of their culture indicate they occupied America between 1500 and 1000 B.C. The second race of people to enter the present United States is open to more speculation. Some historians and archaeologists have concluded that the Hohokam followed the Mound Builders. The Hohokam, a Pima word meaning "departed long ago," was a flourishing society around 300 B.C. These agriculturists and pottery-makers lived in individual houses and cremated their dead. The Pueblos were also early arrivals to the United States between 200 and 1 B.C. It is generally believed that wherever these three races of people traveled some families remained at various stopping places which accounted for the many different tribes scattered throughout the country by 500 A.D.

American Indian tribes are generally classified according to areas of the country in which they lived. Various tribes lived in the Southeast, Northeast, Plains, Southwest, Great Basin, California, and the Northwest. The tribes throughout the various regions were largely nomadic or semi-nomadic people relying basically upon farming, food gathering, and hunting for survival. Some of the Plains Indians were buffalo hunters and their culture was based upon horse nomadism which generally produces in people today an image of the "typical Indian." Indians of the California region did not practice agriculture but some parts of the region contained dependable quantities of acorns and other foods which helped contribute to a relatively stable village life. Perhaps the Northwest coast Indians were the most prosperous in that plentiful supplies of fish contributed to their economic stability.[1]

GAMES OF THE AMERICAN INDIANS

Despite subtle differences in Indian culture brought about by economic conditions, they shared many similarities in religious beliefs and rituals which influenced their daily lives. The function of games was inexorably woven into the social fabric of the American Indians. Not only were they an important feature of religious and ceremonial activities but they served as a major source of entertainment. Culin, in his extensive study of games of the

North American Indians, summarized their chief purpose by stating that, in general, "games appear to be played ceremonially, as pleasing to the gods, with the object of securing fertility, causing rain, giving and prolonging life, expelling demons, or curing sickness."[2] Culin, who identified and described the games of approximately 225 American Indian tribes throughout the United States, identified two general categories and then further subdivided them:

  I. Games of chance
     A. dice games
     B. guessing games
 II. Games of dexterity
     A. archery
     B. javelin or darts
     C. shoot at a moving target
     D. ball game
     E. racing games

In games of chance the dice games were those which depended upon the random fall of the dice or other implements, while guessing games entailed a guess or choice of the player. Generally, the dice games were played in silence while guessing games were accompanied by singing and drumming designed to invoke the aid of the divinity presiding over the game. The guessing games consisted of four types:

1. Those in which a bundle of sticks, originally shaftments of arrows, are divided in the hands, the object being for the opponent to guess in which hand the odd stick or a particularly marked stick is held. . . .
2. Those in which two or four sticks, one or two marked, are held in the hands, the object being to guess which hand holds the unmarked stick. . . .
3. Those in which four sticks, marked in pairs, are hidden together, the object being to guess their relative position. . . .
4. Those in which some small object—a stone, stick, or bullet—is hidden in one of four wooden tubes, in one of four moccasins, or in the earth, the object being to guess where it is hidden. . . . [3]

The games in these categories were played only by men, women, or young adults, and not by children. Children amused themselves with such activities as top spinning, mimic fights, and other imitative sports.

BALL GAME

Lacrosse or the "little brother of war" as it was commonly referred to, originated from the ball game played by the American Indians. An early narrative account of the game was published in 1775 by an Indian trader of some forty years. He described a Choctaw ball game in which the ball used was made from a piece of scraped deerskin, moistened, stuffed hard with deer's hair, and sewed with deer's sinews. The ball sticks, one held in each hand by the Choctaws, were about two feet long with the lower end resembling the palm of a hand laced with deerskin thongs:

Figure 2.1. A choctaw Indian with ball sticks.

The goal here is about five hundred yards in length: at each end of it, they fix two long bending poles into the ground, three yards apart below, but slanting a considerable way outwards. The party that happens to throw the ball over these, counts one; but, if it be thrown underneath, it is cast back, and played for as usual. The gamesters are equal in number on each side; and at the beginning of every course of the ball, they throw it up high in the center of the ground, and in a direct line between the two goals. . . . They are so exceedingly expert in this manly exercise, that, between the goals, the ball is mostly flying the different ways, by the force of the playing sticks, without falling to the ground, for they are not allowed to catch it with their hands. It is surprising to see how swiftly they fly, when closely chased by a nimble footed pursuer; when they are intercepted by one of the opposite party, his fear of being cut by the ball sticks, commonly gives them an opportunity of throwing it perhaps a hundred yards; but the antagonist sometimes runs up behind, and by a sudden stroke dashes down the ball.[4]

Swanton has collated other early descriptions of the game from eyewitness accounts. Contrary to general belief today thousands of participants did not constitute an average game. Twenty to forty players on a team was more typical of play. However, gambling generally accompanied the event:

... They place about twenty of one village against as many of another, and put wagers against each other to very considerable amounts. . . . When they are very much excited they wager all that they have, and, when they have lost all, they wager their wives for a certain time, and after that wager themselves for a limited time.[5]

Although Choctaw women played the game to avenge the loss of their defeated husbands, it was unusual because most of the other tribes did not permit it:

... They play with much skill. They run against one another very swiftly and shove one another like the men, being equally naked except for the parts which modesty dictates they shall cover. They merely redden their cheeks, and use vermillion on their hair instead of powder.[6]

The game also permitted one of the few occasions in which all violence during the game was forgiven. The old men acted as mediators during the game and did not consider it as something over which to fight. One early observer was also informed that "it is the only case in which life is not generally required for life." Although this was true, at times a ball game served as the catalyst to bring old feuds to the surface, or it sometimes encouraged feuds. In two particular instances the game failed to serve as the "moral equivalent for war." About 1790 the first of two ball games was played between the Choctaw and Creeks for possession of a beaver pond and ownership of a specified territory. Both games ended in battle.[7]

The emphasis on ritual was recorded by an observer's account of the day preceding the game in which the two opposing parties of men, women, and children assembled on the playing field:

As night approaches both sides for an hour or more go through a repetition of ceremonies. . . . A mingo seats himself on the ground. . . . A number of girls and young women now come forward and arrange themselves in two parallel lines facing each other. . . . The painted ball players with their ball sticks in hand then come forward, dance and shout around their post, then form a circle at the outer end of the line of women where they clash their ball sticks overhead, then hold them poised erect for a few moments. While they are thus standing in silence, the women, prompted by the mingo, dance and chant a song in a low tone, keeping time with their feet. The song generally is "Onnakma, abi hoke." Tomorrow we will win it.[8]

After chanting this several times the players danced around the post and re-formed their circle at the end of the outer line of the women, where they repeated the same action with their ball sticks. The women continued to dance and chant the same song. The ceremony was repeated twelve times and then the players and women dispersed to participate in revelries and amusements lasting the entire night. Prophets with blackened faces spent the night invoking their magical powers in favor of their home team. In the morning the same ceremonies as conducted the night before were performed by the players and women, but different songs were used. The next several hours were spent posting wagers with the betting parties tieing the articles which they wagered together and placing them on a scaffold. The women were observed to be equal to the men in their enthusiasm toward placing bets. About midday the game was ready to begin:

> Each mingo stations his players, the most expert being placed near the posts of the opposite party as here the struggle is generally the most violent. The rest of the players assembled at the marked spot in the center and some time is spent in betting. This over, a prophet throws up the ball and the play begins. Twelve is the number of rounds usually played. The party that wins a round has the privilege of throwing up the ball, which is done by one of their prophets. The posts of the two parties have lines extending out on each side. The rule is that the posts must be struck on the inside, that is on the split sides, and the ball must fall on the inside of the drawn line; if otherwise, it is not counted. During the play, no outsider is expected to interfere in the play in any manner whatsoever. Should he do this, the party to which the offender belongs is expected to forfeit one round or otherwise make some reparation.[9]

During the actual playing of the game, the prophets would place themselves in the midst of the players and perform certain actions symbolizing the throwing of the sun's rays upon his players' bodies. Because they believed that all life and power came from the sun, infusion of its rays to teammates would help win the day. When the game ended which was generally in one day and sometimes two, the losers, it was reported, would graciously accept their defeat and return to their homes. "It sometimes happened that some of the vanquished party went home half naked, having bet even their clothes on the result of the play."[10]

A variation of the previously described ball game in which the players experienced unsolicited divine intervention was played by the Indians living in Spanish Florida during the seventeenth century. Both religious and civil officials believed that this game of ball, when played by the Christian Indians, was harmful to their bodies, souls, and the peace of the local provinces. The time-honored game was finally outlawed in 1684 after a ten-year campaign against it.[11] The ancient game was played by kicking a small ball against a goalpost and was called by the Spanish "el juego de la pelota," or "the ball game." After one village had challenged another to a game, they would agree on the day, playing site, and the number of players. It was usually played on Sunday from noon until dark with 40 or 50 players on a side wearing loincloths and slippery paint. The goalpost, shaped like a tall flat Christmas tree with a long trunk, was topped by snailshells, a nest and a stuffed eagle for symbolic reasons. The playing field dimensions are unknown. During the game the edge of the playing field contained piles of belongings which were wagered by the Indians who used an elaborate barter system rather than money. The pelota ball was a bit larger than a musket ball and consisted of hard dried hair and mud packed in buckskin. If the ball was kicked against the goalpost it was worth one point, and if it landed in the eagle's nest it counted as two points with eleven points constituting the game.[12]

By 1771, Florida Indians were distinctly called Seminoles and they also played a type of ball game unlike lacrosse known to Indians in other states. An observer described their game which was not usually played in a war-like atmosphere or against other tribes and included men, women, and children:

> Within a circle whose circumference is about thirty feet is erected a pole, which serves as the goal. The players take sides. . . . The object of the game is to strike the pole with the ball, which is knocked with a racquet or stick, which is made of hickory, with a netted pocket made of deer thongs. The ball is tossed up and caught in the netted pocket and then hurled at the pole. The opposing side endeavors to prevent the ball from touching the post.[13]

A score was tallied when the top of the pole was hit but there was apparently no total number of points which determined the conclusion of a game.[14] Although the origin of the racquet is not clear, two racquets, one in each hand, were commonly used by the Seminoles and other Southeastern tribes. A later variation of the thonged racquet was a carved wooden ball stick thought to be uniquely used by the Seminoles. Absence of organized competition was a distinguishing characteristic of the Florida Seminoles with cooperation more accurately exemplifying their work and play.[15]

OTHER GAMES AND ACTIVITIES

In 1844 the fourth edition of George Catlin's drawings and notes about the American Indians was published. He devoted a large portion of his adult life to visiting Indian tribes and preserving on canvas over 3,000 illustrations of their native dress, wigwams, dances, ceremonies, games, and other daily activities.

Catlin visited the Mandan tribe of the Upper Missouri and reported that their games and amusements were similar to other tribes and that Tchung-kee was their favorite diversion:

> . . . two champions form their respective parties, by choosing alternately the most famous players, until their requisite numbers are made up. Their bet-

Figure 2.2. Seminole Indian with carved wooden ball sticks. Courtesy of the Museum of Natural History, University of Florida.

tings are then made, and their stakes are held by some of the chiefs or others present. The play commences with two (one from each party), who start off upon a trot, abreast of each other, and one of them rolls in advance of them, on the pavement, a little ring of two or three inches in diameter, cut out of a stone; and each one follow it up with his 'tchung-kee' (a stick of six feet in length, with little bits of leather projecting from its sides of an inch or more in length), which he throws before him as he runs, sliding it along upon the ground after the ring, endeavoring to place it in such a position when it stops, that the ring may fall upon it, and receive one of the little projections of leather through it, which counts for game, one, or two, or four, according to the position of the leather on which the ring is lodged. The last winner always has the rolling of the ring, and both start and throw the tchung-kee together; if either fails to receive the ring or to lie in a certain position, it is a forfeiture of the amount of the number he was nearest to, and he loses his throw; then another steps into his place.[16]

Figure 2.3. Mandan Indian playing Tchung-kee.

Figure 2.4. Sac and Fox Indians sailing.

Another popular activity of the Mandans was "game of the arrow" where the object was to shoot their arrows into the air using a bow, attempting to see who can send the greatest number before the first one reaches the ground. Not only was this considered to be sport but it also served the practical purpose of sharpening their hunting and fighting skills.

Catlin also observed that the Mandans were expert swimmers with their swimming style differing from that used by what he termed the "civilized world." Here Catlin describes the freestyle stroke of the Mandans:

> The Indian instead of parting his hands simultaneously under the chin, and making the stroke outward, in a horizontal direction, causing thereby a serious strain upon the chest, throws his body alternately upon the left and the right side, raising one arm entirely above the water and reaching as far forward as he can, to dip it, whilst his whole weight and force are spent upon the one that is passing under him, and like a paddle propelling him along, whilst this arm is making a half circle, and is being raised out of the water behind him, the opposite arm is describing a similar arch in the air over his head, to be dipped in the water as far as he can reach before him, with the hand turned under, forming a sort of bucket, to act most effectively as it passes in turn underneath him.[17]

The Sac and Fox Indians usually lived along river banks and streams, and were also expert swimmers and skillful canoemen. Catlin frequently witnessed these Indians sailing their light dugout canoes with the aid of their blankets. The man stood in the bow of the canoe holding a blanket by two corners with the other two under his foot or tied to his waist or leg, while the woman sat in the stern and steered the canoe with a paddle.

The horse-riding feats of the Comanche Indians greatly impressed Catlin. "Racing horses, it would seem, is a constant and almost incessant exercise, and their principal mode of gambling; and perhaps a more finished set of jockeys are not to be found."[18] He went on to describe one particular extraordinary riding skill:

> Amongst their feats of riding there is one that has astonished me more than anything of the kind I have ever seen or expect to see in my life—a stratagem of war learned and practiced by every young man in the tribe, by which he is able to drop his body upon the side of his horse at the instant he is passing, effectually screened from his enemies' weapons as he lays in a horizontal position behind the body of the horse, with his heel hanging over the horse's back, by which he has the power of throwing himself up again and changing to the other side of the horse if necessary. In this wonderful condition he will hang whilst his horse is at fullest speed, carrying with him his bow and shield, and also his long lance of 14 feet in length, all or either of which he will wield upon his enemy as he passes, rising and throwing his arrows over the horse's back, or with equal ease and equal success under the horse's neck.[19]

Puzzled as to how the Comanches were able to suspend their bodies in such fashion he discovered that a short hair halter was placed around the neck of the horse with both ends braided into the mane. The loop made a sling for the elbow which supported the body on the middle of the upper arm permitting the rider to suddenly drop to the horizontal position.

Figure 2.5. Horse riding feat of the Comanches.

The Hopi Indians living in eastern Arizona practiced a kick-ball race which had religious significance as well as a practical function. Devout Hopi who engaged in it were relieved of all sadness and health was renewed. They also believed the cloud deities favored the participants and would send rain rushing as swift as the runners.[20] In 1893 an observer witnessed a race which covered ten to twelve miles over an open course. At a given signal each of the runners kicked a small, hard ball as far in front of him as possible and ran after it. It was reported there was no actual race or keen struggle, but instead each village group stayed relatively together while reaching the finish line.

The Iroquois Indians also participated in games and amusements common to most other tribes, but perhaps they were one of the few tribes to hold funeral games. Athletic contests in honor of their dead were held with prizes offered to those who displayed exceptional feats of physical skill, strength, and agility. Even while contending for victory, participants displayed moderation and reserve out of respect for the departed.[21] One such funeral game was "Cane Rush" in which one youth was given a stick and a prize was offered to anyone else who could take it from him. Climbing a greased pole with a prize such as a kettle or deerskin tied at the top was another example of a funeral game.

Native Americans have distinguished themselves in amateur and professional sport. Among those who first reached international sport competition was Frank Pierce, a member of New York's Pastime Athletic Club. He became the first American Indian to compete in the Olympic Games when he ran the marathon at the 1904 St. Louis Olympics. Four years later Pierce

Figure 2.6. Chunkee stone, a gift of Mr. and Mrs. Howard B. Greene to the Samuel P. Harn Museum of Art, University of Florida. Photo: John Knaub, Instructional Resources, University of Florida. In southeastern North America, Creek and other Indians played a game called chunkee. The game was played by rolling a carved stone and trying to get as close as possible to a mark, much like horseshoes.

entered the marathon at the London Olympics. The Carlisle Indian School was represented by no fewer than three Olympians. The first was Frank Mt. Pleasant who also ran the 1908 marathon. Neither Pierce nor Mt. Pleasant won medals. In 1912 two other Carlisle Indian School students competed at the Stockholm Olympics. Lewis Tewanima of the Hopi tribe was a bronze medalist in the 10,000 meter run. The third Carlisle Indian School student, Jim Thorpe, who has been hailed as the greatest athlete ever, won the Olympic decathlon and pentathlon. Thorpe, a Sac and Fox Indian, later excelled in professional football and major league baseball. Jesse Renick, a Choctaw Indian, played basketball at Oklahoma A & M University, now

Oklahoma State. He continued playing Amateur Athletic Union (AAU) basketball and was a member of the 1948 London Olympic Games team. In 1964, William "Billy" Mills, a $7/16$ Sioux Indian, became the first American gold medalist in the 10,000 meter run. Mills also excelled in AAU competition, setting records in the six mile and 10,000 meter distances. Henry Boucha, a Chippewa Indian, played the 1969–1970 ice hockey season for the Winnipeg Jets and was a member of the 1972 silver medal ice hockey team. After the 1972 Sapporo Olympic Winter Games, he played three seasons for the Detroit Red Wings. He played briefly for the Minnesota North Stars but an eye injury ended his career.[22]

A paucity of Native American women exists at the Division I level of intercollegiate sport, however, that is changing as Ryneldi Becenti and Gwynn Hobbs are leading the way for other women of similar ethnic backgrounds. Ryneldi Becenti, of the Dine' tribe, was a star basketball player at Window Rock High School in Fort Defiance, Arizona, and was the 1989 Arizona Player of the Year. Before entering Arizona State University, she graduated from Scottsdale Community College (SCC) and became the first SCC player to score 2,000 points in a career. The quick guard left her name in the Arizona State University all-time records in three categories. After the 1993 season, Becenti's 396 assists placed her second in that category with 396. She was sixth in steals with 85 and second in three-point field goals with 90.[23]

Gwynn Hobbs, also a guard, completed an impressive basketball career at Navajo Academy in Farmington, New Mexico. She entered the University of Nevada Las Vegas (UNLV) and quickly established herself as a team contributor. Her membership on the Big West Conference All-Freshman team was a signal of future successes. She played on the West team at the 1993 U.S. Olympic Festival and the following year was named to the first-team All-Big West Conference squad. By the 1994–1995 season, she became UNLV's all-time career leader in three-point goals.[24] The basketball careers of Becenti and Hobbs have been enthusiastically followed by Native Americans in the western United States. Perhaps, their inspiration will pave the way for Native American women to enter international sport competition.

SUMMARY

Although it would seem that the games of the North American Indians were greatly varied, after careful study Culin concluded they could be classified in a small number of related groups and that morphologically they were almost identical and universal among all tribes. Their activities may be generally classified according to games of chance and games of dexterity. Upon first discovery it appears as though they only served as amusement or gain; but it is important to note they were also an integral part of the Indians' religious ceremonies designed to please the gods, procure magic, drive out sickness or other evil, produce rain, and induce other beneficial results. Lacrosse originated from a ball game played by the

American Indians in which set rituals were an important part of the game. Variations of the game were played by the Indians living in Spanish Florida during the seventeenth century. Other games and activities of the American Indians were preserved on canvas by George Catlin. The Mandans were expert swimmers and the Comanches excelled in horsemanship. The Iroquois were one of the few tribes to hold funeral games in honor of their dead. The recognition of games by scholars as an essential element of the Indians' cultural milieu has contributed to a better understanding of these first Americans.

REFERENCES

1. Eleanor Leacock and Nancy Lurie (eds.). *North American Indians in Historical Perspective*, New York: Random House, 1971, p. 10.
2. Stewart Culin. *Games of the North American Indians*, Twenty-fourth Annual Report of the Bureau of American Ethnology, 1902–1903. Washington: Government Printing Office, 1907, p. 34.
3. Culin. *Games of North American Indians*, ibid., pp. 31–34.
4. James Adair. *The History of the American Indians*, London: Edward and Charles Dilly, 1775, pp. 399–401.
5. John Swanton. *Source Material for the Social and Ceremonial Life of the Choctaw Indians*, Bureau of American Ethnology, Bulletin 103, Washington: Government Printing Office, 1931, p. 140.
6. Swanton, *ibid.*, p. 141.
7. Swanton, *ibid.*, pp. 141–142.
8. Swanton, *ibid.*, p. 148.
9. Swanton, *ibid.*, pp. 148–149.
10. Swanton, *ibid.*, p. 149.
11. Amy Bushnell. "'That Demonic Game': The Campaign to Stop Indian Pelota Playing In Spanish Florida, 1675–1684," *The Americas*, 35 (July, 1978), p. 1.
12. Bushnell, *ibid.*, pp. 5–6.
13. Minnie Moore-Wilson. *The Seminoles of Florida*. New York: Moffat, Yard and Company, 1910, pp. 101–102.
14. Jean Chadhuri. Seminole interviewer, Big Cypress Reservation. Oral history project, oral history interview, State Museum, University of Florida, May, 1971, p. 5.
15. Harold Lerch and Paula Welch. "A Ball Game Played by the Florida Seminoles During the Green Corn Festival," *Research Quarterly*, 49 (March, 1978), pp. 91–94.
16. George Catlin. *Letters and Notes on the Manners, Customs, and Condition of the North American Indians*, 4th Edition, Volume 1, London: David Bogue, 86 Fleet Street, 1844, p. 132.
17. Catlin, *ibid.*, p. 97.
18. Catlin, *ibid.*, Volume 2, p. 65.
19. Catlin, *ibid.*, Volume 2, p. 65.

20. Elsie Clews Parson. *Hopi Journal of Alexander M. Stephen,* Part 1. New York: AMS Press, 1969, pp. 258–279.
21. Karen L. Smith. "The Role of Games, Sport, and Dance in Iroquois Life," unpublished Master's Thesis, University of Maryland, 1972, p. 73.
22. Bill Mallon and Ian Buchanan. *Quest for Gold the Encyclopedia of American Olympians.* New York: Leisure Press, 1984, pp. 40, 132–33, 154, 326, and 353–54.
23. "Basketball," *Arizona State University Media Guides 1991–1992 and 1992–1993,* pp. 11, 34, 45.
24. Jim Gemma (ed.). "Gwynn Hobbs," *1994–1995 Lady Rebel Media Guide,* Las Vegas: Quality Impressions Printers, p. 11.

Chapter 3

THE COLONIZATION OF AMERICA 1607–1775

THE FOUNDING OF EARLY COLONIES

The first settlers of the "New World," as America was then called, had left their native English soil to escape religious persecution from the Church of England. During the reign of Elizabeth I Puritanism was born from a reaction to irreverence and as opposition to the efforts of the queen to turn the Church into an institution of the state with no strong religious convictions. General political and economic unrest also instigated emigration to North America. Transition from an agricultural to industrial nation caused England's natural sources to wane which also prompted colonization of a new land. Finally, social problems induced by urban growth caused a class unrest forcing many to consider an alternative to life at home. The search for religious freedom, economic and social stability, resulted in the founding of Jamestown, Virginia, in 1607, and the establishment of the Plymouth Colony in 1620. Material sufficiency, however, was to be hard earned over a period of years. In spite of the harsh conditions of life posed by the wilderness, Indian attacks, killing disease, and oftentimes little food, the Pilgrims persevered in scratching out an existence. These successful efforts of the early colonists led to the beginning of the great migration of Puritans to New England in 1630 and the settlement of Boston under John Winthrop and the Massachusetts Bay Company. In the words of one writer:

> The Great Puritan Migration...was the largest and most important of all movements overseas by English people in colonial times.... These Puritans were a hardheaded and dogmatic lot. Tenacious of purpose, they regarded themselves as chosen by God to create a purer church and a City of God in the wilderness.[1]

The influx of immigrants continued and the colonists who founded Maryland in 1634 experienced a minimum of privation compared to their New England counterparts. The winter climate was less severe and settlers were able to obtain supplies from the Virginia Colony. Life became more bearable as they tamed the harsh elements of their new land.

Colonists in Carolina had also established secure living conditions by 1675 in the more temperate climate. Profiting from the early pioneering techniques of others, William Penn founded his colony in 1681 under fewer conditions of hardship. An influx of many wealthy Quaker settlers to the area along with the existing Swedish and Dutch farmers saw the colony of Philadelphia flourishing by 1684.

EDUCATION IN THE COLONIES

Education in the colonies was a reflection of European class standards in that higher learning was reserved for the upper class. People in the lower classes learned the fundamentals of reading, writing, and arithmetic in addition to the skills of artisans or laborers. The most pervasive influence on education came from the colonial middle class who saw the importance of preparation for a productive life. They also sought to gain some of the cultural advantages associated with the upper class. The New England colonies were the leaders in educational development which was in harmony with their religious beliefs. Because of this religious unity it was generally possible to develop a common system of education. In 1647 Massachusetts required that each town having fifty families or more provide a schoolmaster to teach reading and writing to the children. However, this act failed to have the colony-wide effect intended by its authors. Many of the poorer towns elected to pay a fine rather than support a schoolmaster. Those towns having a schoolmaster were careful to identify his many and varied duties as illustrated in this excerpt from a New England "Town Book" dated 1661:

1. Act as court messenger
2. Serve summonses
3. Conduct certain ceremonial church services
4. Lead Sunday choir
5. Ring bell for public worship
6. Dig graves
7. Take charge of school
8. Perform other occasional duties[2]

These duties of the schoolmaster were a reflection of the important relationship the New England colonists saw between religion and education. The effort put forth by the schoolmaster in conducting these duties earned him the respect of the townspeople. Religious differences in the middle colonies made it impossible to develop a unified system of public education. The Southern colonies also experienced religious differences which bred educational diversity. Settlements were widely scattered thereby causing a lack of concentration of people and resources in an area.

WORK AND LEISURE IN THE COLONIES

Small farming was the predominant means of support for New Englanders. Because of climate and soil conditions, men, women, and children had little time for other than long hours of hard work. Men performed the heavier tasks while women made clothes and prepared food. Children were usually called upon to gather grain and tend the livestock. The more prosperous merchants residing along the coastal towns dominated the public affairs of the day.

The strict religious beliefs of the Puritans influenced the limited leisure time of the inhabitants. Most games and amusements were prohibited because they were thought to contribute very little to life in the settlements. Because of harsh living conditions, the quest for economic survival was of paramount importance.

In order to enforce their strict code of conduct, the Puritans passed early laws which regulated personal and public behavior. In essence, no line of distinction existed between " . . . self-regarding sins and crimes against society."[3] From this desire to regulate behavior came a law requiring that each town in Massachusetts have a public house to control the sale of intoxicating beverages and provide for the welfare of travelers. The tavern, called an "ordinary," additionally served as a gathering place for townspeople to conduct public meetings and socialize. Games such as card playing, billiards, shuffleboard, quoits, and ninepins were forbidden in an "ordinary."

Church attendance on Sundays was compulsory and secular activities were forbidden. Wagner has concluded, however, that in spite of this official decree, many of the early settlers were compelled to recreate in their own manner on Sundays. The church synod of 1649 deplored the fact that multitudes in larger towns were not observing the Sabbath. Common evils on the Lord's day were "drinking, mixed dancing, and unlawful gaming." The church expressed grave concern that regardless of fasting days and sermons directed to these evils, reforms were not forthcoming.[4] The clergy took official measures to insure that the holiday of Christmas, which was observed in England, would not survive the Atlantic crossing by banning its celebration, which was viewed as a great dishonor to God. In 1659 anyone found guilty of observing this holiday in Boston by not working or feasting had to pay a fine of five shillings.[5]

In time, economic conditions improved, which helped to bring about a gradual relaxation in some forms of amusements. However, we are reminded that "all merriment was not innocent" and penalties were given to those who indulged in sports or games which fostered gambling, immorality, or drunkenness. Mixed dancing was forbidden as well as theatrical productions, card playing, shuffleboard, billiards, and bowling. Diversions such as fishing or fowling, if done in moderation, were tolerated by the town fathers and clergy as long as they did not lead to "waste of time." By the eighteenth century records began to appear which publicly tolerated recreational amusements in Massachusetts. America's first newspaper, the *Boston News-Letter*, founded in 1704, advertised in 1714 that:

> the Bowling Green, formerly belonging to Mr. James Ivers in Cambridge-Street Boston, does now belong to Mr. Daniel Stevens at the British Coffee

House in Queen-Street, . . . where all Gentlemen, Merchants, and others that have a mind to Recreate themselves shall be well accommodated.[6]

Equestrian novelties for interested spectators were advertised in the Essex Gazette of Salem, Massachusetts, as early as 1771:

Horsemanship, John Sharp, High-Rider and Performer in Horsemanship, late from England, but last from Boston, where he has been performing for some time past, intends to ride for the Entertainment of the People of Salem & c., in the Street by the Upper Burying Ground, near the Alms-House, this Day, if the Weather will permit it; if not, he will perform To-Morrow. — He rides two Horses, standing upon the Tops of the Saddles, with one Foot upon each, in full Speed: — Also three Horses standing with one Foot upon each of the outside ones, and in full Speed: — Likewise one Horse, and dismounts and mounts many Times when in full Speed.[7]

In time, military training days provided a good opportunity for the able-bodied townsmen to participate in various games and contests. In Boston, after the training drill was completed, competition was held in target shooting with prizes ranging from a silk handkerchief to a silver cup. Wrestling, rough-and-tumble fighting, running, and jumping contests were also popular activities.

NEW YORK

New Yorkers engaged in a more active social life than their Puritan counterparts in Boston. Dutch and English immigrants influenced early forms of recreation and sport in New York. European traditions, ethnic food, and special observances were often adapted to the new homeland. Holidays imported by the Dutch were enthusiastically celebrated. Dutch settlers played games such as skittles, an early version of bowling. They also participated in a game that included some of the elements of modern handball and enjoyed board games.

Throughout the year, sociable New Yorkers sought pastimes that were appropriate for the various seasons of the year. Meals were often a highlight of skating and sleighing parties. Deer parks and game preserves maintained by the gentry were similar to those found in England. Expert shooting was admired and rewarded with valuable prizes. A house and a lot were offered on one occasion while a gold watch was awarded in another shooting match.[8]

Amusements and social life in New York were perhaps more acceptable than in any other colony. Favorite activities for the upperclass included fishing, hunting, fencing, horse racing, cricket, boating, carriage riding, and sleighing. In the early 1700s, it was fashionable for aristocrats to attend stage plays, which was in sharp contrast to the actions of New Englanders who viewed the theater as a "house of Satan." The middle class amused themselves with hunting and fishing, skating, sleighing, dancing, and card playing. Two activities considered cruel by many were cockfighting and bearbaiting.

Nevertheless, they were acceptable diversions for some aristocrats as well as common folk.

As early as 1728, the excitement of attending the fair was eagerly anticipated by all classes of people. A close look at a live lion added to the attraction:

> Jamaica Fair opens on Tuesday the 7th of May Instant, and continues four days, where will be exposed to sale variety of Goods and Merchandise, and several fine Horses will be there to be sold. It is expected that the Lyon will be there to be seen.[9]

PENNSYLVANIA

In 1682, the Society of Friends, or Quakers, migrated to Pennsylvania, bringing with them their strict code of beliefs regarding amusements which were similar to the Puritans. Like their Puritan neighbors they sought to live in the New World free from religious persecution. Idleness and certain amusements were considered to be an "abomination unto God" and early laws were passed which regulated personal and group behavior. Temptations to be avoided were those inherent in gambling, stage entertainments, music, and dancing. Oppressing or injuring any part of the animal creation as in cockfighting or horseracing was also against their beliefs. The hunting of animals was considered immoral when engaged in for pleasure and diversion. The education of youth was of serious concern to the Quakers and parents were instructed to sanction only those amusements which did not compromise one's religious principles or virtue. Moral education was in general harmony with current puritanical beliefs which emphasized prohibitions forbidding indulgence in the worldly customs of society. In 1694 Quaker educational policy admonished youth to avoid:

> ...challenging each other to run races, wrestling, laying of wagers, pitching bars, drinking to one another, riding or going from house to house to drink rum or other strong liquors to excess, to jest or talk idly.[10]

In keeping with this policy, parents were given the responsibility to see that their children avoid the corrupt fashions of this "wicked world" by not playing "ranting games." However, as economic conditions improved and with the influx of other groups to Pennsylvania came a greater acceptance of "innocent diversions" such as hunting, ice skating, swimming, and fishing. In 1732 a group of Philadelphians, many of them Quakers, formed the first fishing club in the English colonies. Combining utilitarian and recreational values, the enthusiastic anglers fished along the banks of the Schuylkill River on farm property owned by a club member. The early Quaker influence regulating amusements continued to wane as a greater number of people moved to the region. Amusements such as dancing, bowling, billiards, cock fighting, and horse racing deemed undesirable in the past became increasingly popular in spite of objections of some conservative residents.

Educational practices also reflected the process of change when the esteemed Philadelphian, Ben Franklin, wrote his "Proposals Relating to the Education of Youth in Pennsylvania." He urged youth to run, leap, wrestle, and swim.[11] Franklin was an expert swimmer capable of performing many feats both upon and under water.

THE SOUTH

In the Southern colonies, plantation life was less demanding for the large landholders providing them with more leisure time compared to the New England and Middle colonies. In the early days of settlement much of the work was done by indentured bondservants, but they were gradually replaced by black slaves. Many of the farm implements and shoes and clothing were manufactured on the plantation by some of the slaves who were trained for this work. One of the main crops of the South was tobacco, much of which was exported to England. The Southern colonies maintained a much closer contact with England than did the New England colonies. The South was not entirely plantation country, but also included many families who worked small farms with few or no slaves.

In the Southern colonies, the lines of social stratification were clearly drawn. Social classes consisted of aristocrats, laborers, and black slaves. The class lines often determined the nature of one's sporting activities. In 1674, a tailor in Virginia was fined for entering his mare in a race which was then a sport suitable for only "gentlemen." During the mid 1700s, the gentry of Maryland, Virginia, and Carolina rivaled each other in producing the fleetest thoroughbreds, while less affluent men raced the best horses they owned. From 1765 to 1775 in Maryland, it was fashionable for gentlemen to attend turf events. " ... Annapolis, the abode of elegance and refinement, was resorted to from all quarters at its regular race meetings."[12] Other sporting activities common among southern aristocrats were fox hunting, hunting and fowling, and fencing bouts. Cockfighting was another favorite activity of plantation life which drew spectators of all social classes. Slaves engaged in such diversions as fishing, singing, and dancing.

THE COLONIAL FRONTIER

The westward movement of the early pioneers left little time for anything other than work vital to survival. Hard physical labor and ever watchful guard against Indian attack left the frontier colonist with limited leisure time. Similar hardships were common among those settlers who eventually moved as far west as California and Oregon. Work for men in the era of the colonial frontier centered around harvesting crops, cabin building, and other building. Play was mainly associated with work. Hunting and fishing provided some relaxation while also serving as a source of food. Sharpshooter contests and wrestling matches offered diversion as well as utilitarian value.

During the first century of colonization, many sporting and recreational activities were individual, while cricket and rudimentary soccer drew the attention of those interested in group play. Eventually, as the colonies achieved greater economic stability, especially in the established towns, colonists began to spend more time and money on recreational pursuits. Horse racing became the first popular spectator sport prior to the Civil War.

SUMMARY

The first settlers in America left their native country of England to escape religious persecution, and out of political, social, and economic unrest. Withstanding the hardships of material insufficiency, the early colonists persevered and established Jamestown and Plymouth Colonies in 1607 and 1620. The great Puritan migration, which occurred in 1630, helped to insure the growth and development of towns in the New England, Middle, and Southern colonies.

The New England colonies were leaders in developing a system of education which was in agreement with their religious beliefs. Religious differences in the middle and Southern colonies bred educational diversity making it impossible to develop a unified system of public education. Settlements were also more widely scattered in these areas than in New England, resulting in less concentration of people and resources in one location.

In keeping with their strict religious beliefs, the Puritans prohibited most games and amusements. The harsh living conditions forced them to choose economic survival as being of major importance. Although Sunday church attendance was mandatory and secular activities forbidden, church fathers bemoaned the fact that citizens, especially in the larger towns, were breaking the Sabbath by drinking, mixed dancing, and unlawful gaming. As economic conditions improved some forms of amusements were sanctioned by the town Fathers and parsons such as fishing or fowling if done in moderation. By the eighteenth century, recreational amusements had become openly tolerated in Massachusetts and were advertised in town newspapers. In Boston, military training days offered a good opportunity for the townsmen to engage in various activities such as target shooting, wrestling, and running and jumping contests. The Quakers, unlike their Puritan neighbors, more readily recognized the role of physical activities in the educational development of their children. They supported the Greek ideal advocating a sound mind in a sound body.

Amusements and social life were most acceptable in the New York colony where popular upper class activities consisted of fishing, hunting, horse racing, cricket, boating, carriage riding and sleighing in the winter. The middle class were fond of hunting, fishing, skating, sleighing, dancing, and card playing. Cockfighting and bear baiting appealed to both middle and upper classes of people.

Life for the large landowners in the Southern colonies was less demanding when compared to the New England and Middle colonists, because much of the work was done by indentured bondservants and eventually black slaves. The lines of social stratification were very evident in the Southern colonies: aristocrats, laborers, and slaves. Popular sporting activities for aristocrats were horse racing, fox hunting, fowling, and fencing bouts. Cockfighting was one activity which attracted all three social classes. In sharp contrast, survival was paramount to the frontier colonists pushing westward. Brief respites from the arduous rigors of frontier survival took the form of utilitarian activities such as hunting and fishing. Sharpshooting and wrestling contests were additional diversions which had a practical value. Communal activities centering around house raisings and harvesting parties also served to meet the dual purpose of survival while providing a welcome relief from work.

Throughout approximately the first 100 years of colonization in America many sporting and recreational activities were individual in nature while some games involved group play. As the colonies increased in economic stability, recreation became increasingly more acceptable, especially in the larger, more established towns. Forms of recreation began to change from those which offered active involvement to amusements more passive in nature. Horse racing became the first popular spectator sport.

REFERENCES

1. John Pomfret. *Founding The American Colonies,* New York: Harper and Row, 1970, pp. 23, 161–162.
2. John H. Best and Robert T. Sidwell (eds.). *The American Legacy of Learning,* Philadelphia: J.B. Lippincott Co., 1967, p. 47.
3. J.A. Doyle. *English Colonies in America, Volume 2,* New York: Henry Holt and Co., 1889, p. 63.
4. Peter Wagner. "American Puritan Literature: A Neglected Field of Research in American Sport History," *Canadian Journal of History of Sport and Physical Education,* 8(December, 1977), p. 74.
5. Justin Windsor, (ed.). *The Memorial History of Boston, Volume 1,* Boston: James R. Osgood and Co., 1880, p. 516.
6. Herbert Manchester. *Four Centuries of Sport In America,* New York: The Derrydale Press, 1931, p. 27.
7. Isaac Greenwood. *The Circus,* Washington, D.C.: Hobby House Press, 1898, p. 47.
8. Esther Singleton. *Social New York Under the Georges 1714–1776,* New York. D. Appleton and Co., 1902, pp. 259, 261, 264.
9. *The New York Gazette,* No. 131, April 29 to May 6, 1728, p. 4.
10. Thomas Woody. *Quaker Education in the Colony and State of New Jersey,* New York: Arno Press and The New York Times, 1969, p. 21.

11. Thomas Woody. *Educational Views of Benjamin Franklin,* New York: McGraw-Hill Book Co., Inc., 1931, p. 157.
12. "History of the American Turf, from Eighty Years Since-Best Horses and Co." *American Turf Register and Sporting Magazine,* 6(October, 1834), p. 59.

Chapter 4

EARLY AMERICA AND THE FRONTIER, 1776–1880

Sports and amusements from the end of the Revolutionary War into the late 1880s became more diversified and attracted a greater number of participants. Some sports and amusements were readily accepted, while others, vigorously opposed by lawmakers and clergymen, were slow to gain acceptance. Gouging matches, cock fighting, and other activities of a barbarous nature were eventually outlawed as people began to reject the rough and uncouth elements of society. Amusements were connected to the necessities of life when, for example, people combined a barn raising with dancing, eating, and playing games. Sports were adapted to the areas of the country where people lived. In the west for instance, the natural prairie grass made a suitable track for horse racing. There were even horse races down the main streets of frontier towns. New Americans arriving from Europe and other parts of the world introduced sports, pastimes, and amusements. Many activities became the rage in the east and spread south and west where they were equally popular. With the diffusion of sports and games across the land came deviations in rules.

HORSE RACING

Horse racing was among the first spectator sports which became a popular source of entertainment following the Revolution. By the end of the eighteenth century racing centers were located in New York, Maryland, Virginia, and South Carolina. Growth of the sport did not proceed without opposition. Public racing was prohibited in some states and clergymen attacked it from the pulpit. An illustration of religious disapproval occurred on September 17, 1809, when church goers attending the Elizabeth-Town, New Jersey, Presbyterian Church listened to the vices their minister attributed to horse racing. He cautioned them to "review the long and black catalogue—idleness, gaming, sabbeth-breaking, prophane swearing, intoxication, debauchery, ... cheating, quarrelling, (and) fighting."[1] Horse racing was thought by many to be a source of corruption to the rising generation because it represented an unacceptable defiance of the work ethic. Americans had become accustomed to gaining the necessities of life following long hours of laborious work.

Horse racing was dealt a devastating setback during the Revolutionary

War when many of the finest horses, added to the cavalry, were lost in military action. Through theft and abandonment numerous animals were shifted around randomly, resulting in loss of their identity. From New York to Georgia horse racing and breeding were interrupted during the British occupation. The British took over Brooklyn's Flatland Plains race course where they added bull baiting and other English pastimes to the program. After the Revolution, British cavalry officers who owned some of the fastest horses of the day took them home.[2] Several years passed while horse racing recovered from the effects of the war. Shortly after the Constitution had been ratified, states began enacting laws which impeded as well as prevented racing. Some states set limits on bets. Restrictions on horse racing had negligible effects on reducing gambling debts and stifling interest in the sport.

Racing grew in the United States until the War of 1812. The importation of English thoroughbreds was drastically reduced when "embargoes against commerce with England" were introduced prior to and after the War of 1812.[3] Though war again dampened enthusiasm for the turf hardly had a decade passed upon conclusion of the 1812 conflict when sectional races sparked north-south competition.

THE NORTH VS. THE SOUTH

Opposition to horse racing subsided and sectional races attracted large crowds. A horse race which matched the north's best against the south's representative ignited rivalry among enthusiasts of the turf. On May 27, 1823, the first of several sectional races was held. American Eclipse met the southern horse, Henry, at Long Island's Union Course for a purse of $20,000 a side. An estimated crowd of 60,000 saw Eclipse win two of the three four-mile heats after losing the first heat.[4]

Americans had become enamored with sport and horse racing thrived. Publications featuring turf events contributed to sporting communication. The first was J.S. Skinner's *American Turf Register and Sporting Magazine* which appeared in 1829. Articles on hunting, shooting, trotting races, fishing, and pedestrianism appeared in Skinner's magazine during the 1830s and early 1840s.

On May 10, 1842, a horserace which generated much speculation in English and American sporting circles attracted thousands from all over the country. The purse was $20,000 a side and the race was a sectional match-up, featuring the North's Fashion and Boston, the South's favorite. *The New York Herald* dispatched a special express horse to return its rider to the press as soon as the race ended. *The Herald* boasted of its ability to inform the public of the outcome within thirty minutes after the conclusion of the race.

The roads leading to Long Island's Union Course were jammed with carriages, hacks, wagons, cabs, horsemen, and stump pedestrians. The entire inside of the track was lined with horsemen and other conveyances which brought people to the race. The stands were filled and trees "that overlooked the course (were) groaning with the weight of anxious gazers."[5]

Meanwhile, after eleven o'clock on the morning of the race the Long Island Railroad Company found it impossible to transport the immense number of passengers, but the company continued to sell tickets. A train carrying over 2,000 passengers did not reach the race until after the first heat and hundreds who had purchased tickets set out on foot and reached the course before the train's passengers.

Among the variously estimated 50,000 to 70,000 thousand spectators were members of the United States Senate and House of Representatives, judges and lawyers, as well as the British and American Army and Navy. The "Ladies' stand" was graced with New York City's fashionable belles. Many women were sitting in carriages where they could view the race.[8] The . . . race course was brimming with excitement "when the horses were brought upon the ground, . . . the whole mass of spectators upon the stand appeared to rock to and fro like the ocean's wave, all anxious to get a peep . . ."[7] Prior to the start of the race a crowd tore down a portion of a fence in an attempt to gain a better view. For a time it seemed unlikely that the race would take place. The intruders filled the Jockey Club Stand, reserved for members at a cost of $10.00. For a sum of 200 dollars the proprietor of the course engaged the services of pugulist Yankee Sullivan, to remove the trespassers. Sullivan enlisted the aid of about 50 men who, with locked elbows cleared the course.[8] Fashion won both the first and second four-mile heats. *The New York Herald* proclaimed the North victorious and printed a description of the race soon after it ended. After the race the irate "passengers rolled several (cars) off the track over the hill, and smashed others, while 'a perfect mash' was made of the ticket office."[9]

Apparent concessions for horse racing were made by the nations' lawmakers. In preparation for the intense summer heat the Houses of Congress adjourned while the Capitol building was cleaned and ventilated. "Curiously enough, the adjournment usually (occurred) on the race week, and while the process of cleaning (was) in progress at the Capitol, the legislators (amused) themselves on the course" in Washington.[10]

Women attending some race tracks were accorded special treatment by a "Ladies Committee." The Fashion Jockey Club of New York, the Metairie Club of New Orleans, and the Pioneer Jockey Club of San Francisco designated similar provisions for women beginning with their arrival, whereupon the "Ladies Committee" received the women at the door of their carriages and escorted them to the "Ladies stand" and "attend (ed) to their comforts during their presence."[11]

Readers of *The New York Times* on September 28, 1858, were made aware of the acceptance of women at horseraces when it reported that, "to the right of the Judge's, there was a large number of ladies, who appeared to anticipate much pleasure from the occasion."[12] *The Times* depicted horse racing as an exciting spectator sport which attracted large crowds. Horse racing, among the first organized sports, became firmly embedded in the American sporting scene. Gambling, rivalry, excitement, and diversion for leisure time made horse racing attractive to people of varied backgrounds.

WORK AND RECREATION COMBINED

Long hours and tiresome labor were necessary to produce food, clothing, shelter, and other necessities of life. A combination of work and recreation made the accomplishment of work-related tasks more pleasant for pioneer Americans. Almost anything that brought people together was received with enthusiasm. Where sheep were raised enjoyable activities were frequently combined with sheep shearing. Entertainment and dining made sheep shearing a festive occasion.[13] Quilting parties and other sewing tasks such as making clothes and carpets provided women with a practical form of recreation. They enjoyed the opportunity to talk about the times and no doubt the chance to gossip. House raisings, barn raisings, and corn huskings were other projects which brought people together for work and recreation.

While women met to sew, men gathered late in the afternoon at times during the middle and late 1850s. Social activities generally followed a group evening meal. Books and papers were read aloud and singing often took place. Occasionally an unannounced wedding offered a change for the people. These gatherings were attractive because no one knew what might occur.[14]

EXHIBITIONS

Americans looked for diversions to turn their thoughts from work and the problems they encountered in a developing country. Large crowds flocked to exhibitions where they could view unusual abilities, freaks, and an assortment of rarities. Predominantly influenced by the Congregational Church, Connecticut society from 1818 to the middle of the century experienced restraints on theatrical performances, tumbling exhibitions, and rope dancing, as well as the circus. Both the state legislature and the clergy opposed the circus. Newspapers claimed the circus was vulgar and not beneficial to one's mind or spirit. Traveling menagerie companies, however, were well received. These exhibitions of wild animals were accepted because they were considered educational and enabled people to see nature.[15] For several days in September, 1838, *The New York Herald* informed New Yorkers that for 25 cents, they could see a giraffe, gazelle, antelope, an Egyptian ibex, and a Syrian goat.

Traveling showmen going from village to village entertained and amused the people with novel items in their wagons. One showman reportedly displayed two mummies which he claimed were ancient Egyptians. Electric appliances were unusual and amused those who wanted to experience an electrical shock.[16]

Holidays such as Election Day offered other amusing diversions. Schools and stores closed so people could attend parades and participate in quoits, hunting, fishing, and wicket ball. In the evening a ball was held. Training Day which brought men between the ages of 18 and 45 together to prepare against an invasion was also a festive occasion. Women prepared delicious picnic baskets and:

> after lunch there was the enjoyable period of gossip among the older people while the boys traded marbles and jack-knives. The men and older boys engaged in sports of a boisterous type, such as shooting at marks, horseracing, wrestling, running, leaping, and ball playing. In the meantime the demure little girls walked sedately around the green and exchanged their pennies for peppermint drops.[17]

WORSHIPERS GATHER FOR
RELIGIOUS AND SOCIAL FUNCTIONS

In addition to church attendance and practice sessions for segments of the religious service, church-related social functions became customary for most religious groups. Churches served their members by bringing them together to meet their spiritual and social needs. Singing schools were organized to train church members to sing more effectively and they provided both the young and old with an opportunity to gather in a social setting. The singing school, though popular in various sections of the country during earlier periods was an especially favorite occasion at the beginning of the 19th century.[18]

LEISURE AND SCHOOL ACTIVITIES

Leisure activities were becoming as much a part of the American tradition as organized sports. Some leisure activities were pursued in numerous parts of the country while others were limited to geographic regions by weather and terrain. For example, during the latter years of the 18th century the young people of Albany, New York, enjoyed rural excursions on canals. Different groups would meet at one of the islands where they bent and twined the shrubs to form a shelter. These excursions usually began early in the morning, and shortly after arriving at the island breakfast was prepared. After breakfast the young men fished and hunted birds; while the young women, who usually brought their workbaskets, began working and singing. After the young women prepared dinner, the entire group would pick fruit that was in season to take home for their families.

Another favorite summer amusement of Albany's youth was going to the "bush." A group of young people traveling in open carriages would visit the poor members of the community who lived in the bush. The visitors usually had plenty of good things to eat and were generally well received by the bush people. After dancing, the young people returned home by moonlight.

The sloped streets of Albany provided a natural area for sleighing. Many people enjoyed watching the parade of sleds and it was not unusual for older people to join in the fun.[19] Snowshoeing and skating were other well-liked activities in parts of the country where snow and ice were plentiful.

Traveling in Pittsburgh during the fall of 1806, Thomas Ashe, an English tourist, observed the amusements and noted the seasonal influence on activities:

> In winter, carioling or sleying predominates: the snow no sooner falls, than pleasure, bustle, and confusion, banish business, speculation, and strife; nothing is seen but mirth, and nothing is heard but harmony. All young men of a certain condition provide themselves with handsome carioles and good horses, and take out their favorite female friends, whom with much dexterity they drive through the streets; calling on every acquaintance, and taking refreshment at many an open house. For the night, an appointment is generally made by a large party (for instance, the company of twenty or thirty carioles) to meet at a tavern several miles distant; to which they go by torch-light, and accompanied by music. On arriving there, the ladies cast off their fur pelisses, assume all their beauties, and with the men commence the mazy dance. This is followed by supper, songs, catches, and glees. When the voice of Prudence dispels the charm, they resume their vehicles, and return delighted with the moments which they have thus passed—this is repeated frequently during the snow. The summer amusements consist principally of concerts, evening walks, and rural festivals held in the vicinity of clear springs and under the shade of odoriferous trees.[20]

Cricket was played during much of the nineteenth century but never gained widespread adoption like the more lively game, baseball. The oldest cricket organization in the United States, the St. George's Cricket Club was founded in New York during the early 1830s. Club membership grew and interest in cricket was sufficient enough to purchase land for a permanent location.[21] Another endeavor to further cricket in America occurred at Haverford College near Philadelphia about 1836. Englishman William Carvill, a gardener, invited some students to play. Homemade bats and balls were used and the game flourished until about 1838. It was not revived at Haverford until the mid 1850s. Another Englishman, Robert Waller, started cricket in Philadelphia and was a leader in the formation of the Union Cricket Club in 1842.[22]

During the 1840s, young boys attending academies engaged in a variety of games and sports. They could choose from such activities as marbles, hockey, swimming, archery, cricket, and leap frog. In addition, they enjoyed kite flying and the trundle hoop. They played fives, a game resembling handball which involved players alternately striking the ball against the wall. Trap ball, a bat and ball game, was also popular.[23]

Swimming was given early attention because of its value as a safety precaution and promotion of cleanliness. Later swimming was pursued for its recreational values. An 1818 publication listed several advantages of

Figure 4.1. Cricket, 1842.

acquiring the skill of swimming. In summary, the author suggested that swimming offered:

1. personal security and power to assist someone in distress
2. better health by adding variety to bathing
3. development of manly courage and dispelled fear of the water
4. safer involvement with amusements such as rowing.[24]

Figure 4.2. Trundling the hoop.

CROQUET, THE COURTING GAME

Croquet, among the first activities adopted by American women, was firmly established when the Civil War had concluded. Croquet was inexpensive, easily set up, did not require much space, and was quickly learned. Families played the game and it became a socially acceptable encounter between the sexes. In 1868 a writer for *Harper's Bazaar* referred to croquet as an:

> exquisite game, at which the stakes are soft glances and wreathing smiles, and where hearts are lost and won. At every blow of the mallet Cupid's shafts are driven deeper and deeper into the willing victim . . . [25]

In 1875, manufacturers constructed a set with candle holders on top of each wicket and post enabling "croquers" to play the game in the evenings.[26] Rules were not standardized because manufacturers published their own list of regulations. A meeting in Norwich, Connecticut, in 1882, attended mostly by women, resulted in the formation of the National Croquet Association (NCA). The NCA drew up a tournament at its first meeting and both men and women participated.[27]

EARLY PUGILISTS

The sons of prominent southern families who had studied in Europe are generally credited with activating boxing in America. Boxing was an established British sport by the latter half of the eighteenth century. The sport emerged on the American scene early in the nineteenth century. Having enjoyed boxing in England the young men of the South found a natural rivalry in the black boxers who represented plantations.[28] Interplantation rivalry and wagering intensified the development of the sport in the South. Some slaves won their freedom because of their boxing prowess. They gained their freedom by winning a designated number of bouts and giving their owners a portion of the money accumulated in prizes and wagers. Freed slaves gradually spread boxing northward.

Bill Richmond, a black slave, was born on Staten Island in 1763. General Earl Percy, a commander in the British military, discovered Richmond's boxing ability during the British occupation of New York. Percy arranged private fights for the amusement of his friends. The General took the successful young boxer to England in 1777 where he soon attained fame as a pugilist.[29] Richmond continued his boxing career in England, and although he was never an American champion, he did influence America's first leading black boxer.

Tom Molyneux (sometimes spelled Molineaux) was born in 1784 to a slave family owned by the Molyneux's of Virginia. Both his father and grandfather were fighters. By the early 1800s Tom Molyneux, a free man, had moved to New York. In the early days of boxing blacks engaged in spur of the moment fights for almost any small prize. Molyneux was soon known as the best black fighter in New York. The Virginia born boxer was per-

Figure 4.3. Clerical Instructor. "Now hold the ball firmly with your foot, Miss Scramble, and take care not to hit yourself this time!" Miss Scramble. (who is getting rather bored) "Ah, well, in case I do, suppose you hold the ball for me, Mr. Smiler.!"

suaded to fight the great British champion, Tom Cribb. Molyneux worked his way to England as a sailor and while there trained under the tutelage of Bill Richmond. After a few successful fights Richmond thought his protegé was ready to meet Cribb.[30]

In December, 1810, Tom Molyneux fought the English champion, Tom Cribb. The forty-four round fight took fifty-five minutes. *The London Times* summarized the result: "Both the combatants were dreadfully beaten; and they were almost deprived of sight. The Black gave in rather from weakness than want of courage."[31] Molyneux fought Tom Cribb the following year and lost. He experienced a few successful fights but contracted tuberculosis and died on August 4, 1818, at the age of thirty-four.[32]

Jacob Hyer is generally regarded as the first white pugilist to achieve widespread recognition. He fought Tom Beasley in 1816 in New York City, won the bout, and never fought again. Hyer's son, Tom Hyer, later became the first recognized champion of the United States.[33]

A few prize fights were promoted in northern cities during the 1820s. The sport was not highly organized but devotees of pugilism could name "the best men about town." Excitement at the fights often turned into bedlam. A fight in 1832 near Newark, New Jersey, "terminated in a general row, in which principals, seconds, and spectators, all joined."[34] Local law enforcement officers intervened in fights but unruly crowds ignored attempts to stop contests. The sheriff of Elizabethtown, New Jersey, attempted to stop a fight in 1834 "by reading the riot act, . . . but was unsuccessful."[35] The sport cut across the social strata of America attracting the moneyed class as well as the impoverished. Fights were sometimes held on boats and islands in order to escape law enforcers and the hostile press.

English pugilists traveled to America and stimulated interest in the sometimes dormant American ring. Fistic history is replete with tales of bloody melees. Kicking, gouging, and head butting were common during early boxing matches. An Englishman, James Burke, sailed for America and fought Samuel O'Rourke at New Orleans, May 6, 1836. When O'Rourke's fans realized Burke was going to win the fight they charged the ring with clubs. Burke began defending himself with a knife obtained from one of his friends. He saved his life by seizing a horse and fled the battle. The melee resulted in at least one death and severe injuries to hundreds.[36]

The Tom Hyer—"Country McCluskey" McCleester fight occurred at Cauldwell's Landing, Hudson River, New York, September 9, 1841. The match extended into 101 rounds and at the end of the three hours and five minutes Hyer was the victor.[37] Early boxing matches were characterized by lengthy rounds and few restrictions.

When Thomas McCoy and Christopher Lilly agreed to fight in the fall of 1842, boxing was the rage among many of New York City's inhabitants. Hardly a week passed when a fight was not scheduled at one of the theaters or halls. The McCoy-Lilly fight was held midway between Yonkers and Hastings in Westchester County. It was September 13, 1842 and *The New York Herald* reported that among the several thousand spectators were twenty or thirty Irish women who lived in the vicinity. The Irish who had poured into the country during the 1830s had gained recognition for their pugilistic prowess. It was fashionable to claim Irish ancestry.

McCoy went down first as the crowd cheered the shout, "first blood for Lilly!" "Time" was called before the one hundred twentieth round began.

After two hours and 41 minutes Thomas McCoy was unable to stand. McCoy was dying:

> and in fifteen minutes he had ceased to exist. The excitement upon the ground was intense . . . and many (were) heard (to) exclaim, 'this is the last fight I will ever go to see.'

> His body was placed on top of one of the liquor stands . . . and conveyed . . . on the shoulders of several of his friends from whence it was placed on board the steamboat Saratoga and conveyed to the house of his mother . . . [38]

According to *The Herald,* Thomas McCoy was the first boxer actually killed in the ring although others had later died as a result of injuries sustained while boxing. Amid the uproar which followed the fight were demands by New Yorkers to end boxing. Three days after the fight *The New York Herald* declared "the dreadful result of this battle will put an end to prize fighting in this country for years. . . . "[39] The fatal fight cast boxing deeper into legal difficulties and it was not until bare knuckle boxing was abandoned that legalization of the sport began to occur.

Many young Americans whose prowess was identified in the prize fight ring boarded ships for England in search of better opportunities to box. The exodus from the American fight ring detracted from the development of the sport in this country.[40] Moreover, it was no wonder that boxing was slow to gain acceptance. The bare knuckle brutality brought forth the criminal element in society. Some of the early champions were criminals and their fights were cues for pickpockets to gather. The hoodlum element seemed almost entrenched in the sport.

A TWELVE-YEAR REIGN

In 1841, London-born James Sullivan began a 12-year reign as the best fighter in America. He acquired the nickname "Yankee Sullivan" because he entered the ring with an American flag around his waist. Sullivan had gotten into trouble with the law and was sentenced to 20 years in a British penal colony in Australia. He escaped, headed for the United States, and arrived in San Francisco.[41] Yankee Sullivan's boxing reign ended when he lost the championship to John Morrissey in 1853.

The John Morrissey—John Heenan fight, according to *The New York Times,* was the "engrossing topic" of conversation among "the fashionable and legal, as well as the low . . . " in Buffalo.[42] Followers of the fighters crowded into Buffalo saloons brandishing guns and knives as they bullied their opposing sides. Trains brought spectators from various parts of the country. Steamers transported them to the site of the fight: Long Point, Canada, seventy miles from Buffalo. Morrissey's partisans threatened blood if their hero was defeated. Fearing violence, some spectators stayed away and the fight drew only 1,000 onlookers. After 11 rounds which lasted 21 minutes, Morrissey was declared the winner.[43]

REVISED BOXING RULES CONTRIBUTE TO LEGALIZATION

In 1743, John Broughton, an English pugilist, issued the first code for boxers which permitted almost any method of fighting. The British Pugilists Protective Association announced the London Prize Ring Rules in 1838. When the Marquis of Queensberry presented his rules requiring gloves; rounds of three minutes, rather than rounds that lasted until a fall; and the elimination of such blows as the kidney punch, boxing began to rise above the level of barbaric slug fests. The Queensberry rules were used in England during the 1860s but it was not until late in the 1880s that they came into vogue in America. After 1889 no other American championship was decided with bare knuckles. The adoption of the Queensberry rules by American fighters contributed to the legalization of boxing.[44]

Supported by both the criminal element and the acceptable constituents of society, boxing see-sawed between declarations of legality and illegality in various states. In 1920 professional boxing was formally restored to New York when the Walker Law was passed. Other states patterned legislation of the sport after New York's example.

BOATING

Boats for transportation, recreation, competition, and fishing attracted all classes of people. Boat clubs and rowing associations developed as the population settled in new areas or moved to established cities and towns. In 1838, recreational boating was advertised in the summer issues of *The New York Herald.* Boats could be rented for a day, week, or month.

Indicative of the interest in competition was the boat race announced in the fall of 1838 by *The New York Herald.* New York area clubs could enter a race for six- and four-oared boats. There was also a race for boats not exceeding 22 feet in length with two pairs of sculls or two oars.

New York City was one of the earliest centers of yacht racing and attracted wealthy members. On the tenth anniversary of the New York Yacht Club in 1854, 14 yachts entered the annual regatta.[45] In 1859, an editorialist in *The New York Times* wrote that the " ' . . . June Regatta' had become one of the 'fixed facts' of the Gothamite year."[46] The yacht racing season was welcomed with enthusiasm and offered diversion for the serious competitor and the casual observer.

PEDESTRIANISM

Pedestrianism, a sport originating in England, attracted competitors who attempted to be the first to complete a prescribed distance within a time limit by running and walking. Variations of "ped" races were those which challenged racers to be the first to complete a specified distance. The taxing six-day races, sometimes referred to as "wobbles," were arranged to determine who had the most stamina and could cover the greatest distance. Pedestrian contests were conducted both indoors and out-of-doors. Large crowds attended pedestrian races in the 1830s and 1840s. Races frequently took place on courses constructed for horse racing. Many of those in attendance bet large sums of money. In April, 1835, nine peds raced before a crowd estimated at 16,000 to 20,000 at the Union Course, Long Island. A purse of $1,000 was awarded to Henry Stanard who, with 12 seconds to spare, was the first to cover 10 miles within an hour.[47] An 1844 race reported in the *American Turf Register and Sporting Magazine* held at the Beacon Course attracted a crowd of 30,000. Another race at the Beacon Course during 1844 was advertised in England, Canada, and the United States. Varying accounts of the assembled persons ranged from 25,000 to 35,000. Before the race began

> a dense multitude of Oliver Twists broke through two or three lengths of the palings and filled up . . . the open space in front of the stands, [and] encircled the entire concourse. Nearly 10,000 of these specimens of the tag-rag and bob-tail denizens of New York got admission to the course. . . . [48]

An hour passed before the course was cleared of spectators. Seventeen men entered the race with the objective of covering the greatest distance in one hour. The winner was paid $600.00 and the remainder of the $1,000 was divided among the next three finishers.[49]

Madison Square Garden was the site of six days "go-as-you please" races for men and women. In mid-December, 1879, 22 women vied for the Championship Belt of the World. While most of the contestants were from the United States, England, France, Russia, and Canada were each represented by one walker.[50] On the final evening of the contest, 5,000 spectators cheered Miss Howard, an American, as she completed 393 miles. *The New York Times* reporter noted, "The women who remained on the track to the end showed signs of suffering which were painful to watch.[51]

Followers of pedestrianism in Boston, Brooklyn, Chicago, Pittsburgh, and Washington, D.C. were amazed at the endurance of women walkers. Numerous women's races in 1879 featured walking quarter miles in the same number of consecutive quarter hours. Undaunted by the $1.00 for standing room and $2.00 for reserved seats, a crowd of more than 2,000 jammed into Brooklyn's Mozart Garden, to witness Madame Anderson's final laps of 2,700 quarter miles in 2,700 consecutive quarter hours. An overflow crowd twice as large waited in the street to hear the outcome of the English pedestrian's feat.[52] Six days later, May Marshall of Chicago had begun a walk of 2,700 quarter miles in 2,700 quarter hours in Washington, D.C. Meanwhile, in response to Madame Anderson's accomplishment, the French woman, Exilda La Chappelle, had begun a similar walk for $1,000.[53] After each quarter mile, she immediately retired to her dressing room where she fell on a bed and went sound asleep. A bell jarred her awake and she bounded out of her room and onto the track where she was met with enthusiastic applause. Ten days into the race, La Chappelle was able to complete a quarter of a mile in 3:56.[54] Daily reports in the *Chicago Tribune* kept the readers informed of the number of quarter hours and quarter miles completed, as well as her diet of raw oysters, eggs, and beef tea. Meanwhile, May Marshall had completed her walk with an increase to 2,796 quarter miles in the same number of consecutive quarter hours.[55] The month-long walk ended with La Chappelle agreeing to walk an additional 50 quarter hours to beat the English woman.[56] City officials, men, women, and children attended races featuring women walkers. Some were drawn by curiosity and the social atmosphere which was enhanced by band music. Because few women were featured in sporting events, many women spectators experienced an infrequent opportunity to admire other women with the stamina to excel in such taxing endurance events.

Between 1875 and 1885, professional pedestrians claimed the attention of a large number of the inhabitants in several major American cities. Lack of regulations and exploitation of racers contributed to the demise of pedestrianism. Many of the pedestrians continued their feats into the twentieth century.[57]

People were attracted to pedestrianism because of its uniqueness and its gambling possibilities. While a few women entered pedestrian races, mostly white men dominated the sport. The speedier six-day cycling races eventually replaced professional pedestrianism.

BICYCLES MAKE AN APPEARANCE

The bicycle gained the attention of some Americans following the Civil War. It did not become a prominent method of transportation or leisure activity because the célérifère, a pedaless, low, two-wheeler with a seat, depended on a thrust from the toes or momentum from downward slopes. The early bicycle period was brief. It was characterized by mismanaged patents, failure to pay royalties, and expensive prices for cheaply made bicycles.

Interest in the bicycle waned until the high wheel displayed at the Philadelphia Centennial Exhibition in 1876.[58] Prior to the decade ending in 1880, bicycle manufacturing was intermittent. During a period of fifteen years in 1890, the bicycle industry experienced rapid growth, then decline. In 1890 there were 27 bicycle manufacturers and the number rose to 312 in 1900. By 1905 the bicycle manufacturers numbered 101. During the decade ending in 1900, bicycle production was remarkable. General adoption of the pneumatic tire and society's acceptance of cycling brought two particularly prosperous years from 1894 to 1896. When the demand for bicycles plummeted, many manufacturers began producing motorcycles and automobiles.[59]

Between 1890 and 1895, the bicycle rage caused a rapid expansion of the industry. A decline in the bicycle industry was evident in 1897. In 1889 1,182,691 bicycles were produced and the number decreased to 250,487 in 1904. Meanwhile, demands for the motorcycle showed signs of increasing.

Production of motorcycles in the decade from 1899–1909 increased from 160 to 18,628.[60]

SIX-DAY BICYCLE EVENTS IN THE UNITED STATES

During the 1860s and 1870s, "go as you please" events had attracted a large following in the United States. Hopeful contestants walked and ran a track over a six-day period ranging from Monday to Saturday. By the late 1870s this style of competitive diversion was replaced by a faster and more exciting form of transportation—the bicycle. Attracting the interest of a few hearty Americans, the first six-day bicycle race was held in Chicago starting November 25, 1879, at the Exposition Building. A team of four Americans competed against an English quintet which marked the beginning of six-day cycling events in the United States.[61]

The unique six-day cycling event appealed both to men and women participants. The first American male six-day champion was Albert Schock when in March, 1886, he won the United States Championship by riding a distance of 1,009 miles and three laps in Minneapolis.[62] Madison Square Garden staged its first race for women on February 12, 1889. The field of 12 contestants consisted of 10 Americans, an Irish entry and an English competitor. An American, Miss Starley, earned first place honors by pedaling 624 miles and 2 laps.[63] Women's racing was brought to an end as a result of social pressure and by the efforts of the influential bicycling club, the League of American Wheelmen, which did not approve of contests among females.

Although six-day endurance events were popular, track and road races of varying distances were also in vogue. On Tuesday, November 27, 1894, the beginning of a six-day international bicycle tournament was held at Madison Square Garden which attracted over 1,000 entrants. A featured event included World Sprint Champion A. Zimmerman, from New Jersey, who competed for a share of the $10,000 prize money offered by race promoters.[64] Hopeful entrants were now using bicycles of revolutionary design known as the "Rover Safety Bicycle." Prior to 1885 contestants used the high wheeled "ordinary," but the Rover had two wheels of equal size and was rear-wheeled chain driven. Invented by J.K. Starley in 1885, it became well established and served as the prototype of the modern bicycle.

In 1896, the first continuous twenty-four hours a day six-day bicycle race was staged December 6–11 at Madison Square Garden. Thirty-one competitors entered the event with pre-race favorites being Albert Schock and Teddy Hale. Hale, from Ireland, won first place honors and received front-page coverage in *The New York Times* by cycling a total of 1,910 miles and eight laps bettering Schock's old record by more than 310 miles. Hale earned nearly $5,000 in prize money and endorsements for his winning efforts.[65] The 144-hour race was a supreme test of endurance in which the effects of fatigue and crashes took their toll. During a break in the race the eventual second-place finisher complained to his trainer that "other riders were in league against him, and were continually throwing bricks and sticks at him."[66] Another racer went to sleep on his "wheel" and was rudely awakened when his machine rolled off the track. "He then got a big cigar and while smoking did some lively sprinting. . . . During the day he had five falls."[67] Throughout the entire race Hale slept a total of only eight hours. His daily diet consisted of four pounds of roasted chicken, eight quarts of beef and chicken tea, one pound of boiled rice, one pound of oatmeal, two bowls of custard, fish every other day, milk toast, jelly, tapioca, and two to three pounds of fruit.[68]

In 1898, the era of the individual, twenty-four hours a day, six-day bicycling contests ended because of the severe physical demands it placed upon the contestants. Two years earlier a *New York Times* editorial writer sarcastically remarked that it is an accomplishment to demonstrate that a man astride two wheels can outdistance a hound or horse, thereby making him superior to animals. Commenting on the "saneness" of the sport he continued:

> An athletic contest in which the participants 'go queer' in their heads, and strain their powers until their faces become hideous with the tortures that rack them, is not sport, it is brutality.[69]

In 1899, the event was modified and featured the two-man team style six-day. On December 4, 1899, James J. Jeffries, a renowned heavyweight boxer, served as the official starter for 19 teams of two riders participating in a six-day at Madison Square Garden. Under the new rules the maximum time a contestant could cycle was 12 hours a day. The team of Charles Miller and Frank Waller logged a distance of 2,733 miles and four laps to earn first place honors.[70]

The team style six-day was conducted in the United States from 1900 through the 1930s which encouraged faster races and greater use of tactics. During the 1920s attending a "six" was in vogue for politicians and entertainers and serving as honorary starter was considered a privilege. The Depression greatly curtailed this unique bicycle event and with the onset of World War II they were no longer held. Since that time four six-day races have been staged in the following cities; Chicago (1957), Cleveland (1958), New York (1961), and Los Angeles (1973). All four events were financially unsuccessful.[71] Although this type of racing is no longer widespread in the United States, it is well-received in Europe where about a dozen races are held each year.

THE MEDICAL PROFESSION RECOGNIZES EXERCISE AS A CONTRIBUTOR TO HEALTH

The Journal of Health, first published in Philadelphia in 1830 by an association of physicians, represents an early endeavor to advise its readers of ways to preserve health through exercise. Topics published included commentaries on physical education, gymnastics, calisthenics, and the effects of exercise on health. By 1830 the medical profession was already expressing concern for those who were engaged in sedentary occupations. Walking was regarded as an appropriate exercise for both sexes. However, in the first issue of *The Journal of Health,* caution was expressed about some exercises because it was thought that running and leaping were:

> . . . of too violent a nature to be used by any but those who are already in the enjoyment of health and considerable bodily vigor: and even these cannot be often repeated or continued for any length of time.[72]

Journal readers were instructed to exercise every portion of the body to produce symmetry. In order to enhance symmetry, men when choosing amusements and sports, were directed to avoid using muscles that were employed in their occupations.[73] Reflecting both the constraints of fashion and society in the 1830s, *The Journal of Health* recognized that girls and women would benefit from the same kinds of exercise allowed those of the opposite sex, but the editor was content to publish articles that adapted exercises to females.

In an article entitled "Calisthenics" printed in the February 23, 1831, edition of *The Journal of Health,* women were encouraged to engage in restricted calisthenics such as making evolutions with the arms. While standing on one foot women were instructed to bend the opposite leg without touching the floor. Rope jumping and "battledore" or badminton were also advocated for women. In describing the plight of women because of their inactivity, a writer for *The Journal of Health* warned:

> The consequences are, a greater tendency to stoop, and acquire false and injurious attitudes—deformity of the spine and the like; together with an acquired nervousness of temperament, which makes them, in after years, a prey to dyspeptical and hysterical disorders, and an inequality of spirits distressing to themselves, and often exceedingly annoying to friends and others in whose society they may be thrown. Nor are the monstrous absurdities of their dress, at all calculated to diminish these evils. For fear inaction of the muscles of their chest and back should not be sufficiently enfeebling, tight dresses, under various names, compress those parts, and almost paralyze their action.[74]

Charles Caldwell, a medical doctor, using the term "physical education," at an 1833 assembly of teachers, called for a greater emphasis on the physical development of Americans. Regarding diet he believed "that the thirteen or fourteen millions of people, inhabiting this country, eat more trash, for amusement, and fashion's sake, and to pass away idle time, than half the inhabitants of Europe united."[75]

The medical profession, through its early publications, made some Americans aware of the benefits of sports, games, and amusements long before

Figure 4.4. An acceptable game of badminton.

physical education became an established profession. Physical exercise was regarded as an important contributor to one's general well-being.

FRONTIER AMUSEMENTS AND SPORTS

The westward expansion of the country was accomplished by those who were willing to accept the challenge of settling new land and enduring numerous hardships. The transporting of families was difficult when some trails were negotiable only by horseback. People lived in crudely built homes miles apart from their nearest neighbors. Medical attention was inadequate and little was done to quell the ravages of epidemics. Food was often scarce and attacks by Indians were a constant threat. Because day-to-day necessities demanded so much of their time, frontier men, women, and children had little time for leisure pursuits. Some sports and amusements evolved because they were of a utilitarian nature. The practice of hunting skills served as amusement and improved the hunter's ability to kill game.

HUNTING

Hunting contributed an ample portion to the Western settlers' livelihood. Firearms and a variety of other hunting equipment were used for recreation with both young and old enjoying target practice. Prizes were sometimes awarded to the best marksmen in shooting matches, and wagering added excitement to the event. A group of hunters desiring competition would divide into two parties. A point system was then devised whereby a specified number of points was awarded for shooting a certain animal. At the end of the day they compared what they had shot and declared the winning group. Frequently the losing side prepared dinner for the winners.

Participants in hunts were serious about their sport. Noise among hunters was unacceptable, wrote a contributor to the *American Turf and Sporting Magazine* in 1836 who warned, "a noisy man is never tolerated more than once to join . . . a hunt."[76]

In addition to learning how to use firearms, boys were taught to use the bow and arrow. Another skill which was both utilitarian and recreative was imitating animals. The imitations of wild turkeys often brought animals within rifle range.[77] Throwing the tomahawk was another activity practiced by boys. A tomahawk, having a handle of a certain length, made a specified number of turns in a given distance. With practice a boy could measure a distance with his eye and strike a tree with his tomahawk.[78] Spears made of broken pitchforks were used for spearing fish. The spearsmen continued their amusement after dark by using torches to light up the stream.[79]

HORSE RACING

Frontier horse racing sometimes occurred after a spur of the moment challenge. Stores would close and townspeople would gather on a smooth stretch of land to watch a race. Newspapers announced races arranged in advance. Work horses were often used in races but as tracks were laid out and race horses moved westward the sport took on a more professional air.[80] In some frontier towns race tracks had been established before 1800. "Shooting matches, foot races, and wrestling all had their devotees, each with a stake on the outcome. The stake was usually more than the better could afford, which . . . made the event more exciting. Each contest was accompanied by copious drinking, and sometimes the drinking occurred without the contest."[81]

RACES, GAMES, AND BASEBALL FOR ALL

Some frontier sports were rough and without enforced regulations conducted in a boisterous and barbaric manner. Fist fights, lacking rules, were violent. The contestants kicked, butted, bit, and gouged; and the loss of an eye, and ear, or a finger, was common. Other activities such as cycling and roller skating which became the rage in the east spread west and contributed to acceptable conduct on the part of participants and observers. Ten pin bowling and billiards moved westward in the 1860s.[82]

Foot races were run at various distances by men and boys. Out of town runners would challenge the local talent. In preparation for a race runners attached a load of shot to each ankle. Additional activities which were natural challenge events included the running and standing long jumps and the high jump.[83] Using little or no equipment the sometimes spontaneous frontier competition provided an opportunity to test individual skills and much needed social interaction.

The Civil War brought military men together who sought a respite from the ordeals of war, and baseball provided such a diversion. By the early 1870s men in prairie towns had organized baseball teams. Boys played on the town's junior team.[84] In 1873 Wichita, Kansas had a baseball club for young ladies. They challenged a team having presumably the best players in the Arkansas valley for the victor's belt.[85]

FRONTIER WORK AND RECREATION

Like their counterparts in other parts of the country frontier settlers found work more pleasant when it was combined with recreational activities. In the words of historian Fredric Paxson:

> The loneliness of prairie life made a craving for companionship. . . . The frontier social life may be said to have its beginning at the log-raising that attended the construction of the cabin. . . . When the timbers were ready the neighbors of the countryside would ride in on horseback, from thirty or forty miles away. They made a picnic of the occasion, and the able-bodied men in a few hours . . . piled up the logs and laid the roof. The frontier welcomed the legitimate excuse for such a gathering. Weddings became boisterous and rude, with home-stilled whiskey in an open tub, a drinking gourd at its side.

Funerals lost something of their solemnity when relatives and friends so manifestly welcomed the opportunity to get together. The occasions came infrequently, but when they came there were stores of pent-up loneliness to be relieved.[86]

Cornhusking, maple sugar gathering, harvesting, quilting, sewing, and weaving also brought frontier families together. The men spent the day working, while the women, in addition to working on various projects, prepared the food. Drinking, gossiping, and debating accompanied the other events. In the evening older people continued their conversations while the young people square danced. Even though dancing was generally popular it was opposed by religious groups who judged it as an immoral practice.[87] There were some religious groups who permitted the play party in which floor patterns similar to dance movements were performed in the absence of music. Participants sang such favorites as "Miller Boy" or "Skip to ma Lou."[88] Other occasions which attracted frontier people were singing schools and spelling bees.

SNUFFING OF A CANDLE— BARKING OFF SQUIRRELS—DRIVING THE NAIL

Like numerous other English travelers, John James Audubon provided valuable documentation of early America's political, social, religious, and sport endeavors. Audubon took three journeys through the United States during 1829–1830, 1831–1834, and 1836–1837. He was particularly fascinated with the art of snuffing a candle, barking off squirrels, and driving a nail.

The same rifle which served as a weapon for protection against enemies and as an instrument for food gathering, also provided a means of sporting challenge. Marksmen, standing at a prescribed distance, took aim at a candle in an attempt to snuff it without putting it out. Snuffing a candle provided practice for shooting at night when a torch reflected light from the eye of an animal.

John James Audubon once observed Daniel Boone bark off numerous squirrels with his rifle. In his first observation, Audubon was amazed when Boone hit the piece of the bark immediately beneath the squirrel, and shivered it into splinters, which had produced the concussion that killed the animal and sent it whirling through the air.

Driving a nail was considered a common feat by Kentuckians, and not any greater an accomplishment than shooting off a wild turkey's head, at a distance of 100 yards. A nail was hammered about two-thirds of its length into a tree or post. A marksman usually standing 40 paces from the target attempted to drive the nail. Hitting the nail on the head was satisfactory, whereas bending the nail or even hitting close to the nail was not acceptable.[89]

LEISURE ACTIVITIES OF FRONTIER WOMEN

Substantial time for leisure activities of female members of frontier society even by 1830 was more widely observed among the elderly and young unmarried women. Youthful equestriennes of well-to-do families rode atop side saddles and displayed outstanding riding skills. Elderly women seeking less physical activities attended the shooting matches held by men where they sewed and exchanged stories. Married women, on the other hand, engaged in few activities outside the home. Some evidence suggests that quilting parties and gatherings for cornhuskings and other tasks increased the work of the housewife, since she was responsible for seeing that the guests ate and were made comfortable. The camp meeting was a diversion which gave both married and unmarried women a reason to leave their homes and mingle with those of their own sex. Frontier communities without permanent houses of worship adopted a form of religious service known as the camp meeting. Camp or church attendance was considered a main source of recreation by some women.[90]

Holidays such as the Fourth of July were enthusiastically celebrated on the frontier. The commemoration became less formal with fewer speeches and more informal music. Ball games, horse races, foot races, sack races, and wheelbarrow races were incorporated into the celebration. In addition there were parades and band concerts. Chasing greased pigs and climbing a greased pole were popular events.[91] The celebration of holidays contributed to American tradition, furnished a theme around which activities could be coordinated, and functioned as a rallying point for people of diverse backgrounds.

By the 1880s, sports in Aberdeen, the "hub city," were diverse. Draw poker, baseball, dog fights, boxing matches, horse races, and ice skating were all part of the recreation pursuits of the inhabitants. Gambling was a part of most sports, especially horse racing. Almost everything imaginable was wagered on the outcome of a horse race, even the wearing attire of those placing bets.[92] Spontaneous sport gave way to organized competition and teams. Laws were passed to exclude gambling, and dog fights were banned.

BARBARIC SPORTS AND AMUSEMENTS

Cockfighting flourished despite opposition from some state legislators. It was oftentimes associated with holidays. In Westmoreland County, Pennsylvania during the Christmas holidays of 1819 there was a cock fight for a six hundred dollar purse. The winner was decided after the best three out of five fights.[93] Even the most distinguished citizens frequented the cocking pit. A short distance from the Washington race course and the nation's capital a cock pit was set up in 1842. "The brutal sport was conducted with great science and order . . . without molestation from the police. . . ."[94] Critics of cockfighting judged the sport as a poor reflection on the character of the country and the morals of Washington.

Thousands of dollars changed hands during cock fights. Interstate pittings were common. Large crowds from Kentucky and Ohio gathered in Dayton where "the pit and amphitheatre would scarcely hold the crowd and give room for the fights."[95] The Cincinnati and Dayton Humane Societies were responsible for the closing of the Dayton pit in February, 1895.[96] Like other sports where gambling abounded there were followers of the sport who made great sums of money and there were those who found themselves in debt.

Bear baiting was one of the bloodiest confrontations of animals. A bear, enclosed in a pen, fought five or six dogs. In gouging matches any means of overpowering an opponent was permitted. A man was considered an accomplished fighter if he could gouge out an opponent's eyeball. Cheers would rise from a crowd when a fighter bit off a nose or an ear. Gouging matches were prevalent along the banks of the Ohio, in the southern states, and in the west. As the country became more settled, legislators enacted laws prohibiting these barbaric melees.

In April, 1806, a spur of the moment horse race in Virginia sent the residents of Wheeling scurrying to see the event. Two men who had met in a public house decided to settle an argument on the town race course. Thomas Ashe, who was traveling in the area at the time, was amazed that two-thirds of the population left for the race course as news of the race spread. He was informed by a proprietor that many of the people would remain at the course until nightfall. Ashe arrived after the two men had raced, but the price of a saddle was collected and six contestants were enticed by the prize money to enter another race. Following the race there was a dispute over the wagering and umpires were appointed. The umpires' decision was rejected and a general skirmish ensued. Soon the crowd's attention was drawn to a quarrel between two men, one a Kentuckian, the other a Virginian. The crowd formed a circle around the two men and demanded to know if they were going to "fight fair" or "rough and tumble." Fighting was a common occurrence and always attracted onlookers. In "rough and tumble" fighting no one was permitted to interfere. The fight commenced and few rounds had been completed when:[97]

> the Virginian contracted his whole form, drew up his arms to his face, with his hands nearly closed in concave, by the fingers being bent to (the) full extension of the flexors, and summoning up all his energy for one act of desperation, pitched himself into the bosom of his opponent.... The sky was rent by the shouts of the multitude.... [98]

The Kentuckian was knocked breathless and fell to the ground. The Virginian maintained a firm grasp on his opponent.

> ... He kept his knees in his enemie's body, fixing his claws in his hair, and his thumbs on his eyes, gave them an instantaneous start from their sockets. The

sufferer roared aloud, but uttered no complaint. The citizens again shouted with joy.[99]

Wrapping his arms around the Virginian, the Kentuckian began to squeeze and the two men began to roll as the Virginian encircled his arms around the larger adversary. The Kentuckian snapped the Virginian's nose. He retaliated by tearing the larger man's lip downward toward his chin. The Kentuckian gave up and the winner was carried about atop the shoulders of well wishers.[100]

"This spectacle ended, and the citizens refreshed with whiskey and biscuit, sold on the ground, the races were renewed. . . . "[101] According to a Quaker living in Wheeling, races were held two or three times a week. Race goers from neighboring states were attracted to the spring and fall races which continued without interruption for 14 days.

During the teens of the 1800s "gander pulling" was observed in Louisville, Kentucky. A live gander, its neck greased, was tied to a tree or pole. A horseback rider at full gallop would attempt to pull off the head of the gander and if successful was awarded a prize.[102] In the mid-1830s "gander-pulling" occurred in various parts of the South and Midwest.

Small inns in Virginia and Kentucky, where ruffians were driven by the westward spread of religion and justice, were the site of fights which occurred almost every day. "At such taverns, there were always persons at no loss for a subject of quarrel. The invariable consequences of which were the loss of sight, and sometimes of life. . . . "[103] Entertainment, though vicious in some inns or taverns, was more pleasant in others. Early nineteenth century amusements at taverns included billiards and cards. Gambling made both of these more attractive. Concerts, plays, and balls in cities such as Lexington, Kentucky, and Cincinnati, Ohio, were well attended during this time period.[104]

People living in the city of Natchez of the Mississippi Territory, like those people in the cities of Kentucky, Ohio, Louisiana, and Mississippi during the early 1800s enjoyed many of the same amusements, sports, and pastimes. Balls, concerts, horse racing, billiards, and cards brought people together in socially acceptable forms of recreation.

REVISITING THE OREGON TRAIL 1842–1860

In his study of pioneers who endured the rigors of crossing the continent in cumbersome wagons, Professor Harold Lerch examined leisure and sport among the pioneers. From such sources as diaries, records of the Oregon Pioneer Association, and the *Oregon Spectator,* he has offered the following insights into leisure and sport among the trail goers and eventual settlers of Oregon territory.

The journey along the Oregon Trail was a repetition of long slow day marches, smokey campfires, and monotonous meals. Physical suffering, exhausting labor, and mental anxiety over possible Indian attacks were somewhat alleviated when music, dancing, and humor were included in the daily routine. Survival skills such as hunting and fishing offered diversion and provided a supply of fresh food for the entire party. Some wagon caravans celebrated holidays such as Independence Day. These diversions, aside from offering enjoyment, promoted group cohesiveness resulting in greater member communication, and feelings of security throughout the wearisome and uncertain journey.

Rare impromptu activities were identified in the form of foot races with friendly Sioux Indians who sought provisions at a camp on June 12, 1850. On a second occasion, the Indians and travelers staged a lighthearted snowball battle inspired by snow on July 10, 1850. In general, the westward travelers had neither the time, energy nor inclination to participate in sporting activities during their crossing. Aside from social gatherings around an evening campfire in which music and dancing were most prevalent, the day's journey offered little or no recreative diversion.

Oregon City marked the end of the pioneers' weary trek across the continent. Out of the Oregon territory was to be carved Oregon, Washington, Idaho, and parts of Wyoming and Montana. As settlements and economic prosperity flourished, sport, amusement, and recreation became more common. As early as the 1840s, impromptu horse races were conducted but were not condoned by the press. Racing of another sort was familiar to the area by 1851. Steamboat races prompted a newspaper man to reminisce that they reminded him of watching races on the Mississippi. The presence of steamboats was indicative of the growth and development of the territory's commercial resources and were used to establish regular communication between different points on the Willamette river with Oregon City.

Neither boxing nor bowling were condoned by the *Oregon Spectator*. Nevertheless, they continued to serve as sporting diversions for some in spite of objections by the press. As early as 1846, boxing matches were held in the region with the promise of return engagements. When a second bowling alley was to be constructed in Oregon City, an editorialist wrote that too much time was wasted, but did acknowledge that good citizens were present. In retrospect, the writer was compelled to recognize those good citizens despite attitudinal differences towards acceptable forms of relaxation. Less objectionable pursuits reached the *Spectator's* pages in the late 1850s when curling and sleigh riding were witnessed with novel interest. As the pioneers continued to prosper, social, and religious institutions brought additional stability to the region. Activities became less spontaneous and gave way to more structure when compared to those performed on the Trail. They were indicative of life which flourished amid the certainty of physical safety, and largely within the confines of established social convention.[105]

SUMMARY

From the end of the Revolutionary War into the late 1880s, sports and amusements became diversified and attracted a greater number of participants. Horse racing became an early spectator sport, and by the end of the eighteenth century it was popular in New York, Maryland, Virginia, and South Carolina, while it met with disapproval on religious grounds in other states. Nevertheless, horse racing thrived and was attracting thousands of spectators by the early 1800s. In 1842 a horse race which attracted national and international attention was held in New York and featured the North's best horse against the South's favorite. During this period it was becoming acceptable to accommodate women at some racetracks where a ladies' stand was provided.

Leisure activities such as hunting and fishing were becoming a common part of American life throughout the country. Other pursuits were limited to geographic regions by weather and terrain. Snowshoeing and skating were well-liked in the colder climates. Work and recreation continued to be combined in rural areas with such projects as quilting parties, corn huskings, and barn raisings. Churches began to serve their members not only spiritually but socially by providing both young and old with recreative functions. Americans, in looking for diversions from work in the early 1800s, flocked to exhibitions where they could view unusual novelties provided by traveling showmen. As early as 1830 the medical profession expressed its concern for those engaged in sedentary occupations and reinforced the need for physically active exercise. Walking was regarded as an appropriate activity. Advancing this concept to its ultimate were those engaged in six-day pedestrian races which also attracted large crowds in the 1830s and 40s.

The sport of boxing emerged on the American sports scene early in the nineteenth century. The sons of elite Southern families who had studied in Europe are generally credited for initiating boxing. Some slaves became skilled pugilists and, after earning their freedom because of boxing prowess, gradually spread the sport northward. During the 1820s a few organized prize fights were staged in northern cities with contests sometimes held on boats or islands to escape law enforcement and the hostile press. Bare knuckle contests which sometimes lasted for hours were replaced by the Queensberry rules and the legalization of boxing in America after 1889. During the second quarter of the nineteenth century boat and yacht clubs increased in number and attracted the interest of the wealthy class. By the end of the Civil War, croquet, among the first activities engaged in by American women, was firmly established and represented a socially acceptable form of recreation between the sexes. Pedestrianism reached its zenith in the 1830s and 40s, and eventually gave way to six-day bicycle events and other races of varying distances. As early as 1830 the medical profession recognized exercise as a contributor to health by publishing *The Journal of Health* in Philadelphia.

The westward movement by pioneers brought with it the challenge of settling new land amidst numerous hardships. Sports and amusements were utilitarian in nature, offering a diversion from the daily rigors of life, while maintaining necessary survival skills. Activities took the form of shooting matches, tomahawk throwing, and the imitation of wild animal calls. For the most part frontier sports were rough and generally without regulations as in rough-and-tumble fighting in which no holds were barred. Like colonists in other parts of the country the settlers found work more pleasant when combined with a social element. Cornhusking, harvesting, and weaving parties brought families together for work and recreation. Holidays were also enthusiastically celebrated on the frontier with a variety of games and activities which served as a rallying point for people of diverse backgrounds. Sports and amusements, more barbaric in nature, were also part of the frontier life. Cockfighting flourished despite opposition from some state legislators, and bear baiting was a common occurrence. Gouging matches between men were eventually prohibited by law as the country became more civilized.

REFERENCES

1. John M'Dowell. *Sermon of Horse Racing.* Elizabeth-Town, New Jersey: Isaac V. Kollock, 1809, p. 12.
2. William H.P. Robertson. *The History of Thoroughbred Racing in America.* New York: Bonanza Books, 1964, p. 28.
3. Robertson, *ibid.,* pp. 31–32.
4. "Memoranda of the Race Between Eclipse and Henry," *The New York Herald,* May 10, 1842, p. 1.
5. "Result of the Great Race," *The New York Herald,* May 10, 1842, p. 1.
6. J.S. Skinner. "The Fashion and Boston Match," *American Turf Register and Sporting Magazine.* 13 (July, 1842), pp. 367–368.
7. "Result of the Great Race," *The New York Herald,* May 10, 1842, p. 1.
8. "Result of the Great Race—The South Against the North—The North Victorious," *The New York Herald,* May 11, 1842, p. 2.
9. Henry William Herbert. *Horse and Horsemanship of the United States and British Provinces of North America, Volume 1.* New York: Stringer and Townsend, 1857, p. 290.
10. "Racing-Gambling and Other Amusements-Business of Congress-The Navy-Visit of Pipelayers," *The New York Herald,* May 10, 1842, p. 1.
11. Henry William Herbert. *Frank Forrester's Horse and Horsemanship of the United States and British Provinces of North America, Volume Two.* New York: Stringer and Townsend, 1857, pp. 531–560.
12. "Sporting Intelligence," *The New York Times,* September 28, 1858, p. 4.
13. Esther Alice Peck. "A Conservative Generation's Amusements," *The Maine Bulletin.* 40 (April, 1938), pp. 104–105.
14. Robert B. Weaver. *Amusements and Sports in American Life,* Chicago: The University of Chicago Press, 1939, pp. 29–30.
15. Peck. "A Conservative Generation's Amusements," *op. cit.,* pp. 1–2.
16. Weaver. *Amusements and Sports in American Life, op. cit.,* p. 29.

17. Peck. *op. cit.,* p. 20.
18. Weaver. *op. cit.,* p. 26.
19. Weaver, *ibid.,* pp. 19–20.
20. Thomas Ashe. *Travels in America, Volume One.* London: John Abraham, 1808, pp. 52–53.
21. Charles A. Peverelly. *The Book of American Pastimes.* New York: Charles A. Peverelly, 1866, p. 23.
22. William Rotch Wister. *Some Reminiscences of Cricket in Philadelphia Before 1861.* Philadelphia: Press of Allen, Lane and Scott, 1904, pp. 6–9.
23. No author. *The Book of Games, or a History on Juvenile Sports, As Practiced at the Different Academies.* Philadelphia: Crolius and Cladding, 1842, pp. 16, 20–21.
24. J. Frost. *The Art of Swimming; A Series of Practical Instructions, on An Original and Progressive Plan by Which the Art of Swimming May be Readily Attained with Every Advantage of Power in the Water.* New York: P.W. Gallaudet, 1818, pp. 1–3, 5.
25. "Croquet," *Harper's Bazaar.* 1 (October 24, 1868), p. 827.
26. Everett Dick. *The Sod-House Frontier, 1854–1890.* Lincoln, Nebraska: Johnsen Publishing Co., 1954, p. 282.
27. Wells Twombly. *200 Years of Sport in America: A Pageant of a Nation at Play.* New York: McGraw-Hill Book Co., 1976, pp. 60–61.
28. Alexander Johnson. *Ten and Out!* New York: Ives Washburn, 1927, pp. 5–6.
29. Nat Fleischer. *Nat Fleischer's All-Time Ring Record Book.* Norwalk, Connecticut: O'Brien Suburban Press, 1941, p. 29.
30. Johnson. *op. cit.,* pp. 6, 13, 18–19, 21.
31. "Pugilism," *The London Times,* December 19, 1810, p. 3.
32. Nat Fleischer. *The Heavy Weight Championship.* New York: G.P. Putnam's Sons, 1949, p. 33.
33. Fleischer. *ibid.,* p. 41.
34. "Prize Fighting in the United States," *The New York Herald.* September 24, 1842, p. 2.
35. *New York Herald. ibid.*
36. *New York Herald. ibid.*
37. "Appendix Containing Short Sketches of Hyer Sullivan, and Morrissey," *Life of William Poole.* New York: DeWitt and Davenport, 1855, pp. 68–69.
38. "The Ring-Prize Fight Between Lilly and McCoy—Death for McCoy in the Ring." *The New York Herald,* September 14, 1842, pp. 2, 5–6.
39. "City Intelligence." *The New York Herald,* September 16, 1842, p. 2.
40. Fleischer. *op. cit.,* p. 41.
41. Johnson. *op. cit.,* p. 24.
42. "The Fight for the Championship," *The New York Times,* October 22, 1858, p. 5.
43. *The New York Times, ibid.*
44. Johnson. *op. cit.,* pp. 7, 14, 16–17.
45. "The Regatta," *The New York Times,* June 2, 1854, p. 4.
46. "The Yacht Club Regatta," *The New York Times,* June 1, 1859, p. 4.
47. "The Great Foot Race." *American Turf Register and Sporting Magazine.* 6 (May, 1835), p. 478, and "The Great Foot Race," *American Turf Register and Sporting Magazine.* 6 (June, 1835), p. 518.

48. Ibid. *American Turf Register and Sporting Magazine.* 15 (November, 1844), p. 685.
49. Ibid., pp. 685, 689.
50. "Ladies International Tournament," *The New York Times,* December 15, 1879, p. 5.
51. "Miss Howard Wins the Belt," *The New York Times,* December 21, 1879, p. 5.
52. "A Great Pedestrian Feat," *The New York Times,* January 14, 1879, p. 6.
53. "Pedestrianism," *Chicago Tribune,* January 21, 1879, p. 5.
54. "Pedestrianism," *Chicago Tribune,* February 5, 1879, p. 5.
55. "Pedestrianism," *Chicago Tribune,* February 19, 1879, p. 8.
56. "Pedestrianism," *Chicago Tribune,* February 23, 1879, p. 7.
57. John A. Lucas. "Pedestrianism and the Struggle for the Sir John Astley Belt, 1878–1979," *The Research Quarterly.* 39 (October, 1968), pp. 588, 593–594.
58. Charls A. Pratt. "A Sketch of American Bicycling and Its Founder," *Outing.* 18 (July, 1891), pp. 342–347.
59. Robert H. Merriam. "Bicycles and Tricycles," *Special Reports of the Census Office Manufactures, 1905 Part IV.* Washington, D.C.: Government Printing Office, 1908, p. 289.
60. "Bicycles, Motorcycles and Parts," *13th Census of the United States Taken in the Year 1910, Vol. 10.* Washington, D.C.: Government Printing Office, 1913, pp. 825, 827.
61. "Racing on Bicycles," *The New York Times,* November 25, 1879, p. 5.
62. "The Bicycle Record Beaten," *The New York Times,* March 14, 1886, p. 7.
63. "Women on Bicycles," *The New York Times,* February 12, 1889, p. 2.
64. "Training for Big Races," *The New York Times,* November 23, 1894, p. 6, and "Exciting Bicycle Races," *The New York Times,* November 28, 1894, p. 6.
65. "Hale Wins the Big Race," *The New York Times,* December 13, 1896, p. 1.
66. Ibid.
67. "Schock Out of the Race," *The New York Times,* December 10, 1896, *p. 2.*
68. "After the Six-Day Race," *The New York Times,* December 14, 1896, p. 2.
69. "A Brutal Exhibition," *The New York Times,* December 11, 1897, p. 8.
70. "Six-Day Bicycle Race On, *The New York Times,* December 4, 1899, p. 2, and "Miller and Waller Win," *The New York Times,* December 10, 1899, p. 11.
71. Joe Kossack. "Six Days of Bicycling," *Bike World,* 2 (August-September, 1973), pp. 22–25.
72. "Gymnastic Exercise," *The Journal of Health,* 1 (January 13, 1830), p. 132.
73. "Variety in Exercise," *The Journal of Health,* 1 (April 20, 1830), p. 245.
74. "Calisthenics," *The Journal of Health,* 2 (February 23, 1831), p. 191.
75. Chares Caldwell. *Thoughts on Physical Education: Being a Discourse Delivered to A Convention of Teachers in Lexington, Kentucky on the 6th and 7th of November, 1833.* Boston: Marsh, Capen and Lyon, 1834, pp. 51–52.
76. "Racing and Sports in the West," *American Turf and Sporting Magazine,* 8 (October, 1836), p. 66.
77. Weaver. op. cit., p. 50.
78. Weaver. ibid., p. 51.
79. Dick. op. cit. *The Sod-House Frontier 1854–1890.* p. 283.
80. Dick. ibid., pp. 278–279.
81. Rober E. Riegel. *America Moves West.* New York: Henry Holt and Co., 1947, p. 105.

82. Dick. op. cit., pp. 279–280.

83. Dick. ibid., pp. 279–280.

84. Dick. ibid., pp. 280–281.

85. "City and County News," *The Wichita Eagle,* February 13, 1873, p. 3.

86. Frederic L. Paxson. *History of the American Frontier 1763–1893.* Boston: Houghton Mifflin Co., 1924, p. 115.

87. Riegel. *America Moves West.* op. cit., p. 104.

88. Dick. op. cit., p. 372.

89. John James Audubon. *Delineations of American Scenery and Character.* London: Simpkin, Marshall, Hamilton, Kent and Co., 1926, pp. 59–62.

90. William Forest Sprague. *Women and the West: A Short Social History.* Boston: The Christopher Publishing House, 1940, pp. 57–59, 62, and Harold Preece. *Living Pioneers the Epic of the West by Those Who Lived It.* Cleveland: The World Publishing Co., 1952, p. 179.

91. Dick. op. cit., pp. 379–380.

92. Carl C. Stewart. "Thrilling Horse Race of Pioneer Days Is Recalled," *Aberdeen American News,* June 1, 2, 1931, sec. E, p. 6.

93. J. W. Cooper. *A Treatise on Cocking, Giving a History of the Various Breeds of Imported and American Game Fowls.* Media, Delaware County, Pennsylvania: Cooper and Vernon, 1859, p. 83.

94. "Racing-Gambling and other Amusements—Business of Congress—The Navy— Visit of Pipelayers," *The New York Herald,* May 10, 1842, p. 1.

95. "An Interstate Cocking Main," *The National Police Gazette: New York,* February 16, 1895, p. 3.

96. Ibid.

97. Thomas Ashe. op. cit., pp. 223–225.

98. Ashe. Ibid., p. 26.

99. Ashe. Ibid., p. 227.

100. Ashe. Ibid., p. 228.

101. Ashe. Ibid., p. 229.

102. Henry Bradshaw Fearnon. *Sketches of America.* London: Longman, Hurst, Rees, Orme, and Brown, 1818, p. 247.

103. Ashe. op. cit., p. 231.

104. Thomas Ashe. *Travels in America, Volume Two.* London: John Abraham, 1808, pp. 149, 178–179.

105. Harold A. Lerch. "Pioneer Expressions of Sport and Leisure on the Oregon Trail 1842–1860," Houston: AAHPERD Convention, History Academy Symposium, 1982.

Chapter 5

URBANIZATION AND INDUSTRIALIZATION IN THE UNITED STATES, 1850–1890

In 1800, the United States was primarily an agricultural nation. However, one of the most dramatic changes was the transfer of a large proportion of wealth and population from rural areas to an urban setting. By the mid-nineteenth century, America experienced this phenomenal industrial and urban growth which influenced the sporting and leisure-time activities for all classes of citizens.

INDUSTRIALIZATION

Industrial growth can be linked to a variety of causes but many authorities agree that the factor which served as a major catalyst was the transportation-communication network. Most of the early railroads were designed as short-run lines in order to serve the needs of the larger cities. However, the passing of the Pacific Railways Acts by Congress in 1862 and 1864 authorized subsidies for railway construction which encouraged intense rivalry among towns and cities across the country to connect with a cross-country line. Although often plagued by economic difficulties and cut-throat competition, some cities prospered financially from the railroads while others suffered. Nevertheless, by 1880 the outline of our contemporary railway network was etched on the face of America. Because of this new national transportation system, and the accompanying spread of telegraph and telephone lines, large-scale manufacturing was developed which made the factory an important part in the nation's network of urban economic and geographic development.

Aside from a national system of transportation and the rise of manufacturing, another major factor contributing to industrialization was the agricultural revolution. Notwithstanding the "good times" and bright lights in the cities, the development of new methods of farming contributed markedly to America's changing life-style by reducing the need for farm labor.[1] Essentially, the newfound use of machinery lightened the farmer's work while also making it possible for one man to do the work of ten leaving the remaining nine men to seek their livelihood in the cities.

URBANIZATION

Industrialization influenced urbanization in that it required labor which further increased the size of cities. It must also be recognized that urbanization contributed to industrialization due to the concentration of population which provided a ready-made labor force. Aside from economic development the effects of industrialization also produced major social consequences. Rural America alone did not make up all of the urban population. Immigrants came to the United States in overwhelming numbers during the latter part of the nineteenth century. From 1850 to 1900 over sixteen million men, women and children arrived in America.[2] Metropolitan areas experienced rapid growth and by 1860 the population in eight cities exceeded 100,000 with New York already passing the 1,000,000 mark.[3] These early arrivals to American cities in large numbers oftentimes provided nearly half the entire labor force of the central business districts with a typical work day lasting about 12 hours. Under far less than favorable working conditions a machinist, considered to be a skilled worker, earned a daily wage of $1.61 in 1860 and unskilled laborers received $1.03. By 1880 skilled workers were paid $2.45 for their day's efforts while the unskilled workers made $1.32.[4] The eight-hours-a-day work movement began to gain momentum about 1842. Employees in government navy yards and municipal workers in some larger cities were the first to profit from it by the 1860s.[5] Home living conditions of the immigrant in the cities offered little relief from the hardships of daily work. Leaving boarding-houses as soon as possible, families settled in old private residences which had been converted into tenements. Three basic elements dictated where the immigrant would live in such cities as New York. It was essential to be close to one's place of employment, housing had to be inexpensive, and it was a source of comfort and help to live with neighbors of the same ethnic background. For the city dweller in Europe who migrated to America, it was not much of a change to live in an apartment which lacked proper plumbing, lighting, and ventilation. However, those who came from rural areas such as Ireland or southern Germany had to make a difficult adjustment to city conditions:

> Instead of the fresh country air, he breathed the foul miasma of cramped and insalubrious quarters... there was little but gloom and darkness.... When water for bathing and washing had to be fetched from street pumps or near-by wells, bodily cleanliness was more of an ideal than a reality. Not only was it impossible to bathe, but insufficient space and air hindered home laundering. ... Nearly all the old buildings, and many of the newer ones, lacked toilet facilities. Back-yard, wooden privies were common, but they could not accommodate the large number of inhabitants they were intended to serve. Through overuse and improper care, the privies remained a constant menace to health, and their contents, instead of being drained or carried away, frequently overflowed to the surface and created breeding places of disease.[6]

Aside from inferior living quarters the newly arrived urbanite found little wholesome outside space in which to relax and play.

EARLY PLAYGROUNDS IN URBAN SOCIETY

With the transformation of the United States from a rural-agrarian to urban-industrial society came the dawning realization of the need for municipal playgrounds and recreational centers. Three major factors attributed to this movement which had its early beginnings before 1900. First, the population shifted from rural to urban areas causing overcrowded living conditions. Second, the reduction of working hours offered greater opportunity for recreational pursuits and finally, mobility was increased because of improved travel facilities.

Early impetus for public recreation areas came from civic and social workers who recognized the lack of suitable opportunities for constructive play experiences of young and old alike living in congested cities. They provided funds and established the first public playgrounds in their attempts to build favorable public opinion which was to eventually lead to governmental support of public recreational facilities. The playground movement began prior to 1900 in the larger cities with Boston leading the way as early as 1868. In 1889 the famous Charlesbank outdoor gymnasium was established by the Boston Park Department which represented an early serious effort by a city to recognize and provide for the play of young children.[7] Other major cities such as Philadelphia, Chicago, Baltimore, and New York followed Boston's example by developing similar playgrounds. In keeping with this early trend to encourage constructive use of leisure time, New York City was the first to earmark their school buildings as community recreation centers in 1898.

Even though economic conditions were improving slightly for the city dweller, the hours of work were still long and money was scarce. In spite of early efforts to establish playgrounds and recreation centers, little if any attention was given to the social welfare of the city worker. Although the playground and recreation movements made limited headway in meeting the needs of an ever-growing urbanized society in the latter part of the 1800s, it was to mushroom by the twentieth century in response to the ever-increasing pressures of urban sprawl and technological advancement. In 1906 the Playground Association of America was founded by Dr. Luther Gulick, city school supervisor of physical education in New York City, and Dr. Henry Curtis who was a pioneer playground worker in Washington, D.C.

INVENTIONS AND THE RISE OF SPORT

Historian John R. Betts concluded that the impact of invention had a major influence on the rise of sport in the second half of the nineteenth century. By 1900 sport was a commonly recognized element in the daily lives of millions of Americans which was largely brought about, according to Betts, by the development of the steamboat, railroad, telegraph, improvements in the printing process, electric light, streetcar, camera, bicycle, automobile, and the mass production of sporting goods.[8]

Steamboat

The steamboat was a common carrier of sports crowds to major horse racing events as well as outdoor sporting events which were held along the eastern seaboard and in the Mississippi Valley. In the 1850s, for example, the steamer Natchez was chartered to bring stables of horses to New Orleans for upcoming races. It also transported turf enthusiasts. "The fine steamer Natchez starts this evening for the scene of action, and this favorite will doubtless be crowded with interested parties to the contests," boasted *The New Orleans Times Picayune.*[9] In 1869 a prizefight was staged near St. Louis and the steamboat Louisville was engaged for the noisy excursion to ringside 26 miles away at Foster's and Bridewater Island.[10] During the early and middle years of the nineteenth century the steamboat played a major role in promoting a rising interest in horse racing and other outdoor sporting activities.

Railroad

The development of a railroad network was also instrumental in bringing the sporting scene to Americans throughout the nation. In 1830, there were 23 miles of railroad in operation in the United States, but this grew to 52,864 miles in a 40-year period. Twelve years later by 1882 it had more than doubled to 114,928 miles of operational railroad throughout the country.[11]

As early as 1838 racing horses were being transported by rail. By 1851 Kentucky became the breeding center for thoroughbreds and the railways served to help establish this recognition. In the 1870s Western turfmen were sending their horses to races in the east. Railroad companies realized the advantage of encouraging the racing public and did so by cooperating with the Kentucky Derby officials and organizers of agricultural fairs in promoting excursions by train to racing events.

Baseball clubs, mainly organized throughout the East and Midwest, made use of the railway network in the 1870s. The National League which was organized in 1876 relied upon the railroad and its continuing development to help popularize the game of baseball which it did throughout the years to come. Intercollegiate athletics also depended upon the railroad to transport teams and their followers to football, baseball, rowing, and track and field contests. The railroad helped to bring boxing and cycling into greater public view as well as carry rod and gun enthusiasts into the rural preserves using branch train lines. So pervasive was the railroads' influence that "by the closing years of the century virtually every realm of sport had shared in the powerful impact of the railroad on American life."[12]

Public amusement parks were promoted by railroad companies as they increasingly recognized their economic value. By 1896 it was estimated that at least 100 companies had established parks of their own for the sole purpose of increasing their passenger business. Two of the most noted examples were the Toledo and Detroit Electric Railway Companies. An elaborate enterprise was engaged in by the Toledo Company when they constructed a $65,000 casino on the shores of Lake Erie, in a large park which they owned. The Detroit firm enjoyed "phenomenal patronage" at their five-acre Boulevard Park where a grandstand seating over 8,000 people was constructed. General entertainment themes included such epic "plays" as the "Last Days of Pompeii, Carnival of Venice, and Capture of Vera Cruz." A stage complete with painted background and props in the foreground enhanced the play. Actors pantomimed their roles which depicted athletic contests, pageants, races, and ballets, with the finale being spectacularly pyrotechnic in nature.[13]

Telegraph

In concert with railway development came the establishment of telegraph lines throughout the country. Invented in 1844, the electric telegraph played a major role in disseminating news to all parts of the nation. During the early years sporting events were not extensively reported due to the cost of telegraphic messages, however, as early as 1849 a prize fight was reported from Maryland as being a brutal encounter. Over the next decade several boxing matches received wide coverage by telegraph.

As sporting news expanded telegraphy in time made it possible to provide accounts of baseball games, horse races, boxing matches, and regattas. By 1870 many metropolitan newspapers published daily reports of sporting events. In the 1880s sport was such an everyday topic for discussion by almost everyone, that newspapers expanded their coverage using telegraphic messages from distant parts of the country.[14]

Printing Improvements

Numerous inventions improved the printing process which encouraged the mass production of the daily newspaper. Of course sporting news was an important part of its contents. The publication of sporting books also increased, and the books were concerned with such topics as athletics, hunting, camping, canoeing, yachting, angling, mountain climbing, and cycling. The athletic almanac was also developed with A.G. Spalding and Brothers becoming the leading authority on rules of play. A few writers directed their talents toward developing athletic themes during the 1870s, and by the 1890s there was a demand for boys' athletic stories.[15]

Incandescent Light

The development of the electric light bulb by Thomas A. Edison in 1879 initiated a new era for participants in athletics and spectators alike. In November, 1885, *Harper's Weekly* described in festive detail the third annual show of horses held in Madison Square Garden which lasted five days. The reader was also treated to a description of the Garden and mention of electric lights:

> ... gaudy with festoons of racing flags and brilliant streamers, lighted at night by hundreds of electric lights, and at all times thronged with handsomely dressed ladies, was, as may be imagined, an attractive place for all classes of the community.[16]

Figure 5.1. The New York Athletic Club's reception room.

Electric lighting improved facilities in YMCAs, school gymnasiums, and athletic clubs. The New York Athletic Club was brilliantly lighted and the gymnasium was described as being "light and airy." It was a far cry from the dismal atmosphere which surrounded early indoor sport. Emerson's words, "beauty is its own excuse for being," were used to lend support to the belief that ... "fine surroundings will not do an athlete any harm ... "[17]

Indoor baseball was also born during the age of the electric light when it was first played by several New York regiments in an armory. Of course baseball by gas light or candlelight was judged impossible. "With the electric light, however, all is different." Baseball was just one of the many recreational games made possible by the electric light.[18]

Lights were used by the city of Boston in conducting athletic events. On February 15, 1890, the Boston Athletic Association held its first indoor track and field meet of the season in the hall of the Massachusetts Mechanics' Association. Several thousand spectators watched approximately 600 amateur athletes compete under the "lights" for five hours in the largest meet of its kind ever held in Boston.[19] Electric lighting enhanced the night life in the cities by encouraging people to attend indoor sporting events after completion of the workday.

Streetcar

The electric street car was instrumental in showing city dwellers the route to the countryside. In 1890 there were only 144 electric railways in a total of 789 street lines. About 3,000 of the 32,500 cars were electric. By 1899 there were over 50,600 electric cars with the mileage of electric railways increasing from 1,300 to nearly 18,000.[20]

Figure 5.2. Indoor baseball.

At the beginning of the twentieth century, the ever growing interest in games and amusements by people in thousands of towns and cities was greatly stimulated by the development of rapid transit systems. Park amusement circuits for street railway companies had already been developed in such cities as Kansas City, Minneapolis, St. Paul, Grand Rapids, Duluth, St. Louis, Milwaukee, Rock Island, Davenport, and Des Moines.

Photography

Development of the Eastman Kodak camera in the late 1880s made it possible for pictures to be taken and used as photographs in sporting magazines and eventually in the newspapers. In 1872 Eadweard Muybridge was an important link in motion picture history when he successfully proved that a trotting horse was not always in contact with the ground. By setting up a battery of 24 cameras alongside a track the movements of a horse was successively photographed. By 1879 Muybridge's photographs had attracted international attention. He eventually developed a monumental study of 11 volumes entitled *Animal Locomotion,* which contained 100,000 photographs of horses, athletes, birds in flight, and other living subjects. With his pictures he showed the work and play activities of men, women, and children of all ages. He captured for interested viewers such actions as pitchers throwing a baseball, batters hitting the ball, and athletes performing record-breaking events.[21]

By the 1880s, the motion picture was refined and proved to be one of the most popular attractions at the penny arcades. For the newly arrived immigrant to the cities, as well as those living in small rural communities, the moving picture served as an agency for information and as a nominally priced form of entertainment. Morris writes:

> In the slums of the great Eastern and Middle Western cities there were herded vast immigrant populations. Largely unfamiliar with the English language, they could not read the newspapers, magazines, or books. But the living pictures communicated their meanings directly and eloquently. To enjoy them no command of a new language was essential. They made illiteracy, and ignorance of American customs seem less shameful; they broke down a painful sense of isolation and ostracism. Dwellers in tenements, workers in sweatshops, could escape the drabness of their environment for a little while, at a price within their means. They could learn about their adopted country, see the water come tumbling over Niagara Falls, the spectacular architecture of the Pan American Exposition at Buffalo, the funeral of President McKinley, the inaguration of President Theodore Roosevelt. They could participate in little dramatic incidents: a budding courtship interrupted; a chase; a comic altercation between Happy Hooligan, the disreputable tramp, and a smug member of the prosperous class . . . [22]

Bicycle

The bicycle took America by storm in the 1880s. Bicycle enthusiasts were instrumental in establishing a consciousness in America for the construction of good roads which influenced the development of our highway system. A

Figure 5.3. Urban America, 1890s.

cycling club, the League of American Wheelmen, were leaders in helping to bring about legislation for good roads, and by 1900 over half the states had new and improved highway legislation. Key mechanical principles of the bicycle were also used to help develop the automobile. For example the pneumatic tire, ball bearings, hub braking, and the tangential spoke made it possible for its development. Many bicycle manufacturers were among the first automobile makers because they found it relatively easy to adapt their machinery to build motor cars.

Bicycling served to carry people to and from their work and it revealed the pleasures of the surrounding countryside. It also became a means for seeking adventure. One such daring young man was Thomas Stevens. Leaving San Francisco April 22, 1884, on a 50-inch bicycle, he toured the world until completing his trip December 17, 1886, at Yokohama, Japan. Actually wheeling about 13,500 miles Stevens recounts an impromptu bicycle-horse race while in Turkey enroute to a village:

> ... I overtake a zaptieh also enroute to Angora who is letting his horse crawl leisurely along ... The zaptieh is, of course, delighted at seeing me thus mount, and not doubting but that I will appreciate his company, gives me to understand that he will ride alongside to Angora. For nearly two miles that sanquine but unsuspecting minion of the Turkish Government spars his noble steed alongside the bicycle in spite of my determined pedalling to shake him off; but the road improves; faster spins the whirling wheels; the zaptieh begins to lag behind a little, though still spurring his panting horse into keeping reasonably close behind; a bend now occurs in the road, and an intervening knoll hides us from each other; I put on more steam, and at the same time the zaptieh evidently gives it up and relapses into his normal crawling pace, for when three miles or thereabout are covered I look back and perceive him leisurely heaving in sight from behind the knoll.[23]

Bicycles of the 1890s consisted of a large front wheel with cranks and pedals. A curved "backbone" with a saddle attached to it connected the front wheel to a smaller rear wheel. In 1889 the dangerous high wheel was replaced by the "safety" which had two wheels of the same size. Eventually a drop frame was also designed for the ladies who could, if desired, purchase a folded screen which attached to the front of the bicycle in order to keep the feet and ankles from view when mounting or riding the bicycle.[24] Within a few years, however, the "horseless carriages" which were beginning to make occasional appearances on the roads ended the bicycle craze.

Automobile

The automobile was one of the last inventions of the nineteenth century with its earliest use taking the form of racing. In the 1890s, a number of car manufacturers such as Haynes, Ford, Packard, Pierce Arrow and Buick were established. In 1895, Herman H. Kohlsaat, publisher of the *Chicago Times-Herald,* sponsored the first automobile race in America. The event helped to

Figure 5.4. An 1890 wheelman.

bring recognition to the gasoline motor as the proper source of motor power. European auto races attracted American drivers to endurance and speed contests which in turn attracted pioneer manufacturers. The auto makers recognized the publicity gained from the races as reported by the newspapers.[25]

Finding machinery work preferable to plowing on his father's farm, a young man named Henry Ford moved from Dearborn to Detroit, Michigan. Out of a job, Ford with the help of three men, built a racing car and challenged the reigning auto-speed king, Alexander Winton. The ten-mile race was held in 1902 at Grosse Pointe, Michigan, which Ford won in 13 minutes, 23.2 seconds. He then built two identical racers equipped with four cylinders and having 80 horsepower. One of the cars named "999," after the Empire State Express locomotive, was so fast that both Ford and a co-worker dared not drive it at top speed. Looking for a driver courageous enough to tame the spirited "999," Ford hired a fearless bicycle rider named Barney Oldfield to be his race driver. Although he had never driven an automobile, Ford and a friend taught him how to drive in a week. In an auto race at Grosse Pointe, the "999" with Oldfield at the tiller jumped into the lead and won by a half mile. Capitalizing on this win, the Ford Motor Company was formed on June 16, 1903.[26] The company was a success from the start and in a little over 15 months from the date of incorporation, it had paid dividends totaling 100 percent of the issued capital stock.[27]

PRODUCTION OF SPORTING GOODS

In the 1850s, sporting accessories such as archery equipment, guns, fishing tackle, and billiard tables were made by individual craftsmen. Prior to the Civil War methods for the mass-production of goods had not yet been established. Economically the sporting goods business did not assume major importance in the nineteenth century. However, by the end of the century A.G. Spalding and Brothers was nationally recognized as the leader in the manufacture and sales of sporting goods. Branching out into a variety of sports in the 1880s, Spalding monopolized the market by absorbing other smaller companies.[28]

In the latter years of the century, department store catalogues began to advertise sporting goods. In 1895, for example, the Sears, Roebuck and Company's catalogue contained 507 pages offering the usual items plus others such as shoes, women's garments, wagons, stoves, furniture, china, and glassware. The second most important space allocation consisting of 83 pages was devoted to weapons and fishing equipment.[29] By 1905, a variety of sporting goods could be purchased from the Sears catalogue in addition to guns and fishing tackle. Now advertised were such items as snow skis, croquet sets, tennis racquets, boxing gloves, footballs, sleighs, baseball equipment, and bicycles. Items which sold especially well were boxing gloves, baseball equipment, and bicycles. Sears issued a special bicycle catalogue and also devoted six pages to bicycles and accessories in the 1905 general catalogue. The featured model was "The Celebrated Three-Crown Nickel Joint Napoleon Bicycle" which sold for $13.85. Ladies were encouraged to buy "The Josephine" equipped with "combination rubber pedals, mud and chain guard, handsomely striped, varnished and laced to match color of frame. Price, $14.35."[30]

America, in the latter half of the nineteenth century, experienced a rapid rise in technological developments. Commensurate with an ever-increasing reduction in long working hours, Americans increasingly turned their interest to sport and recreational activities. The leisure time habits of millions of city and rural citizens were directly influenced by urbanization, industrialization, and the age of inventions.

SUMMARY

By the mid-nineteenth century, America was experiencing rapid industrial and urban growth which influenced the sporting and recreational activities for millions of Americans. Two major factors contributing to industrial growth were the development of a national transportation-communication network and the agricultural revolution. Industrialization influenced urbanization in that the required labor force greatly increased the populations of cities. By 1860, eight cities exceeded over 100,000 residents with New York passing the 1,000,000 mark. Immigrants provided nearly all of the labor required of the central business districts in American cities.

With the development of the United States to an urban-industrial society came the need for municipal playgrounds and recreational centers. The playground movement began in the larger cities with Boston initiating action as early as 1868. In 1889 the Charlesbank outdoor gymnasium was developed by the Boston Park Department. Similar playgrounds were constructed by other major cities, however, this movement made little headway until the twentieth century.

Inventions had a major influence on the growth of sport in the second half of the nineteenth century. By 1900, sport had achieved a more acceptable place in American society. It was largely brought about by the development of the steamboat, railroad, telegraph, printing process, electric light, streetcar, camera, bicycle, automobile, and the mass production of sporting goods. In the 1850s and 60s the steamboat played a major role in promoting horse racing and other sporting events. In 1830 there were 23 miles of railroad in operation which had grown to 114,928 miles by 1882. Baseball clubs and intercollegiate athletics used the railroad to bring the sporting scene to Americans throughout the nation. Railroad companies also promoted public amusement parks to increase their passenger business. The telegraph made it possible to disseminate news, and by 1870 many metropolitan newspapers were publishing daily reports of sporting events. Improvements in the printing process encouraged the production of sporting books and stories with athletic themes. The incandescent light initiated a new era for athletes and spectators. Electric lighting improved facilities in YMCAs, school gymnasiums, and athletic clubs. The streetcar provided a means for city dwellers to go to the countryside where amusement parks awaited them. Photography made it possible for pictures to be taken and used as photographs in sporting magazines and newspapers. Motion pictures became an interesting attraction at penny arcades especially for the newly arrived immigrant, because it served as a source for information and entertainment. Bicycle enthusiasts helped to bring about the establishment of good roads, and by 1900 over half the states had passed improved highway legislation. Automobile development first took the form of racing which helped to establish the gasoline engine as the proper source of motor power. The early efforts of the auto racing industry later provided Americans living in the twentieth century with a means of private transportation. The mass production of sporting goods lent economical access to an increasing variety of equipment with which men, women, and children could enjoy sporting and leisure activities. The leisure time habits of Americans were influenced by urbanization, industrialization, and inventions.

REFERENCES

1. Lane L. Miller. *The Urbanization of Modern America.* New York: Harcourt Brace and Javanovich, Inc., 1973, pp. 27–35.
2. U.S. Department of Commerce, *Historical Statistics of the United States, Part I,* Washington, D.C.: Bureau of the Census, September, 1975, pp. 105–106.
3. *U.S. Bureau of the Census, Thirteenth Census: 1910,* Washington, D.C.: U.S. Government Printing Office, 1913, p. 80.
4. U.S. Department of Commerce, *Historical Statistics of the United States, Part I,* Washington, D.C.: Bureau of the Census, September, 1975, p. 165.
5. John Commons (ed.), and others. *A Documentary History of American Industrial Society, Volume IX,* Cleveland: The Arthur H. Clarke Company, 1910, pp. 277–278.
6. Robert Ernst. *Immigrant Life in New York City, 1825–1863.* New York: 1949, p. 51.
7. Clarence E. Rainwater. *The Play Movement in the United States,* Chicago: University of Chicago Press, 1922, p. 72.
8. John R. Betts. "The Technological Revolution and the Rise of Sport, 1850–1900," *The Mississippi Valley Historical Review,* 11 (September, 1953), pp. 231–255.
9. "Natchez Races," *The New Orleans Times Picayune,* December 10, 1859, p. 4. and "They're coming," *The New Orleans Daily Picayune,* December 1, 1855, p. 2.
10. "The Prize Fight Near St. Louis," *Wilkes' Spirit of the Times,* June 19, 1869, pp. 276–277.
11. *Statistical Abstract of the United States, No. 6,* 1883, Washington: Government Printing Office, 1884, p. 160.
12. Betts. "The Technological Revolution and the Rise of Sport," *op. cit.* pp. 238.
13. "Fireworks As A Park Attraction," *The Street Railway Journal,* 12 (May, 1896), p. 317.
14. Betts. *op. cit.* pp. 238–239.
15. Betts. *ibid.* pp. 242–243.
16. "The Horse Show," *Harper's Weekly,* 29 (November 14, 1885), p. 743.
17. "The New York Athletic Club," *Harper's Weekly,* 29 (February 14, 1885), p. 109.

18. "In-Door Base-Ball," *Harper's Weekly,* 34 (March 8, 1890), p. 179.
19. "Athletics In Boston," *Harper's Weekly,* 34 (March 1, 1890), p. 171.
20. Gilson Willets. *Workers of the Nation. Volume One,* New York: P.F. Gollier and Son, 1903, p. 498.
21. Waldemar Kaempffert (ed.). *A Popular History of American Invention.* New York: Charles Scribner's Sons, 1924, pp. 424–425. and Robert T. Taft. *Photography and the American Scene,* New York: The Macmillan Company, 1942, pp. 406–407.
22. Lloyd Morris. *Not So Long Ago,* New York: Random House, 1949, p. 29.
23. Thomas Stevens. *Around the World on a Bicycle, Volume I,* New York: Charles Scribner's Sons, 1887, p. 318.
24. Mark Sullivan. *Our Times, The United States – 1900-1925,* New York: Charles Scribner's Sons, 1926, p. 241. and Arthur M. Schlesinger. *A History of American Life – The Rise of the City, 1878-1898, Volume X,* New York: The Macmillan Company, 1933, pp. 312–313.
25. Betts. *op. cit.* p. 253.
26. Reginald M. Cleveland and S.T. Williamson. *The Road Is Yours,* New York: The Greystone Press, 1951, pp. 196–197.
27. Lawrence Seltzer. *A Financial History of the American Automobile Industry,* Boston: Houghton Mifflin Company, 1928, p. 91.
28. Betts. *op. cit.* p. 245.
29. Boris Emmet and John Jeuck. *Catalogues and Counters – A History of Sears, Roebuck and Company,* Chicago: The University of Chicago Press, 1950, p. 38.
30. David L. Cohn. *The Good Old Days,* New York: Simon and Schuster, 1940, pp. 454–455.

Chapter 6

THE WOMEN'S RIGHTS MOVEMENT

FROM SENECA FALLS TO LEGISLATION

The women's rights movement in the United States stemmed from discriminatory practices encountered by some American women while they were in England. The movement had a profound influence on political, social, economic, and religious development in this country; but it initially had little effect on sport and physical education for women. The crusade was inaugurated before physical education was acknowledged as a beneficial part of women's education. Although leaders of the movement occasionally spoke in favor of physical activity, much of their time was absorbed by their endeavors to achieve women's franchisement. Although white women such as Susan B. Anthony, Lucretia Mott, and the Grimke sisters, Angelina and Sarah, worked to improve the plight of women, some daring black women such as abolitionist, Sojourner Truth voiced their opinions for women's rights. Mary Church Terrell, another black woman, led the way in helping other black women improve their status.

Women were confronted with public discrimination when they were denied the right to speak at the World's Anti-Slavery Convention in London during June 1840. Thus, the early participants in social reform were acquainted with the crusade for emancipation which affected both slaves and women. Lacking the freedom of open expression and forced to sit behind a curtain at the convention, Lucretia Mott and Elizabeth Cady Stanton who were members of the American delegation, vowed to hold a women's rights meeting when they returned to the United States. Their plans reached fruition when the First Women's Rights Convention was held at Seneca Falls, New York, July 19–20, 1848.[1]

The mid-nineteenth century woman, in addition to lacking voting power, was denied freedom to pursue interests that extended beyond the care of her home. Those that joined the women's movement sought "to acquire an education, to earn a living, to claim ... wages, to own property, to make contracts, to bring suit, to testify in court, to obtain a divorce for just cause, to possess her children, (and) to claim a fair share of the accumulations during marriage."[2] Throughout their struggle to achieve basic rights for women, suffragists were the object of ridicule, hate, and ongoing discrimination. They were criticized by their families and friends and some were

Figure 6.1. The champions of woman's suffrage.

imprisoned. In spite of hardships, patrons of the women's movement worked tirelessly to help women join the mainstream of American life.

THE OMISSION OF PHYSICAL ACTIVITY

Feminists who assembled at Seneca Falls concentrated on seeking reforms in areas that directly affected their freedom to function in society. Although there were some early concerns for the generally low status of women's health and the benefits of physical exercise, women's rights advocates omitted physical activity from their resolutions. Physical activity was not a prominent alternative for feminine expression in the late 1840s. Vestiges of the Victorian belief which portrayed women as fragile creatures whose responsibilities were confined to the home and family lingered into the twentieth century. Sport did not reflect the ideals of the Victorian image because vigorous physical activities were considered unladylike for girls and women. Rather than condoning organized sport for women, society favored as an alternative "feminine" oriented recreational pursuits such as walking, horseback riding, bathing, and sleigh riding. The sphere of women gradually expanded as they asserted themselves and fought to gain entry into all aspects of life that affected their well-being.

The well-known Catherine Beecher was a proponent of education and calisthenics for women who may have sparked a more pronounced interest in physical activity among women's rights workers had she chosen to join their crusade. Beecher, however, was a conservative and objected to the overt actions of feminists which brought ridicule to them. In a letter dated April 26, 1844, Beecher wrote: "the elevation of my sex by the opening of a profession for them as educators of the young is the first object of earthly interest in my mind—the theme of my daily nursing and nightly dreams—the enterprise to which every energy is consecrated...."[3] In 1851, she acknowledged that American women suffered from unjust laws and customs. She explained that "what is now sought by the Woman's Rights party in this country..., can be secured by far safer, less objectionable, and more efficient methods, than those they are now pursuing."[4] Beecher believed the feminists' actions offended many conservatives and that women could achieve equality through a less conspicuous campaign. Beecher was influenced by the strict societal dictates of the first half of the nineteenth century which accorded women a drastically inferior status to men. Women were omitted from political roles and few had economic resources. Religious groups opposed the practice of women speaking before mixed audiences and the custom was carried over into society. Catherine Beecher accepted many restrictions on her sex and was known to have men read her speeches. In 1871, Beecher remained steadfast in her dissapproval of suffrage for women. She argued that it was contrary to Christian beliefs and that "with the gift of the ballot, comes the connected responsibility of framing wise laws to regu-

Figure 6.2. Bathing—A "feminine" activity.

late finance, war, agriculture, commerce, mining, manufactures, and all the many fields of man's outdoor labor."[5]

THE BLOOMER CONVENTION

Another setback to women engaging in physical activity occurred when the bloomer costume was first worn by a few daring feminists. Although wearing the bloomer costume was not the major issue at the National Women's Rights Convention at Syracuse, New York, in the fall of 1852, widespread controversy over proper attire for women ensued. Elizabeth Smith Miller brought public attention to the bifurcated skirt, but it was Amelia Bloomer who promoted the costume in *The Lily* and whose name was adopted to the fashion innovation.

Some women recognized the inappropriateness of their voluminous dress for work and physical activity. Reminiscing about an attempt to bring about dress reform, Elizabeth Cady Stanton, staunch feminist leader questioned:

> How can you . . . ever compete with man for equal place and pay with garments of such frail fabrics and so cumbrously fashioned, and how can you ever hope to enjoy the same health and vigor with man, so long as the waist is pressed into the smallest compass, pounds of clothing hung on the hips, the limbs cramped with skirts, and with high heels the whole woman thrown out of her true equilibrium.[6]

Figure 6.3. Simple ball games were approved during the 1840s.

Stanton blamed the impediments of fashion for curtailing running, rowing, skating, and climbing trees. Furthermore, Stanton faulted the "crippling, cribbing influence of costume" for much of the poor health and ill temper among women.[7] The corset was condemned by medical doctors who warned that waist constriction impeded circulation and displaced viscera. The "artificially reduced waist" was accepted by fashion-conscious women who endured waist cinching until well into the twentieth century.

The bloomer was a striking departure from traditional dress and remedy for the constrictions of costume and it brought forth public outrage making its wearers the subject of insult. Bloomers were not immediately popular in New York City and other cities. Soon after their debut "ladies of irreproachable character, walking in the streets of New York, accompanied by their husbands and brothers, (were)... hissed and hooted."[8] *The New York Times* in response to the bloomer crusade suggested that "if a gentleman... were to promenade Broadway in a bonnet or petticoat, he would very justly meet with general attention. Why should the ladies expect to commit similar departures from custom with greater impunity?"[9]

Thus, another opportunity to encourage physical activity among the female populace during the early days of the women's rights movement was thwarted. The bloomer, upon its introduction, was discarded by many women at a time when dress reform was long overdue. Public ridicule of wearing apparel and criticism directed at an overt suffrage campaign was too much to bear for even some of the most staunch supporters of the women's movement.

THE CIVIL WAR DELAYS THE WOMEN'S RIGHTS MOVEMENT

In 1861, when the fight between freedom and slavery gripped the North and the South, women's rights activities were abandoned. Instead women from the North and South exerted their energies in war relief work. They labored in hospitals, on the battlefield, harvested crops, and taught school. The National Women's Rights Conventions which helped spread the women's rights movement were not held during the Civil War.[10] The war transformed women's lives and moved many for the first time from the confines of their homes. They showed others and revealed to themselves that they were capable of performing demanding tasks by assuming roles once assigned to men and performing crucial services.

After the Civil War, women expected equality for former black slaves and themselves but they were disappointed. Unfortunately a split among backers of women's rights occurred in meetings of the American Equal Rights Association (AERA). The AERA was organized after the Civil War "to secure Equal Rights to all American citizens, especially the Right of Suffrage, irrespective of race, color, or sex."[11] In the May, 1869, meeting of the AERA Stanton called for a women's suffrage amendment and most moderate feminists opposed it. Elizabeth Cady Stanton and Susan B. Anthony then organized the National Woman Suffrage Association (NWSA). The moderates organized the American Woman Suffrage Association (AWSA) in November 1869.[12] The division in the women's movement caused frustration and stymied the movement. A reunion did not occur until two decades later.

THE WOMEN'S CHRISTIAN TEMPERANCE UNION

Meanwhile, another organization which advanced the rights of women was the Women's Christian Temperance Union (WCTU) established in 1874. Countless women bore the brunt of alcohol's effects on their husbands. The temperance crusade was widespread and emotionally appealing. Although of short duration the temperance movement united many women and drew attention to another of their distressing situations. Mary A. Livermore, a WCTU worker, portrayed the movement as:

> the anguished protest of hopeless and life-sick women against the drunkenness of the time, which threatened to fill the land with beggary and crime, and forced women and children to hide in terror from the brutality of the men, who had sworn to be their protectors. The liquor dealers were entrenched in the law, sheltered by the courts, and protected by the strong arm of the government. There was no redress for the wronged and outraged woman.[13]

The WCTU advocated women's suffrage and contributed substantial sums of money to the movement. The temperance crusade gave women another opportunity to leave their homes. It expanded their interests outside the home and increased their contacts with people. The organization also ignited opposition to suffrage by the liquor interests.[14]

In 1890, the two women's suffrage organizations the AERA and the NWSA merged and became the National Woman Suffrage Association (NWSA). Elizabeth Cady Stanton, newly elected president of the NWSA, was still earnestly pleading for women's right to vote.[15]

PHYSICAL ACTIVITY AND
THE THREAT OF BEING OSTRACIZED

The time-consuming work of the women's movement and the general feeling of oppression among women left little time for physical exercise of a recreational nature. Although women's rights advocates recognized the necessity of physical activity and its benefits, they never launched a visible campaign that promoted national acceptance of sport or physical exercise for women. In essence women who were in positions to advance physical activity were engulfed by their burdensome problems that demanded immediate attention. While sport and physical exercise were important, the time to bring them into American society was a long way off. It was widely accepted that women, because of their more delicate physical, emotional, and psychological makeup, were not subject to the same valuable contributions toward over-all health and well-being which their brothers realized through vigorous physical activities.

There were, however, during the course of the women's movement, people who provided further explanation as to why women did not pursue exercise. In 1882, Elizabeth Cady Stanton suggested that improper dress and diet as well as social customs and restrictions impaired the health of women. She observed that city school girls were seldom seen in gymnasiums or on playgrounds. Stanton contended that the threat of being ostracized kept many women from engaging in physical activity. In the early 1800s women were denied "the distractions of business, politics, and out-door amusements, which help to fill up a man's life and change the current of his thoughts . . . "[16]

At the NWSA Convention in 1893, Ruth C.D. Haven, in her speech, "The Girl of the Future," envisioned women with opportunities to select careers. She predicted payment of appropriate wages and that women would have some "leisure for recreation."[17] By the turn of the century inequalities that had plagued women since the Seneca Falls Convention were disappearing. Victorian constraints were fading and women had become more outspoken. The professions were slowly admitting women and job opportunities were expanding. Men and women found new freedoms in an urban society which was a contrast from the more restricted rural life. Industrial America was rapidly changing and influenced by people of varied races, religions, and culture. Those who benefitted most from the new-found freedoms in an urbanized society, the advances in industrialization and technology, and leisure activities, were middle class wives.

Meanwhile, turn of the century women physical educators, though not large in numbers, were teaching the strategies of basketball, then a novelty sport. Most were content to advance physical education programs which accentuated participation by all. They shunned the highly competitive male athletic model. They were not compelled to join the women's movement which demanded radical reforms. In essence they were designing their own programs and for the most part encountered few obstructions. By comparison to women who were seeking societal reforms they experienced little discrimination.

The reality of women achieving the freedom to express their opinions at the ballot box took place in November 1920. The time seemed favorable for proponents of women's suffrage to direct their attention to other needs of women. In the Fall of 1920 several women's organizations met for the purpose of promoting the physical health of females. Representatives of the National Woman Suffrage Association, the National Women's Trade Union League, the Young Women's Christian Association, the National Women's Christian Temperance Union, and the General Federation of Women's Clubs agreed to promote physical health among women. Those in attendance at the New York City meeting recommended the use of recreation and health centers for educating women about the importance of emotional as well as physical health.[18] Women were urged to wear work clothing and leisure attire which allowed freedom of movement. Abandonment of the corset was recommended. An appeal to shoe manufacturers called for design to fit the natural form of the foot.[19] The women's movement waned during the conservative political climate of the 1920s. There was a decline in reform and the national promotion of physical health by a conglomerate of women's organizations failed to materialize.

In spite of the conservative political climate, more women were participating in physical activities. They were aware of the benefits of exercise and society was receptive to their participation in certain sports. They flocked to the beaches and engaged in other outside activities such as tennis and golf. Women had transformed from fragile creatures into healthy and physically active members of society. They were recognized for their accomplishments as leaders in reform movements and in sports. Among the notable achievers of the mid-1920s was Gertrude Ederle. When Ederle swam the English Channel in 1926, she not only became the first woman to accomplish the feat but her 14 and one-half hour swim bettered the time of the five previous male swimmers by two hours and three minutes. *The Literary Digest* proclaimed: "women got the vote . . . and now they hold the greatest of all swimming records, despite the fact that their champion, Miss Ederle, still lacks two years of voting age." In recognition of Ederle's achievement, Carrie Chapman Catt, a leading proponent of women's suffrage, reflected: "It is a far cry from swimming the Channel to the days to which my memory goes back, when it was thought that women could not throw a ball or even walk very far down the street without feeling faint."[20]

REAWAKENING OF THE WOMEN'S MOVEMENT

The reawakening of the women's movement in the 1960s coincided with the national crusade for improving the plight of oppressed minority groups. Women in the 1960s amid the civil rights movement and opposition to the Viet Nam conflict, began to seek improvements. They demanded an end to job discrimination and called for the elimination of class distinction of women. Women resented certain responsibilities such as serving as secretaries at meetings or making the coffee for office workers. They voiced disapproval of heretofore stereotyped roles. They wanted freedom to choose beyond the role expectation which depicted them as mothers who were to accomplish housework related skills.

ATHLETICS FOR WOMEN, A VISIBLE ALTERNATIVE

Sportswomen of the 1960s were playing volleyball and basketball out-of-doors because men controlled the gymnasiums for varsity athletic programs. Other sportswomen were playing in outdated gymnasiums because new facilities were almost always constructed for male athletes. These women who were members of the playday and sportsday generation, were ready to join the women's sports movement. Some of these women had participated in the more competitive AAU sports programs. Others, without approval from college and university physical educators, joined city sports conferences conducted by recreation departments. Denied collegiate athletic competition, these former playday participants wanted highly skilled girls and women to have the opportunity to excel at sports. As students they dared to defy the wishes of faculty members and by the mid-1960s had demanded to coach athletic teams as well as have an extensive competitive season.

Legislation, considered a boon to the women's sports movement by some and to others a destructive influence on men's sports, has produced radical changes in athletic and physical education programs. The controversial Title IX of the Education Amendments of 1972 states:

> No person in the United States shall on the basis of sex, be excluded from participation in, be denied the benefits of, or be subjected to discrimination under any education program or activity receiving Federal financial assistance. . . . [21]

The law, originally introduced in 1971 as an amendment to the Civil Rights Act of 1964, following Congressional debate and charges, emerged as Title IX. Guidelines for the implementation of Title IX have specified that physical education classes are to be coeducational and that males and females must be given an equal opportunity to participate in athletic programs. Furthermore, classes that heretofore were traditionally conducted for one sex, such as auto mechanics and home economics, by law are required to admit both sexes. Separate departments of physical education for men and women have combined. Athletic scholarships previously awarded to men were offered to women.

ATHLETIC SCHOLARSHIPS

A lawsuit that jolted sportswomen throughout the United States was prompted by Elaine Gavigan. Before her retirement in 1982, Gavigan was the women's tennis coach and physical education instructor at Broward Community College (BCC) in Florida. Prior to the Association of Intercollegiate Athletics for Women (AIAW) restrictions on scholarships, BCC and Marymount College, another south Florida institution, had offered tennis scholarships to women. Vehement objections to scholarship recipients entering the 1972 Florida Commission of Intercollegiate Athletics for Women (FCIAW) state tennis championships were voiced by coaches from nonscholarship institutions. As debate over the athletic scholarship issue swept the state, coaches offering financial assistance feared their athletes would be barred from the state championships. Fern "Peachy" Kellmeyer's team from Marymount College in Boca Raton, was a contender for the state title. Meanwhile, the scholarship issue was to be resolved at the April, 1972 meeting of the

FCIAW. Elaine Gavigan had read about the passage of Title IX in a newspaper article. She explained:

> I told Peachy about Title IX and said what we need is a sympathetic lawyer who will champion our cause on the basis of discrimination as explained in Title IX. About a week later, she called and said ... Ted Hainline would take our case free of charge, but I would have to meet him and explain ... [Title IX].[22]

After a heated debate in April, 1972, the FCIAW voted to uphold the AIAW guidelines which prohibited athletic scholarships. Gavigan recalled the meeting:

> Feelings ran deep. The atmosphere was charged with emotion, but at all times the issue was dealt with in an open and professional manner. I walked out of the meeting to hide my bitter disappointment. I remember saying that there really wasn't any reason for my presence since the rest of the meeting time would be spent in planning the state tournament which we would not be allowed to attend.[23]

The lawsuit prompted by Gavigan was filed in the United States District Court of the Southern District Court of Florida in 1973. The class action suit, with Kellmeyer's name listed first, called for an end to the discriminating rules of the AIAW, which prohibited athletic scholarship recipients from participating in AIAW sponsored competition.[24] AIAW legal counsel, realizing that Kellmeyer and Gavigan would win their case, recommended that the AIAW change the scholarship rules. In his letter to Elaine Gavigan, Hainline wrote:

> So, the rule was changed. We win the case by default—so-to-speak.
> I must say, however, that the representatives of the defendants, and their counsel, were most courteous and cooperative. When I went to Washington, D.C. to discuss this matter with them, I expected the "hate reception," but received just the opposite.
> The case will be dismissed.[25]

In a statement released by the AIAW in April, 1973, during Carole Oglesby's presidency, the end of conservatism in women's sports was signaled by a statement which read in part:

> Times are changing, and we must change with them. The consciousness of women as to their rights and privileges has been raised, and the whole theory of protecting women from exploitation, of paternalistic action "for their own good," has been a casualty of the student movement and the women's movement.[26]

Women have made remarkable gains in achieving the right to function more fully as members of society. Nearly every sector of society has been affected by organizations and individuals who have worked to improve the status of women. Education, politics, legislation, religion, and sport have been influenced by the women's movement. There are still inequities experienced by women and sport provides an example. While Title IX caused the expansion of sports programs and provided the basis for dramatic changes in girls' and women's sports, gender equity remains a problem in the 1990s. Furthermore, the declining number of women coaches and administrators remain as challenges which will continue beyond the year 2000.

SUMMARY

The women's movement in the United States had little initial effect on sport and physical education for women. The First Women's Rights Convention was held in 1848 to seek reforms in areas affecting their freedom to function in society. Since physical activity was not a major concern of feminists in the 1840s, resolutions pertaining to health and exercise were omitted. The Victorian belief still prevailed which portrayed women as fragile creatures with responsibilities confined to the home and family. Only such "feminine"-oriented activities as walking, bathing, and sleigh riding were socially acceptable. Catherine Beecher was an advocate of exercise for women; however, she did not join the feminists' crusade. She believed that women could gain equality through less conspicuous means and that feminist actions offended many conservatives.

During the Civil War, women's rights activities came to a halt when women turned their energies to war relief work. The war helped to expand the scope of women's lives in that it took them from the confines of their homes to perform crucial services. They worked on the battlefield, in hospitals, taught school, and harvested crops. After the Civil War, feminists expected equal rights by law but a division in the movement stood in the way of their goal. In 1890 the AERA and the NWSA merged to become the National Woman Suffrage Association.

Although advocates of women's rights supported the benefits of physical activity, they did not institute a visible campaign to promote the national acceptance of sport or physical exercise for women. By the turn of the century Victorian ideals were fading and women were more outspoken. Job opportunities were expanding commensurate with the growth of the country's urbanized and industrial society. After women earned the right to vote in 1920, proponents of women's suffrage turned their attention to promoting the physical health of females. Several women's organizations convened in the fall of 1920 to discuss ways of achieving this purpose, but failed to materialize during the conservative political climate of the 1920s. In the ensuing years more women were participating in physical activities because of the social and healthful benefits.

The women's movement reawakened in the 1960s amid opposition to the Viet Nam War and the civil rights movement. A principal theme was to abolish stereotyped sex roles and have the freedom to choose beyond traditional role expectations. In the women's sports movement legislation brought about changes in athletic and physical education programs.

REFERENCES

1. Elizabeth Cady Stanton, Susan B. Anthony, and Matilda Joslyn Gage (eds.). *History of Woman Suffrage, Volume One.* Rochester, New York: Charles Mann, 1889, pp. 50, 60–62.
2. Susan B. Anthony and Ida Husted Harper (eds.). *The History of Woman Suffrage, Volume Four.* Rochester: Susan B. Anthony, 1902, p. xiii.
3. Personal letter, C.E. Beecher, April 26, 1844. Courtesy Rutherford B. Hayes Library, Fremont, Ohio.
4. Catherine Esther Beecher. *The True Remedy for Wrongs of Women.* Boston: Phillips, Sampson, and Co., 1851, pp. 21, 23.
5. Catherine E. Beecher. *Woman Suffrage and Woman's Profession.* Hartford: Brown and Gross, 1871, pp. 5–7.
6. Stanton. *History of Woman Suffrage, Volume One. op. cit.,* pp. 469–470.
7. Stanton. *History of Woman Suffrage, Volume One, ibid.,* p. 470.
8. "Bloomerism," *The New York Times.* January 31, 1852, p. 4.
9. "Bloomerism." *ibid.,* p. 4.
10. *History of Woman Suffrage, Volume One, ibid.,* p. 747.
11. Elizabeth Cady Stanton, Susan B. Anthony and Matilda Joslyn Gage (eds.). *History of Woman Suffrage, Volume Two.* Rochester, New York: Charles Mann, 1889, p. 182.
12. Barbara Deckard Sinclair. *The Women's Movement: Political, Socioeconomic, and Psychological Issues.* New York: Harper and Row, 1975, p. 263.
13. Mary A. Livermore. *The Story of My Life.* Hartford: A.D. Worthington and Co., 1897, p. 578.
14. Sinclair, *op. cit.,* p. 266.
15. *History of Woman Suffrage, Volume Four. op. cit.,* p. 159.
16. Dio Lewis, Elizabeth Cady Stanton, and James Read Chadwick. "The Health of American Women," *North American Review.* 135 (December, 1882), pp. 511, 516.
17. *History of Woman Suffrage, Volume Four, op. cit.,* p. 210.
18. Willystine Goodsell. *The Education of Women: Its Social Background and Its Problems.* New York: Macmillan Co., 1923, pp. 291–292.
19. H.A. Stewart. "I Didn't Know That—Did You?" *The Ladies Home Journal 37* (April, 1920), p. 72.
20. "How a Girl Beat Leander at the Hero Game," *The Literary Digest,* 90 (August 21, 1926), pp. 56, 67.
21. United States Department of Health, Education and Welfare, HEW Fact Sheet, June, 1975, p. 1.
22. Questionnaire completed by Elaine Gavigan, January 31, 1984.
23. Ibid.
24. Case Number 73-21-CIV–NCR filed by Theodore R. Hainline, 1–4.
25. Letter to Elaine Gavigan from Theodore Hainline, April 17, 1973.
26. "Policies on Women Athletes Change," Association for Intercollegiate Athletics for Women, April 2, 1973, 1–2.

Chapter 7

AMERICAN TURNERS

merica's sporting and physical education heritage owes much to the German immigrants who came to the United States in the early part of the nineteenth century. Sport and physical activity has undergone continuous expansion throughout the twentieth century. Adaptations have occurred as various ethnic groups settled and produced a blending of ideas and practices.

GERMANY'S RISE FROM HUMILIATION TO NATIONAL PRIDE

On October 14, 1806, the Prussian army was soundly defeated by Napolean's forces at the Battle of Jena. Backed by a state riddled with corruption and inefficiency, the once mighty army under Frederick the Great was nearly annihilated by the French. With the treaty of Tilsit in 1807 Prussia surrendered approximately one-half of its territory and population to her conquerors, thus eliminating her as a major European power. However, with the arrival of the second half of the century came a resurgence of national German pride. Of major importance was the total reorganization of education with one primary aim of instilling a new national pride in Germany's people. In the early 1800s the church was relieved of its schooling function and secular education became a responsibility of the state. Subjects such as history, geography, speech, arithmetic, and music were taught with a pedagogical as well as patriotic emphasis. Physical exercises were also of major importance because of their health and military values.[1]

FRIEDRICH LUDWIG JAHN (1778–1852): THE FATHER OF GERMAN GYMNASTICS

Friedrich Jahn was a patriot who believed that the German people could rise from their humiliating defeat in 1806 through a rejuvenation of their Teutonic values. Unaccustomed to autocratic rule, Jahn was considered to be a liberal crusader who wanted to see the semi-independent states more closely unified with constitutional liberty replacing monarchial rule.

Jahn, a staunch supporter of personal freedom, held that the development of the individual was of utmost importance. In seeking to implement his vision of freedom and growth, Jahn organized athletic clubs for the purpose of developing physical fitness and national pride in German Youth. These clubs were called "Turnvereins," stemming from the German verb "turnen," meaning "to do gymnastic exercises." Every Turner or club member participated in such activities as apparatus work, running, jumping, fencing, swimming, and group games. The singing of patriotic songs was also an integral part of the program. The important task of providing leadership in an athletic club was given to the gymnasium instructor. From Jahn's book, *The Art of Gymnastics* which served as the Turner's manual, Emmett Rice through Jahn describes in detail the ideal conduct of an instructor:

> He must set a good example for the youth on the playground and in the gymnasium; during his work period practice self-denial in all indulgence which might be imitated by youth; not assume an attitude of snobbishness or superiority, but be sociable and congenial and continue so always; as the one who enforces the rules and regulations, be the first to follow them; not consider himself above them but, on the contrary, he should be severest with himself in their enforcement; not try to excel or even equal all excellent performers; quietly and modestly endeavor to improve himself; guide and direct the conversations of the youth into instructive and entertaining channels, so that neither by word nor suggested deed, they become objectionable; avoid the appearance of the usual schoolteacher dignity and in his behavior and intercourse be friendly and yet earnest, and mix cordiality and dignity; clearly show that he is enthusiastic about the seriousness of his work and is not following it from sheer vanity and mercenary selfishness; know how to live and mingle with his pupils and all others who have been entrusted to his care, so that they will respect his manliness and love him for his humanness; discover the latent characteristics and peculiarities and encourage the blossoming virtues; administer all activity among his pupils as an older friend, a director, a judge, a counselor, and cautioner.[2]

Educators throughout the land followed Jahn's teachings which gave rise to the national growth of Turner Societies.

The War of Liberation (1813–1815) ensued with a rekindled national spirit. The French army under Napolean was defeated at the Battle of Leipzig by Prussia, Austria, and Russia. In 1815 France once again suffered defeat by Prussia and England at the Battle of Waterloo. Although the nobility were in agreement with Jahn in wanting their country to be free from French dominance, they became fearful of his liberal political philosophy after the War of Liberation. Jahn and other patriots sought democracy which was a direct threat to the autocratic rule of the monarchs. However, the various German states remained largely independent of one another as monarchies. Undaunted, the Turners continued their political affairs in highly visible fashion calling for a democratic constitution and greater freedom of individual thought and action. Their efforts were met with stiff opposition. Turnvereins were outlawed by the crowned heads and its members were forbidden to hold meetings. Jahn himself was imprisoned for five years and released in 1824. Throughout this period of political turmoil many Turners fled the country and sought refuge in America bringing the Turnverein concept with them.

GERMAN GYMNASTICS BROUGHT TO AMERICA

In the fall of 1823, Joseph Cogswell and George Bancroft started an experimental school in Northhampton, Massachusetts. Named the Round Hill School, its educational aim according to Geldbach, in the words of Cogswell and Bancroft, was "to preserve the health and improve the morals and the mental powers."[3] The founders believed that one means of achieving these aims was through a regular physical education program. The Round Hill School was the first institution in America where physical activity was an integral part of the school curriculum. Dr. Charles Beck, a former pupil of Jahn, was employed as an instructor in Latin and gymnastics. In 1825 he founded an outdoor gymnasium for the school. Although the Round Hill School was forced to close in 1832 primarily due to financial problems, a budding interest in German gymnastics had developed in America.

Charles Follen, also a pupil of the celebrated Jahn, came to America in 1824 with Beck and helped establish the first public gymnasium in Boston. Opened in 1826, Follen served as its first supervisor for almost a year. He was also the first person to teach gymnastics in an American college. Although a German instructor at Harvard, he met informally with his students instructing them in the art of gymnastics.

Follen was succeeded as supervisor of the Boston gymnasium by another arrival from Germany named Francis Lieber who had been personally recommended by Jahn. Lieber also opened a swimming school in Boston which may have been the first of its kind. By 1828 public interest in gymnastic exercises had waned and the Boston gymnasium was closed in that same year.

It is difficult to explain the abrupt demise of this exercise movement when one considers the enthusiasm with which it was first received. It may be speculated that one major cause was the fact that most Americans worked at maintaining what appeared to be a satisfactory level of existence. Work hours were long and demanding leaving little time or inclination for seemingly frivolous exercise. Perhaps yet another reason may be because German gymnastics in America lacked the political spirit of nationalism which was so much a part of the German Turnverein. Finally, Beck, Follen, and Lieber were scholars in their own right, relying primarily on their academic capabilities to make a living and their work in gymnastics was only an avocation.

TURNVEREINS ORGANIZE IN AMERICA

During the 1830s and 1840s, German migration to the United States steadily increased. The yoke of the monarchs had become unbearable, tossing all parts of Germany into revolution. The failure of the liberal revolutionists in 1848 and 1849 brought thousands of political and social refugees to the land of freedom in search of a new home. The new arrivals settled in the larger cities forming closely knit communities which enabled them to more readily adjust to their new environment as well as preserve their own customs.

Friedrich Hecker was among those to leave the homeland. He was a hero of a defeated republican uprising in south Germany. Hecker established a temporary home for the first German-American Turnverein in the United States. It was organized November, 1848, in Cincinnati, Ohio. A week later a group of men who were former followers of Hecker met in Hoboken, New Jersey and planned a New York Turnverein. Another early Turnverein was organized in Louisville, Kentucky in 1850. Other societies rapidly followed and within three years approximately twenty-five Turnvereins with a total membership of nearly 2,000 existed in 11 states. Four Turnvereins located in New York, Philadelphia, Baltimore, and Cincinnati contained about half of the total membership. By 1860, over 150 societies were in existence with membership totaling between 9,000 and 10,000 of direct German origin. Turnvereins were now operating in 27 states.[4]

In these early years the Turnverein was more than just a place for exercise. In 1887, the president of the North American Turnerbund (Union of Turnvereins) summarized its political and social function:

> In these Turner halls thousands of Germans were converted into good American citizens, for they soon discovered that this was the free country which had been their ideal. . . . Turner halls soon became the schools for the diffusion of knowledge of American politics and political economy. Thus German Turners became American citizens, and soon the Turner Bund made it obligatory that every one of its members should declare his firm intention to become an American citizen. . . . Besides the bodily exercises, they held at their meetings debates and lectures on religious, social and political questions.[5]

The Turners transplanted many of their customs, but they were also willing to accept the responsibilities found in their new homeland. True to their ideals of freedom, the Turners took an official antislavery stand in the shadow of approaching Civil War, but support was not unanimous. In 1855, the Houston Turnverein withdrew from the National Turnerbund which was formed in 1850, because its members favored the abolition of slavery. Societies in South Carolina, Georgia, Alabama, Texas, and Virginia also withdrew from the national organization soon afterward. The total seceding membership was only 175 out of a total southern membership of 782.

In October, 1860, the Turnerbund National Executive Committee, located in Baltimore, urged Turnvereins throughout the country to support the

OUR NEW HOME

Schlich Engraving Co.

LOOMIS AND HARTMAN
ARCHITECTS

310 East Broadway   ·   ·   Louisville, Kentucky

Figure 7.1. The Louisville Turners opened a new building on their sixty-seventh anniversary. Courtesy of Forrest P. Steinlage, Louisville, Kentucky.

Republican platform and vote for Lincoln in the coming elections. The advice was generally heeded, even in the slave states. During the spring of the same year the national office was destroyed by a mob when Turnverein members refused to lower the national flag above their building and replace it with the state flag. Most of the Turnverein members were forced to flee the city, leaving the Turnerbund without a national clearinghouse. With Civil War imminent, each Turnverein throughout the country was left to function on an independent basis.[6]

TURNERS SERVE IN THE CIVIL WAR

The call for volunteers by President Lincoln was met with immediate response by the Turners. Approximately 75 percent of all Turners in the United States were in active service. From the Turnverein in St. Louis, three full companies, "Well drilled and completely equipped, were ready to take the field at once."[7] Members of the Southwest known as the "Western Turnregiment" formed the Seventeenth Missouri Regiment. The Twentieth New York State Volunteer Regiment contained 1,200 formed into three companies of Turners from the Eastern seaboard states. "Their return to New York City on May 10, 1863, reduced in numbers to 460 by two years of

Figure 7.2. Interior of Louisville Gymnasium. Courtesy of Forrest F. Steinlage, Louisville, Kentucky.

service, was the occasion of great rejoicing among the entire German population."[8] A large part of the Ninth Ohio Volunteer Infantry consisted of over half the Cincinnati Turner membership as well as Turners from neighboring cities. In Philadelphia eighty-six volunteers out of a membership of approximately 260 helped form the Twenty-ninth New York or Astor Regiment. By April 17 a company of 105 Turners were ready to march from Chicago. A second company was organized soon afterward. Company C of the Fifth Wisconsin Regiment contained Turners from Milwaukee and other Wisconsin Turnvereins. They were known as the "Turner Rifles." Approximately 50 years later Leonard commented on the war's effect on membership:

> Many societies were so reduced in numbers by enlistment that they found it necessary to disband, and effort was everywhere centered on the support of those who were hastening to the field, or had already gone. The roll of Turner dead is a long and honorable one.[9]

From 1861 to 1865, the Turnerbund was largely dormant and it maintained only a marginal existence.

REORGANIZATION AND GROWTH

Post-war development of the National Turnerbund first took the form of reorganization. In April, 1865, 58 Turnvereins sent delegates to Washington for the national convention. The details of reorganization were completed and the name of the organization was changed to the North American Gymnastic Union with headquarters in New York. The main objective of the Union was to promote physical training.

Over the next 20 years (1866–1886) the number of Turnverein Societies increased from 96 to 231 with membership rising from 6,320 to 23,823. The number of boys in classes grew from 3,317 to 13,161, while the girls increased from 120 to 3,888.[10] By the dawn of the twentieth century the number of American Turners had steadily grown. In 1903 there were 35,757 men with membership distributed throughout 250 societies. Of this number 5,586 were considered active members who were regular participants in gymnasium exercises. A program for men over 40 years of age found 2,041 members enrolled. Women were no strangers to the program in that 5,368 were counted as active members. There were also 2,418 men between the ages of 14 to 18 enrolled in the intermediate classes. Children's classes consisted of boys and girls ranging from ages five to 16. There were 18,724 boys and 11,307 girls actively engaged in the program, of which 5,289 were children of other than German parentage. The adult classes met twice a week during the evenings for one or two hours with children's classes meeting twice a week after regular school hours. Many societies also organized special clubs for their members in such activities as fencing, sharpshooting, swimming, bowling, singing, and dramatics.[11]

NATIONAL TURNFESTE (GYMNASTIC FESTIVAL)

In 1851, the first National Turnfeste or gymnastic festival was held in Philadelphia. They were conducted almost yearly for the next 30 years. After 1881 they were patterned after the time period of the Olympic Games and held every four year.[12] Attended by members throughout the United States, competition was held in track and field, games, mass drills, dancing, singing, dramatics, literary and declamatory exercise.[13] In keeping with the early Greek ideal, winners of the competition were awarded wreaths of laurels or oak leaves. Diplomas were also given as recognition of superior achievement. The fact that the Turners combined physical exercise with mental training was a reflection of the Greek ideal which sought to develop a sound mind in a sound body for a better society. Thus, the Turners, as did the Greeks, used the gymnasium for physical exercise as well as a meeting place for discussing affairs of state, philosophy, poetry, and other pertinent questions of the day.

Credence to the benefits of the Turners' system of physical and mental development of its members was given by Dr. Dudley Sargent, Director of Hemenway Gymnasium at Harvard University. A guest observer of the Twenty-sixth Gymnastic Festival held in Milwaukee in 1893, Sargent was impressed with the fact that 3,000 participants came to the Festival from as far away as California, Louisiana, and Massachusetts. Participants consisted of young and middle-aged men, women, and children. True to the concerns of the time Sargent expressed his concern for the "fairer sex":

> The great interest taken by women in physical training and the importance to the race of having this sex maintain its physical vigor would seem to warrant almost every encouragement. They should certainly be invited to appear in class exercises from the city where the festival is held, but whether they can come from distant cities and mingle with profit in the festivities of a four-day's tournament are questions that the governing board can afford to ponder over.[14]

Sargent reinforced the need for greater development of the lower limbs, and the heart and lungs. He noted that the Tournament now included the 100 yard run, pole vault, running, high and broad jump, and hop, step, and jump which was important to increasing these functional capacities.[15]

Dr. Edward Hartwell, Director of Physical Training in the Public Schools of Boston, also praised the July 21–25 Festival of 1893:

> No other association in the country . . . could have accomplished the like; for the simple reason that singleness of purpose, readiness to cooperate for common ends, thoroughness of organization, practical efficiency and intelligent leadership, such as have characterized the North American Gymnastic Union for years cannot be found in any like measure elsewhere in America.[16]

The operating structure of the National Turnfeste as well as each individual society stemmed from a philosophy which differed vastly from that of athletics which was becoming firmly entrenched in American life. Advocating the Greek ideal of all-around development, the Turners took a contrasting view of the growing tide of specialization and commercialism associated with athletics in the United States. In clarifying their position, Dr. Henry Hartung, in an article written in 1903, referred to the work of Gutsmuths, who is known as the Grandfather of Physical Education. In his book, *Gymnastics for the Young*, written in 1793, Gutsmuths praised the German system:

> We are not athletes, and our youths shall neither knock out their teeth nor crush their ribs; they shall neither kill others nor wrench their own limbs. In our exercises we seek health, not its destruction; we seek strength, not the unfeelingness of the cannibal; we strive for manly sense and courage, not for unrestrained wildness and license.[17]

Hartung then expressed his own view:

> It would be a deplorable fact, indeed, if the present indulgence in unlimited and unqualified athletics, with its professionalism and mercenary character, should become the ruling passion in our educational institutions, high and low. Our manhood would degenerate, our gymnastic ideals would be buried, and with the hailing of the modern gladiator we would see approaching the decadence of our country.[18]

However, athletics continued to flourish giving birth to a nation of spectators— a phenomenon antithetical to the goals of the Gymnastic Union.

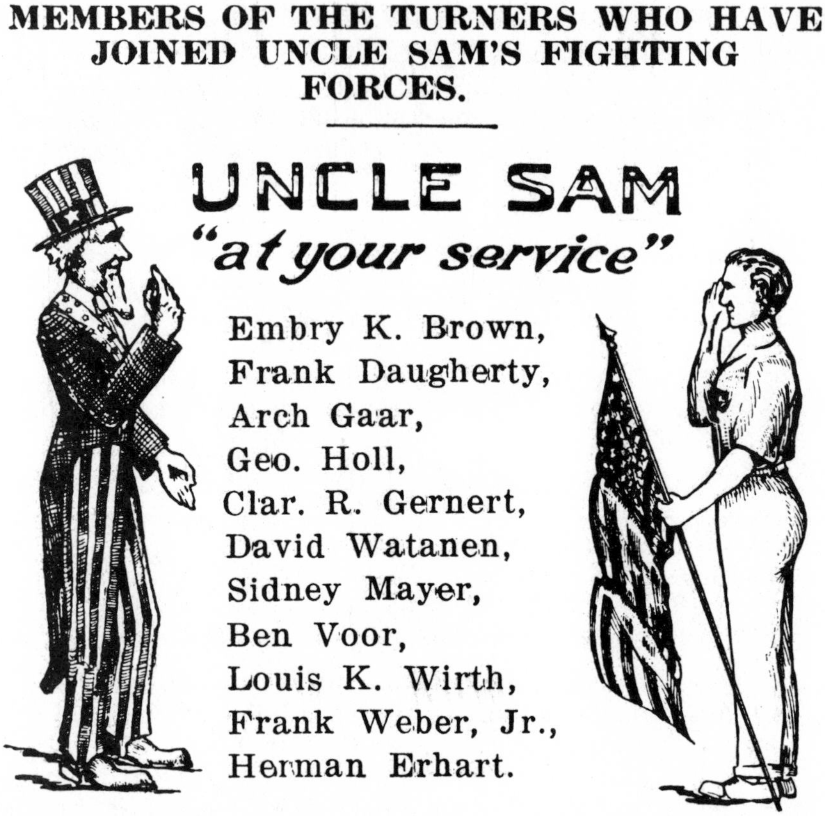

MEMBERS OF THE TURNERS WHO HAVE JOINED UNCLE SAM'S FIGHTING FORCES.

UNCLE SAM
"at your service"

Embry K. Brown,
Frank Daugherty,
Arch Gaar,
Geo. Holl,
Clar. R. Gernert,
David Watanen,
Sidney Mayer,
Ben Voor,
Louis K. Wirth,
Frank Weber, Jr.,
Herman Erhart.

Figure 7.3. Courtesy of Forrest P. Steinlage, Louisville, Kentucky.

TURNERS IN WORLD WAR I

With the entrance of the United States into the war against the central powers, the Americans of German origin were in a position to demonstrate their loyalty. After the declaration of war, the North American Gymnastic Union's Executive Committee sent a delegation to Washington offering their facilities to help train men drafted into the service.[19]

On an individual basis, 692 Turners volunteered for service, and 1071 members were drafted. Of this number 217 (12.3 percent) were exempted or rejected leaving 1546 men in the service. It is interesting to note that only 10.65 percent of the drafted Turner members were rejected for not being physically fit compared to a 33 percent rejection rate for drafted non-Turner members.[20] Various causes reported for nonfitness were poor eyesight, heart trouble, underweight, overweight, small stature, and general weakness.[21] The benefits of regular physical exercise made an apparent difference between those fit and unfit for the war effort.

Once again during a war, the activities of the Societies had suffered a setback. At the 27th Convention held in Louisville, Kentucky in 1919, the Executive Committee stressed concern about the future direction of the American Gymnastic Union in light of anti-German sentiment expressed throughout the country:

> We are standing today on the threshold of a momentous decision. Whatever the outcome, let us look hopefully into the future. May it bring peace and happiness for nations and individuals. May the bitter hatred which the war engendered vanish forever, and may confidence and respect between nations and individuals be again established. May future generations profit by the sad experience of our time.[22]

Prior to World War I, the American Turners had been instrumental in promoting German gymnastics in public school physical education. With Germany's defeat, however, greater acceptance of German gymnastics in the public schools appeared to be waning.

TURNERS INTRODUCE GYMNASTIC EXERCISES IN THE PUBLIC SCHOOLS

By the early 1900s, there were more than 34,000 Turners in America distributed in memberships through 258 societies.[23] Vitally interested in securing a well-rounded education for their youth, the German-Americans sought to instill physical development as an integral part of the public school offering.

In keeping with this aim, specially trained teachers were prepared by a central normal school established in November, 1866, in New York City by the North American Gymnastic Union. The one-year course included the history and purpose of the German Turner, the anatomy and aesthetics of gymnastics, first aid, gymnastic nomenclature, theory of the different systems, and practical instruction with special emphasis given to training boys and girls. Throughout the next 18 years the school was moved from New York to Chicago, and then to Milwaukee graduating a total of 113 men. The first woman completed the course in April, 1878, with two more graduating in 1879.[24] Offering their services free of charge, the efforts of these early teachers were instrumental in the inclusion of German gymnastics in the school curricula in many cities, mostly in the Midwest. Schools in the cities of Cleveland, Cincinnati, St. Louis, Indianapolis, and Milwaukee and others offered the German system of exercise partially because a great number of German Americans had settled in the region, thereby giving it popular support.

On a national level, the Turners were also visible. Turner leaders joined the Association for the Advancement of Physical Education formed in 1885 and informed its membership of German gymnastics by giving lectures and providing exhibitions. The Turners also published the periodical *Mind and*

Figure 7.4. Women's class—Louisville Turnverein—1917. Courtesy of Forrest P. Steinlage, Louisville, Kentucky.

Figure 7.5. Men's class—Louisville Turnverein—1917. Courtesy of Forrest P. Steinlage, Louisville, Kentucky.

Body initiated in 1894, which was then written in English.[25] Publication of *Mind and Body* ended in 1936.

The Turners served as a primary agent in helping to establish physical education as a permanent part of the public school curriculum. They were instrumental in helping to pass state legislation requiring physical education in the schools of California in 1866, and Ohio in 1892. In 1897, Wisconsin enacted state legislation requirements with North Dakota and Pennsylvania passing legislation in 1899 and 1901.[26] The latter part of the nineteenth century was a time in which the German system of exercise was at its height in America. The American Turners were a vital and dynamic force in helping to establish early legislative support for physical education in the nation's schools.

THE NORTH AMERICAN GYMNASTIC UNION

Although the German American Turnverein still exists in the United States, its membership has drastically declined. Just before World War I, over 40,000 men, women, and children were American Turners. As of January 1, 1974, the membership had decreased to 14,852.[27] Probable causes for decline may be attributed to a backlash resulting in America's wars with Germany, a waning of German heritage by German-American descendents resulting in their "Americanization," and the scattering of the German-American population throughout the country.

By 1995, American Turner membership had stabilized and included 13,500 members in 63 clubs or societies throughout the United States.[28] The National Turnfeste, now the National Festival of the American Turners, is held every four years in the year preceding the Olympic Games. The July 5–9, 1995 National Festival in South Bend, Indiana, featured competition in volleyball, fencing, tennis, racquetball, golf, swimming, diving, gymnastics, track and field, and cultural events. Competitors range in age from teenagers to those over 60. The official publication, *American Turner Topics,* informs members of current events.

Each society operates as an autonomous body owned and managed by its members. Program development is based on the objectives and needs of each society. While Turner groups promote physical fitness rather than the development of elite athletes, competitive programs are also offered. Annual national tournaments in volleyball, basketball, gymnastics, softball, swimming, and golf attract the more serious competitors.[29] Survival of the American Turners can be attributed to programs provided for all age groups, autonomy of each club, opportunities to gather at national tournaments and the national festival, and involvement of the membership in making program decisions.

SUMMARY

America's sporting and physical education heritage was greatly influenced by German immigrants who came to America in the early part of the nineteenth century. Friedrich Jahn was a staunch supporter of individual freedom who organized Turnvereins in Germany to develop fitness and national pride. After the War of Liberation (1813–1815) Jahn and other patriots advocated democracy which threatened the autocratic rule of the monarchs. Turnvereins were outlawed by the monarchs with Jahn himself being imprisoned for five years. During this time of political turmoil many Turners fled their native country to live in America bringing the Turnverein concept with them.

In 1823, the Round Hill School in Massachusetts included gymnastics as an integral part of the school curriculum. A former pupil of Jahn's named Charles Beck was employed as an instructor of Latin and gymnastics. Although the Round Hill School closed nine years later, an interest in German gymnastics had developed in America. Charles Follen was also a Turner who helped to establish the first public gymnasium in Boston which opened in 1826. He served as its supervisor and was the first person to teach gymnastics in an American college. Francis Lieber was another arrival from Germany who succeeded Follen as supervisor of the Boston gymnasium. He opened a swimming pool in Boston which may have been the first of its kind. Public interest in gymnastics soon waned and the Boston gymnasium was closed in 1828.

Throughout the 1830s and 1840s, German migration to America steadily increased. Friedrich Hecker was among those to leave his homeland. He established a temporary location for the first German-American Turnverein in the United States in 1848. By 1860, Turvereins could be found in 27 states with a membership between 9,000 and 10,000 of direct German origin. Turnvereins were more than just a place for exercise in that they served to educate its membership about American politics as they prepared to assume the responsibilities of citizenship. During the Civil War American Turners accepted this responsibility in that approximately 75 percent were in active service. From 1861 to 1865 the Turnerbund was largely dormant.

After the war, the National Turnerbund was renamed the North American Gymnastic Union with the main purpose of promoting physical training. Over the ensuing years the number of Turnverein societies increased from 96 in 1866 to 250 in 1903. Men, women, and children were among those who engaged in gymnasium exercises. Many societies offered special activities for their members such as fencing, swimming, sharpshooting, bowling, singing, and dramatics. The National Turnfeste, or gymnastic festival, began in 1851 and was conducted almost yearly for thirty years. After 1881 they were held every four years with competition in track and field, games, mass drills, dancing, singing, dramatics, literary and declamatory exercises. The Turners sought to combine physical exercise with mental training which was a reflection of the Greek ideal and in contrast to the ever increasing growth of specialization and commercialism associated with athletics in the United States.

The Turners were dedicated to securing a well-rounded education for their youth by including physical development as part of the public school curriculum. To meet this aim the North American Gymnastic Union established a teacher training school in New York City in 1866. The school was moved throughout the next 18 years to Chicago and then Milwaukee graduating a total of 113 men. The first woman completed the year-long course in 1878 and two more women graduated in 1879. These early teachers were instrumental in establishing German gymnastics in the schools of such midwestern cities as Cleveland, Cincinnati, St. Louis, Indianapolis, and Milwaukee. The Turners played an important role in helping to secure early legislative support for physical education in the public schools. After World War I anti-German sentiment caused a waning of acceptance toward the inclusion of German gymnastics in the nation's schools.

Present-day membership has drastically declined in the German American Turnverein. Before World War I there were over 40,000 members but by the early 1970s membership had decreased to less than 15,000. Causes for decline may be attributed to America's wars with Germany, a waning of German heritage by German-American descendents, and the scattering of the German-American population throughout the country. By the 1990s the membership had stabilized at 13,500.

REFERENCES

1. Ellwood P. Cubberly. *A Brief History of Education.* Boston: Houghton Mifflin Company, 1922, p. 318.
2. Emmett A. Rice. "The American Turners," *Journal of Health and Physical Education,* 5 (April, 1934), p. 3.
3. Erich Geldbach. "The Beginnings of German Gymnastics In America," *Journal of Sport History,* 3 (Winter, 1976), p. 236.
4. Fred E. Leonard. "German-American Gymnastic Societies and the North American Turnerbund," *American Physical Education Review,* 15 (December, 1910), pp. 618–619.
5. H.M. Starkloff. "Paper by Dr. H.M. Starkloff," *Proceedings of the American Association for the Advancement of Physical Education November 25, 1887,* Brooklyn: New York, Rome Brothers, Steam Printers, 1887, pp. 30–31.
6. Leonard. "German-American Gymnastic Societies and the North American Turnerbund," *op. cit.,* p. 622.
7. Leonard. *ibid.,* p. 623.
8. Leonard. *ibid.,* p. 623.
9. Leonard. *ibid.,* p. 623.
10. Leonard. *ibid.,* p. 624.
11. Henry Hartung. "The Present Condition of Gymnastics and Athletics in the

North American Gymnastic Union," *American Physical Education Review,* 8 (December, 1903), pp. 276–277.

12. Leonard. *op. cit.,* pp. 622–625.

13. Rice. *op. cit.,* p. 6.

14. Dudley A. Sargent. "Report of Dr. D.A. Sargent," *Twenty-Sixth National Festival of the North-American Gymnastic Union (Turnerbund) Milwaukee, Wisconsin, July 21-25, 1893,* St. Louis, Missouri: Published by the Executive Board, 1893, p. 12.

15. Sargent. "Report of Dr. D.A. Sargent," *op. cit.,* p. 13.

16. Edward M. Hartwell. "Report of Dr. Edward M. Hartwell," *Twenty-Sixth National Festival of the North-American Gymnastic Union (Turnerbund) Milwaukee, Wisconsin, July 21-25, 1893,* St. Louis, Missouri: Published by the Executive Board, 1893, p. 16.

17. Hartung. "The Present Condition of Gymnastics and Athletics in the North American Gymnastic Union," *op. cit.,* p. 279.

18. Hartung. *ibid.,* p. 279.

19. *Proceedings of the 27th Convention of the American Gymnastic Union, Louisville, Kentucky, June 22-24, 1919,* p. 2. (no publishing information)

20. "Statistics Bearing on Members of the North American Gymnastic Union in Service," *American Physical Education Review,* 23 (November, 1918), p. 501.

21. *ibid.,* p. 502.

22. *Proceedings of the 27th Convention of the American Gymnastic Union, Louisville, Kentucky, June 22-24, 1919,* p. 4.

23. Fred E. Leonard and George B. Affleck, *The History of Physical Education,* Philadelphia: Lea and Febiger, 1947, p. 310.

24. Leonard. *ibid.,* pp. 625–626.

25. "Notes and Comments," *Mind and Body,* 25 (February, 1919), p. 461.

26. Session Laws of American States and Territories, California—section 55, March 24, 1866; Ohio-House Bill No. 457, January 1892, p. 276; Wisconsin—No. 16, S, March 23, 1892, p. 137; North Dakota—S.B. 126, March 8, 1899, p. 113; and Pennsylvania—No. 15, March 8, 1901, p. 49.

27. Henry Metzner. *History of the American Turners,* Rochester, New York: National Council of the American Turners, 1974, p. 32.

28. Telephone interview, Shirley Luckhardt, National Secretary, American Turners, April 27, 1995.

29. "Join the American Turners," pamphlet of the American Turners.

Chapter 8

FROM GYMNASTICS TO
AMERICAN PHYSICAL EDUCATION

Physical education in the United States during the latter half of the nineteenth century was characterized by several European gymnastics systems. Partisans for each system were vying for preeminence in physical training institutions. The two primary rivals for supremacy in physical training programs were the German and Swedish gymnastics systems. Francois Delsarte designed a series of gestures to accompany oratory which became known as the Delsarte system. It was expanded in America and was practiced in schools for young ladies and in the YWCA as a form of gymnastics during the late nineteenth century. The Delsarte system was less known than the Swedish and German systems. The YMCA also contrived a gymnastics program. A combination of other systems were practiced to a lesser extent.

In general, from 1865 to 1900, American physical education was guided largely by European influences. Holding the attention of school and nonschool groups, the main objective was to promote better health through exercise, thereby enhancing the quality of life. The means of reaching this goal was not readily agreed upon by advocates of the various systems which prompted a great deal of oftentimes bitter controversy producing what became known as the "battle of the systems." In his government report, James Boykin presented his view of the dilemma physical education faced when considering the German and Swedish systems. He cautioned that up to this time the rivalry between the two systems was beneficial because it helped to bring gymnastics more prominently before the educational public than ever before. Boykin predicted the struggle to gain public favor would be detrimental to the cause that both systems served. He astutely reasoned:

> With what confidence can an American board of education adopt the one system of gymnastics when a large and able body of experts pronounce it "without rational or physiological foundation," and with what trepidation will they approach the other system when an even larger number of equally able men assert, with their greatest physiologist, that "only the half-educated are impressed by it" And what comfort can they gain by turning the eclectic system when both parties sneer at them as 'heterogeneous conglomerations?'[1]

Because these systems defined the nature of physical education during this period in American history, a closer look at their characteristics is warranted.

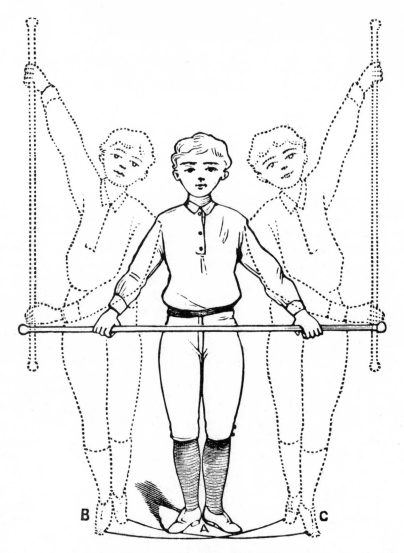

Figure 8.1. Wand exercise, 1888.

GERMAN–AMERICAN SYSTEM

Although the essential principles of German gymnastics remained constant, its adherents modified their practices somewhat in accordance with the American perspective of exercise. Three unique features were claimed to exist in this system. It emphasized general body development, instruction to a large number of students at one time, and teaching progression from simple to more complex movements.[2]

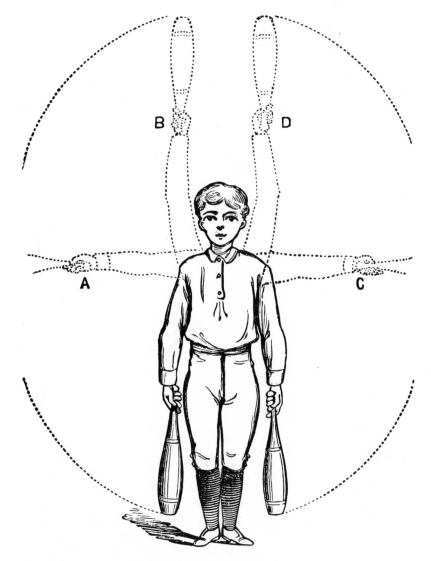

Figure 8.2. Indian club exercise, 1888.

Six classes of exercises described this system:

1. Marching in various forms.
2. Calisthenics using short and long wands, dumb-bells, rings, and clubs.
3. Fancy steps, mainly for girls which used many movements ranging from a gallop to complicated forms performed by expert dancers.
4. Apparatus work on such equipment as the horizontal bar, parallel

bars, long and side horse, rings, ladders, poles, ropes, balance boards, pulley weights, and vaulting table.

5. Popular gymnastics such as high, far and deep running, hop, step and jump, running, putting the shot, javelin and discus throwing, swimming, skating, fencing, boxing, wrestling, and shooting.

6. Games and plays.[3]

A typical lesson would begin with a series of free exercises performed in a rhythmical manner. Class exercise on the apparatus then followed with a change of apparatus coming next. The lesson then ended with exercises of the individual's own choosing.

SWEDISH SYSTEM

Swedish gymnastics was developed by Per Henrik Ling who established the Royal Gymnastic Central Institute at Stockholm in 1814. Ling's system was introduced to the United States by Baron Nils Posse who was a graduate of the Gymnastic Central Institute. Coming to Boston in 1885, he and Hartvig Nissen, who arrived two years earlier, were instrumental in promoting Swedish gymnastics among interested Americans. Mrs. Mary Hemenway was a Boston philanthropist who provided financial support for the newly established Boston Normal School of Gymnastics which trained teachers in Swedish gymnastics. In 1890, the Boston schools adopted Swedish gymnastics, while other schools, mainly in the Eastern cities, followed Boston's example:

1. *Introductions.* These consisted of simple exercises at the beginning of the lesson to gain muscular control and establish proper body position and carriage.

2. *Arch-flexions.* They were backward-flexions of the trunk designed to straighten the dorsal region of the spine and push the chest forward which was extended to increase the chest capacity.

3. *Heaving movements.* Various exercises were done from a hanging position in order to develop the upper part of the chest and the arms.

4. *Balance movements.* Because the two preceding exercises were quite vigorous, the series of movements offered a change of pace. They were intended to produce good coordination and graceful posture.

5. *Shoulder-blade-movements.* Consisting of various arm-movements, they were designed to place the shoulder-blades in correct position.

6. *Abdominal exercises.* They stressed the abdominal walls which promoted digestion.

7. *Lateral trunk movements.* Consisting of rotations and sideway flexions they were designed to promote general blood circulation.

8. *Slow leg movements.* They provided a rest from the preceding exercise and could be omitted if one was not too tired from doing the lateral trunk movements.

9. *Jumping and vaulting.* These exercises promoted general elasticity of the body.

10. ***Respiratory exercises.*** Consisting of deep inhalation and exhalation, they were accompanied with arm movements which expanded and contracted the chest in even rhythm with the act of breathing.[4]

A modified system of Swedish gymnastics was practiced by the Sokols who were of Czechoslovakian origin. They founded the Bohemian Gymnastic Union in Chicago in 1878.

Figure 8.3. Swedish system, school gymnastics.

GERMAN VS. SWEDISH SYSTEM

Although German gymnastics had been introduced to the United States almost 50 years earlier than Swedish gymnastics, Ling's system of exercise began vying for supremacy over the German system. A national rivalry developed between the two systems to such an extent that a "Conference on Physical Training," was held in Boston, November 29 and 30, in 1889. It was hosted by concerned individuals and groups to bring the systems to the

Figure 8.4. Swedish system, school gymnastics.

public's attention. Over 2,000 people attended the conference held at the Massachusetts Institute of Technology. The United States Commissioner of Education presided over the gathering. Speakers explained and debated the training systems and analyzed physical education ideologies. The Physical Training Conference of 1889 was a milestone in the physical education profession. Not only was the conference organized by two women, it also brought national attention to the profession. The leaders of the era met together and concentrated on the issues affecting the profession. Philanthropist Mary Hemenway and Amy Morris Homans, director of the Boston Normal School of Gymnastics (BNSG), planned and directed the conference. Isabel C. Barrows edited the papers and discussions of the 1889 Conference.

In a concluding act of business immediately before the Conference adjourned, Luther Gulick, M.D., Director of the Physical Department of the Young Men's Christian Association, Springfield, Massachusetts, presented the following unanimously accepted resolution:

> Resolved, That the most cordial thanks of this Conference be extended to Mrs. Hemenway and to Miss Homans for the generosity and large-mindedness that led them to undertake and guide this Conference; and to express our conviction that not only the Boston public schools, but the whole cause of physical education in America, has received a great impetus from this meeting, which is the result of our labors.[5]

A major point of contention between the proponents of the two systems was that the Swedish advocates claimed their system was based upon sound physiological principles with exercises then being developed in line with these principles. They questioned the validity of the German system by citing its lack of scientific rationale. A proponent of the German system responded to the charge with a pragmatic reply:

> I have at different times exercised with professional anatomists and physiologists through an entire term at the gymnasium of Eiselin. I can't recall that any opportunity presented itself to apply our theoretical knowledge to the exercises in which we vied with each other, because there exists the same chasm between such views and exercises as there is between theory of voice and singing. A knowledge of the muscles and nerves, the combination of forces, and the classification of levers unquestionably assists the teacher of gymnastics in the same manner that an understanding of John Mueller's doctrine of the compensation of the forces of the larynx is of benefit to the instructor of vocal music. The teacher of music is not thereby enabled to tell his scholar how he is to proceed in order to produce a certain tone, and in the same way the anatomic-physiological knowledge is of no avail in the gymnasium.[6]

Disciples of the German system charged that the Swedish method was dull and too formal, did not possess recreational values, and was deficient in social and moral training. Swedish adherents countered by charging the German system used too much music, was too recreational, and did not provide for correcting specific problems and weaknesses.

In retrospect, it may be confirmed that both systems made a creditable contribution to the development of physical education in the United States. The German system introduced many gymnastic games which were recreational, and Swedish gymnastics stressed free exercise for public school children as opposed to apparatus work. These were especially desirable because most public schools had only classroom space in which to exercise.

CONTRIBUTIONS OF DR. DUDLEY A. SARGENT

Dr. Sargent, director of Hemenway Gymnasium in Cambridge, Massachusetts, is credited with making some original contributions to the development of physical education. The "Sargent System," a term used to set the principles apart from the German and Swedish systems, is not accurate because he advocated use of both systems, his own principles, and other activities:

Figure 8.5. Interior view of the Hemenway Gymnasium.

What America most needs is the happy combination which the European nations are trying to effect; the strength-giving qualities of the German gymnasium, the active and energetic properties of the English sports, the grace and suppleness acquired from the French calisthenics, and the beautiful poise and mechanical precision of the Swedish free movements, all regulated, systematized, and adapted to our peculiar needs and institutions.[7]

Sargent's unique contribution to physical education was the development of appliances having different heights and weights which were adaptable to the strength of the person using it. As one's strength developed, resistance could be increased. He designed such appliances as chest developers, leg machines, and finger machines. In all, he developed 40 different pieces of equipment in which to exercise the specific muscle groups of the shoulders, neck, back, trunk, arms, fingers, legs, and feet. Sargent was not guided by a profit motive in developing this equipment but his concern rested with providing trustworthy equipment instead.

His appliances were soon introduced to school, college, and athletic club gymnasia throughout the United States. The YMCA conducted basically an eclectic program and also used Sargent's apparatus. By 1892, many of his inventions were being used by approximately 350 institutions in the United States.[8]

A program governing exercise and running is found in Sargent's 1897 handbook. Emphasis is on progression using his appliances for the most part, and running as well as other movements. Selected excerpts, much of which is timely in the twentieth century follow:

1. Take a 15-minute walk before breakfast.
2. Avoid severe mental work after 9:00 P.M. Use the gymnasium and walk from one to three miles late in the evening.
3. Fill the lungs frequently and exercise vigorously, so that a profuse perspiration is brought about before the allotted task is finished.
4. When subjected to unusual mental or emotional excitement, increase the time and amount of exercise, using chiefly the muscles of the lower limbs.
5. Give your whole attention to the exercise in which you are engaged. Execute every movement with accuracy and precision. Be conscious of the muscles you are using, and become for the time a devoted admirer of your own physique.
6. Confine yourself to minimum weights and light exercise for three months; but increase the rapidity of the movements as fast as possible.
7. While using the apparatus for local development, contract and then completely relax as many muscles as possible.
8. Prolong the time but not the amount of exercise. Do not increase the minimum weight before reaching the maximum number of times. Take long, slow walks.

Running Track (The track was 19³/5 laps to a mile)

1. Walk at a moderate pace twelve laps to the right, then twelve to the left, swinging the leg from the hip instead of the knee, and landing equally on the ball of the foot and heel.
2. Walk one lap, gently increasing the speed on the second lap, until you walk into a run; run four laps to the left, then four to the right; and settle into a walk again.
3. Start on a steady run at slow speed and keep it up, without varying the gait, for twenty-four laps, running twelve laps each way.
4. Begin with a walk of one or two laps; then settle into a run of moderate speed, and keep it up for 20 laps, putting on maximum speed at the fifteenth lap, and gradually slowing down after that to a walk on the twenty-first, which it will be desirable to continue for four laps or more. Reverse regularly the order of running.[9]

Through Sargent's well-respected efforts which reflected an exact and scientific approach, physical education gained in respectability and professional status.

THE DELSARTE AND THE YMCA SYSTEMS

Francois Delsarte was a Frenchman who devoted his life attempting to formulate the laws of aesthetics. A vocal and dramatics teacher, he never came to America but his ideas were first introduced in this country by a former student, S. Mackaye in 1869. Delsarte found that certain poses and gestures could be best taught through physical exercises, however, he was not interested in developing a system of gymnastics exercises. Nevertheless, his methods were accepted by elocution and dramatics teachers who claimed health and poise were the outcome of this form of exercise. A student of the system described its purpose:

> to harmonize mind and body; to put the soul back into the whole body; to maintain equilibrium of all the functions and principles of being; to render the body plastic; to free all the channels of expression; to remove constrictions that interfere with the flow of emotion to all the parts.[10]

The method used such techniques as relaxation and deep breathing exercises in conjunction with emotions as denoted by various body poses. Although this system lacked a sound supporting rationale it was quite popular in its day.

The Young Men's Christian Association developed its own system of physical conditioning which was a combination of light and heavy exercises borrowed from different sources. The primary goals of the YMCA program were to develop strength, general health by obedience to the laws of health, and moral development.[11] An instructor named Robert J. Roberts was instrumental in developing and promoting the YMCA system of exercise which was enthusiastically received by its membership.

THE NEW PHYSICAL EDUCATION

As the struggle between German and Swedish gymnastics continued into the early 1900s, there became apparent a growing dissatisfaction with physical education in the United States being dominated largely by these two systems. In 1894, Boykin speculated that at some future time there would be an American system of physical training based upon the combined American experience in this field:

> The progress of the evolution toward an American system even in the last few years, may be distinctly seen, expecially in school gymnastics; for, have not the Germans begun to adopt the Swedish ideas of the day's orders and systematic progression, and have not the Swedes aimed to make their gymnastics more attractive ... and have not the professed followers of Delsarte adopted exercises that are plainly muscle makers as well grace givers? And do not they all utilize much that comes from the old English sports, from calisthenics, from Dio Lewis, and from Dr. Sargent?[12]

In 1910, Dr. Thomas D. Wood of Columbia University charged that the existing program was ineffective because of three major reasons:

1. It purported to achieve postural and corrective results through formal movements in class exercises which are unsatisfactory. With the exception of individuals needing remedial exercises, it would prob-

ably be more advantageous to employ more natural and spontaneous exercises.

2. There was too much attention placed upon the body to the detriment of one's personality and attitude development.
3. The activities developed abilities not closely related to the activities of daily living, therefore, the time and effort given them are not justified.[13]

Wood's philosophy of physical education was undoubtedly influenced by a new trend in education in which the focus shifted from subject matter to child development, needs, and interests. Educational leaders such as William James, G. Stanley Hall, Charles Eliot, Edward L. Thorndike, William Kilpatrick, and John Dewey believed that play was essential in the education of children. Wood applied this line of thinking to the development of the "new physical education" which took the form of a "natural" program of activities consisting of games and sport to nurture the intellect as well as foster moral and social well-being. In 1927, Wood, in coauthorship with Rosalind Cassidy, published *The New Physical Education*[14] which describes in detail the natural program of physical education. Wood's philosophy inspired one of his students named Clark Hetherington who was Wood's assistant at Stanford from 1893 to 1896. Hetherington was a scholarly man who held several influential positions during his lifetime career in sport and physical education. Known as the "modern philosopher of physical education," he was instrumental in further defining and establishing the new physical education. One of his many contributions was developing a theory of play and establishing it as fundamental education. He put his ideas into practice with the founding of the Demonstration Play School sponsored by the University of California at Berkeley, in 1913. Enrolling children ages four through twelve, school was held three hours a day for six weeks during the summer. Hetherington organized the child's activities in line with developmental interests which consisted of the following categories: big muscle activities (gymnastics, games, athletics, dancing); manual activities (construction with blocks to expression using a variety of materials); environmental and natural activities (excursions and nature experimentations); dramatic activities; rhythmic and musical activities; social activities; vocal and linguistic activities (expressing thoughts and feelings); and economic activities (familiarization with social forms of exchange).[15] The school was highly successful and attracted the attention of educators nationwide. The program flourished until 1934 when the University discontinued it because of financial difficulties.

In the ensuing years, support for the natural program and its ramifications couched in philosophy, content, method, student achievement, teacher's role, and evaluation advocated by Wood and Hetherington continued to grow. The natural program was further expanded and promoted in the 1930s, 1940s, and 1950s by two able proponents, Dr. Jesse F. Williams of

Columbia University, and Dr. Jay B. Nash of New York University. Williams, a medical doctor, coined the well-known statement in one of his most famous articles that education is "through" the physical rather than education "of" the physical and that "modern physical education . . . is based upon the biologic unity of mind and body."[16] In his philosophy which taught that an individual was a unified organism, the purpose of education and physical education was to prepare citizens for democracy. He believed that through games and sports each student could learn those values approved by society. Williams was a prolific writer of books and articles who profoundly influenced the conduct of physical education. J.B. Nash's philosophy likewise reflected the wholistic nature of the individual in that there is no such thing as physical activity apart from thinking and feeling, with the latter also entailing its physical counterpart.[17] Nash was concerned with the ultimate well-being of the individual not only in the physical sense as identified by organic vigor and neuromuscular skills, but in sound character and emotional development too. Through these early leaders and subsequent spokesmen and women, emphasis in physical education was redirected from the "physical" to "education," thereby bringing its goals into harmony with those in education. While contributions in philosophical, curricular, and methodological procedures enhanced the professional status of physical education over the years, marked gains were additionally being made in research and measurement with early efforts dating back to the 1850s.

TESTS AND MEASUREMENTS IN PHYSICAL EDUCATION

The beginning of tests and measurements in American physical education is attributed to the association of William Augustus Stearns, D.D., president of Amherst College and Edward Hitchcock, M.D. In his inaugural address on November 22, 1854, Stearns spoke of the importance of physical activity and recognized the need for an organized physical education program. The inclusion of physical education in the college curriculum was even referred to as the most consequential innovation of his presidency. In his annual reports to the trustees, Stearns repeated his plea for physical education.[18]

Amherst was the first college in the United States that established a faculty position of hygiene and physical education. A gymnasium was constructed in 1859, and in 1860 the Board of Trustees voted to establish a physical education program. John W. Hooker, M.D., became the first teacher in the new department, but because of ill health he resigned. In 1861, Edward Hitchcock, a Harvard graduate, was offered the position of Professor of Hygiene and Physical Education. Hitchcock's pioneer work in tests and measurements began in the fall of 1861. He initiated a collection of data that included age, weight, chest girth, arm girth, forearm girth, lung capacity, and pull ups. The body measurements of students served as a basis for prescribed exercises designed to develop body symmetry. Additional measurements were added during the period between 1861 and 1880. Hitchcock was a pioneer in anthropometrics and the first practitioner of scientific measurement in physical education. His collection of data was widely used and helped to establish a sound basis for improving tests and measurements.[19]

DECLINE OF ANTHROPOMETRIC MEASUREMENTS

From 1880 until about the turn of the century, Dr. Dudley Allen Sargent's influence was evident in tests and measurements. He eventually reached the conclusion that body size and muscle measurement was not a reliable indicator of an individual's power and working capacity. Sargent, while still a medical student at Bowdoin College, was the gymnasium director and gymnastics instructor at Yale. In 1873, he introduced a strength test to determine "the efficiency of men in handling their weight by their arms as a preliminary qualification for proficient work in heavy gymnastics."[20] Sargent refined his strength test to include speed and endurance which was used as a minimum requirement for athletic participation. With questions still unanswered, Sargent concluded in 1913 that strength measurement did not reveal any information concerning one's potential power. "We are soon taught by experience that there is in most men an unknown equation which makes for power and efficiency which has never been determined and which can only be measured by an actual test."[21] With the invention of such measuring devices as the spirometer and dynamometer, attention was directed from symmetry and size to an individual's work performance. Sargent, realizing that body size and muscle measurement were inadequate data for determining one's physical power and working capacity, favored the dynamometer as well as cardiovascular activities for testing strength and endurance.[22]

In September, 1879, Sargent was appointed Director of the Gymnasium and Assistant Professor of Physical Training at Harvard. In January, 1880, Sargent introduced the physical examination and the Harvard Strength Test to his students. From the total score on the test items a summary of a man's "all-around ability" was indicated. In addition, Sargent believed the strength test was indirectly a test of the individual's physical condition. Sargent used the strength test to determine a student's fitness to participate in athletic contests and eliminated those who were unfit for athletics. An "all-around strength (test) was decided upon, because this seemed the most common factor required in all forms of physical activity."[23] In 1887, Sargent published "The Physical Proportions of the Typical Man," which attracted wide interest. In his article, Sargent introduced his Anthropometric Chart based on the measurements of 10,000 individuals. The objective of the chart was: to furnish the youth of both sexes with a laudable incentive to systematic and judicious physical training by showing them, at a glance, their relation in size, strength, symmetry, and development to the normal standard.... [24] Measurements from Sargent's chart were used as a basis for

Figure 8.6. Amherst College Gymnasium.

making life-size plaster figures of the "typical" American college man and woman which were exhibited at the 1893 World's Fair in Chicago.

Interest in strength testing culminated in the intercollegiate strength tests which were ratified by physical directors from fifteen colleges in 1897. The man having the highest total score based on strength of back, legs, forearms, lungs, upper arms, and chest was declared the champion strong man of the colleges. The institution having the highest rating determined by the total score of its top 50 men was awarded the institutional championship. During this time the development of muscular power as a means of strengthening and improving the structure as well as function of the body was considered an important objective of physical education.

Because of Sargent's influence, the Harvard Strength Test became an intercollegiate event. In May of each year, institutions published the records of their 50 strongest men. The man with the best score was declared the collegiate champion and the college producing the highest total score was awarded the strength trophy. The competition, however, fell into disrepute when it was discovered that testing apparatus had been tampered with to produce better scores. Records were falsified and "ringers" were entered in the competition.[25]

DECLINE OF STRENGTH TESTING

Strength testing fell into disfavor because it did not indicate a level of endurance or heart and lung development. It was also thought that a man could become muscle-bound, thereby hindering skillful movements. Many athletes believed that preparing to take a strength test would interfere with successful participation in varsity athletics.

Toward the end of the century, enthusiasm for measuring power and working capacity began to wane. Earlier the anthropometric basis for testing had been criticized because size and symmetry gave no indication of one's strength. In the succeeding era of testing, anthropometric-plus-strength approach was criticized because the strong body was not necessarily efficient.[26] Testing individual movement ability began to attract the attention of researchers. Luther H. Gulick performed early work in this area in 1890 using such events as the 100-yard dash, 12-pound hammer throw, running high jump, pole vault, and mile run. Other achievement tests followed using similar events.

EMPHASIS SHIFTS TO POSTURE

Accurate posture measurement was developed by the end of the nineteenth century. An instrument designed to record posture was a tracing device contrived by John H. Kellogg in 1890.[27] Kellogg's apparatus consisted of a frame which held a pencil in such a way that the pencil could be moved vertically and longitudinally, at right angles to a blackboard. An individual stood against a paper covered backboard, and an outline was traced on the paper by moving the pencil around the end of the person's body. Other means of recording posture were developed over the next two decades but Jesse H. Bancroft's Triple Test of Posture involving no measuring instruments, was particularly suitable for use in schools. The test was based on a subjective rating on one's posture while standing, marching, and exercising. Bancroft described the Triple Test in her 1913 edition of *The Posture of School Children* and advocated its use once a month in the 1924 edition of the book.[28]

In 1915, Dr. Clelia Duel Mosher and Professor E.P. Lesley of the mechanical engineering department of Leland Stanford Junior University, developed the schematograph. Mosher, like her predecessor at Oberlin College, Dr. Delphine Hanna, had collected anthropometric data on college women and was not content with physical training procedures which were used for men and then adapted to women. She therefore attempted to improve posture examinations. The apparatus, a reflecting camera, having clear rather than ground glass of an ordinary camera, produced an individual's image. Thin paper or cloth was placed on the glass and the subject's posture was drawn with pencil or pen. The instrument was designed for use by the medical examiner for the admission of women to colleges and gymnasiums as well as for other physicians.

TESTING PHYSICAL CAPACITY, MOTOR ABILITY AND ACHIEVEMENT

After World War I, researchers turned their attention to developing a variety of tests for use in physical education. In the early 1920s, the University of Oregon devised a test of physical efficiency. The introduction of statistics by Frederick R. Rogers in the collection, analysis, and interpretation of data proved an invaluable aid to progress in tests and measurements. Rogers proposed a system of scoring physical capacity tests which provided an index of general athletic ability. David K. Brace measured motor ability with a 20-item test in 1927, and W.W. Tuttle reported on the Pulse-Ratio test in 1931 which dealt with the ratio of the resting pulse rate to the rate after exercise. Other research efforts in the 1930s involved physical skill differences, organic capacity, body typing, maturation studies in children, and physical fitness.

Early in the 1930s, Jesse Williams categorized physical education tests into classification tests and achievement tests. Classification tests were used to determine an individual's capacity in relation to a standard. Achievement tests measured what the individual could do which included the knowledge and skills possessed at the time the test was administered.[29] By the late 1930s, physical education tests had increased in number and variety. Physical educators in some parts of the country were administering physical capacity tests and achievement tests. In addition to skill tests there were diagnostic, motivation, knowledge, and appraisal tests. Testing programs were not widespread when Mabel Lee challenged physical educators to " 'test, teach, test' until the average pupil attains the standard."[30] She predicted that:

> the day of killing time with whistle-blowing drawn-out calling of rolls, and teaching without lesson plans or attainment standards will be over when the physical education teacher is required to prepare her pupils to meet high graduation requirements.[31]

The Harvard Step Test was introduced in 1943. It indicated physical efficiency and was based on the assumption that an estimate of capacity to perform hard work should be required of the individual. It required the subject to step up and down on a 20-inch platform at 120 counts per minute.

TESTING IN THE LATTER PART OF THE TWENTIETH CENTURY

During the 1950s and 1960s, physical fitness testing occupied the attention of the profession. Subjective evaluations in the form of cumulative records, personal checklists, skill rating, questionnaires, and anecdotal records were employed but never gained widespread use. Motor skill tests in various sports were conventional procedures in students' evaluations. Test results also called attention to curricular content and caused some physical educators to scrutinize the products of their programs. Statistical procedures became more widely practiced during this period. Evaluation of varying teaching styles and procedures were used.

Testing and measurement have been a vital part of American physical education. While early physical educators appeared preoccupied with what might seem elementary testing by twentieth century standards, they have contributed to the establishment of a scientific rationale for the profession. Some universities have acquired sophisticated equipment and have established testing centers in order to evaluate human performance. Investigation of varying environments and the effects on sports participation have been especially beneficial to athletes.

PHYSICAL EDUCATION AND THE DEPRESSION

The Great Depression of the early 1930s adversely affected public education. By the summer of 1933, the public school system faced perhaps the most serious crisis in its history when budgets were being drastically cut and schools were forced to close or shorten class hours. It disrupted the education of some 2,000,000 children and caused many teachers to lose their jobs or suffer salary cutbacks of up to 50 percent.

Conservatives publicly voiced their opinions and demanded a return to the "3 R's," while such special subjects as physical education, art, and music were considered "frills" which should be dropped from the curriculum. As a result, many of these so-called "frills" were eliminated or curtailed in many parts of the country. James E. Rogers, Director of the National Physical Education Service, urged physical educators at the grass roots level to meet the crisis by working harder and giving extra time to professional duties. Rogers emphasized that community involvement also contributed to job security. Volunteer service to one's community through the promotion of play days and festivals was encouraged in order to establish much needed contacts with city officials.[32] Rogers also reported, after visiting 32 communities of varying sizes in 12 states, that physical educators who were certified to teach an additional subject were being retained and some programs were reinstated when it was pointed out that state laws required physical education.[33]

Although the Depression severely affected the nation's educational system, its effects helped to improve teacher education requirements. Before 1930, only a few states required more than one year of college in order to become an elementary school teacher,[34] whereas a decade later most states required two to four years of professional preparation. The depression also brought about the establishment of adult education agencies and directed national attention on the problems of youth. The federal government acted to help youth by establishing the Civilian Conservation Corps (CCC) and the National Youth Administration (NYA).

The CCC was established in the spring of 1933 to furnish employment and training for unemployed youth. The first work camp was established on April 17 of the same year in George Washington National Forest near Luray,

Virginia, under the supervision of the United States Service. The first CCC enrollees were housed in army tents until permanent barracks were built. In time the standard CCC camp consisted of 22 buildings which included the barracks, a dining hall, an education, and a recreation building. In a five-year period of program operation, over 2,000,000 young men and war veterans were provided with new opportunities in the CCC camps. The types of work carried on by the CCC were in the areas of forest protection and conservation, soil conservation, recreational developments, aid to grazing and wildlife, flood control, reclamation, drainage, and emergency rescue activities. By 1938, in recreational developments alone, more than 160 camps were established in 69 national parks totaling 7,222,460 acres. Some 655 camps were developed in 777 state parks which totaled 2,728,253 acres.[35]

The National Youth Administration was established within the Works Progress Administration by executive order of June 26, 1935. Taking in youth 16 to 25 years of age, it was developed to give young adults an opportunity to finish school or learn a trade which would ultimately give them a chance to work and earn a living. Four major divisions of the program consisted of student financial aid, employment for out-of-school youth on work projects, vocational assistance for those seeking jobs, and recreation and leisure-time activities. During its eight-year operation, 2,700,000 young people were given job experience and training on projects producing useful goods and services.[36] Some youth were employed as a work force in the construction of such athletic and recreational facilities as stadiums, tennis courts, and swimming pools.

From 1932 to 1937, the federal government spent approximately a billion and a half dollars in building and improving permanent recreational facilities in the United States. During the years of the 1930s the profession of physical education began to align itself with the new purposes of leisure-time preparation. The Depression and its economic hardships had helped to hasten the advent of leisure time for millions of Americans.

Recreational pursuits and informal activities such as swimming, picnicking, miniature golf, and boating became popular during the 1930s largely because they were inexpensive during a time of economic hardship. Because juvenile delinquency was now an even greater national problem, community youth agencies such as the YMCA, YWCA, Boy Scouts, Girl Scouts, and others sponsored organized activity programs in support of constructive leisure-time activities. Many church-sponsored recreation programs were hard-hit by the Depression and by 1936 it was estimated that 21,000 rural churches throughout the country were forced to close with one major factor due to financial hardships. Although city churches were a bit more fortunate, many of their social service and recreation programs were abandoned due to lack of funds.[37] One church-sponsored program, the Catholic Youth Organization (CYO) founded in 1930, flourished by promoting the sports of boxing and basketball. Later CYO sports programs included more sports in which thousands of young men and women have participated.

A NATIONAL ORGANIZATION

While the basis for American physical education was being formulated by adherents to various gymnastics systems, a far-sighted young gymnastics instructor at Adelphi Academy in Brooklyn, New York, initiated the founding of a national physical education organization. Dr. William G. Anderson invited noted people throughout the country having a common interest in teaching and exercise to attend a meeting. On November 27, 1885, forty-nine people assembled at Adelphi Academy and a national association was founded and named the Association for the Advancement of Physical Education (AAPE). Dr. Edward Hitchcock from Amherst College served as its first president. A year later the organization changed its name to the American Association for the Advancement of Physical Education. During these first few years the membership was small, but it steadily increased. At the tenth annual convention held in 1895, the Association voted to permit the establishment of local societies.

In 1903, the membership of now over 1,000 voted to change the national association's name to the American Physical Education Association (APEA). Continuing to grow in influence, it amended its structure of local societies to national sections identifying a specific phase of physical education. Sections were being organized in such areas as Normal Schools and Professional Training, Gymnastic Therapeutics, and Anthropometry. By 1930, other sections such as Research, Recreation, and the Section on Women's Athletics were in existence. At this time new district organizations had been completed which were the Eastern, Midwest, and Southern. The Northwest was organized a year later and the Southwest came into existence in 1935. A Central District was developed from the Midwest in 1933. In 1930 *The Journal of Health and Physical Education* replaced two earlier publications, the *American Physical Education Review,* which had been published by the Association from 1896 to 1929, and the *Pentathlon* initiated in 1928 by the Mid West Society. The publication of the *Research Quarterly* at this same time also helped to contribute to the growing national influence of the APEA. The *Quarterly* publishes completed research in the areas of biomechanics, growth and development, health, history and philosophy, measurement and research designs, motor learning, neurophysiology, physiology of exercise, psychology of sport, recreation, sociology of sport, and teacher preparation curriculum and instruction. The periodicals are now called *The Journal of Physical Education, Recreation and Dance* and the *Research Quarterly for Exercise and Sport.*

The American Alliance for Health, Physical Education and Recreation (AAHPER), formerly the APEA until 1937, provides physical educators with professional direction and public visibility. Convention programs, special task forces, and workshops are conducted on contemporary issues and topics of concern to professionals in the field. Youth sport programs, drugs in sport, public health and the conduct of physical education programs at all levels of instruction are but a few of the many areas of concern.

The expansion and broad range of interest areas served by the AAHPER was evident when in 1974 it reorganized into seven associations. They are the American Association for Leisure and Recreation; American School and Community Safety Association; Association for the Advancement of Health Education; Association for Research, Administration, Professional Councils, and Societies; National Association for Girls and Women in Sports; National Association for Sport and Physical Education; and National Dance Association. At the same time the organization's name was changed from the "American Association" to the American Alliance for Health, Physical Education, and Recreation. In 1979 "Dance" was added to the title and the organization is now officially recognized as the American Alliance for Health, Physical Education, Recreation, and Dance (AAHPERD). Six associations within the Alliance now serve the profession and include: American Association for Active Lifestyles and Fitness (AAALF), American Association for Leisure and Recreation (AALR), Association for the Advancement of Health Education (AAHE), National Association for Girls and Women in Sport (NAGWS), National Association for Sport and Physical Education (NASPE), and the National Dance Association (NDA).

Other professional physical education organizations have been formed by concerned individuals and groups since 1885, all of which have contributed to the development of physical education. The Society of College Gymnasium Directors was founded in 1897, which was an organization exclusively for men. It became the College Physical Education Association in 1935, and was eventually recognized as the National College Physical Education Association for Men (NCPEAM). The American Academy of Physical Education (AAPE) was organized in 1904 to recognize those who were conducting scientific work in the area of physical training. An organization for women was formed in 1924 called the National Association of Physical Education for College Women (NAPECW). In the spring of 1910, Amy Homans invited some physical training directors to Wellesley College to determine the status of physical training. The group continued to meet annually and in 1915 organized the Association of Directors of Physical Education for Women. A constitution was accepted in 1916 and dues were one dollar a year. In 1917, the Middle West Society of College Directors of Physical Education was founded. The Western Society for Physical Education of College Women was organized in 1922 and in 1924 a national organization became a reality.[38] Directors or department heads made up the membership until after World War II when all faculty ranks were invited to join. Mabel Lee recalled that the director meetings enabled the early leaders to learn about their new positions in the absence of their faculty members. In a move to combine professional efforts, and influenced by Title IX legislation, the NCPEAM and NAPECW merged in 1978 to form the National Association for Physical Education in Higher Education (NAPEHE).

MOVEMENT EDUCATION

The beginnings of movement education in the United States can be traced to Margaret H'Doubler at the University of Wisconsin. In 1925, H'Doubler emphasized the necessity for an all-inclusive understanding of the body in motion through the harmonious union of all parts of the mind and body. She began using the term movement education in 1946. H'Doubler's concern for a lack of in-depth understanding of movement among those studying in the profession was also the concern of the National Association of Physical Education for College Women (NAPECW). The NAPECW recognized the deficiency of movement ability among many college women. Because of these two concerns the NAPECW in conjunction with three summer workshops in 1956, 1960, and 1964 studied and identified their position regarding movement education.

Further impetus to movement education occurred in the summer of 1956 at the first Anglo-American Workshop in Yorkshire, England. American physical educators were familiarized with England's philosophy of movement education. The English approach reflected the emphasis on the uniqueness of the individual child in the learning process.[39] The English concept of movement education has had an impact on elementary school physical education primarily through the teacher preparation institutions. Its implementation varies depending on the teacher's interpretation of the concept.

THE PROFESSION

The physical education profession, through publication, conventions, and workshops is assisting professionals in the field to conduct school programs in American society. Materials and aids for teachers of elementary, middle or junior high school, and high school physical education have been published to enhance program quality. AAHPERD and other organizations sponsor conventions and workshops which serve as incentive for encouraging its membership to keep abreast of current trends and practices. Conducting on-going research continues to be an important function of professional organizations. For example, an AAHPERD Research Consortium has been developed in order to improve research efforts and more effectively coordinate the research activities of the six national associations of the Alliance. An Alliance project ultimately designed to benefit a nonschool population is the Project on Aging. The purpose of this project is to increase the number and quality of professional preparation programs dealing with the health and well-being of older people.

As society becomes increasingly oriented to technology, citizens are being confronted more than ever before with sedentary lifestyles. Many Americans have acted to counteract this condition by participating in a variety of exercise forms.

THE AAHPER BECOMES INVOLVED WITH
THE NATIONAL CONCERN FOR PHYSICAL FITNESS

Prior to the early 1950s, the development of fitness in physical education programs was given major attention only during periods of threat to the national security. Post World War I and II trends indicated that once peace was restored the emphasis on fitness waned as programs returned to activities which fostered a more natural play element. Change was soon to be evident when a published study stimulated national concern about physical fitness during a peaceful time in the nation's history. In 1953, Dr. Hans Kraus and Ruth Hirschland published the results of their study, "Muscular Fitness and Health" in the *Journal of Health, Physical Education, and Recreation* using the Kraus-Weber tests.[40] The Kraus-Weber tests were previously developed by Hans Kraus and S. Eisenmenger-Weber, and used in earlier studies. Consisting of six items, the tests were designed to measure minimum strength and flexibility of the trunk and leg muscles. They were administered to over 4,000 American youths six to 19 years of age. A comparable number of European children of the same age were then tested. It was discovered that almost 58 percent of the American youth failed one or more of the test items compared to a failure rate of approximately 9 percent of their European counterparts. The startling conclusion was publicized by the media throughout the country. The general public, educators, medical doctors, and government officials questioned why such a major difference existed between the two groups. Kraus and Hirschland offered an explanation:

> European children do not have the benefit of a highly mechanized society; they do not use cars, school buses, elevators or any other labor saving devices. They must walk everywhere. Their recreation is largely based on the active use of their own bodies.[41]

The findings and implications of the Kraus-Hirschland report were eventually brought to the attention of President Dwight D. Eisenhower. His concern for the lack of fitness in American youth prompted him to call for a National Conference on Physical Fitness which was held in June, 1956, at the United States Naval Academy. Its purpose was to develop ways in which the federal government could promote youth fitness programs throughout the country. From this conference evolved the President's Council on Youth Fitness and a President's Citizens Advisory Committee.

Recognizing and encouraged by federal support, the American Association for Health, Physical Education, and Recreation (AAHPER) held a Youth Fitness Conference on September 1956, in Washington, D.C. Leaders of the profession developed program guidelines aimed at improving the fitness of the nation's youth. Two years later the AAHPER Fitness Testing Project was under way which led to the development of the AAHPER Youth Fitness Test and the first national norms ever established by the Association.[42] The test project became a part of Operation Fitness-USA which was developed by the AAHPER to symbolize and promote physical fitness throughout the country. Operation Fitness-USA has been instrumental in serving as a means for promoting and implementing fitness-related projects among interested groups in the nation.

With the inauguration of President John F. Kennedy in 1961 came not only his personal concern for fitness, but a national concern. Soon after he took office, President Kennedy called a National Conference on Physical Fitness in Youth which was held in February, 1961, in Washington, D.C. The conference convened to answer two key questions: how could the federal government best support youth fitness programs, and what was the most effective way to work with state and local groups in promoting fitness? President Kennedy possessed a keen commitment to promote the nation's fitness and he took the opportunity to present his views to the public in many ways. Writing in *Sports Illustrated* as President-Elect, he stated in his article, "The Soft American," that a lack of physical fitness in the American people was a threat to national security:

> Physical fitness is as vital to the activities of peace as to those of war, especially when our success in these activities may well determine the future of freedom in the years to come. We face in the Soviet Union a powerful and implacable adversary determined to show the world that only the Communist system possesses the vigor and determination necessary to satisfy awakening aspirations for progress and the elimination of poverty and want. To meet the challenge of this enemy will require determination and will and effort on the part of all Americans. Only if our citizens are physically fit will they be fully capable of such an effort.[43]

Two years later he wrote a second article for *Sports Illustrated* entitled "The Vigor We Need" in which he reemphasized the importance of national fitness as well as provided a summary of the government's involvement in fitness.[44]

During the Kennedy Administration, the President's Council on Youth Fitness was reorganized. It worked in cooperation with a variety of agencies such as the American Medical Association and especially the AAHPER. With time and successive leadership, the President's Council evolved as an agency having broader functions. In 1968 it became the President's Council on Physical Fitness and Sports. The Council conducts a comprehensive fitness promotion program and is engaged in a myriad of activities involving conducting clinics, carrying on research, providing educational resources, and promoting legislation. Many agencies have contributed to the organization and growth of fitness programs in the United States; however, three have played a major role in its development: the President's Council on Physical Fitness and Sports; the American Alliance for Health, Physical Education, Recreation, and Dance; and the American Medical Association.

SUMMARY

During the latter half of the nineteenth century, physical education in the United States was characterized by a variety of gymnastic systems. Two main rivals were the German and Swedish systems. In 1889, a Conference on Physical Training was held in Boston to bring the systems to the public's attention. Both systems contributed to the development of physical education in the United States by the introduction of recreational games and free exercises. Dr. Dudley Sargent's unique contribution to physical education were pieces of exercise equipment such as chest and leg developers. Physical education as a profession gained status from Sargent's contributions which reflected a scientific approach. The Delsarte system of exercise, which was short-lived, used such techniques as relaxation and deep breathing exercises. The YMCA established its own system of physical conditioning which was eclectic in nature.

In the early 1900s, Dr. Thomas Wood pioneered the "new physical education" which consisted of a "natural" program of activities comprised of games and sport. Clark Hetherington, the "modern philosopher of physical education," was instrumental in developing a theory of play and establishing it as fundamental education. Through the 1930s, 1940s, and 1950s, the natural program was expanded by Dr. Jesse F. Williams and Dr. Jay B. Nash. Williams coined the statement that education is "through" the physical rather than education "of" the physical. Nash's philosophy likewise reflected the holistic nature of the individual which included not only physical health, but sound character and emotional well-being.

Progress was being made in research and measurement with efforts beginning in the 1850s. Dr. Edward Hitchcock began work in tests and measurements in 1861 at Amherst College. From 1880 until the turn of the century, the influence of Dr. Sargent was evident in tests and measurements. Interest in strength testing was keen during the 1890s but it was eventually criticized because it did not indicate heart and lung development. The earliest test of movement ability was devised by Luther Gulick in 1890. During the prewar decade, physical educators directed their attention to tests concerned with posture, ability, fitness, and cardiovascular endurance. World War I stimulated specific interest in physical fitness testing because of the need to evaluate military personnel. By the late 1930s, there were a greater number and variety of physical education tests to measure motivation knowledge, skills, achievement, and physical efficiency.

The Great Depression adversely affected public education. Physical education programs struggled to survive with some programs being retained with the help of the American Federation of Labor, the American Legion, the Turnvereins, and Sokols. Although the depression severely affected education, three of its specific effects were beneficial. It upgraded educational requirements for teachers, many agencies for adult education were established, and the Federal Government dealt with the nation's youth problems through such agencies as the Civilian Conservation Corps (CCC) and the National Youth Administration (NYA). During the 1930s, the physical education profession began to align itself with leisure-time preparation.

A national physical education organization was founded in 1885 which was initiated by Dr. William G. Anderson. In 1903, the membership had grown to over 1,000 and had changed its name to the American Physical Education Association (APEA). It continued to grow in membership and influence with national sections becoming part of its structure. By 1930, there were such sections as Anthropometry, Research, and the Section of Women's Athletics. In the 1930s, new district organizations occurred which were the Eastern, Mid West, Central, Northwest, Southern, and Southwest. The addition of two publications, *The Journal of Health and Physical Education,* and the *Research Quarterly* in 1930 helped to contribute to the growing influence of the association. The organization is presently titled The American Alliance for Health, Physical Education, Recreation, and Dance (AAHPERD) which consists of associations pertaining to leisure; safety; health education; research; administration, and professional societies; girls and womens sport; sport and physical education; and dance. Other professional organizations have been formed by concerned groups and individuals and have contributed to the establishment of physical education as a profession.

The AAHPERD became involved with a national concern for fitness as a result of the Kraus-Hirschland study published in 1953. Its startling results prompted the federal government to sponsor a National Conference on Physical Fitness in 1956. From this conference evolved the President's Council on Youth Fitness. Encouraged by federal support, the AAHPERD held a Youth Fitness Conference in 1956 for the purpose of developing program guidelines to improve fitness levels of the nation's youth. Two years later the association developed a youth fitness test with national norms. During President John F. Kennedy's administration the President's Council on Youth Fitness was reorganized, and in 1968 it became the President's Council on Physical Fitness and Sports. The President's Council, the AAHPERD, and the American Medical Association have played a major role in organizing and conducting physical fitness programs in the United States.

REFERENCES

1. James C. Boykin. *Physical Training.* Washington, D. C.: Government Printing Office, 1894, p. 521.
2. Boykin. ibid., p. 544.
3. William A. Stecher. "The German System of Physical Education." Paper read at the 7th Annual Meeting of the American Association for the Advancement of Physical Education. Philadelphia, (April 7–9), 1892, p. 11.
4. Baron Nils Posse. *How Gymnastics Are Taught in Sweden.* Boston: T. R. Marvin and Son, Printers, 1891, pp. 24–25, 28, and Boykin, *Physical Training,* pp. 540–541.

5. Isabel C. Barrows (ed.). *Physical Training Conference 1889.* Boston: George H. Ellis Press, 1889, p. 132.

6. Boykin. op. cit., pp. 550–551.

7. Excerpts from an address by Dr. Dudley A. Sargent before the Physical Training Conference, 1889. Reported by Boykin, *Physical Training,* p. 555.

8. Boykin. op. cit., pp. 550–551.

9. Dudley A. Sargent. *Handbook of Developing Exercises.* Cambridge: Harvard University, 1897, pp. 5, 17.

10. F. Townsend Southwick in *Werner's Magazine,* June, 1893. Reported by Boykin, *Physical Training,* p. 557.

11. C. Howard Hopkins. *History of the YMCA in North America,* New York: Association Press, 1951, pp. 246–251.

12. Boykin. *op. cit.,* p. 523.

13. Thomas D. Wood. *Health and Education,* Part I, Ninth Yearbook of the National Society for the Study of Education. Chicago: University of Chicago Press, 1910, pp. 81–82.

14. Thomas D. Wood and Rosalind F. Cassidy. *The New Physical Education.* New York: Macmillan Company, 1927.

15. Clark W. Hetherington. "The Demonstration Play School of 1913," *Annual Report of Regents of the Smithsonian Institution 1914.* Washington: Government Printing Office, 1915, pp. 701–707.

16. Jesse F. Williams. "Education Through the Physical," *The Journal of Higher Education,* 1 (May, 1930), p. 279.

17. Jay B. Nash. *Physical Education: Its Interpretations and Objectives.* Dubuque: William C. Brown Company, 1963, pp. 93–94.

18. Thomas Le Duc. *Piety and Intellect at Amherst, 1865–1912.* New York: Columbia University Press, 1946, pp. 128–129.

19. Kenneth D. Miller. "A Critique of Tests and Measurements in Physical Education," Unpublished dissertation, University of Michigan, 1948, pp. 13–14.

20. Dudley Allen Sargent. "Twenty Years' Progress in Efficiency Tests," *American Physical Education Review.* 18 (October, 1913), p. 454.

21. Sargent, *ibid.,* p. 452.

22. Dudley A. Sargent. "Strength Tests and the Strong Men of Harvard," *American Physical Education Review.* 2 (June, 1897), pp. 108–109.

23. Sargent, "Twenty Years' Progress in Efficiency Tests," *op. cit.,* pp. 452–453.

24. Dudley A. Sargent. "The Physical Proportions of the Typical Man," *Scribner's Magazine,* 2 (July, 1887), p. 11.

25. Miller. "A Critique of Tests and Measurements in Physical Education." *op. cit.,* pp. 22–23.

26. Miller, *ibid.,* pp. 22–24.

27. John Harvey Kellogg. "The Value of Exercise as a Therapeutic Means in the Treatment of Pelvic Diseases of Women," *Transactions of the American Association of Obstetricians and Gynecologists,* 3 (1890), pp. 328–330.

28. Jesse H. Bancroft. *The Posture of School Children.* New York: Macmillan Co., 1924, pp. 197–200.

29. Jesse Feiring Williams. *The Principles of Physical Education.* Philadelphia: W.B. Saunders Co., 1932, p. 443.

30. Mabel Lee. *The Conduct of Physical Education.* New York: A.S. Barnes Co., 1937, p. 269.
31. Lee, *ibid.,* p. 269.
32. James E. Rogers. "Meeting the Crises," *Journal of Health and Physical Education,* 3 (October, 1932), p. 37.
33. James E. Rogers. "How Has the Depression in Education Affected Physical Education?" *Journal of Health and Physical Education,* 5 (January, 1934), pp. 12–13, 57, 58.
34. Benjamin W. Frazier. *Professional Education of Teachers, Chapter 14,* Biennial Survey of Education in the United States 1928–1930. 1 Washington: United States Government Printing Office, 1931, p. 10.
35. Robert Fechner, Director, Civilian Conservation Corps. *Objectives and Results of the Civilian Conservation Corps Program.* Washington, D.C., 1938, pp. 1, 2, 6, 15.
36. Federal Security Agency War Manpower Commission. *Final Report of the National Youth Administration—Fiscal Years 1936-1943.* Washington: United States Government Printing Office, 1944, p. 234, and National Youth Administration, *Some Facts About Youth and the NYA.* Washington, D.C.: United States Government Printing Office, 1937, n.p.
37. Frederick W. Cozens, and Florence S. Stumpf. *Sports In American Life,* Chicago: The University of Chicago Press, 1953, pp. 104–105.
38. Dorothy S. Ainsworth. "Women's College Directors' Societies," *Journal of Health and Physical Education,* 3 (May, 1932), pp. 3–4.
39. Kate Ross Barrett. "Early Reference to Movement Education," Unpublished manuscript, 1969, pp. 2–4.
40. Hans Kraus and Ruth P. Hirschland. "Muscular Fitness and Health," *Journal of Health, Physical Education, and Recreation,* 24 (December, 1953), pp. 17–19, and Hans Kraus and Ruth P. Hirschland, "Minimum Muscular Fitness Tests in School Children," *Research Quarterly,* 25 (May, 1954), pp. 178–188.
41. Kraus and Hirschland, *ibid.,* p. 18.
42. *American Association for Health, Physical Education, and Recreation, Youth Fitness Test Manual.* Washington, D.C.: American Association for Health, Physical Education, and Recreation, 1961.
43. John F. Kennedy. "The Soft American," *Sports Illustrated,* 13 (December 26, 1960), p. 16.
44. John F. Kennedy. "The Vigor We Need," *Sports Illustrated,* 17 (July 16, 1962), pp. 12–15.

Chapter 9

TEACHER PREPARATION

Public education in America is based upon the democratic ideal which guarantees equality of opportunity for everyone. Free public school education for all students has served as the basis for preparing a citizenry to effectively function as contributing members of society. The American public school has been acclaimed for teaching citizenship to poor, rich, immigrant, and native-born students. Early curricula, once narrow in scope, have evolved to meet the demands of a complex society.

Legislation requiring school attendance was first enacted in 1852 in Massachusetts, and by 1918 compulsory attendance was mandated by all the states. Prior to 1852 only those students who had the academic ability, interest, and finances were educated. However, compulsory attendance brought with it multidimensional problems. Teachers were confronted with the task of educating students having a wide range of intellectual capabilities, needs, and interests. As a result, it was inevitable that attention would be given to the selection and preparation of teachers. It would also be recognized at a later time that the physical needs of these students would be of importance in providing them with a more well-rounded education.

THE BEGINNING OF TEACHER TRAINING
IN PHYSICAL EDUCATION

The North American Turnerbund established a teacher-training institute in 1861 at Rochester, New York, but it soon closed because of the Civil War and did not reopen until after the war. In 1861 Dio Lewis established the Normal Institute for Physical Education in Boston and he is generally recognized as giving the first major impetus to preparing teachers of physical education in the United States. The first course began July 5, 1861, and lasted 10 weeks at which time seven men and women graduated. Members of the first faculty were Thomas Hoskins, M.D., Professor of Anatomy; Josiah Curtis, M.D., Professor of Physiology; Walter Channing, M.D., Professor of Hygiene; and Dio Lewis, M.D., Professor of Gymnastics. The following year an elocution department was added, chaired by Professor T.F. Leonard.[1] Regular instruction was provided in anatomy, physiology, hygiene, and gymnastics. A course offered in January 1862, included the principles of the "Swedish Movement-Cure" developed by Per Henrik Ling of Sweden which was devoted to treating such chronic diseases as curvature of the spine, paralysis, and other maladies. The students were drilled twice a day and they were expected to learn at least 200 different exercises as well as exhibit skill in leading a small class. The course cost $75.00 including a $5.00 matriculation fee and $10.00 for the diploma. Ladies were given a 25 percent discount on the fees because of the "unjust disparity of compensation" between male and female labor.[2]

Dio Lewis edited and published *Lewis New Gymnastics and Boston Journal of Physical Culture.* For the sum of $1.00 patrons could subscribe to this early "advocate and expounder" of physical education. An advertisement for the periodical boasted, "If it does not prove the means of revolutionizing the public mind on physical training, then we are mistaken."[3] Such advertisement was an extension of Lewis' dynamic personality. He was a polished and convincing public speaker, however, most of his ideas concerning exercise were not original but taken from many different sources. Dio Lewis' school remained in existence for seven years and graduated 421 men and women. These graduates met much of the immediate need for gymnastics instructors in the Eastern cities and eventually other parts of the country. There was no real demand for physical education teachers in the public schools until 1885 when Kansas City included physical education in its schools under the leadership of Carl Betz who was an American Turner. The Normal School conducted by the North American Turnerbund, a German gymnastics and social organization, was reestablished after the Civil War and many of their graduates had begun to introduce physical training primarily in the public schools of Midwestern cities.

During the fledgling years of physical education the profession was closely allied with the medical field. The benefits espoused by early leaders were derived from calisthenics and gymnastics and were medical in nature. Most American physical educators were medical doctors and did not pursue pedagogical degrees. As physical education became a part of the public schools the ties with the medical profession became less distinct.

TEACHER TRAINING SCHOOLS BECOME MORE PREVALENT

Prior to 1880, the development of teacher training had been modest. The idea of preparing more competent teachers of physical education now began to assume increasing importance. Greater attention was being given to curriculum development, the teaching staff, facilities, and qualifications of teacher training candidates. Six schools are noteworthy because they offered two years of theoretical and practical course work. They were:

Dudley A. Sargent's Normal School, Cambridge, Massachusetts, 1881
William G. Anderson's Normal School, Brooklyn, New York, 1886
The Physical Department of the International Young Men's Christian
Association Training School, Springfield, Massachusetts, 1887

The Boston Normal School of Gymnastics, Boston, Massachusetts, 1889
The Posse Normal School of Boston, Boston, Massachusetts, 1890
The Normal School (conducted by the Turnerbund), Milwaukee, Wisconsin, 1892

Summer schools were also developed and assumed an important role in the early training of teachers. The Harvard Summer School was begun in 1887 by Sargent. The Chautauqua School of Physical Education at Chautauqua Lake, New York, started in 1886 under the supervision of Dr. William G. Anderson and Dr. Jay Seaver. Many teachers attended these two prominent schools.

Sargent's school, founded in 1881, was only for women who were studying in the Harvard Annex, which was later to become Radcliffe College. The school was moved to Boston and in later years the program was opened to men. The effectiveness of Sargent's teacher training methods was reflected in the fact that up to 1920, nearly one-third of 9,656 individuals graduating from 28 teacher training institutions were from The Sargent School. Thus, one out of every three graduates training in physical education were from that institution.[4] A second private normal school, the Brooklyn Normal School for Physical Education, was founded by Dr. Anderson who was instrumental in forming the Association for the Advancement of Physical Education in 1885. In 1892, Anderson moved his school to the Yale University gymnasium in New Haven, Connecticut. Another institution which made an important contribution to early teacher training was the YMCA which established a physical education department at Springfield in 1887. In 1890, a second YMCA training school was established in Chicago. These two training centers eventually became known as Springfield College and George Williams College. In 1905, Springfield College was authorized by the state of Massachusetts to grant a bachelor's degree in physical education after three years of successful study, and a master's degree after four years of study. In 1920, Springfield College had the next higher number of graduates which totaled 885. That is, one individual out of every eleven graduates of teacher training institutions was from Springfield.[5]

The Boston Normal School, founded in 1889, where teachers of Swedish gymnastics were trained, was financially sponsored by Boston philanthropist Mrs. Mary Hemenway. The first class graduated in 1891 with 13 members. Amy Morris Homans was director of the school from its inception until her retirement in 1918. She played an important role in the development of physical education because of her excellent administrative ability, high standards, and professional vision. She invited Constance Applebee to introduce field hockey and was responsible for outfitting the first public school kitchen in the United States.[6] In 1909, under her leadership the school became the Department of Hygiene and Physical Education at Wellesley College in Massachusetts. During Miss Homans' 80th year one of her former students recalled:

> She impressed on her students a professional attitude toward their work—they
> must be dignified in appearance and manner, they must be thorough students,
> combining theory and practice at a time when only the latter was stressed. . . . [7]

During Miss Homans' career, she influenced many young women, two of
whom became Presidents of the American Physical Education Association.
Mabel Lee was elected the first woman president of APEA in 1931 and her
Wellesley classmate, Mary C. Coleman, served as president of the Association during 1933–1934.

In 1890, Baron Nils Posse, from the Royal Gymnastic Central Institute in
Stockholm, established a second Swedish training school in Boston. Posse
endorsed varied styles of teaching:

> the teacher of to-day follows no set form, no ready-made system, but applies
> the laws which Nature dictates; his effort is to make men and women, not
> puppets with a smattering of useless book-learning. His method varies with his
> classes, and text books become merely tools to assist in making the framework
> around which mind and character are built. [8]

Posse also provided advice for conducting a lesson in gymnastics. The
instructor was to explain and show every new movement to the class but not
do the exercises with them. Using this procedure, the instructor could watch
for and correct any mistakes the students might make. [9]

The South's first normal institute which prepared physical educators was
H. Sophie Newcomb Memorial College, the coordinate college of Tulane
University of New Orleans. The liberal arts college was founded by Josephine
Louise Newcomb in 1886, to honor her daughter. In October of the following
year, 150 students began their education in the school established for white
women. In 1891, a Boston educated woman from New Orleans, Clara Gregory
Baer, became the first physical educator at Newcomb College. She had
attended Emerson College of Oratory, the Boston School of Expression, and
graduated from the Posse Normal School of Physical Education. By the
1893–1894 academic year, the South's first teacher certification program in
physical education was offered. In 1907, a four-year physical education
degree program was established, another first in the South. While teacher
preparation was phased out by 1925, Newcomb College remains a part of
Tulane University and a legacy to the pioneering efforts of Clara G. Baer.
By 1925, other larger institutions with more resources were offering degrees
in physical education. [10]

The early origin of teacher training schools was due largely to private
initiative and capital. A new era of teacher training appeared on the horizon
with increasing attention given to curriculum content and pedagogy. Within
this larger general movement in education, the place of physical education
in the schools began to take perspective and become more visible. Early
leaders such as Sargent and Anderson had provided the impetus for the
development of teacher training programs.

TEACHER TRAINING BECOMES ACCEPTED
IN HIGHER EDUCATION

Before 1900, teacher preparation was largely a responsibility of private normal schools with colleges and universities having little influence in the training of teachers. An early exception was noted in 1891 when Leland Stanford Junior University formed a Department of Physical Training and Hygiene. The program was directed by Thomas D. Wood, and offered professional training in physical education for prospective teachers. The program consisted of about 35 semester hours of credit in such offerings as health, basic science, physical education theory, activity courses, and special work of an investigative nature.[11] More states passed laws establishing the function of physical education in the public schools, creating a need for a greater number of trained teachers. In 1930 there were more than 200 institutions offering four-year professional courses in physical education leading to a bachelor's degree.[12] Just prior to 1900, the University of Nebraska, the University of California, Oberlin College, the University of Missouri, and the Normal College at Ypsilanti, Michigan were among the early institutions to include a professional curriculum in their course offerings. As the turn of the century approached there was no standardization of curricular content in colleges and universities that prepared physical education teachers. The end of World War I was a major factor which promoted state legislation requiring the teaching of physical education in the public schools. The number of qualified teachers was far less than the demand. A 1920 survey indicated that 143 men and 722 women were studying to become physical education teachers. It was estimated that 1000 men and 1500 women were needed to fill immediate positions.[13] To meet this demand more colleges and universities began to offer professional preparation programs. The number of institutions offering teacher training rose from 20 in 1918 to 295 in 1944 with the number increasing to 361 in 1946.[14] By 1950, there were more than 400 colleges and universities which offered a specialty in the teaching of physical education.

As the decade of the 1930s began, Darwin Hindman, of the Ohio State University, recommended that teacher training institutions consider:

1. implementing a series of courses to prepare elementary school teachers to teach physical education
2. providing courses for school administrators which will inform them of the purpose and needs of physical education programs
3. how the physical education minor could be improved to meet the needs of most teachers who were teaching more than one subject.[15]

In general, physical educators agreed that elementary school physical education was important but secondary and college physical education received most of the attention at teacher training institutions. Because of the Depression teachers were frequently called upon to teach more than one subject.

Teacher training institutions then, of necessity, had to prepare instructors for the job market demand.

TEACHER STANDARDIZATION

Teacher education curricula were designed independently and although there were some similarities, they lacked standardization. In 1931 the Department of School Health and Physical Education of the National Education Association authorized the appointment of a national committee to develop standards for evaluating institutions preparing teachers of health and physical education.

In 1935, Blanche Trilling of the University of Wisconsin emphasized better evaluation knowledge for prospective physical educators. In addition to knowing how to teach a variety of dances, games, and sports skills, Trilling believed teachers of the mid-1930s should "manipulate with ease frequency distribution, normal probability curves, coefficients of correlation, probable errors, standard deviation, and T-scale scores."[16] Trilling contended that knowledge of the appropriateness of measuring devices, skillful use of measuring instruments, interpretation of the results were essential for effective physical education programs.

PROFESSIONAL PREPARATION CONFERENCES

A National Conference on Undergraduate Professional Preparation in Health Education, Physical Education, and Recreation was held at Jackson's Mill, West Virginia, in May, 1948. The Jackson's Mill Conference emphasized the importance of a general curriculum and the need for competency in achieving curriculum objectives. The focus on teacher preparation in physical education envisioned for the 1950s was on the development of many skills and much knowledge.[17] Criteria which have influenced the development of undergraduate teacher education programs throughout the 1950s and into the 1960s were formulated at the Jackson's Mill conference. A similar conference was held to standardize graduate programs in January, 1950, at Pere Marquette State Park in Illinois.

In 1962, another Professional Preparation Conference for undergraduate education was held in Washington, D.C. During the 1960s teacher preparation programs were designed to develop the generalist who could teach varied and sequential physical education activities. Students majoring in physical education who had skill deficiencies were expected to acquire skills in those areas. In addition, coeducational experiences were recommended for students in professional preparation programs. Competencies essential for teaching elementary school physical education were considered an important phase of the undergraduate curriculum.[18]

TEACHER PREPARATION IN THE 1970S

In 1972, a National Conference on Professional Preparation of the Elementary Specialist was held at Lake of the Ozarks, Missouri. During the decade of the 1970s, elementary school physical education reflected the English influence which was introduced into the United States by women physical educators who had studied in England. Budget cutbacks in school systems resulting from voter refusal to approve school bonds as well as the recession of the mid-1970s resulted in fewer teaching positions. The overabundance of teachers in nearly all subjects caused some teacher preparation programs to develop course offerings in nonteaching areas. Physical education graduates of the late 1970s were prepared to assume positions in physical fitness centers and other nonschool agencies, such as senior citizen residences. The advent of Title IX produced rapidly expanding interscholastic programs when girls teams became more prevalent than ever before. Teacher preparation institutions offered specializations in athletic administration, athletic training, and coaching.

During the 1980s, more career choices were available to students and departments of physical education prepared students to meet the demands of the changing job market. General curricula were replaced by more specialized courses of study in a variety of areas. The names of departments and colleges were changed to reflect the diverse areas of study. Many Colleges of Health, Physical Education, and Recreation became Colleges of Health and Human Performance. Faculty members in Departments of Physical Education in Colleges of Education renamed their academic areas and many chose Departments of Exercise Science or other names to indicate expanded areas of study. By the 1990s, fewer students chose to teach physical education. During the 1995 AAHPERD Convention, Dr. John Schleppi spoke of the diversity of program offerings:

> Instead of a Department of Physical Education we are additionally a department of exercise science [offering] sport management, recreational leadership, prephysical therapy, nutrition, health services . . . or combinations . . . [of these programs]. The alternative career choices, following a nonteaching tract, have led to significant changes within departments of physical education. As an example, where I am employed, at the University of Dayton, less than 20% of the majors are in the traditional physical education program.[19]

Graduates of these programs often continue in graduate school before taking positions in professional sport, athletic training, wellness centers, physical rehabilitation programs, or athletic administration. Some students choose an exercise science program to prepare for careers in sport law and sports medicine.

SUMMARY

Dio Lewis established the Normal Institute for Physical Education in Boston in 1861 and is generally recognized as giving the first major impetus to preparing physical education teachers in the United States. His school remained in existence for seven years with graduates meeting much of the immediate demand for gymnastics instructors. No real demand for physical education teachers existed in the public schools until 1885 when Kansas City included physical education in its schools under the leadership of Carl Betz, an American Turner. The Normal School, conducted by the North American Turnerbund, was reestablished after the war and many graduates had begun to introduce physical training in the public schools of Midwestern cities.

After 1880, the preparation of physical education teachers began to assume greater importance. Increased attention was being given to curriculum development, the teaching staff, facilities, and qualifications of teacher training candidates. Six schools were noteworthy during the 1880s because they offered two years of theoretical and practical course work. Up to 1920, nearly one-third of 9,656 individuals graduating from 28 teacher training institutions were from The Sargent School. Two YMCA training schools eventually became Springfield College and George Williams College. Amy Morris Homans directed the Boston Normal School which became the Department of Hygiene and Physical Education at Wellesley College in Massachusetts. Early teacher training schools were due largely to private initiative and capital.

Prior to 1900, teacher preparation was generally conducted by private normal schools with colleges and universities having little influence on teacher training. As more states passed laws recognizing the importance of public school physical education, the need for a greater number of trained teachers became evident. Among the first institutions to include a professional curriculum in their course offerings were the Universities of Nebraska, California, Missouri; Oberlin College; and the Normal College at Ypsilanti, Michigan. After World War I, there was a greater demand for qualified physical education teachers. To meet this need more colleges and universities began to offer professional preparation programs. Program standardization became evident and in 1948 a National Conference on Undergraduate Professional Preparation in Health Education, Physical Education, and Recreation was held at Jackson's Mill, West Virginia. The Conference emphasized the importance of a general curriculum and the need for competency in achieving curriculum objectives. During the 1960s, teacher preparation programs were designed to develop the generalist who could teach a variety of activities at various grade levels. During the 1970s, the teaching of elementary school physical education reflected an English influence which was introduced to the United States by women physical educators who had studied in England. Economic difficulties caused a decline in public school teaching positions. Specialization became more prevalent and some teacher preparation programs developed course offerings for nonschool positions such as those found in physical fitness centers and senior citizen residences. During the 1980s and 1990s, more specializations developed and revealed a break from traditional offerings.

REFERENCES

1. Fred Eugene Leonard. "The 'New Gymnastics' of Dio Lewis (1860–1868)," *American Physical Education Review,* 11 (June, 1906), pp. 90–91.
2. Leonard, *ibid.,* pp. 91–92.
3. Dio Lewis (ed.). *Lewis New Gymnastics and Boston Journal of Physical Culture,* 1 (March, 1861), p. 79.
4. Bruce L. Bennett. "Contributions of Dr. Sargent to Physical Education," *Research Quarterly,* 19 (May, 1948), p. 87.
5. Bennett, *ibid.*
6. Fanny Garrison. "Amy Morris Homans—An Appreciation," *The Sportswoman,* 5 (February, 1929), p. 7.
7. Garrison, *ibid.,* p. 7.
8. Baron Nils Posse. "Modification of the Swedish System of Gymnastics to Meet American Conditions," *Physical Education,* 1 (November, 1892), p. 169.
9. Baron Nils Posse. "Suggestions on Physical Culture," University of North Carolina at Greensboro, The Wellesley Physical Education Collection, p. 9, n.d.
10. Joan Paul. "H. Sophie Newcomb Memorial College," *Journal of Physical Education and Dance,* 65 (March, 1994), pp. 53–54.
11. Walter Kroll and Guy Lewis. "The First Academic Degree in Physical Education," *Journal of Health, Physical Education and Recreation,* 40 (June, 1969), p. 73.
12. Walter C. John. *National Surveys of the Office of Education Chapter 20,* Biennial Survey of Education in the United States 1928–1930. 1 Washington: United States Government Printing Office, 1931, p. 11 and, Marie M. Ready and James Frederick Rogers, *Hygiene and Physical Education, Chapter 10.* Biennial Survey of Education in the United States 1928–1930, 1 Washington: United States Government Printing Office, 1931, p. 21.
13. Elmer Berry. "Problems in Recruiting of Teachers of Physical Education," *American Physical Education Review,* 25 (June, 1920), p. 235.
14. H. Harrison Clarke. "Select Your Physical Educator With Care," *Education History of American Physical Education and Sport* 68 (April, 1948), p. 465.
15. Darwin A. Hindman. "Some Needs in Physical Educator Teacher Training," *Journal of Health and Physical Education.* 2 (April, 1931), pp. 8–9.
16. Blanche M. Trilling. "A Twenty-five Year Perspective on Physical Education Needs," *Journal of Health and Physical Education,* 6 (May, 1935), p. 7.
17. *Professional Preparation in Health Education, Physical Education and Recreation Education, Report of a National Conference.* Washington, D.C.: American Association for Health, Physical Education, and Recreation, 1962, pp. 131–132.
18. *Professional Preparation, ibid.,* pp. 61–62.

19. John Schleppi, "The History of Physical Education and Sport: What Should We Teach?" American Alliance for Health, Physical Education, Recreation and Dance Convention, Portland, Oregon, March 31, 1995.

Chapter 10

THE EVOLUTION OF DANCE IN AMERICA

Dance, like many social, religious, and political convictions, resulted from contributions made by numerous peoples who brought their ideas and cultural heritages to America. As was true of other forms of amusement, entertainment, and art it did not progress without opposition. Some religious groups such as the Quakers and Puritans were instrumental in having regulations passed which forbade dancing. In contrast, the Shakers, another religious group, sanctioned dancing because it was considered an act of worship. Contemporary dance choreographers have looked into the past and have incorporated Shaker movements in their choreography.

In addition to the importation of European dances and their American adapations, professional performers helped to establish such European dance forms as the ballet. Ballet dancers from France, Santo Domingo, and later dance companies from the Soviet Union had an impact on the popularity and technical perfection of American ballet.

Black slaves continued their dances on southern plantations and made original contributions to the development of jazz and tap dancing by learning how to clog from European immigrants. Initially their dances were religious in nature but in time they became secular. The clog consisted of almost no arm and body movement with the head held rigid, while the feet beat rapid tatoos on the ground. The slaves added the loose swing of body movement and changed the beat to syncopated off-rhythm. They also made contributions to other dance forms adapted from American and West Indies dances. Recognized styles of dance in America today may be traced back to European influences and even further to native Americans.

DANCE AND THE NATIVE AMERICANS

Dance for the American Indian was an essential ingredient to existence itself in that it was performed in association with the life elements of fertility, war, crop growing, hunting, death, and rebirth. These first American performers did not dance with the main purpose of imparting theatrical intent. Arthur Todd identified this important difference by pointing out that the Indian danced for intrinsic reasons quite apart from the performance factor. For example, the Indian's crops and very life depended upon rain, which made taking part in the rain dance purposeful. It was this inner

150

need for communication with the gods which prompted the primal desire for expression. Secondly, dance was not performed for aesthetic reasons and it was passed from generation to generation not as a technique but through participation. A major contribution of Indian dance was that its movements originated from inner compulsions which were translated into visible dance forms. Although of early origin, this concept of inner expression has served as the basis for contemporary comparisons commonly made between native American and modern dance.[1]

A characteristic common to most Indian dances is the straight posture of the back while held in the upright position with the knees bent. Although there is not a great deal of arm movement, the head is commonly in various positions such as well back, lifted high, or bowed slightly forward. It has been noted that various head movements represent the flight of graceful birds. Early observers were especially impressed with the dancing abilities of the Plains Indians, particularly the Sioux, who had the greatest variety of dances. Because they were hunters and warriors their dances differed in spirit and character from many other tribes who relied principally upon agriculture to support life.

The Indians' bitter struggle with the United States government which eventually resulted in removal to reservations, dealt a severe blow to their forms of dance. In those early years dancing was generally viewed by government authorities as suspicious, warlike behavior, and it was therefore suppressed. The ban on dancing helped stifle the religious, social, and political life of the Indians because dance was such an inexorable part of their lives. A new government policy inaugurated in 1934 removed the ban on dancing, but for many tribes it came too late because most of the old ceremonial dances were already extinct.[2] For many years to come Indian dances were staged at circuses, carnivals, and Western movies and shows with only a theatrical billing. Two pioneer non-Indians were instrumental in introducing the dance art of the American Indian to audiences both in the United States and Europe. Reginald and Gladys Laubin lived with the Plains Indians and learned ceremonial dances which were very nearly forgotten from the old men of the tribes. An Onondaga Indian of the Iroquois Nation named Tom Two Arrows has also been successful in bringing his native dances to national and international audiences.[3]

The contributions that native American dances have made to the art both directly and indirectly are still being realized. They have served as a source of inspiration for the contemporary performer while also stimulating further investigations into their significance and forms. Aside from attempts by some to preserve the purity of these ethnic dance forms, their essence has also served as the theme for other theatrical activities.

DANCE IN COLONIAL AMERICA

By the beginning of the eighteenth century, many of the hardships associated with the founding of a new country had been conquered. Small farms were established and merchant ships were traveling the seas in trade with England. Public education began to establish itself in New England while the Southern colonies left the education of their children to the families who could afford it. As the colonies flourished economically, politically, and socially, there arose more leisure time for cultural pursuits and amusements.

Although the Puritans did not actively establish an American dance culture, they were not totally anti-dance as some authorities would believe. They accepted what the Bible had to say about dancing and did not approve of men and women dancing together, or dancing which generated an attitude of licentiousness. Also, professional actors, singers, acrobats, or dancers were looked upon suspiciously by the Northern colonists as an immoral group of people who did not earn their living by the accepted trades and business enterprises of the day.[4] On the Southern plantations, however, the prevailing attitude differed in that the owners would stage lavish balls usually lasting for days.

By the middle of the century professional troupes came from Europe to treat the American colonists to plays and dances in spite of official objections. In 1774, the first Continental Congress passed a resolution which advocated the closing of all public places of amusement. At the onset of the American Revolution the British actors who had been performing in New York, Philadelphia, and Baltimore hastened back to their native country. When the war was over an actor, named Lewis Hallam who had been popular in the colonies prior to the Revolution, returned to Philadelphia in 1784. The government was still opposed to the theater and Hallam was unable to secure a license in order to produce plays. Undaunted, Hallam gathered together a small company and proceeded to provide entertainments which were disguised as "lectures." It was during one of these "lectures" in 1784 that John Durang, presumably self-taught, made his debut at age 17. He went on to become the first American to win widespread recognition as a dancer. Although he danced many roles and even did some choreography, he became most famous for his Hornpipe dance. The tune was composed by an acquaintance of Durang's, a German born dwarf named Hoffmaster who was a talented musician and prominent figure among the artistic group in New York. Durang's Hornpipe, an ancestor of the modern tap dance, is described:

A Sailor Hornpipe—Old Style

1. Glissand round (first part of tune).
2. Double shuffle down, do.

3. Heel and toe back, finish with back shuffle.
4. Cut the buckle down, finish the shuffle.
5. Side shuffle right and left, finishing with beats.
6. Pigeon wing going round.
7. Heel and toe haul in back.
8. Steady toes down.
9. Changes back, finish with back shuffle and beats.
10. Wave step down.
11. Heel and toe shuffle obliquely back.
12. Whirligig, with beats down.
13. Sissone and entrechats back.
14. Running forward on the heels.
15. Double Scotch step, with a heel Brand in Plase. (sic)
16. Single Scotch step back.
17. Parried toes round, or feet in and out.
18. The Cooper shuffle right and left back.
19. Grasshopper step down.
20. Terré-a'terre' (sic) or beating with toes back.
21. Jockey crotch down.
22. Traverse round, with hornpipe glissade, bow and finish.[5]

By 1789, the anti-theater law in Philadelphia was repealed and the stage troupe could now legally announce their performance. Durang celebrated by dancing for his audience none other than a Hornpipe! Later he developed variations of this dance and even performed it on the tightrope and around eggs placed on the floor. Although Durang was a dancer possessing natural talent which he developed through his associations with trained artists, the fact that he was the only American born artist in Hallam's troupe enhanced his popularity.

THE SHAKERS

Ann Lee, an Englishwoman, first established the Shakers near Albany, New York, during the Revolutionary War. A religious sect, they became known as Shakers because of their peculiar shaking movements used during worship. Communes were built in eastern New York, parts of New England, and in Kentucky and Ohio. By 1845, their numbers reached nearly 6,000 but by the middle of the first decade of the twentieth century a sustained decline was evident. Complicated dances and marches were introduced at various times and were observed by sectarians during Sunday society meetings. The Shaker dances, borrowed by sectarians, provided a recreational function but Shaker theologians insisted on justifying dancing as an act of worship. Sectarians interpreted Shaker marching as "the unity and discipline of the group, and the proximity but physical separation of the lines of male and female dancers represented the group's maintenance of celibacy in the face of temptation."[6] Abstaining from sexual relationships, the group worked to develop a sin-free society. Through their dancing, sin was supposedly shaken from their bodies. The Shakers did not perform mixed couple dances and they did not contribute to the theater dance of their era. They exhibited the concept of religious dance, and provided a basis for creativity on the part of twentieth century dance choreographers.

DANCE OF THE AFRICAN SLAVES IN AMERICA

Slaves danced on plantations where they lived and, when given passes, were allowed to visit other plantations where they danced. An English visitor observed that slaves sometimes danced for the entertainment of their owners. After a dinner in the spring of 1861 the older children were summoned to dance and were rewarded with lumps of sugar.[7]

Some dances were patterned after the motions of animals. The Pigeon Wing, a dance resembling the movements of the bird, apparently was performed on numerous plantations. Other animal dances, probably derivatives of African dances, were the Buzzard Lope, Turkey Trot, and Snake Hip. Dances were incorporated into such work projects as corn shucking and quilting. Weddings and Christmas were also times for dancing.

The Juba, of African origin, involved stamping, clapping, and slapping of arms or other body parts as a substitute for musical instruments. The use of drums was eventually prohibited by plantation owners because they believed that revolutionary messages could be sent among blacks. The patting rhythm was known as "Patting Juba" which provided rhythm for dancing and became very popular when drums were banned.[8] The Juba was primarily a competitive dance of skill and began when a participant stepped into the circle of dancers and performed a skill. A member of the opposite sex joined in the performance of the skill while the other dancers clapped and encouraged the competitors by singing. It was a well-liked plantation dance and Juba music evolved. The "Big Apple" may have been influenced by the Juba.[9]

Another dance performed on plantations was the "chalk-line walk" which later became nationally known as the "cake-walk." Performed in couples, it sometimes involved walking on a path with a pail of water balanced on the participants' heads. The couple having the most erect posture, and spilling the least amount or no water, won the contest. In later cake walk contests the "fanciest" walker would win a cake. After slavery ended the cake walk became in vogue throughout the country. It was introduced at the Centennial of American Independence in Philadelphia in 1876, and the winning couple was awarded an enormous cake. Minstrel shows included the cake walk and contributed to the popularity of the dance. Black minstrel companies often set aside an evening and offered a prize to the best local couple. Competition, cash prizes, presentation of cakes, as well as sociability made the cake walk a novel craze. The Prize Cake Walk Contest became a common event in New York City and national championship contests were held in Madison Square Garden. Cake walk contestants were judged on time, style, and execution. The *National Police Gazette,* a leading sports paper during this era, awarded medals to the winners.[10]

By the end of the nineteenth century and the beginning of the following century, the cake walk reached the height of its popularity. In addition to minstrel shows and Madison Square Garden competition, the cake walk was performed in vaudeville shows. Some authorities gave credit to the Cake Walk competition for the emergence of the expression, "that takes the cake."

TAP DANCING AND MINISTREL SHOWS

The ancestors of the modern tap dances are African shuffling foot movements consisting of relaxed knees with a crouching posture and syncopated footwork adapted from European jigs and clogs.[11] Slaves on the plantations were to modify the clog dances of the English and Irish to suit their own indigenous form of expression which was religious in nature. It was from this unique form of dance that many public entertainers gained a wealth of material from which to stage their performances called Negro minstrels.

They reached the height of popularity in the late 1850s and 1860s. It was a fashionable form of entertainment for fifty years and lingered well into the twentieth century.[12] About a quarter of a century after the introduction of minstrel shows blacks began appearing in the minstrels.

Vocalists, instrumentalists, and comedians provided entertainment for minstrel goers. Frequent advertisements in the *New York Herald* encouraged attendance by children for half price. One notice in the *Herald* read: "Woods Minstrel Hall has been newly ventilated, and an ice water fountain erected in the centre, making it the coolest place of amusement in the city. Admission, 25 cents; children under 12 years, half price."[13]

Many of the minstrel acts became standard features. In the center, the dignified interlocutor, with characters such as Mr. Bones and Mr. Tambo on either side provide side-splitting comedy. Other humorous imitations of the town blacks upon whom the minstrel was patterned, were heard in songs with musical accompaniment. A variety of acts were presented in which minstrel members exhibited their specialties. "A clog-dance was always in order, although the mechanical precision . . . was wholly foreign to the characteristics of the actual negroes whom the minstrels were supposed to be representing."[14] The first part of the show generally consisted of songs, jokes and grand walk-around. The second part, the " 'olio' or mixture was usually- . . . made up of vocal and instrumental music, dances, specialties, a hoedown, and stump speeches. In the grand finale the entire company participated in farcical afterpieces."[15]

Matthews cited three reasons for the decline of the minstrel show. First, he suggested that its failure may have been a result of the inaccurate portrayal of black men. Some minstrel shows strayed far from black culture with their

Irish brogue and even German dialect. Second, the exclusiveness of masculine entertainers eliminated additional appeal and show variety with the omission of women. Third, the program generally followed by most minstrel shows was monotonous and could not match the competition of the music hall and variety show which appealed to the public.[16]

While the minstrel show met its demise, the art of tap dancing flourished in the 1930s and 1940s and is still practiced, but it is not highly visible. One of the greatest early dancers to help establish tap was a black man, Bill "Bo Jangles" Robinson. Not necessarily confined to the stage, tap dancing was also popular during the late 1930s and early 1940s in school physical education programs especially in the southeastern part of the United States. Tap dancing is recognized as an art in itself. However, with the rise of ballet, jazz, and modern dance which all began to be combined in movie and Broadway choreographies in the 1930s and 1940s, tap dancing declined.

VAUDEVILLE

Vaudeville, the American variety show, was probably influenced by English performers. As early as 1769, some Philadelphia comedians toured the east in what is recognized as an early form of vaudeville entertainment. New York opened its first "vaudeville house" in the late 1840s and vaudeville became a favorite form of entertainment by the middle of the nineteenth century.

A typical show included jugglers, magicians, acrobats, instrumentalists, and monologists. The highlight of the show was generally a:

> . . . soft-shoe number preceded by a small boy in uniform who would, with a pontifical gesture, toss a cornucopia of sand before the footlights, to prepare the floor for a gala team of dancers in linen suits, straw boaters and glistening canes.[17]

In the early 1930s, it was evident that vaudeville was declining. The radio offered performances by top vaudeville stars and their shows could be enjoyed in the comfort of homes without charge. Movies and television further contributed to the demise of vaudeville shows, and another era in American entertainment ended.

FROM BALLROOM TO SQUARE DANCING

In the 18th century, French dancing masters came to colonial America bringing with them indigenous dances of their homeland. Although not all colonists, especially in New England, approved of dancing, the French masters were well received in the larger cities of New York and Philadelphia. They were especially welcome in the Virginia colonies where dancing was an important part of social life and essential to the training of "ladies and gentlemen." These dance instructors came to America in even larger num-

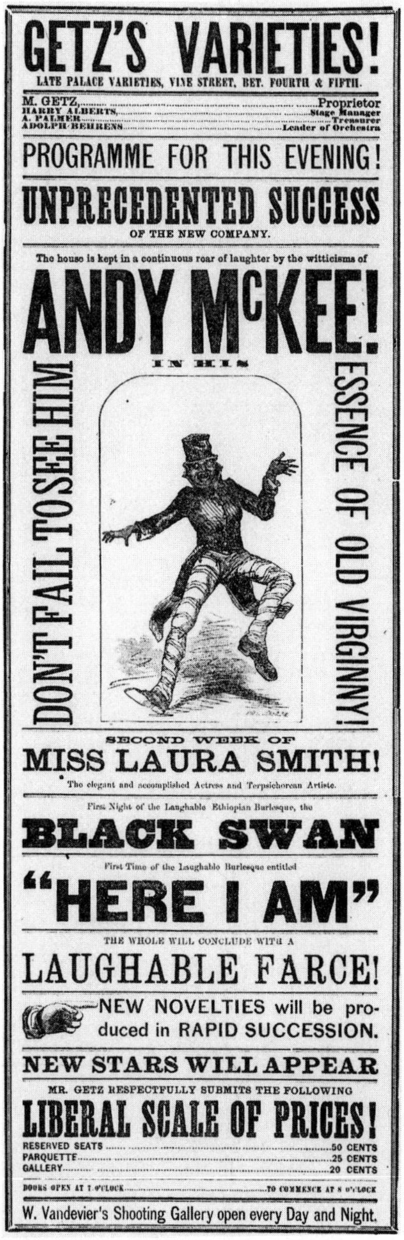

Figure 10.1. Courtesy of Belknap Collection, University of Florida, Gainesville, Florida.

Figure 10.2. Courtesy of Belknap Collection, University of Florida, Gainesville, Florida.

bers after the revolution and introduced highly polished and sophisticated set dances called "quadrilles." It was fashionable for socially elite colonists to attend "balls" which were formal occasions where dancing was a featured part of the evening. These "balls" were private affairs, and those in attendance knew one another well or had been properly introduced.

By the early 1850s, upper class New Yorkers typified the popularity of ballroom dancing prompting one observer to comment that it "was the one great article in the code of the fashionables to which all other amusements . . . were subordinate."[18] A "grand dress-ball" at a hotel was held once a week and two "undress-balls" or "hops" were well attended. The "hops" were more informal but most of the fashion-conscious wore formal attire. Public parlors were usually filled with dancers when there were no hotel dances.[19]

> From 1910–1920, pantomimic animal dances and dance-songs with instructional lyrics became standard ballroom fare. The explicitness of pantomimic action in animal dances and instructions in dance-songs gradually diminished until the steps of the foxtrot bore little if any resemblance to the movements of a fox, and the lyrics for the Charleston gave little if any instructional aid in the performance of America's favorite dance during the twenties. With the Charleston, the distinction between dancing-to-do and dancing-to-watch was erased, and on a professional level, ballroom and tap merged with performers inventing tap-Charleston.[20]

The origins of square dance in America may also be traced back to the *quadrilles*, a French term for a square dance formation of four couples. While the quadrilles were being performed by the more genteel members of society, itinerant dancing masters were teaching less sophisticated quadrilles to the working class in rural areas of the country. As immigration to the New World steadily increased, country people from England and Scotland came to America settling south along the chain of Appalachian mountains. They brought with them vigorous round and chain dances which spread across the American frontier. Although one can find in square dances traces of the quadrilles, round and chain dances, with the passage of time it has developed its own unique characteristics.

Square dance is practiced throughout the United States with similarities in fundamental movement, form, and technique. The "shuffle" step is basic to all sections of the country and easily learned. The clog step, also used, is especially prominent in North Carolina square dances. However, differences in square dance exist throughout various regions in such features as tempo, promenade position, and style.

JAZZ

Africans appeared on the American mainland early in the seventeenth century and they remained in bondage for one century and nearly three-quarters of another century. But even the unfairness of their enslavement could not stifle the continuation of their dances. They perpetuated their rhythmical activities by stomping on the ground, clapping hands, and singing songs.

In a two-volume doctoral dissertation tracing the derivation of jazz dance, Russella Brandman showed that jazz resulted from a blending of African, European, West Indian, and American dance and musical forms. Brandman's study revealed:

> The blending process was instigated by the unfortunate institution of slavery and was nurtured by the cross-exposure of slaves and masters to each others' religious and social customs as well as to the related music and dance. The immediate results of this blending prior to the Civil War led to the introduction of some White characteristics into Black communal dance forms and to the appearance of Black elements in White social dances. Music underwent the same sort of process, so that syncopation began to appear in marching and church music as well as in dance tunes. After the Civil War, the further diffusion of black and white cultures allowed the blending of the above hybrids plus an increased fusion of Black and White elements. . . . [21]

The result of the combination of black and white dance elements, according to Brandman's research, produced the earliest jazz forms which included the cake walk, minstrel and ragtime dances, Dixieland jazz, and blues styles in music. These dances were most popular around the turn of the nineteenth century.

The development of jazz, as we know it today, was given additional impetus by the 1923 musical, "Runnin' Wild," which led to the Charleston craze. It swept the country and prompted people to participate rather than spectate. Next came the lindy hop, which originated in Harlem around 1928 and today is considered by dance historians to be a jazz classic. A basic step was done in closed partner position and then the couple would separate to perform solo improvisations. By 1939, the jitterbug had evolved from the lindy when air steps or acrobatic lifts became increasingly popular.

Jazz was influenced in the 1930s and 1940s by such talented performers as Busby Berkeley, Gene Kelly, and Fred Astaire. Astaire's dancing style, smooth and elegant, became his trademark. He furthered the development of jazz dance with his use of the arms, hands, and horizontal and vertical space. By the 1950s, "modern jazz" had emerged and was best illustrated in Jerome Robbins' landmark musical, "West Side Story." One important advancement in dance had been made in that it was used as a medium for developing the story and to define characters and express emotions. In the 1960s, the "Twist" and its successors, the "Frug" and "Watusi" emphasized torso manipulation rather than fancy footwork with all contact between partners removed. Since the 1960s many other "different" dances have appeared, sharing the common characteristics of torso action over footwork and solo performance with no contact between partners.[22]

Even in its early days, jazz appeared in dance works. Initially viewed as a novelty, it eventually gained greater acceptance as a medium for expression.

Jazz dance is now an established art form for the concert stage and appears in many styles ranging from sophisticated to primitive in nature.

BALLET

The early history of ballet in America generally consisted of visiting European artists who performed European ballets. Few American dancers were trained in this art form requiring long, arduous preparation and it was not until the 1940s that American companies were established.

The first ballets performed in America were probably staged by Alexander Placide and his wife in Charleston, South Carolina in 1791. The Placides, trained in acrobatics, pantomime, tight rope dancing, and classic ballet, had previously appeared in Paris and Santo Domingo. In January, 1792, they travelled to New York City and presented a "Dancing Ballot" (sic) titled "The Bird Catcher." The cast included John Durang, America's first professional dancer.[23]

Numerous ballets were presented in the theaters of Boston, New York, and Philadelphia during the latter part of the eighteenth century. The first serious ballet given in this country was a French work, "La Foret Noire," in Philadelphia on April 26, 1794. Madame Gardie, an accomplished dancer from Santo Domingo, made her American debut in the April performance. Gardie was noted as both a dancer and mime who won great popularity in New York, Boston, and Philadelphia. Unfortunately, she died tragically when her husband, despondent over his inability to contribute to his wife's support, stabbed her to death in August, 1798.[24]

In the early 1800s, American audiences were introduced to extraordinary classical dancing by Europeans. New York City's Park Theater engaged the talents of a French ballet master in 1821. Interest in ballet grew even more with the visit of a French dance company. By the 1840s, ballet in America had acquired great popularity, primarily because skilled European artists dominated the American scene.

The opening of the Metropolitan Opera House in 1883 focused attention on American ballet. A school was founded in 1909 which provided the basis for developing American talent. A year later, the Russian ballet dancer, Anna Pavlova, considered the greatest dancer of her time, debuted at the Metropolitan Opera House. She was enthusiastically received and elevated ballet in America to an even higher level with her flawless execution and stage presence. Pavlova continued her American tours and made her last appearance in this country during the 1924–25 season.[25]

George Balanchine is credited with raising the New York City Ballet to international prominence. Born in St. Petersburg, Russia, he was named Georgi Balanchivadze. The dance scholar, Lincoln Kirstein, became Balanchine's patron and cofounder of the City Ballet. In 1934, a year after Balanchine immigrated to the United States, they established the School of American Ballet. The American Ballet's first tour encountered financial difficulty and

Figure 10.3. La Vern Porter Dance Troupe. Left to right: La Vern Porter, Karen Stevens, and Carla Pittman. Photographed by Daniel White. Courtesy of La Vern Porter.

the two men agreed to an association with the Metropolitan in 1935. Three years later, the union ended when Balanchine objected to the Met's conservative style of management. For eight years following the collapse of his company, Balanchine choreographed for Broadway shows and films.

In 1946, after Lincoln Kirstein had returned from World War II, he established the Ballet Society. This small group, drawn from the School of American Ballet, debuted on November 20, 1946. Balanchine created an acclaimed ballet for the opening of the struggling Ballet Society. Later, the Ballet Society became a constituent of the City Center, which operated the Mecca Auditorium and was renamed the New York City Ballet. Balanchine achieved wider recognition in the 1950s when the public was more receptive to his pure dance ballets. The New York City Ballet reached a wider

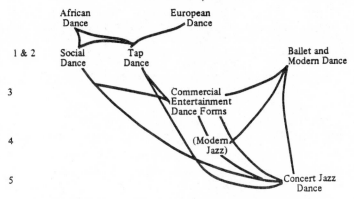

"Evolutionary Pathway of Jazz Dance, in the United States"

Key: 1: African communal dance body movement + European couple formation and footwork = jazz social dance.

2: African shuffling + European jigs and clogs = tap.

3: Jazz social dance + tap = more varieties of jazz dance in commercial entertainment.

4: Jazz, tap, and/or combination entertainment forms + ballet and modern dance = more hybrid entertainment forms (modern jazz).

5: Social dance, tap, various entertainment forms, modern jazz + ballet and modern dance = concert jazz dance.

Figure 10.4. Courtesy of Rusti Brandman, University of Florida, Gainesville, Florida.

audience when it moved to the New York State Theater at Lincoln Center and Balanchine was at his peak. Balanchine died in 1983, leaving an artistic legacy for generations to come. He was recognized as one of the greatest choreographers in the history of ballet.[26]

MODERN DANCE

Three visionary American artists, Isadora Duncan, Loie Fuller, and Ruth St. Denis, broke away from the rigid European dance traditions of the early 20th century. The pioneering trio was recognized as great artists in Europe and the United States. They led the way for the creative and emotional expression in modern dance. Born in San Francisco in 1880, Duncan's first dance appearance was at the age of 15. She is credited with introducing a modern version of classical dance which emphasized interpretative dancing. At first, Isadora Duncan's appearance in wisps of sheer fabric draped about her body and bare limbs were considered shocking. Duncan's view of dance was introduced more widely when she opened dancing schools in several European cities and in the United States. Her appearances in unusual costumes accentuated with long flowing scarves focused attention on her unique style of dancing. Duncan was revered in France not only because she was a great dancer but for allowing her home to be used for war relief work during World War I. Isadora Duncan's life ended tragically on September 14, 1927, near Nice, France. A long silk scarf wrapped around her neck, streaming in long folds, became entangled in the rear wheel of an open automobile and strangled her.[27]

Less than four months later Loie Fuller, known for her flowing robes and serpentine dances, died in Paris, France, on New Year's Day in 1928. Fuller was born in Fullersberg, near Chicago, in 1870, a town named after her ancestors. At the age of 13 she became a temperance lecturer and quit a year later when she went barnstorming in Shakespearean plays. Eventually, Fuller found her niche in dancing. Her use of color and changing lights conveyed great emotion to her audiences in the United States, England, and France. During World War I, her charitable work for the Allies won praise in France, Belgium, and Rumania. After the war she established a school of dancing in Paris and sent troupes to the United States.[28]

Ruth St. Denis' career spanned well over half a century. Various years of her birth in Newark range from 1877 to 1880. St. Denis, the last of the modern dance trio, died on July 21, 1968, in Los Angeles. She was known as the First Lady of American Dance and first received instruction from her mother who schooled her in the Delsarte method of poses and postures. She was paid $20.00 a week when her dancing career commenced in 1894. In the late 1920s, she and Ted Shawn were receiving fees as high as $3,500 a week.

Influences on her expressive dance came from varied sources. She visited Paris and saw a number of dancers including Loie Fuller. The writings of Mary Baker Eddy attracted St. Denis to Christian Science. Religious inspiration and a desire to make dancing more creative apparently united when she saw a picture of the goddess Isis on a poster displaying Egyptian Deities cigarettes. St. Denis saw power and beauty in the goddess and began to study Eastern dances. In 1906, she presented her first dance recital of original choreography. A series of matinee dates, sponsored by society women, was followed by a European tour.

By the 1909–1910 season, Ruth St. Denis became the first solo dancer to appear at a New York theater in an evening performance. Prior to her evening engagement, dance had been an afternoon event with little fanfare. In 1914, Ruth St. Denis married Ted Shawn and they organized the Denishawn Company and Denishawn School in 1915. Among the Denishawn students were Martha Graham, Doris Humphrey, and Charles Weidman. Denishawn Schools were established throughout the United States and became the basis for modern dance in this country. The Denishawn era ended in 1931 when Ruth St. Denis and Ted Shawn separated.

During World War II, St. Denis resided in Hollywood and aided the war effort by working in the Douglas aircraft factory.[29] Isadora Duncan and Loie Fuller contributed to the war effort during World War I by leading rallies to raise funds. The three dancers made an impression on modern dance because of their creativity, desire to break from tradition, and futuristic vision.

A second generation of modern dancers evolved from the Denishawn School in the 1930s and 1940s. Martha Graham, Charles Weidman, Doris Humphrey, Helen Tamiris, and Hanya Holm carried on the creative tradition established by Ruth St. Denis and Ted Shawn. During the 1950s, 1960s, and 1970s, a third generation of modern dancers prospered from the influence of such performers as Graham, Humphrey, Weidman, and others.

Among these were Erik Hawkins, Merce Cunningham, and Paul Taylor who all studied under Martha Graham and have since formed their own companies, each known for its distinctive personal style. Hawkins is noted for his "pure poetry" of movement while Cunningham's compositions are said to be more intellectually interesting rather than emotionally arousing. Taylor is associated with avante-garde ideas presented within the content of traditional theater. Humphrey and Weidman served as sources from which José Limon derived his dance technique considered to be humanistic and in exaltation to the spirit of mankind. Limon's style has been taught over the years at the Juilliard School in New York and colleges throughout the country.[30]

Contemporary modern dance trends may best be described in terms of those artists who strive for revolutionary change as opposed to other performers more content to dance within the traditions of their mentors or on less revolutionary paths of their own. Twyla Tharp typifies the performer who seeks innovative change in that she has used her eclectic dance training to develop a healthy irreverence for tradition. Her movement style is composed of quick footwork, floppy torso, and arm movement with unusual changes in direction and quality. Many other contemporary artists study other dance and movement forms such as ballet, jazz, yoga, and various martial arts styles. Numerous dance groups such as LaVern Porter's Dance Troupe perform throughout the country and thrive on the interest directed to the performing arts evident in the 1970s and 1980s.

In addition to seeking unique forms of individual expression, new types of dance performances may be found within the realm of the innovator's repertoire. Steve Paxton is credited with developing "contact improvisation" which:

> . . . explores momentum, weight support and transference, touch and balance, especially with reference to falling and rolling and to the moving of two bodies together. As a performance form, contact is extremely casual. The audience becomes involved in the actual physical movement of the performers rather than in an aesthetic illusion created by the dance.[31]

DANCE IN EDUCATION

Dance first appeared in the public schools in America in the form of folk dance at about the turn of the century. Elizabeth Burchenal, America's famous folk-dance authority, was instrumental in introducing dance to public education as a form of recreation. Folk-dancing is a viable part of most elementary and middle or junior high school physical education programs throughout the country.

Many surveys have been conducted investigating the extent and nature of dance education in the United States. In 1938, a national survey was conducted by the Bennington School of Dance to determine the status of modern dance in education. It was discovered that modern dance was being enthusiastically promoted under the auspices of physical education in especially large high schools. Although the program favored the girls, efforts were under way to cultivate the natural interest of boys as well.

The study also revealed that the vast majority of colleges and universities offered instruction in some form of dancing, and approximately two-thirds of these offered modern dance mostly within the department of physical education although in some institutions dance was transferred to the department of fine arts.[32]

The preparation of dance teachers was pioneered by Margaret H'Doubler and Martha Hill. H'Doubler developed the first dance major in the United States in 1926 at the University of Wisconsin at Madison. In 1934, a school of dance was opened at Bennington College in Vermont. Hill was director of dance for years at Bennington College and New York University, and later head of the dance department at the Juilliard School in New York City. With the development of dance as a major course of study at their respective institutions, these early pioneers prepared the first teachers who went out to other schools and colleges to more firmly establish the place of modern dance in education.

By the late 1970s, dance education had expanded so much in Higher Education that both the *American Alliance for Health, Physical Education, Recreation and Dance,* and *Dance Magazine* publish directories to college and university dance programs. The prospective student of dance can select institutions throughout the country which offer intensive courses for degree candidacy or as a minor field of study. Additionally, dance may be taken as part of an interdisciplinary major, or as a concentration within other degree programs. Elective liberal arts credit may also be earned. Some universities have professional companies in residence.

Accountability in education was more evident as the 1980s gave way to another decade. By the 1990s, the National Dance Association of the AAHPERD had an established Choreography Evaluation Project (CEP). The CEP serves to evaluate dance faculty "... who are in need of outside professional evaluation of their choreographic work for retention, promotion, [or] tenure.[33] Universities continue to offer undergraduate and graduate dance programs; however, many programs are housed in academic units such as the fine arts. Research in choreography theory, curriculum, and Laban movement analysis are among the areas of research in higher education. Dance offers many opportunities for experiences in cultural diversity and interdisciplinary studies.

SUMMARY

American Indian dance was performed in association with the life elements of fertility, war, crop growing, hunting, death, and rebirth. Native Americans danced to communicate with their gods. Dance was passed from generation to generation through participation. The contributions of Native

Americans to contemporary art are still being realized and have served as an inspirational source for contemporary performers.

The Puritans in Colonial America did not actively establish a dance culture. By the middle of the eighteenth century, professional European troupes entertained American colonists with plays and dances in spite of objections. After the American Revolution, British actors returned to Philadelphia and produced plays which were disguised as "lectures." In 1784 John Durang made his debut and eventually became the first American to win widespread fame as a dancer. He became most famous for his Hornpipe dance. By 1789 the anti-theater law in Philadelphia was repealed and stage troupes could legally announce their performances.

The Shakers were a religious sect which became established during the Revolutionary War. Living in communes in New York, New England, Kentucky, and Ohio their numbers reached nearly 6,000 by 1845. During Sunday society meetings they performed dances and marches as part of their worship. Through dancing, sin was supposedly shaken from their bodies as they strove to develop a sin-free society.

Figure 10.5. Modern dance in education. Courtesy of Rusti Brandman. Photograph by Chander Rogear.

African slaves danced on plantations in America giving rise to such dances as the pigeon wing, buzzard lope, snake hip, and turkey trot which were patterned much like the motions of animals. The juba was African in origin and a competitive dance of skill. Another plantation dance was the chalk line walk which eventually became known as the cake walk and the "fanciest" walker would be awarded a cake. After the abolition of slavery it was in vogue throughout much of the country reaching its zenith by the end of the nineteenth century and the beginning of the following century.

Tap dancing is derived from African shuffling foot movements adapted from European jigs and clogs. From this African expression performed by plantation slaves many entertainers culled material from which to stage their performances termed Negro minstrels. Minstrels reached their height of popularity in the 1850s and 1860s, lingering into the twentieth century. Although minstrel shows are no longer produced, the art of tap dancing flourished in the 1930s and 1940s and is still visible today, although not highly practiced.

Vaudeville was an American variety show influenced by English performers. Philadelphia comedians toured the east as early as 1769 with a form of vaudeville entertainment. A typical show featured jugglers, magicians, acrobats, instrumentalists, and monologists. By the early 1930s vaudeville as a form of entertainment had declined with radio, movies, and television, bringing this era to a close.

In the eighteenth century, French dancing masters came to colonial America and introduced set dances called "quadrilles" where they were especially well received in New York and Philadelphia. Socially elite colonists attended "balls" where dancing was a featured part of the evening. By 1910 pantomimic animal dances and dance songs with instructional lyrics were common ballroom fare. With the arrival of the Charleston in the 1920s, the distinction between dancing-to-do and dancing-to-watch was erased.

The origins of American square dance stem in part from the quadrilles. Less sophisticated quadrilles were being taught by itinerant dancing masters to people in rural areas of the country. English and Scottish settlers brought round and chain dances which also spread throughout the frontier. In time, square dances have developed their own unique characteristics.

Jazz resulted from African, European, West Indian, and American dance and musical forms. Early jazz stemmed from the cake walk, minstrel and ragtime dances, Dixieland, and blues style in music. The Charleston craze gave way to the lindy hop which is considered to be a jazz classic. By 1939, the jitterbug had evolved complete with acrobatic lifts. "West Side Story" was a landmark musical in the 1950s for jazz in that it was used as a means for story and character development. Jazz dance is now an established art form and ranges from sophisticated to primitive in nature.

Early ballet in America consisted of visiting European artists with Boston, New York, and Philadelphia hosting numerous programs during the latter part of the eighteenth century.

In 1909, a school was founded which provided impetus to the development of American ballet artists, but few professional performances were given in the United States until the mid-1930s. Touring Soviet companies and the organizing American Ballet Company in 1934 revived ballet interest in America. In 1941, the American Ballet Company was disbanded but it helped to further promote ballet by developing some excellent dancers and choreographers. In the 1970s ballet flourished in New York City and some other major cities showing supportive trends.

Modern dance was born from a desire on the part of Isadora Duncan, Loie Fuller, and Ruth St. Denis to break away from what were considered by these visionary artists to be stuffy European traditions. Each of these early artists developed an individual approach to dancing which was based upon the freedom of movement principle in an expression of individuality. St. Denis formed a small company featuring herself and Ted Shawn. The Denishawn company was instrumental in promoting modern dance throughout the United States for 16 years. From the Denishawn school arose dancers of the 1930s and 1940s such as Martha Graham, Charles Weidman, Doris Humphrey and others who established themselves as leaders of dance in theatre and education. A third generation of dancers appearing in the 1950s, 1960s, and 1970s have benefited from the influence of Graham, Weidman, Humphrey and others to form their own distinctive styles. Contemporary modern dance trends take the form of revolutionary change or along the more traditional paths established by their predecessors.

A prevailing form of dance in contemporary education is modern dance. As early as 1938, it was being promoted in especially the larger public high schools by physical education programs. A majority of colleges and universities also offered instruction in some form of dancing. The preparation of dance teachers was pioneered by Margaret H'Doubler and Martha Hill with H'Doubler developing the first dance major in the United States in 1926 at the University of Wisconsin at Madison. The current prospective student of dance can select from institutions throughout the country to pursue a degree in dance or as a minor field of study.

REFERENCES

1. Arthur Todd. "4 Centuries of American Dance," *Dance Magazine,* 23 (September, 1949), pp. 18–19, 30.
2. Felix Cohen. *Handbook of Federal Indian Law.* Washington: United States Government Printing Office, 1942, pp. 175–176.
3. Walter Terry. *The Dance in America.* New York: Harper and Row, 1956, p. 219.
4. Terry, *ibid.,* p. 24.
5. Lillian Moore. "John Durang, The First American Dancer," *Dance Index,* 1 (August, 1942), pp. 121–125.

6. John McKelvie Whitworth. *God's Blueprints: A Sociological Study of Three Utopian Sects.* Boston: Routledge and Kegan Paul, 1975, pp. 33, 69, 242, 244.
7. William Howard Russell. *My Diary North and South Volume I.* London: Bradbury and Evans, 1863, p. 181.
8. Tom Fletcher. *The Tom Fletcher Story — 100 Years of the Negro in Show Business!* New York: Burdge and Co., 1954, p. 18.
9. Katherine Dunham. "The Negro Dance," *The Negro Caravan.* ed. by Sterling A. Brown, Arthur P. Davis, and Ulysses Lee. New York: Dryden Press, 1941, pp. 997–998.
10. Fletcher, *op. cit.*, pp. 19, 103, 105, 107.
11. Russella Brandman. "The Evolution of Jazz Dance from Folk Origins to Concert Stage," Unpublished dissertation, the Florida State University, 1977, p. 516.
12. Lynne Fauley Emery. *Black Dance in the United States from 1619 to 1970.* Palo Alto: National Press Books, 1972, p. 203.
13. "Amusements," *New York Herald,* August 1, 1852, p. 3.
14. Brander Matthews. "The Rise and Fall of Negro Minstrelsy," *Scribner's Magazine,* 57 (June, 1915), pp. 756–757.
15. Bernard Sobel. *A Pictorial History of Vaudeville.* New York: Citadel Press, 1961, pp. 33–34.
16. Brander Matthews. "The Rise and Fall of Negro Minstrelsy," pp. 758–759.
17. Sobel, *A Pictorial History of Vaudeville,* pp. 20, 24, 27.
18. C. Astor Bristed. *The Upper Ten Thousand: Sketches of American Society.* New York: Stringer and Townsend, 1852, p. 128.
19. Bristed. *The Upper Ten Thousand, ibid.,* p. 129.
20. Russella Brandman. "The Evolution of Jazz Dance from Folk Origins to Concert Stage," *ibid.,* pp. 516–517.
21. Russella Brandman, *ibid.,* pp. 515–516.
22. Russella Brandman. Historical Notes on Jazz: From Cake Walk to Concert, unpublished manuscript, University of Florida, Gainesville, 1980, pp. 1–2.
23. Lillian Moore. "John Durang, the First American Dancer," *Dance Index,* 1 (August, 1942), pp. 127–128.
24. Moore, *ibid.,* p. 130.
25. Anna Pavlova Dies at Height of Fame," *The New York Times,* January 23, 1931, pp. 1, 16.
26. Anna Kisselgoff. "George Balanchine, 79, Dies in New York," *The New York Times,* May 1, 1983, Sec. I, pp. 1, 42.
27. "Dancer Was Writing Her memoirs," *The New York Times,* September 15, 1927, p. 4.
28. "Chicago Dancer Dead in Paris; World Famous," *The Chicago Tribune,* January 3, 1928, pp. 1, 6.
29. "Ruth St. Denis, Pioneer of Modern Dance Is Dead," *The New York Times,* July 22, 1968, pp. 1, 35.
30. Russella Brandman. "A History of Modern Dance Through Its Makers," Unpublished manuscript, University of Florida, Gainesville, 1980, p. 3.
31. Brandman. "A History of Modern Dance Through Its Makers," pp. 4–5.
32. Mary Shelly. "Facts and Fancies About the Dance in Education," *Journal of Health and Physical Education,* 11 (January, 1940) p. 18.
33. "The Choreography Evaluation Project," National Dance Association Pamphlet.

Chapter 11

THE INFLUENCE OF WARFARE ON
PHYSICAL EDUCATION AND SPORT
1861–1973

Militaristic themes have been evident in physical education and sport in the United States during times of war. However, developing and maintaining a combat-ready level of fitness is antithetical to the central purposes of education and has never met with wide-spread approval in the United States. The military training regime is based upon the concept of fitness and unfaltering obedience to commands. By contrast, fitness through education stresses that organic development is a natural by-product of self-willed participation in activities and games which further enhance social development and emotional well-being. Nevertheless, the periods of armed conflict in the nation's history have consciously influenced our exercise programs to conform to a theme which solely emphasized military readiness.

THE CIVIL WAR

During the Civil War, there was a distinct emphasis upon military training which largely replaced physical training programs. As early as December, 1861, efforts were made to introduce infantry drills in the public schools of New York and other city school systems. In 1863, Boston school students were experiencing military drill. After the War the government encouraged schools and colleges to maintain and develop military drill as a regular part of the school curriculum. Although continuing at some educational institutions, it was met with criticism by leading spokesmen of the day. They argued that physical training had received a new impetus due to the rapid rise of athletic games and contests, and the real object of military drill had lost its significance when the war ended. Furthermore, military training was deemed an inferior form of exercise by Dudley Sargent, Director of Hemenway Gymnasium at Harvard University and a leading spokesman of the day. Writing in the *Boston Medical and Surgical Journal* in 1886, his principal objection to military drill as physical exercise was that it did not suitably meet the physiological demands of the body. He pointed out that this form of exercise was essentially one-sided, favoring the specific development of muscles to the exclusion of those on the other side of the body. Sargent concluded his argument by reinforcing his major premise in that military drill failed to increase respiration and quicken the circulation to any desired degree.[1] Identifying and defining our national character was also a point of contention when comparing the two systems of exercise. At the third annual meeting of the *American Association for the Advancement of Physical Education* in 1887, J.W. Seaver, M.D., wrote that the average American youth sought more to exercise than dull and routine work. He judged them to be more eager for the excitement that competition offers. Seaver contended:

> ... It is this innate love of competition that makes us a commercial, an enterprising nation. We measure ourselves with others and find where we are weak and fortify ourselves; we find where they are weak and we outstrip them. Our popular athletic games then are real educators and prominent factors in building up national character.[2]

By 1899, it was estimated that less than 5 percent of the country's high schools offered military training. Athletic and recreational pursuits obviously contained elements which were favorable to a large segment of the population, including the Civil War soldier who actively engaged in them.

ATHLETIC AND RECREATIONAL PURSUITS
OF CIVIL WAR SOLDIERS

In the late 1860s and the 1870s, Americans were enthusiastically engaged in sport. Prior to this time there were virtually no organized sports as we know them today. Foster Rhea Dulles, in his well-known book, *America Learns to Play,* wrote that this sudden interest in sports was a phenomenon difficult to explain, but the first glimmer of interest began in the decade prior to the Civil War. As the nation became more urbanized there were less work-play occasions such as barn raisings and husking bees. As a result, many observers realized that this loss of exercise was detrimental to the growing nation's well-being. Certain writers and other leaders of the period directed their energies to encourage more active participation by the American people in outdoor games. Perhaps the game leading the way was baseball, which was spreading to the four corners of the country by the late 1850s. Women of this era did not engage in extensive sports participation.[3] Skating, however, was an exception throughout the winter of 1859 when thousands of men and women ice skated in the parks. Herbert Manchester, in *Four Centuries of Sport in America,* took particular note concerning its benefits for the ladies:

> At Boston most of the young ladies skate, and skate well. ... No doubt much of the health and fresh complexion which distinguish Northern belles arise from this favorite pursuit.[4]

Another emerging activity of increasing interest prior to the Civil War was horseback riding, especially popular in the Southern States with men and many women. Dulles believed that the beginning of growth of interest

Figure 11.1. Thousands were attracted to skating in the 1860s.

in participation in sports arose from the nation's basic need for outdoor exercise to conserve national health. The sponsorship of social leaders helped a great deal to crumble the barriers which had previously stood in the way of the development of organized sports. Games appealing to nearly everyone had finally been invented or developed.

The outbreak of the Civil War temporarily halted the growth of the nation's sports and recreational activities, but for the Union and Confederate soldiers these activities were a welcome part of camp life. Contrary to popular thought, life for the Civil War soldier was not one of constant fighting. In fact, relatively little time was spent on the battlefield in actual combat. A common enemy of both armies was boredom, and once camp duties were completed soldiers were forced to develop their own forms of entertainment. David Samuel Crockett has identified the sport and recreational practices of Union and Confederate soldiers which included combatives and a variety of games and sports.

Boxing was considered a "manly" sport in which bare knuckle contests were fought under some form of rules. Boxing served not only as a form of exercise for the soldiers but as a means of settling disputes. Both Union and Confederate troops attended cockfights. Two roosters, usually armed with spurs, fought one another to the death amid shouts of encouragement inspired by monetary wagers. Fencing was especially pursued by the officers and cavalry troops because the foot soldier did not carry a saber in his arsenal of weapons. It was considered to be a more dignified activity than other sports such as wrestling that were engaged in by the enlisted men of both armies.

Boating and fishing were natural activities for many soldiers because bivouacs were located near a water supply whenever possible. Aside from its enjoyable features, fishing served to supplement the soldiers' diets, which were considered to be rather meager. Swimming was enjoyed by officers and enlisted men because of its intrinsic features, which promoted fun and relaxation during the heat of summer campaigns. Swimming also gave a soldier the rare opportunity to rid himself of the dirt and grime due to long marches and battle.

An activity that was especially encouraged for all soldiers was target shooting, since it directly related to the war effort. Conducted almost always on a competitive basis, awards were sometimes given to the best shots. Hunting stemmed from the dual motive of seeking sporting pleasure as well as from a desire to increase the food supply.

Baseball was the most popular game played by both sides during the war. Because it was not a standardized game it was played in numerous ways with different rules. The equipment was makeshift in most instances. A bat, for example, may have been a board or trimmed tree branch with a yarn-wrapped walnut serving as the ball. Other games and activities included tenpins, soccer, horse racing, quoits, foot races, and the throwing of heavy weights. Gymnastic activities were especially prevalent among the Union troops, which had a large number of German immigrants in their ranks.

TABLE GAMES, MUSIC, AND SNOWBALL BATTLES

The recreational game indulged in most during the war was card playing. Widespread among both Union and Confederate troops, gambling was most commonly associated with the favorite games of poker, cribbage, euchre, seven-ups, chuck-a-luck, keno, and faro. Checkers and chess were played by men in both armies with checkers being most favored. Bank playing, singing, and dancing were favorite pastimes of both the Union and Confederate troops.[5] Another diversion which took place during the winter months was described by a writer in 1878: "Johnny, when in winter quarters, was sometimes afflicted with ennui, and in default of other antagonist, was forced into systematic devices for the killing of time. Snow-ball battles, between whole brigades, arrayed in line, and with colors flying, were frequent . . . (and) he sometimes resorted to the distraction of amateur theatricals."[6] Another light-hearted form of entertainment was found in the: "charms of music rendered by certain of their numbers who were accomplished fiddlers, and many a "stag dance," under the noble sycamores, served to beguile the evening hours between retreat and tatoo."[7]

In the decade following the Civil War, members of the disbanded armies entered preparatory schools and colleges. They had realized the benefits of

Figure 11.2.

physical training during the war and continued their involvement in sport while pursuing their education.[8] Civil War soldiers were instrumental in disseminating baseball throughout the land and establishing it as America's national game.

WORLD WAR I

When World War I broke out in Europe in 1914, the United States was not particularly concerned about threats to its national security. However, as the course of events passed, neutrality changed to active involvement by April, 1917. Once again the question of military training in the schools emerged in a time of national crisis. In an address delivered before the City Club of Chicago on March 23, 1917, Clark Hetherington stated the prevailing attitude of educators in response to the question, "Shall military training be given our youth?" Citing almost unanimous agreement among leading educators in condemning military training in the schools, he reminded his audience that even the most militaristic nations of Europe do not use military training during the years of youth. Instead they rely upon physical training in preparation for military service. Representing the collective opinions of physical educators throughout the country, Hetherington reinforced his point:

Figure 11.3.

> . . . There is no gain in vital vigor, strength, or skill that is not given in a vastly higher degree in the gymnastics, games, and athletics natural to youth. The vitality and skill required by the soldiers are developed best, not by a military training in youth, but by a premilitary physical training.[9]

A number of schools did offer military training in place of physical training during and after the war. Sanctioned by the national government, the War Department authorized a military training camp program for physical directors in high schools and colleges, and for officers of the Volunteer Training Corps and Reserve Militia. The object of the camp, which contained an enrollment of 244 men throughout 15 states, was to train the physical directors to carry on their work in the schools and colleges.[10] The government also encouraged the high school volunteer movement which provided high school boys with military training. In 1918, approximately 30,000 boys were in the program which was distributed throughout fifty-two cities and towns.[11]

ATHLETICS AND THE WAR EFFORT

A conference held in Washington by the National Collegiate Athletic Association (NCAA) in August, 1917 reaffirmed the government's interest in the continuation of athletics and games during the war. In his address to the conference Secretary of War Newton D. Baker emphasized that the country viewed the college athletic program as a means of preliminary training for potential military officers. He believed that sports promoted physical development, team unity, and served as a recreational outlet during military camp life.[12] During the war years the athletic emphasis was altered in that they became more informal with fewer coaches being employed. There was less time given to practice and game schedules were reduced.

The Young Men's Christian Association (YMCA) was instrumental in promoting and developing athletics and games for men in the army and navy during the war. With the purpose of providing rest and relaxation from the stressful effects of battle, an effort was made to meet the needs of the largest possible number of soldiers. A wide variety of activities were engaged in, the most prevalent being swimming, basketball, soccer, volleyball, boxing, and wrestling.

Women in the profession of physical education were called upon to lend their expertise in the war effort. The surgeon general's office initiated a corps known as Reconstruction Aides with the task of helping mental and physical rehabilitation of disabled soldiers returning from France. Plans were made to establish training centers with approved schools of physical education being utilized in preparing women to enter the corps. Marguerite Sanderson, president of the Boston School of Physical Education, was appointed supervisor of the newly developed corps.[13] In another capacity, there were corps of mounted policewomen throughout the country on duty at munition plants and on guard patrolling various war work areas.[14]

EFFECTS OF THE WAR UPON PHYSICAL EDUCATION AND SPORT

Approximately one-third of the men drafted for armed services for World War I were rejected for medical reasons. In view of this startling and uncomplimentary fact, the profession of physical education was criticized by certain groups for neglecting the health needs of the nation's youth. Professor C.W. Savage from Oberlin College, reacting to this criticism, identified new directions for physical education in 1919. He emphatically stated that in the colleges physical education must no longer consist of hygiene lessons and health gymnastics, or medical examinations with a prescription of exercises for specific individuals. Instead, the two fundamental objectives of health and education for all students were identified as being of major importance.[15]

Postwar consciousness of the need for better health and fitness for all served as a major impetus for required programs of physical education. Although the movement for state laws mandating that physical education be required in the schools began in the 1890s, little progress had been made prior to the war. However, by 1930, physical education requirements could be found in 39 states. Many athletic and intramural programs were also in operation throughout the country. In an effort to forget the horrors of war, the country returned to the joys of physical activity as indicated in this poignant poem:

> Back from the smoke and flame,
> Where the lines of steel were gleaming,
> They come once more to the Game
> They knew in their ancient dreaming;
> Safe from the rain-soaked moors
> Where only a shell might greet them,
> They come to the Great Out-Doors,
> Where never a ghost shall meet them.

> For they've finished up their slogging through the midnight and the
>   rain,
> Where they stumbled through the darkness over bodies of their slain,
> Where they left their mates behind them who had paid the final debt,
> And they'd like to play forever where a fellow might forget.

> Back from the Argonne nights
> And each gray dawn that follows;
> Back from the bitter fights
> In Flanders' haunted hollows;
> Back from the dug-out floors
> Where mud and the gray rats found them,
> They come to the Great Out-Doors
> With the breath of June around them.

> For they've finished up their hiking through the endless rains of
>   France;
> They have made their final sortie and have known their last advance;
> They have known their share of horror where the steel was red and
>   wet,
> And they'd like to play forever where a fellow might forget.[16]

Americans returned to sport with a different outcome in mind. No longer was its sole purpose to toughen and ready men for the severe test that war imposed. Instead, to participate was a reward in itself. It served as a healing balm to help physically and mentally restore a weary nation.

WORLD WAR II—SCHOOLS AND COLLEGES CONTRIBUTE TO THE WAR EFFORT

On December 7, 1941, the United States was again embroiled in conflict when the Imperial Air Force of Japan bombed Pearl Harbor. The surprise attack shocked the nation and left no recourse except to retaliate with full force. The armed forces and civilian population of the United States was mobilized in what was to be a life or death struggle for the salvation of the democracy.

The question of whether or not military drill should take the place of physical education during this war period was no longer an issue as it once was during the Civil War and World War I. In a letter to the United States Commissioner of Education John W. Studebaker, Secretary of War Henry L. Stimson stated that military drill should not replace physical conditioning in the schools and colleges. Stimson said that physical conditioning was of fundamental importance to the making of a good soldier and that military drill could be learned once recruits were inducted into the armed forces. In keeping with this conclusion Carl A. Jessen, from the United States Office of Education, identified for teachers of physical education the types of activities which are best suited for developing and improving physical fitness:

Figure 11.4. Courtesy of Alice Lord Landon, 1920 Olympic diver. The World War I troop transport, *Princess Matoika* sailed to Antwerp with the 1920 American Olympic team. Many World War I service men were team members.

1. Hard-driving competitive sports and games involving physical contact.
2. Swimming
3. Tumbling
4. Boxing and Wrestling
5. Strenuous 'setting-up' exercises
6. Hiking and pitching camp
7. Jumping and running
8. Skiing[17]

Under the admonishment that "hard soldiers cannot be developed by soft methods," Jessen urged teachers of health and physical education to promote good health and fitness in youth because it was essential to premilitary training.[18] A government-sponsored program supporting these broad aims was the High School Victory Corps which consisted of preinduction training for the armed forces and civilian war services. Voluntary in nature, the general purpose of the organization was to prepare students for essential war services upon graduating from school. Specific program emphases were given to:

1. Guidance into critical war services and occupations.
2. Wartime citizenship training.
3. Basic instruction in mathematics and science.
4. Preparatory training for industry, agriculture, and the community-service organizations.
5. Preflight training in aeronautics.
6. Special pre-induction courses for the Army, such as fundamentals of electricity, shopwork, machines, radio code, Army clerical procedures, military drill.
7. Special war-fitness programs of physical and health education.[19]

In a 1943 survey conducted by Cassidy and Kozman, it was determined that 23 states were actively promoting the High School Victory Corps and its physical fitness programs. Twenty-one other states were emphasizing wartime physical education programs which focused upon physical fitness. Thus, 44 of the 48 state offices of education were involved with reorganizing and improving physical education programs to meet wartime needs.

They identified trends in physical education programs due to the war. An analysis of state plans revealed:

1. A greater awareness of the importance of physical fitness for boys and girls with a broader application of the term. It included the absence of organic defects and communicable disease, the normal functioning of all body organs, and good mental health.
2. Program attention was given to the older high school boys, then to other boys and finally to girls. The boys and girls programs became more separated.
3. Various insignia were used to motivate students towards higher fitness levels.
4. Formalized discipline and routine responses to commands.
5. Health education plans calling for medical examinations with a follow-up of findings. Nutrition and immunization were emphasized.[20]

There appeared to be greater interest in the construction and use of strength and endurance tests; and games, sports, and dance continued to remain a part of the program.

Action was being taken at the college level with the organization of a committee appointed by the United States Commissioner of Education. Of the 29-member committee, 13 members were physical educators from various colleges and universities around the country. Neils P. Neilson, Executive Secretary of the American Association for Health, Physical Education, and Recreation (AAHPER) was included as a member of the committee. One of the committee's main activities was the preparation of a wartime physical fitness program manual for colleges and universities.[21] Emphasis was placed upon increasing the student's endurance and strengthening the muscles of the trunk, arms, and legs. Activities such as combatives, swimming, ditch jumping, wall scaling, obstacle relays, tumbling, running, and fundamental conditioning exercises were stressed for all men.

Fitness for girls was an important topic even though it was recognized that their needs differed in that they were active on the "home front." Because of the war, women experienced two major work changes. Not only were they typists and store clerks but mechanics, welders, painters, riveters, and any number of other trades not ordinarily engaged in by the majority of women. Secondly, the 24-hour production day forced many women to work long hours including night shifts. By 1943 over 15 million women were working in industry, many of whom were lacking in strength and endurance. Therefore, the general program fitness goals for women stressed improving physical conditioning, how to stay well on the job, responsibility, and teamwork.

In recognizing the various roles of women in the war, the National Association of Physical Education for College Women held a "Victory Through Fitness" workshop in June 24–30, 1943, at the University of Wisconsin. One main purpose of the workshop was to assist female physical educators in helping young women to better understand their role in war and peace. The audience of 100 listened to and participated in such topics as the needs of the WAACS and WAVES, problems of women in industry, and the role of women in war and peace.[22]

A PATRIOTIC ERA

It was a patriotic era; large numbers of men and more women than ever before answered the call to serve their country. Men and women physical education graduates joined the armed forces. Organizations such as the YMCA and the Young Women's Christian Association (YWCA) provided leadership for the conduct of leisure activities. Professional journals and periodicals read by the general public called for unified support of the war effort. Manufacturers of numerous items incorporated war support into their advertisements. Women instructors in the WACS, WAVES, and SPARS introduced servicewomen to numerous conditioning activities and sports. Their appreciation of sports was enhanced and many continued sports participation after being discharged from the service.

Military physical educators returning to the public schools after the war profited from teaching large groups and improvising equipment and playing areas. However, leaders in the profession cautioned against too much emphasis on conditioning and regimented classes. War veteran athletes, many of whom had participated in inter and intrapost competition, raised the caliber of athletic competition in the post-war era.

EFFECTS OF THE WAR UPON PHYSICAL EDUCATION

In January, 1945, draft statistics indicated that four and one-half million men were found unfit for military service because of physical and mental defects.[23] About 700,000 had remediable defects which had not been corrected. The American Medical Association challenged the findings by stating that the standards of physical fitness for military service were considerably higher than those required for everyday civilian life. Nevertheless, as in World War I, the profession of physical education was criticized by some for failing to develop an acceptable level of fitness in the nation's youth. Delbert Oberteuffer responded to this criticism by saying that it was unwarranted and illogical for the following reasons:

1. The vast majority of rejections such as eyes, hearing, hernia, teeth, disease, illiteracy, psychological, nutritional, and orthopedic had nothing to do with physical education programs.
2. Failure to correct remedial defects was due to the inadequacy of correlation between school appraisal services and home or community corrective efforts.
3. Many of the disabilities were the by-products of imperfect genetic matching and would appear under any circumstances unless mating was done arbitrarily on a genetically scientific basis.
4. The methods used to discover disabilities in this war were more searching than in former wars.
5. Where musculoskeletal deficiencies were found, especially muscular weakness, physical education may be held accountable. However, until there is an hour of daily activity in all schools for 12 years, physical education cannot be held entirely responsible.[24]

The war prompted changes in high school and college physical education programs. High school administrators showed an increased interest in physical education; a greater number of boys and girls were enrolled in classes having more time allotment; and academic credit was given. In colleges and universities programs now emphasized physical and organic strength, aquatics, and a wider variety of skill activities. Many schools had established a two-year requirement and offered credit toward graduation. There was an increased emphasis on health programs.

THE KOREAN CONFLICT

From 1950 to 1953, America was again at war. Initially, the American involvement in Korea was reminiscent of World War II. Food and clothing shortages were anticipated and scores of Americans stocked their pantries and closets. Employers feared workers would be employed by defense industries and raised wages. Once the limited involvement of American troops was realized and partial wage and price controls were imposed by the government in 1951, the cost of living stabilized. In general, most aspects of the economy increased during the conflict. Americans experienced some consequences of intervention in Korea when, for example, home construction declined because of shortages of building materials. The Korean War did not impose the drastic changes at home as World War II had done. Restrictions were imposed on the construction of physical education and recreation facilities. Equipment production was reduced because of the need for such materials as rubber and leather. Copper, aluminum, and steel were in great demand for military use. Gymnasiums which were used primarily for instructional purposes were generally approved, however, provisions for spectator seating were omitted. In addition, multipurpose buildings for auditorium-gymnasium-lunchroom use were given consideration. The Office of Education was not authorized to approve swimming pool construction. Availability of steel lockers, playground equipment, and materials for hard surfacing was drastically reduced.

In the February 1952 issue of the *Journal of Health, Physical Education and Recreation,* members of the three professions were informed of the wartime implications for their respective fields:

1. To develop healthy citizens, because of the ever present need for the conservation of our most precious resource—the human being!
2. To develop a knowledge and understanding of self-preservation techniques in the event of possible biological warfare.
3. To provide an effective physical fitness program for all students.
4. To provide student participation in all Civil Defense planning to develop emotional stability and a feeling of security.
5. To provide opportunities for development of good leadership which is of vital importance in the civil defense program.
6. To stress wise use of leisure time, which is recreation, in these times of tension.[25]

Physical educators were urged to emphasize certain aspects of physical education which could contribute to the war effort. Physical fitness and survival skills for self-protection which included wrestling, tumbling, games, and sports were recommended. Leadership opportunities and group activities were considered essential physical education experiences for wartime America. Furthermore, social recreation skills appropriate for use during prolonged air raid drills in evacuation centers which did not necessitate the use of special equipment were proposed. Circle games, singing games, guessing games, and folk dances were suggested social recreation activities.

AAHPER officers and members participated in meetings called by the National Conference for Mobilization of Education and the American Council on Education. In cooperation with the United States Office of Education the American Association for Health, Physical Education, and Recreation prepared Defense Information Bulletins on health, fitness, first aid, and home nursing.

In support of the national emergency declared by President Harry Truman, a Mobilization Conference for Health, Physical Education, and Recreation was held in Washington, D.C., March 19–21, 1951. The AAHPER, the Office of Education, the Federal Security Agency, under the auspices of the National Conference for Mobilization of Education convened the special meeting for the mobilization of health education, physical education, and recreation. The overall purposes of the conference were to identify the needs created by the national and international situation and to determine how the AAHPER could offer assistance through local and state planning.

VIETNAM, AN UNDECLARED WAR

In 1963, over 16,000 American soldiers were in Vietnam and the number rose to 550,000 in 1968. It was not until January 1973 that a cease-fire was announced. Many Americans questioned the presence of their countrymen in Vietnam during an "undeclared" war. American society in the late 1960s, influenced by an unpopular war, was also a time of turmoil. Assassinations of national leaders, violent acts against civil rights workers, urban disorders and destruction, campus demonstrations, and divided opinions over the Vietnam conflict made the decade of the 1960s a turbulent era.

THE COUNTERCULTURE IN THE 1960S

There was an accent on youth boosted by the baby boom generation of the 1940s and 1950s who were teenagers and young adults. Neatly groomed youth of the 1950s were largely replaced by the long-haired "hippie" culture of the 1960s. It was a time of "doing your own thing," justified as long as one did not harm others. Sexual permissiveness, experimentation with drugs, rock music, and political radicalism was subscribed to by those who joined the hippie movement. Hippies detested the conformity of the establishment but in many ways exhibited conformity in dress, speech, and political opinion. Thousands of youths fled to Canada and Sweden rather than serve a country whose war involvement they refused to support.

Sport and physical education, steeped in adherence to conservatism, self-discipline, and tradition, was influenced by the youthful freewheeling members of society. Male athletes challenged the requirement to wear their hair short and some were dismissed from teams for not adhering to restrictions on hair length or facial hair. Such rules as uniform requirements for physical education majors were challenged by some students who rejected control over what they wore.

SUMMARY

Periods of war in the nation's history have caused athletic and physical education programs to reflect a military theme. During the Civil War military training largely replaced physical training programs. Although the Civil War temporarily halted the growth of the nation's sports and recreational activities, the Civil War soldier actively engaged in them. They took the form of combatives, swimming, and games such as baseball, soccer, and foot races. Card playing was the most popular recreational game. Other pastimes were singing, snow-ball fights, and "stag" dancing. After the war men of the disbanded armies were instrumental in helping to spread sport and recreational activities throughout the country.

During World War I, the question of military training in the schools again became an issue. Sanctioned by the government, a small number of schools offered it in place of physical training. The continuance of college athletics was encouraged by the government and viewed as a means of preliminary training for potential officers. The YMCA was instrumental in promoting athletics for military forces and conducted a program of varying activities such as swimming, basketball, volleyball, boxing, and wrestling. One role for women physical educators was in the Reconstruction Aides corps with the purpose of providing mental and physical rehabilitation of disabled soldiers. Postwar consciousness was directed to the need for improved health and fitness for Americans which helped provide impetus for state legislation requiring programs of physical education in public schools.

In World War II, the question of military drill replacing physical education in schools and colleges was no longer an issue. Secretary of War Henry L. Stimson stated that physical conditioning was fundamental to preparing a good soldier, and military drill could be learned upon induction to the armed forces. In a 1943 survey 44 of 48 state offices of education were involved with adapting physical education programs to meet wartime needs. The various roles of women in the war were recognized in a "Victory through Fitness" workshop conducted by the Association of Physical Education for College Women in June, 1943. In 1945 draft statistics indicated a high percentage of men were unfit for military service because of physical and mental defects. The physical education profession was criticized for failing to develop an acceptable level of fitness in military age youth. However, leaders of the profession found this criticism unjustified. Post-war changes in physical education centered around the establishment of required programs, a wider variety of skill activities, and credit towards graduation.

The Korean War did not induce drastic changes in the United States as in World War II. Limitations were set on the construction of physical education and recreation facilities, and equipment production was reduced. Physical educators were encouraged to emphasize to their students physical and survival skills for self-protection. Also proposed were appropriate social recreation skills for potential prolonged air raid drills. The AAHPER cooperated with the United States Office of Education in preparing Defense Information Bulletins on health, fitness, first aid, and home nursing. In March, 1951, a Mobilization Conference was held in which the AAHPER, Office of Education, and Federal Security Agency convened to determine how the AAHPER could provide assistance through local and state planning.

Vietnam, an "undeclared" war by the United States, was seriously questioned by many Americans during the late 1960s. The unpopular war helped to create a time of national turmoil marked by assassinations of national leaders, violence against civil rights workers, campus demonstrations, urban destruction, and divided opinions concerning America's presence in Vietnam. The hippie culture of the 1960s was characterized by sexual permissiveness, drug experimentation, rock music, and political radicalism. Sport and physical education, reflecting the conservative elements of society, was challenged by the youthful, liberal members of society. Policies in sport and physical education came under attack by those who were attempting to bring about change.

REFERENCES

1. Dudley A. Sargent, "The Effects of Military Drill on Boys with Hints on Exercise," Reprinted from *Boston Medical and Surgical Journal,* September 16, 1886, p. 9. Cambridge: A. A. Waterman and Co., 1886.
2. Jay W. Seaver. "Military Training As An Exercise," *Proceedings of American Association for the Advancement of Physical Education,* Third Annual Meeting, Brooklyn, November 25, 1887, pp. 20–21.
3. Foster Rhea Dulles. *America Learns to Play.* New York: D. Appleton-Century Co., 1940, pp. 182–185.
4. Herbert Manchester. *Four Centuries of Sport in America 1490-1890.* New York: The Derrydale Press, 1931, pp. 131–132.
5. David Samuel Crockett. "Sports and Recreational Practices of Union and Confederate Soldiers," *Research Quarterly,* 32 (October, 1961), pp. 335–347.
6. Allen C. Redwood. "Johnny Reb at Play," *Scribner's Monthly.* 17 (November, 1878), p. 35.
7. Allen C. Redwood. "The Fortunes and Misfortunes of Co. 'C,'" *Scribner's Monthly,* 17 (February, 1879), p. 530.
8. Edward Mussey Hartwell. "Athletics Stimulated by War," *Circulars of Information of the Bureau of Education.* Washington, D.C.: Government Printing Office, 1886, p. 106.
9. Clark W. Hetherington. "Shall Military Training Be Given Our Youth?" Washington, D.C.: Government Printing Office, 1917, p. 6.
10. E.C. Delaporte. "Military Training Camp for Physical Directors," *Mind and Body,* 25 (October, 1918), p. 251.
11. A.M. Hitch. "Military Training in Secondary Schools." *Mind and Body,* 25 (September, 1918), p. 216.
12. Palmer E. Pierce. "The Problems of Athletics in Colleges and Schools Under Present War Conditions," *American Physical Education Review,* 22 (October, 1917), p. 447.

13. "Corps of Women Will Help 'Rebuild' Disabled Soldiers," *American Physical Education Review,* 23 (February, 1918), p. 127.
14. Theodora Sohst. "Women Up," *Country Life,* 37 (November, 1919), p. 51.
15. C.W. Savage. "Lessons from the War for Physical Education in Colleges," *American Physical Education Review,* 24 (April, 1919), p. 190.
16. Grantland Rice. "The Return to Sport," *Country Life,* 36 (June, 1919), p. 40.
17. "Meeting the Teacher Shortage in Wartime Physical Education," *Journal of Health and Physical Education,* 14 (October, 1943), p. 416.
18. Carl A. Jessen. "The Best Kind of High School Training for Military Service," *Journal of Health and Physical Education,* 13 (September, 1942), p. 431.
19. John W. Studebaker. "Our Schools Serve the War Effort," *Journal of Health and Physical Education,* 14 (November, 1943), pp. 482–483.
20. Rosalind Cassidy and Hilda Clute Kozman. "Trends in State Wartime Physical Fitness Programs," *Journal of Health and Physical Education.* 14 (September, 1943), pp. 357, 392–393.
21. Committee Appointed by the U.S. Commissioner of Education. *Handbook on Physical Fitness for Students in Colleges and Universities.* Washington, D.C.: U.S. Government Printing Office, 1943.
22. National Association of Physical Education for College Women. "Victory Through Fitness Workshop," University of Wisconsin, Madison, June 24–30, 1943, pp. 14–29.
23. Wartime Health and Education Report to Senate Committee on Education and Labor, Washington, D.C.: U.S. Government Printing Office, January, 1945, p. 1.
24. Delbert Oberteuffer. *School Health Education.* New York: Harper and Row, 1949, p. 356.
25. "Mobilization News," *Journal of Health, Physical Education and Recreation,* 23 (February, 1952), p. 47.

Chapter 12

MEN'S SPORTS PROGRAMS

Much of the organization of men's sports programs in the United States can be attributed to the efforts of the Young Men's Christian Association (YMCA), private athletic clubs, and college students. The American YMCA was founded because concerned individuals wanted to help young men living in the larger cities develop their manhood in Christian virtue. Leaders of the movement discovered that religion and exercise were a compatible union. Private athletic clubs were instrumental in providing opportunities for members to partake of contemporary sporting practices which promoted interest in various forms of competition. College students provided the initiative in institutions of higher learning and, money in fledgling days, to conduct competitive sporting events which were to ultimately attract highly trained athletes and enthusiastic spectators.

THE YOUNG MEN'S CHRISTIAN ASSOCIATION

The beginning of the Young Men's Christian Association can be traced to England during the 1840s when the city was looked upon as "the center of wealth, refinement, and religious power . . . (and) the headquarters for the forces of evil."[1] George Williams was an Englishman concerned about young men separated from friends and families after they had moved to the cities. Williams believed city life caused young men to shun their religious beliefs and tempted them to engage in vice. George Williams, in an effort to meet the needs of urban young men, founded the YMCA in London in 1844. Because of the growth of cities, the YMCA spread throughout the world.

· During the middle of the nineteenth century, "the problems created by the influx of an enormous unevangelized population, roused the church to strenuous endeavor in New York City.[2] Dutch, Presbyterian, Episcopal, and Roman Catholic churches were among the religious affiliates which contributed to the spiritual life of New York City. However, "its theaters, saloons, and vicious resorts allured the young men from the cheerless boarding-houses, and . . . the crowded tenement districts. The gates of sin stood wide."[3] George Petrie was an importer from New York who visited London in 1851 and became acquainted with the work of the YMCA. In 1852, George Petrie founded the American YMCA in an atmosphere of urban expansion, mechanical invention, and religious fervor.[4] The American YMCA, like its British counterpart, was founded to promote religion among young men who had moved to the city. Soon after the YMCA was founded the first black Association was established in Washington, D.C., in 1853. It was many years thereafter before interracial work was initiated in the Association. The movement also spread to German immigrants, American Indians, Chinese, Japanese, French, Scandinavian, and Dutch young men.[5]

THE BEGINNING OF YMCA PHYSICAL WORK

In 1869, the New York YMCA opened a gymnasium. Initially, the gymnasium was considered an attraction which would entice young men into joining the Association. Recognizing that gymnasium activities promoted health and physical development, the Association established a department for physical activities. The inclusion of the gymnasium in New York led to the establishment of nationwide physical training departments in the association.[6] By 1885, there were over 100 YMCA gymnasiums in the United States. Equipment in these early gymnasiums was first geared to circus stunts but then equipment for light gymnastics was added.

Figure 12.1. The New York YMCA Gymnasium, 1870.

Gymnasiums were constructed faster than they could be supplied with qualified directors. Utilization of the gymnasium for Christian work was a problem for the YMCA. Associations found it difficult to obtain directors who were schooled in Biblical doctrine, and therefore some experienced difficulty integrating the physical work with other activities. There were some gymnasiums operating apart from their Associations with separate members and entrances. Retired boxers and circus performers were sometimes hired to conduct the gymnasium activities. Luther Halsey Gulick was the dominant influence in the physical training work of the YMCA. Gulick was influenced by Dr. Delphine Hanna at Oberlin College and the Sargent School of Physical Training. He received a medical degree from New York University in 1889. Dr. Gulick was associated with the YMCA for 16 years as the first secretary for physical work of the International Committee. For 10 of those 16 years he served as director of the gymnasium department of the training school at Springfield, Massachusetts. Gulick devised the well-known YMCA inverted triangle symbolic of the unity of body, mind, and spirit.

Dr. Gulick designed the curriculum for the training of physical work secretaries and elevated the position to professional status. By 1895 57 men had graduated from Gulick's course of study. Gulick resigned from his Springfield position in 1900. He then became a principal in a Brooklyn high school and from 1903 to 1908 Dr. Gulick served as Director of Physical Training in the New York City public schools. He aided in founding the Campfire Girls and the Boy Scouts.[7]

THE ATHLETIC CLUB MOVEMENT

The New York Athletic Club (NYAC), founded in September, 1868, and patterned after the London Athletic Club, was the first organization of its kind in the United States. The NYAC and similar athletic clubs that followed became the primary vehicle for sports participation among male city dwellers. The NYAC engaged in early competition with Columbia College students and in November 1868 scheduled a track meet with the Scottish Caledonian Club of New York.[8] Through Caledonian Clubs, first organized in 1853, the Scots activated interest in track and field with their Caledonian Games. The NYAC added field events and promoted rowing during its initial years of operation.

In the 1870s and 1880s, the athletic club movement spread to diverse sections of the country. The Louisville Athletic Club opened memberships to men, women, and children. The Staten Island Cricket Club had a building for ladies[9] as did New York's Berkeley Athletic Club. Other clubs such as the Pastime Athletic Club of St. Louis opened their facilities for women on certain days of the week.[10] Early in its history the NYAC requested its members to bring ladies to competitive events "in order that athletics might be made as respectable as they were in England."[11] Other athletic clubs constructed grandstands for ladies so they could grace the games with their presence.

In 1879, the National Association of Amateur Athletes of America (NAAAA) was organized and NYAC rules were adopted by the NAAAA. The NAAAA

Figure 12.2. The New York Athletic Club.

lost its power when the NYAC and several other clubs formed the Amateur Athletic Union of the United States in 1888. Two years after its founding the AAU claimed jurisdiction over 64 clubs, having a membership of 33,000 men. The Turnvereins were affiliated with the AAU and the total membership in 1890 was 83,000.[12]

The Athletic Club movement was spawned in an era when Americans were joining societies, unions, leagues, and associations. Athletic clubs were prime movers in the advancement of amateur athletics. The Manhattan Athletic Club reflected the purposes of the movement by directing its efforts to promote:

athletism among the toilers of the growing city. The first and most immediate- . . . (purpose) was to provide within the city limits a track and grounds and the second was to provide a club house with gymnasium and other opportunities for the encouragement of social intercourse . . . [13]

Elaborate facilities for the clientele, members of the upper class, were selling features for new members. In the mid-1880s the NYAC's four-story building housed six bowling alleys, a rifle range, swimming pool, reception hall, parlor, reading room, billiard rooms, restaurant, 1,000 lockers and bathing facilities, sparring room, and a gymnasium. Twenty-two laps around the running track in the gymnasium equaled a mile.[14]

TENNIS, BADMINTON, AND GOLF

While the athletic club movement was continuing to permeate the cities, tennis, badminton, and golf became established in the United States. Although Mary Outerbridge is credited with introducing tennis in 1874, James Dwight is referred to as the "father of American tennis." Some authorities claim that the match played by Dwight and Fred Sears at Nahant, Massachusetts, in the summer of 1875 was the first match played in the United States. Both men wore boots and raincoats as they played the informal game in the rain. Dwight continued to promote tennis and was the United States Lawn Tennis Association (USLTA) president for 21 years.[15]

Badminton or "battledore" was played in India and England about the same time during the nineteenth century. The game was called "poona" in India and badminton in England. Three socialites from New York City learned to play badminton in the late 1870s. Bayard Clarke was acquainted with the game in India. The other two men, E. Langdon Wilks and J. Norman de R. Whitehouse, learned to play in England. In 1878 they organized a club in New York City. The club served as a gathering place for the upper class. There was little emphasis on badminton. In 1884 the membership reached 400. The following year the club was disbanded and reorganized in 1886. Week-end games at the club were festive affairs. Shuttlecocks of varying colors were used on the nine courts. Red and gold pennants, the club colors, adorned the standards which held the nets in place. Players enjoyed tea, sandwiches, and cakes as they rested.[16] Badminton gradually spread to numerous cities in the United States. But by the 1970s, it had failed to attract the vast number of followers as had other racket sports. Acceptance of the game has been deterred by its reputation as a backyard game involving little skill. On the whole, the majority of Americans have remained unaware of the quickness and vigorous nature of the game.

EARLY GOLFING CLUBS IN THE UNITED STATES

John G. Reid, known as the "father of American golf," came to the United States from his native Scotland and settled in Yonkers, New York. Reid is credited with establishing the first golf club in this country. Although the game had been introduced to these shores as far back as the latter part of the eighteenth century, 100 years were to pass before it was to become firmly established. Using a set of golf clubs and some golf balls shipped from

Figure 12.3. Newport, a popular tennis site.

Scotland, Reid assembled a small group of his friends in a Yonkers cow pasture in February, 1888. They laid out three short holes and played a friendly match. Soon they laid out a six-hole course and played often, sometimes to the amusement of onlookers. On November 14, 1888, Reid proposed to his regular golfing partners that they establish an organization to regulate their new sport. With unanimous agreement they titled their group the St. Andrews Club of Yonkers, named after the famous club in Scotland, and elected Reid as their president. In 1892, the city fathers voted to extend a street through the course, so the club moved to a 34-acre apple orchard where they developed a six-hole course. A year later, in 1893, the country's first 18-hole course was built in Chicago. The Yonkers club grew, and by 1897 the club moved to Mt. Hope, New York, where an 18-hole course was constructed.[17]

Converts of the game soon formed other clubs. In 1889, a group of Englishmen organized the Middlesborough Club and built a nine-hole course in Middlesborough, Kentucky. By 1894, six- and nine-hole golf courses could be found in Patterson, Lakewood, New Brunswick, and Montclair, New Jersey; Tuxedo, Newburgh, White Plains, and Long Island, New York; Newport, Rhode Island; Greenwich, Connecticut; and Chicago, Illinois.[18]

CONTROVERSY PROMOTES THE
UNITED STATES AMATEUR TOURNAMENT

Six years after golf had been introduced to the United States, enthusiasts of the Newport Golf Club in Rhode Island decided to hold a tournament to determine the best amateur players in the country. In September, 1894, invitations were sent to the handful of clubs which had been organized mainly on the East coast and in the Midwest. Twenty players entered the tournament with three favorites coming from Boston, St. Andrews, and Chicago. The contestants were to play 18 holes a day for two days. Charlie McDonald from the Chicago Club was one of the favorites to capture the 36-hole tourney, but he lost to W.G. Lawrence from the Newport Club who carded a total score of 188. McDonald claimed he lost on a technicality when he was forced to take a two-stroke penalty after one of his drives landed against a stone wall bordering the course. Furthermore, he contended that the championship should be decided by match play, as was done in Great Britain, and not medal play. The St. Andrews Club took the initiative and in October of the same year held a match play tournament extending invitations to 27 clubs. Twenty-seven golfers accepted with McDonald losing to Laurance Stoddard from St. Andrews on the opening hole of a "sudden death" play-off, the first in American history. Once again the outspoken McDonald publicly voiced his opinion when Stoddard was named as the national champion. McDonald insisted that the tournament could not be regarded as a National Championship because it was not sanctioned by all of the clubs in the country. Recognizing the validity of his contention, a meeting was called by noted golf enthusiasts for the purpose of establishing a nationally recognized authority to govern the conduct of the game. Thus, the United States Golf Association was founded in order to make and enforce rules, settle disputes, and organize tournaments.

In October, 1895, the newly founded association staged its first United States National Amateur Championship at the Newport Golf Club. The tournament drew 32 players, each playing an 18-hole match in a bid for the championship match, which was contested over 36 holes. Charlie McDonald, playing this time in an "official" tournament, became the first national amateur golf champion in the United States.[19]

A GOLF TOURNAMENT FOR THE WEEKENDERS

A victory by a remarkable 20-year-old over two of the game's greatest stars was to help further popularize the game of golf in America. The scene was the 1913 United States Open Championship at Brookline, Massachusetts. Young Francis Ouimet, emerging from a field of 170 American and European entrants, bested England's stars Harry Varden and Ted Ray in the final match with a 1 over par 72 compared to Varden's 77 and Ray's 78. Patrons of *The New York Times* read about Ouimet's stunning victory:

... a tall slender youth ... outplayed and outnerved not only Varden and Ray in the play-off, a wonderful fact in itself, but succeeded in battling his way through the largest and most remarkable field of entrants that ever played for an American title.[20]

Ouimet's triumph was heralded from coast to coast and with it came an even greater appeal to the game for Americans everywhere. It had lost its exclusive image as a sport for only the wealthy.

As municipal courses mushroomed throughout the country, the United States Golf Association offered an enthusiastic public tournament all its own in which USGA amateurs and professionals were ineligible. On August 28–31, 1922, the first Amateur Public Links Golf Championship was played in Toledo, Ohio. The first winner of the 136-member field was 19-year-old Edmund R. Held of St. Louis. The following year team competition was also held in addition to an individual title. Eighteen teams participated in the 1923 Washington, D.C. tournament with Chicago taking team honors. By 1938, two courses were added to handle the 247 starters at Cleveland, Ohio, and in 1939 the USGA introduced sectional qualifying due to the large number of entrants. In 1959 the tournament produced its first black champion when William Wright of Seattle defeated Frank Campbell of Jacksonville, Florida. Wright was a student at Western Washington College of Education in Bellingham at the time of his victory.[21]

INTERCOLLEGIATE SPORTS PROGRAMS HELP TO QUELL DISRUPTIVE BEHAVIOR

Prior to the inclusion of intercollegiate athletics as a part of campus life, disorderly conduct among college students was a problem frequently dealt with by administrators. Fights between students and their town rivals sometimes grew into serious confrontations. A professor recalled an incident in which a cannon was brought to campus and pointed toward some college buildings. On another occasion, amid a conflict between students and firemen, the death of a fire fighter by a gun shot sent a wave of panic among students who barred and bolted their dormitories.[22] There were college literary societies, fraternities, religious functions, and informal physical activities before the introduction of organized sports, but students still found time for mischievious behavior.

Intracampus sports contests, and later more organized intercollegiate athletic programs, helped to quell the disruptive behavior of students. Town and gown riots disappeared, gate stealing declined, and leisure hours were supplemented with athletic participation of spectatorship at sports events. Rowing, baseball, cricket, football, and track and field were the first intercollegiate sports. Socialization by students at athletic contests and intense rivalries among colleges generated enthusiasm for intercampus athletic events.

ROWING

In the spring of 1843, four boats were purchased by Yale students who wanted exercise and recreation. The popularity of rowing soon led to the formation of boat clubs. In 1852, the first intercollegiate rowing event occurred when Yale and Harvard raced. In that same year, the "Yale Navy," a consolidation of all boat clubs, was formed. Richard M. Hurd, who had studied the history of college athletic programs, attributed the introduction of college student athletics to an enterprising railroad man who wanted to advertise the new Boston, Concord, and Montreal Railroad.[23] Thus, intercollegiate athletics emerged from a business venture and became dependent on profits much like business arrangements.

In 1858, Harvard took the lead in arranging for an intercollegiate regatta. Yale, Trinity in Hartford, Connecticut, and Brown in Providence, Rhode Island, agreed to enter the race. A Yale rower drowned in 1858 just before the event, and the first intercollegiate crew championship was postponed until July 26, 1859. Lake Quinsigamond at Worcester, Massachusetts, was selected as the site of the course.[24] *The New York Times* estimated that 10,000 people witnessed the regatta. Yale raced the 3-mile distance in 19 minutes, 14 seconds, beating Harvard by 2 seconds.[25] Intercollegiate rowing had aroused an enthusiastic following among first generation spectators. The second regatta on July 24, 1860, was also rowed on Lake Quinsigamond. It was the last regatta for ten years in which more than two colleges took part. Anticipating the threat of Civil War, the Harvard and Yale faculties suspended the rowing contests between the two colleges until 1864.[26] From 1852 to 1860, Harvard and Yale rowed six races under varying conditions on three different courses. So keen was the Harvard-Yale rivalry that in 1864 standard boat races between the two universities were inaugurated on Lake Quinsigamond, near Worcester, Massachusetts, even though the Civil War continued. Harvard culminated its five successive victories over Yale by venturing into international competition in 1869. The Harvard crew traveled to England where the University of Oxford ended Harvard's record of consecutive victories. The Harvard-Yale regatta inspired the first sensational newspaper accounts of intercollegiate competition. Athletic rivalry, crowd excitement, special trains, the cheers, and displays of the college colors initiated by rowing became a part of other collegiate sports.[27] Rowing achieved a prominent place at a number of colleges throughout the eastern part of the country. It was a novelty for students and townspeople to attach their allegiance to crews and celebrate their victories. When the Columbia University crew returned to New York City after a victory in 1874 intercollegiate regatta "they were received like a conquering army, with music, procession, and the booming of cannon."[28]

In 1871, the Rowing Association of American Colleges (RAAC) was established and included most of the institutions in New England as well as a few in New Jersey and New York. The RAAC was plagued with a continual turnover of membership and varied standards for participation. One regatta might have included seventeen crews and the next only seven. Harvard and Yale dominated the RAAC and colleges took sides. The Harvard-Yale rivalry disrupted the membership of the RAAC. The intense rivalry, together with the difficulty of conducting the race, and judging so many crews led to frequent disputes. Yale and Harvard withdrew from the RAAC in 1876. A few colleges unsuccessfully attempted to continue the Association.[29] Rowing continued to be a part of collegiate sports programs but was primarily confined to the eastern states.

BASEBALL

The first intercollegiate contest occurred on July 1, 1859, between Amherst and Williams at the Pittsfield Baseball Club in Pittsfield, Massachusetts. Arrangements for the game were made through the mail. It was agreed that each team would furnish its own ball and that the game would be limited to 65 runs. The playing field was surrounded by spectators five to six deep. Amherst won the game by a sizeable margin.[30]

Cricket, the next collegiate sport, was first played as an intercollegiate contest by Haverford College and the University of Pennsylvania in 1864. It was natural for the first intercollegiate cricket match to occur in Pennsylvania, where the sport had been introduced nearly three decades earlier and had acquired some enthusiastic followers. Cricket, however, never achieved the widespread popularity of baseball.

Most institutions of higher education fielded college nines. Since the introduction of rowing no other sport had generated the excitement of baseball. It was a low budget sport and a rallying point for students in the spring. On many campuses class competition culminated with a championship game and served as a feeder system to the university nines. In the late 1880s, preparatory schools including Phillips Andover Academy at Andover, Massachusetts; the Philliks Exeter Academy at Exeter, New Hampshire, and the Boston Latin School of Boston, Massachusetts, furnished freshman players for university teams. Questionable practices were used to induce players to join and remain on teams. Some coaches did not wish to part with outstanding players and encouraged them to return to campus and pursue postgraduate studies. Spectators flocked to college baseball games. One writer was particularly impressed with the spirited crowds at Harvard and Yale:

> The attendance is the very finest to be seen anywhere. The spectacle of the ladies radiant in their array of their favorite colors is alone worth the trouble of attending. The students are seated on opposite sides of the field, and from the very first appearance of their favorites to the last out in the game they make the air ring with encouraging cries, which are kept up not only with every play, but with the calling of every ball and strike. The game fairly bubbles over with enthusiasm if the score is at all close. Every fine play of the home club is greeted with continued cheering that often interrupts the game.[31]

Baseball afforded students another opportunity to show their college allegiance by displaying school colors and yelling their favorite cheers.

About the time football was introduced as an intercollegiate sport, athletic programs had attained a recognized position on college campuses. Student involvement as managers, as athletes, and loyal followers firmly implanted athletic programs in institutions of higher learning. Critics of intercollegiate sports had little impact on attempts to deter the development of competitive athletics.

FOOTBALL

A primitive football game existed on campuses long before the first intercollegiate game was played. A free-for-all game was played with an inflated bladder inside a leather case. Teams of varying numbers attempted to kick the ball into a make-shift goal or across an end line.

Princeton and Rutgers initiated the first college football match-up at New Brunswick, New Jersey. A soccer-like game was played. Tackling was not permitted nor was running with the ball allowed. Players kicked the ball or batted it with their hands. A point was scored when the ball was sent between the goal posts at any height. A cross bar was not used.[32] On the morning of November 6, 1869, a train crowded with students steamed out of Princeton, New Jersey, bound for the first intercollegiate football game. A three-game series between Princeton and Rutgers was to be played on Saturday afternoons.[33] There was no admission charge and spectators perched on a broad fence surrounding the field as they sang college songs and yelled cheers. Before the game began the captains discussed the variations in rules used by the two colleges and came to an agreement about how the game was to be played. Uniforms were not worn. The players merely removed their hats, coats, and vests. The Rutgers men added a little color by wearing scarlet turbans.[34] Princeton "bucked" or kicked the ball which had been placed upon a mound of earth. "The . . . Rutgers men pounced upon it like hounds . . . "[35] and won the game by scoring 6 goals to Princetons' 4. Both teams gathered for a dinner following the game.

The second game was played a week later on Saturday, November 13, 1869, at Princeton with Princeton winning 8 to 0. The third game was not played because the faculty members of both Princeton and Rutgers objected to the excitement of the contests which distracted students from their studies.[36]

TRACK AND FIELD

Track events were first established as a part of crew regattas. Some authorities place the first intercollegiate track event at Saratoga, New York in 1873. There was also a 2-mile foot race in Springfield, Massachusetts, the same year. During the intercollegiate regatta at Springfield on July 17, 1873, in which 11 crews entered, there was a three-crew freshmen race, a baseball game between Harvard and Brown, and a two-mile footrace for the Bennett Cup. Runners from Amherst, Cornell, Dartmouth, Harvard, and Canada's McGill College were slated to compete. The footrace was scheduled to begin before the baseball game, but the large crowd making their way to see the race gathered around the baseball nines. The baseball teams could not resist the opportunity to play before a large number of spectators and the game soon commenced. The crowd, thinking the footrace had been postponed, burst out with critical remarks. Judges of the footrace appeared and there was a rush for the grandstand. Before the race there was a discussion and disagreement about the McGill College students' amateur status. It was decided that the only requirement for the race was student status at a college. The runners from Dartmouth and Harvard withdrew. A half-mile track was used and the remaining three runners assembled. The Canadian won and the runner from Cornell finished second. Before the race ended the runner from Amherst threw himself face down on the ground. "He was surrounded by friends and attendants, who administered restoratives, wrapped him in rugs, and placed him in a carriage."[37]

On the front page of the July 18, 1873 edition of *The New York Times,* six of seven columns were devoted to the collegiate sports events in Springfield. Trains had conveyed team partisans to the sporting events. Merchants closed their stores at noon to enjoy the holiday occasion. Thousands of spectators gathered for the three-sport event; some waved colored ribbons for their favorite teams.

In 1874, 1875, and 1876, track and field events were scheduled as appendages of the Intercollegiate Crew Regatta.[38] The growing acceptability of sport as a viable part of college life was evident when in 1876 the Intercollegiate Association of Amateur Athletes of America (IC4A) was organized. It is the oldest collegiate athletic association and continues to conduct track and field championships.

RUGBY FOOTBALL

In the spring of 1874, the captain of Montreal's McGill University challenged Harvard to play two football matches. One match was to be played using the All-Canada code or a modification of rugby and the other using Harvard's rules. Harvard's rules resembled a version of rugby rather than soccer. The Harvard faculty would not permit its students to leave the campus to engage in a contest, and both games were played in Cambridge. There was an admission charge of 50 cents which was used to defray the cost of entertaining the visitors. The first game was played using Harvard's rules on May 13, 1874. Harvard won the game and the following day the first intercollegiate rugby football game was played in the United States with neither team scoring a goal. The rugby rules were enthusiastically received, and in the fall of 1875, Harvard abandoned its old game and adopted rugby.

Harvard challenged Yale to play a game of modified rugby rules. As a result of a meeting prior to the November 13, 1875, game in New Haven, a special set of rules was drafted in which concessions were granted to Yale by Harvard. The modifications were called the Concessionary Rules. The contest stimulated interest in the sport in New Haven even though Harvard won the game.

The centennial of American independence in 1876 also represents the year in which the Americanized version of football was adopted from the rules of rugby. Most colleges had approved the use of Rugby Union Rules but were playing with variations. The purpose of the November 1876 meeting was to establish a uniform set of rules. Princeton was responsible for assembling representatives of the Intercollegiate Football Association and a modified interpretation of the rugby rules was adopted.[39] Yale, Harvard, and Princeton led the way in Americanizing British rugby into football.

UNDERGRADUATE CONTROL OF ATHLETIC PROGRAMS

Prior to 1880, athletic programs were generally organized under the jurisdiction of undergraduates. Preparation of teams and coaching techniques was not sophisticated. Training tables were nonexistent and uniforms were not elaborate. Faculty members, alumni, and sometimes undergraduates filled the coaching ranks. Although some college athletic clubs helped to defray travel expenses, athletes assumed most of the financial obligations for contests away from their own campuses. Equal opportunity for competition regardless of financial status was not practiced prior to 1880. Those students having the financial means participated in intercollegiate athletics.

At Yale, students elected their sports managers and with a graduate treasurer received and disbursed athletic moneys. Each manager was responsible to his captain and Yale University. Members from the preceding year's team elected the team captain. The captain coached the team and along with the manager was responsible for the team's success. Occasionally a former captain or star athlete would return for a weekend and help the team get ready for a game.[40] Students secured the foundation for men's athletics in higher education whereas their female counterparts in later years were participants rather than organizers of sports programs.

In the 1880s, special prominence on campus was accorded the captain of the various sports teams. He was usually the most influential man in his class and held in awe by the younger students. A team member was also held in high regard as recounted by a writer in 1889:

> It is worth while to train for the nine and go through all the trouble that it entails for the advantages derived from it, for the reputation of the best scholar in the class does not amount to much compared to that of the crack ball tosser. At Harvard and Yale, the member of the university nines, as well as the freshmen players, are distinguished by the wearing of a specially prepared ribbon on a straw hat.[41]

Even the prestige of a college was enhanced by its athletic teams and their successes on the playing field. Though hampered by problems such as lack of continuity when student sports leaders graduated, athletic programs garnered staunch support from alumni, students, and townspeople. Sports were continually elevated to the status of intercollegiate competition.

FACULTY INTERVENTION IN INTERCOLLEGIATE SPORT

Student enthusiasm for intercollegiate sports and later patronage from townspeople and alumni contributed to the acceptance of sports as a dominant part of higher education. On the other hand, college faculty members, alarmed at the extent that athletic programs absorbed the interest of students, took steps to regulate and even eliminate college athletics. In 1871, the Harvard and Yale faculties exercised their influence and succeeded in prohibiting intercollegiate soccer matches. Another move, perhaps in desperation, was the 1878 agreement among 12 colleges which established contests in "public speaking, essay writing, and exercises in Greek, Latin, mathematics, and mental science" in what may have represented an attempt by the faculties to squelch the students' enthusiasm for athletics.[42] In 1882, the Harvard faculty objected to the number of baseball games played away from campus and appointed a faculty committee to examine the athletic program. The committee recommended the appointment of a standing committee on athletics which would report annually to the faculty. In addition, the college president was advised to address other colleges and encourage the elimination of competition with professional baseball clubs. Brown, Dartmouth, Princeton, and Amherst agreed to withdraw their teams from professional competition.[43]

While other sports gathered momentum and garnered enthusiastic followers, some colleges continued to express disapproval over the rules of football and player behavior. In November 1883, the Harvard College Committee on Athletics informed the captain of the football team that there would be no further intercollegiate competitions until improvements in the rules were made. Rules in the 1883 season permitted such actions as hacking, tripping, throttling, and striking an opponent with a closed fist. A player was not sent from the field until he had committed three "first offenses." Although the rules were improved, the Harvard Committee on Athletics, after attending four games in 1884, was convinced that a gentlemanly spirit was lacking. The committee observed numerous fights which they described as brutal. In one game a player was thrown out-of-bounds and was struck in the face as he was attempting to rise. Meanwhile his adversary triumphantly returned to the field with the ball. After hearing the committee's report, the Harvard faculty in December 1884, voted 24 to five to prohibit football.[44] Less drastic measures to control football occurred at other colleges. In the fall of 1883, Harvard College failed to persuade the Yale College faculty to call a meeting of college representatives to discuss intercollegiate athletic problems. Harvard then called a conference in New York on December 28, 1883. Yale, Princeton, Columbia, the University of Pennsylvania, Williams, Trinity, and Wesleyan sent representatives. A committee was appointed to devise a plan for joint control of intercollegiate sport. The committee presented eight resolutions which prohibited such practices as using professional athletes as coaches, and it limited competition to institutions that adopted the resolutions. In addition, the committee proposed a four-year limitation to a student's eligibility for competition. The resolutions were discussed at a second conference and sent to the faculties of 21 colleges. Harvard and Princeton were the only institutions that adopted the resolutions.[45] On the surface colleges were in favor of athletic reform but had difficulty agreeing on how improvements were to be accomplished.

THE DEVELOPMENT OF ATHLETIC PROBLEMS

The regulation of intercollegiate sport was dealt a major setback when colleges refused to accept the proposed resolutions. The problems in college athletics might have been minimized had institutions been willing to assume more responsibility for the conduct of their athletic programs. Although firmly entrenched in American education but without a governing body, intercollegiate sports programs became plagued with abuses.

The rapid growth of intercollegiate competition was partly responsible for some of the problems associated with athletics. In essence, the enforcement of regulations, the training of teams, an appropriate number of contests commensurate with educational pursuits, and the preparation of coaches and officials lagged behind the expansion of athletic programs. Initially, sports in the colleges were looked upon as amusements whose participants were expected to assume the costs. Increased interest in athletics brought dependence on money for program maintenance. Lacking the financial backing of their educational institutions students soon realized the marketability of a successful sport. Winning teams brought visibility, community support, and increased gate receipts.

When athletics became ingrained in commercialism, the purpose shifted from health-related benefits to winning. Friendly competition developed into intense rivalry. Student bodies became sources of revenue and enthusiastic rooters. Team backers were constantly searching for schemes to produce winners. After graduation, star athletes were brought back as assistant coaches. Coaches, students, and alumni worked to entice promising athletes to attend their institution. Some athletes were offered money to leave rival institutions and play for other teams. Players were given expensive uniforms and equipment for their sport. The training table and free room rent became an established part of athletic programs. The financially successful student organized athletic programs and their unparalleled popularity also brought prestige to the community. Businessmen were especially inclined to accept athletic programs as a commercial enterprise.[46] Profit making athletic programs became an essential ingredient for survival. The developing sports programs lacked a national parent organization and general regulations governing competition. Without a governing body and a system of monitoring infringements, abuses in sport and particularly football continued.

INTERCOLLEGIATE ATHLETICS ON TRIAL

From the 1880s until well into the twentieth century, the pros and cons of men's intercollegiate athletic programs were a frequent topic of debate. It was generally accepted that intercollegiate athletics were not inherently harmful to participants but the undue emphasis on winning resulted in questionable practices to achieve victory. Critics of intercollegiate sports programs blamed improper management for the woes of athletics.

Specifically the partisans argued that: (1) the training and preparation for contests involved beneficial exercises, (2) the adherence to game rules taught obedience to authority, (3) participation in athletics developed character and fostered leadership, (4) campus disorder was decreased because sports provided outlets for physical energy, (5) athletic contests produced an enthusiastic atmosphere on college campuses, and (6) athletes broadened their experiences and improved by competing against athletes from other colleges.

In contrast, opponents of intercollegiate sports claimed that: (1) athletic programs required excessive time of participants, (2) excitement of contests distracted students from their studies, (3) gambling on contests was an evil, (4) disorders often occurred at the conclusion of contests, (5) physical activity benefited only a small proportion of the students, and (6) athletic programs were too expensive.[47] Overemphasis on winning, the use of "ringers," and illegal recruiting were added to the woes of athletics. Objectionable practices in intercollegiate athletic programs became known as "evils." Several generations of critics perpetuated the "evils in athletics." In general, the arguments against intercollegiate sports changed little over the years.

LACROSSE ORGANIZED WHILE DEBATES OVER FOOTBALL CONTINUE

In the midst of debates concerning the value of football, lacrosse gained participants. During the early 1880s Yale, Harvard, and New York University played lacrosse. The game was introduced by Canadians who had moved to New York. It spread along the east coast and as far south as Georgia.[48] In 1882 the Intercollegiate Lacrosse Association (ILA) was formed. The ILA reorganized in 1926 and was named the United States Intercollegiate Lacrosse League (USILL). Later, "Association" was substituted for "League." For many years Baltimore was the center of lacrosse in the United States.

INTERSCHOLASTICS

By the 1890s, boys' interscholastic athletics were the prototype of their older counterparts in men's intercollegiate sports programs. Physical training teachers generally coached the teams. In 1903, Dr. Luther Gulick was instrumental in founding New York City's Public School Athletic League (PSAL). In 1910 the PSAL concept of faculty-directed athletics had been accepted by 17 other cities. The New York City schools were divided into districts for competition. There was a Girls' Branch, and total PSAL membership in 1910 was over 150,000.[49] Since the turn of the century interscholastic athletics have become an important part of extracurricular activities in both public and private schools.

GOVERNANCE OF ATHLETIC PROGRAMS

By the end of the century three types of athletic governments existed. Some programs enlisted the cooperation of alumni with undergraduates, and faculty input, while other colleges used a dual plan whereby faculty and undergraduates shared the administrative duties. Schools with strong student traditions left the management of athletics in the hands of the students.[50] Men's athletic programs which had been almost entirely governed by students were being transformed into more sophisticated operations.

PHYSICAL EDUCATORS EXPRESS DISAPPROVAL

Clark W. Hetherington, while at the University of Missouri, blamed the lack of educational influence for the problems in athletics. In the June, 1907 *American Physical Education Review* he wrote: " . . . I insist that all the turmoil over athletics is due ultimately to incorrect concepts of their place and function in college life and to weak student-faculty organizations for their administration."[51] Writing in the same publication four years later, Dudley A. Sargent of Harvard College, while stating that institutions and participants benefited from athletic programs, also raised objections to certain practices. Sargent opposed the exaggerated importance of athletics and the questionable methods employed to field winning teams. Furthermore, he believed colleges and universities were remiss in spending excessive amounts of money on athletes, while providing very little in their budgets for the physical education of the majority of students. Sargent favored faculty control of college athletic programs to insure benefits to participants.[52] The popularity of college athletics made faculty initiated reforms a controversial and perplexing problem.

Figure 12.4. Princeton and Yale, 1890.

FOOTBALL, THE WOE OF ATHLETICS

Football received the brunt of the criticism levied against intercollegiate competition. Numerous articles describing the detrimental effects of intercollegiate football appeared in periodicals published during the closing years of the nineteenth century. Objections, both vocal and written, continued into the twentieth century. In addition to the "evils" associated with intercollegiate sport, football injuries and fatalities in particular raised the ire of physical educators, politicians, medical doctors, and the general public. Nevertheless, football programs expanded and coaching careers flourished or withered depending on victory or defeat.

Controversies associated with intercollegiate competition reached a zenith in 1905. Drastic reform was essential to control the abuses in football which seemingly spread like an epidemic. Charges of proselytism of star players and professionalism among college players were rampant. The exaggerated importance of athletics in college life, the excessive amounts of time devoted to athletics, and the sometimes near savage-like behavior of student bodies distressed educators.

THE NATIONAL COLLEGIATE ATHLETIC ASSOCIATION

In December, 1905, a meeting of representatives of colleges and universities met to discuss intercollegiate athletics. The meeting was endorsed by President Theodore Roosevelt, an avid football fan and prominent exponent of the vigorous life. Football was the primary target for reform and there were some representatives who favored the elimination of the game. The purpose of the newly formed Intercollegiate Athletic Association (IAA) centered on " . . . the regulation and supervision of college athletics throughout the United States, in order that the athletic activities in the colleges and universities may be maintained on the ethical plane in keeping with the dignity and high purpose of education."[53]

The establishment of the IAA was the first nationwide attempt to unite colleges and universities who were interested in proving the conduct of athletic programs. Abuses in football were a major factor in the formation of the IAA which became the National Collegiate Athletic Association (NCAA) in 1910. Football received most of the adverse publicity because of the deaths that had occurred as a result of football injuries.

When the IAA met in New York City in 1906, the consensus of opinion was that the standard of competition had indeed improved. The new organization was dedicated to accomplishing its purpose by informing college students of the ideals of amateur sport and by strictly adhering to these ideals.[54] At the 1908 meeting of the IAA, it was evident that the Association was making inroads into the control of collegiate sports in the United States. Three factors contributed to the overall improvement of sports programs. First, the annual IAA Convention provided delegates with an opportunity to meet and discuss athletic programs. Second, speeches made at the IAA meetings were published in newspapers, the *American Physical Education Review,* and in college and university publications. Third, by having elected rules committees which in 1908 included football and basketball, participants' safety and standardization of rules were advanced.[55]

THE CALL FOR FOOTBALL REFORM CONTINUED

Chancellor James Roscoe Day of Syracuse University, while addressing representatives of the Intercollegiate Athletic Association at the fourth annual convention, declared:

> Killing men by football is a comparatively recent invention. It was played in this country for many years without fatalities. The first man killed shocked us, but it was said that he was not trained or was organically weak. Three or four men killed and then a dozen and now fifteen in the colleges and secondary schools in a year is the march of death which has become more deadly by improved rules.[56]

Chancellor Day earnestly called for an elimination of the "fatal features" in football.

During the 1910 football season, the National Collegiate Athletic Association, in an attempt to eliminate some dangerous aspects of the game, implemented several rule changes:

1. Prohibiting pushing and pulling the ball carrier.
2. Maintenance of a seven-player line of scrimmage to prevent mass play off the tackle.
3. Abolishing interlocked interference.
4. Elimination of blocking when a player is attempting to catch a forward pass.
5. Prohibiting crawling with the ball.
6. Minimizing danger to backs during an on-side kick by requiring a kicked ball which had hit the ground to go at least 20 yards beyond the line of scrimmage before the offense could be considered on side.
7. Elimination of the diving tackle.
8. Prohibiting both sides, when the ball was kicked, from interfering with an opponent in an area 20 yards beyond the line of scrimmage.
9. Reducing playing time by 10 minutes, introducing a three-minute rest in the middle of each half, and allowing a man to leave a game when he became tired and return at the beginning of any subsequent quarter.[57]

Each year the NCAA convened, rules were implemented to make football safer. Control over such abuses as falsifying academic records provoked considerable discussion. The pressure to win often outweighed the adherence to rules and regulations.

ALUMNI INTERVENTION

Amherst, like other colleges, was unable to control intercollegiate sports. An enthusiastic alumni group organized an Athletic Board in 1890 to offer assistance and direction to the sports program. By the mid-1890s few regulations were in operation. There were no restrictions on player eligibility and students deficient in grades were permitted to play. Athletes of questionable academic status continued to play for an indefinite number of years. Faculty members exerted little control over scheduling, but after the turn of the century they began to influence the conduct of the athletic program.[58] The problems associated with Amherst athletics were not peculiar to that institution. Conditions in athletics were ready for more stringent supervision.

A CHANGE IN MANAGEMENT

Early in the twentieth century, college officials recognized that they, rather than students, should assume the management of athletic programs. Midway through the first decade of the twentieth century colleges were showing evidence of their increased involvement in athletics, and financial supervision was assumed by faculty and alumni committees.[59] Athletic programs had reached a level of complexity which required personnel who could devote more time to coaching, training, scheduling, and financial affairs.

As the expansion of college athletics occurred in the 1880s, changes in management occurred. The control and management of sports and games by undergraduates gave way to hiring of coaches who developed their responsibilities into more technical roles. More sports were introduced, training was improved, and trainers were hired. Equipment increased in amount, complexity, and cost; and uniforms became more common. Funding from gate receipts and contributions became a necessity in order to meet the rising expense required to conduct athletic programs. Financial assistance was solicited from alumni who responded with generous contributions. Alumni soon began to use their financial clout as a means of influencing the policies of college athletic programs. The long recognized problems associated with athletics were subject to ongoing reform as the twentieth century approached.

BASKETBALL

The game of basketball was added to intercollegiate programs during the 1890s. James Naismith, a young instructor at the Springfield, Massachusetts YMCA, was asked by the director, Dr. Luther Gulick, to teach a class of men who were not responding to marching, calisthenics, or apparatus work. It was the winter of 1891 and there were only a few indoor games, such as three-deep, prisoners' base, and long-ball, which were not appealing to the YMCA men. A game which could be played inside during the winter months was needed. Naismith attempted to modify some existing games. Football, soccer, and lacrosse were modified for indoor play but were unsuccessful. After much trial and error, Naismith devised 13 rules. He originally intended to use boxes for goals but was given peach baskets by the building superintendent. Naismith nailed the baskets to the lower rail of the balcony at either end of the gymnasium. The 18 men in the class were divided into two teams.[60] The 13 rules were fastened to a bulletin board:

1. The ball may be thrown in any direction with one or both hands.
2. The ball may be batted in any direction with one or both hands (never with the fist).
3. A player cannot run with the ball. The player must throw it from the spot on which he catches it; allowance to be made for a man who catches the ball when running at a good speed.
4. The ball must be held in or between the hands; the arms or body must not be used for holding it.
5. No shouldering, holding, pushing, tripping, or striking, in any way the person of an opponent shall be allowed; the first infringement of

this rule by any person shall count as a foul, the second shall disqualify him until the next goal is made, or, if there was evident intent to injure the person for the whole of the game, no substitute allowed.

6. A foul is striking at the ball with the fist, violation of Rules 3, 4, and such as described in Rule 5.

7. If either side makes three consecutive fouls, it shall count a goal for the opponents. (Consecutive means without the opponents in the meantime making a foul.)

8. A goal shall be made when the ball is thrown or batted from the grounds into the basket and stays there, providing those defending the goal do not touch or disturb the goal. If the ball rests on the edge and the opponent moves the basket, it shall count as a goal.

9. When the ball goes out of bounds, it shall be thrown into the field and played by the person first touching it. In case of a dispute, the umpire shall throw it straight into the field. The thrower-in is allowed five seconds. If he holds it longer it shall go to the opponent. If any side persists in delaying the game, the umpire shall call a foul on them.

10. The umpire shall be judge of the men and shall note the fouls and notify the referee when three consecutive fouls have been made. He shall have power to disqualify men according to Rule 5.

11. The referee shall be judge of the ball and shall decide when the ball is in play, in bounds, to which side it belongs, and shall keep the time. He shall decide when a goal has been made, and keep account of the goals, with any other duties that are usually performed by a referee.

12. The time shall be two 15 minute halves, with five minutes rest between.

13. The side making the most goals in that time shall be declared the winners. In case of a draw, the game may, by agreement of the captains, be continued until another goal is made.[61]

The game was an immediate success. Some of the students went home during the Christmas holidays and introduced it to their local YMCA's. The first printed rules appeared in the January 1892 YMCA publication, the *Triangle.*[62] The Amateur Athletic Union, the National Collegiate Athletic Association, and the National Federation of State High School Athletic Associations sponsored tournaments and disseminated rules, thus providing further impetus to the growth of basketball. By the early 1930s it was the leading intramural sport in colleges and universities.

In 1894, the Intercollegiate Fencing Association (IFA) was organized. College physical education programs, influenced by European countries included fencing, and the sport became a natural addition to the collegiate competition. Two years after the IFA was founded, intercollegiate swimming competition began. Though these sports did not attract the following of the more dominant sports of baseball and football, they provided additional competitive opportunities. Intercollegiate swimming programs have been especially important in developing international competitors.

VOLLEYBALL

William C. Morgan was an 1894 graduate of the YMCA Training School at Springfield, Massachusetts, who became the physical director at the Holyoke, Massachusetts YMCA. Finding that basketball was too exhausting for the businessmen in his class, Morgan developed the game of volleyball, then called "mintonette" in 1895. Luther Gulick invited Morgan to bring some players to Springfield for an exhibition game. Dr. Alfred Halstead of the Springfield faculty named the new game volleyball. The rules were published and it was not long before volleyball was played in YMCAs throughout the country.[63] Colleges and universities adopted volleyball and included it in physical education, intramural, and athletic programs. The game received further exposure during World War I when over 1,000 athletic directors in the United States and abroad included volleyball in their programs.

GYMNASTICS

Gymnastic exhibitions were conducted by colleges as early as 1870. After the AAU assumed control of gymnastics and several other sports in 1888, it offered the colleges rules for gymnastics competition. There is a discrepancy in the date of the first college gymnastics meet. Some authorities recognize the meet at the University of Chicago on March 5, 1898, as the first intercollegiate gymnastics meet, while others credit the meet at New York University on March 22, 1899, as the first of its kind.[64] Called a "red-letter day in the history of Western college athletics by *The Chicago Tribune,* the indoor sports competition on March 5, 1898, featured gymnastics, track and field, fencing, and wrestling events. A meeting of the Western Intercollegiate Athletic Association was held in conjunction with the meet. Trains arriving in Chicago were filled with athletes from the Midwest.[65] The meet was referred to as Amos Alonzo Stagg's circus and considered a great success. Stagg went to the University of Chicago in 1892 and coached there for 41 years. Sharing the program with three other sports, the gymnasts "risked breaking their necks on the rings, bars, and vaulting horses . . . "[66] and contributed to the circus-like atmosphere with their performance and colorful tights. At times the gymnastic events were interspersed with other sports and forced into the background. Gymnastic competition included the horizontal bar, side horse, long horse, rings, tumbling, and club swinging. There was also an exhibition of club swinging by an athlete from the University of Minnesota. The University of Wisconsin won the gymnastics competition.[67]

Collegiate gymnastic competition progressed slowly because of the enthusiasm generated by team sports. Despite the team sports movement, leagues in the early 1920s included gymnastic meets. The major leagues were the Eastern Intercollegiate League, the Western Conference (Big Ten), and the Pacific Coast Intercollegiate Athletic Conference. In 1928, the NCAA attempted to standardize rules, but because each league had a set of rules, it was not until 1931 that national rules were adopted. A national meet was scheduled in 1934, but because few colleges could attend, the meet was cancelled. In 1938 the first NCAA national gymnastic meet was held. The National Association for Intercollegiate Athletics (NAIA) was founded that same year for the purpose of governing athletics in small colleges.

During World War II, most colleges eliminated gymnastics competition. Following World War II, interest in gymnastics grew and the NCAA national championship meet resumed in 1948. Explanations accounting for the renewed interest in gymnastics include the concern for physical fitness sparked by the war and the development and use of the trampoline.[68]

BOXING'S TENURE AS AN INTERCOLLEGIATE SPORT FOR HALF A CENTURY

In 1919, Pennsylvania State University organized its boxing program and scheduled a match with the University of Pennsylvania. According to *The New York Times* the Penn State-Pennsylvania match-up was the nation's first dual collegiate meet. Penn State also hosted the first Eastern tournament in 1924 and the first national tournament in 1932.[69]

In 1924, R. Tait McKenzie, Chairman of the NCAA Boxing Rules Committee, reported that the successful intercollegiate boxing meet at Pennsylvania State College in which five teams competed was proof that boxing could become an intercollegiate sport. McKenzie was hopeful that gambling and other evils associated with the professional prize fight ring would not become part of intercollegiate boxing.[70]

Nevertheless, boxing did become a controversial sport not only at the intercollegiate level, but within the physical education program. In 1950, Carlton R. Meyers reported on the status of boxing in institutions of higher education. Meyers based his study on responses received from 620 of the 794 institutions he surveyed. During the decade beginning with the 1939–1940 academic year, 41 institutions discontinued intercollegiate boxing. During the 1948–1949 academic year, 59 institutions sponsored intercollegiate boxing. Forty percent of the institutions that dropped the sport did so because of lack of qualified personnel, limited facilities and equipment, and declining student interest.[71]

Pennsylvania State University, first to initiate intercollegiate boxing in 1919, eliminated the sport from its athletic program in May, 1954. Athletic director E.B. McCoy cited "public apathy and scheduling difficulties..." as reasons for abandoning the sport. Penn State placed third in the 1954 NCAA national tournament which was won by the University of Wisconsin.[72] After 23 years of competition, the University of Maryland dropped boxing because of the difficulty in finding teams to schedule. The ruling became effective at the conclusion of the 1955 season.[73]

Tragedy struck the 1960 NCAA championship when Charles Mohr, a

University of Wisconsin boxer, was knocked out in the second round of a title bout. Despite brain surgery, he died. In the wake of this unfortunate event, collegiate boxing teams were eliminated at San Jose State, Wisconsin, Sacramento State, and Washington. San Jose State won the title three times and the remaining teams earned points in the 1960 tournament. On January 8, 1961, the executive committee of the NCAA voted to eliminate boxing championships. The committee cited the small number of collegiate teams as a primary reason for discontinuing the national championship. Declining interest in intercollegiate boxing and possibly public sentiment following the death of a boxer in the 1960 NCAA finals contributed to the discontinuance of intercollegiate boxing altogether.

INTRAMURALS AND SPORTS CLUBS

Intramural sports became a part of institutional programs just prior to World War I. The term "intramural" comes from the Latin words "intra" meaning within, and "muralis" which means wall. The program consists of competitive sports, and recreational games and activities voluntarily played by college or high school students within their respective institutions.

Early intramural programs developed out of a need not met in physical education or athletic departments. The inclusion of games and sports into physical education programs in the early twentieth century served as a catalyst for the intramural movement. Additionally, athletic departments permitted their facilities to be used for intramurals with the early intent of using them as a source for recruiting for varsity teams. Program benefits were recognized by Ohio State and the University of Michigan when both institutions appointed intramural directors in 1913. As interest grew and programs expanded in the 1920s, a broader ideal, which encompassed a wider variety of sports accommodating individual needs and more opportunities for participation, was in vogue.

In 1919, the expansion of intramurals took a large stride forward when Elmer D. Mitchell was appointed director of intramural sports at the University of Michigan. He also wrote the first textbook on the subject, *Intramural Athletics,* in 1925. Mitchell was considered to be the "father of intramurals" by many; and because of his influence, the first intramural sports building was constructed at the University of Michigan in 1928. In the high schools, intramural activities had begun to appear by 1925 but were not to be firmly established for another five years. Major attention was still being given by coaches and physical educators to the development of standards in interscholastic athletics. Once these standards became established, attention was turned to the sporting needs of students in general. Most high school intramural programs were modeled after those in colleges and included such activities as football, basketball, baseball, swimming, and tennis.

Intramurals have gained wide acceptance throughout the nation's schools and colleges. Initially consisting of organized competitive sports, it has expanded to include informal physical activities. Many programs offer individual and dual activities such as sailing, hiking, racquetball, squash, frisbee throwing, bowling, and jogging. Sports clubs may also be found as an adjunct to many programs which provide additional opportunities for instruction, competition, healthful exercise, and social interaction.

Since the late 1950s, there has been a resurgence of the sports club concept that was prevalent in mid-nineteenth century institutions before intercollegiate sports were firmly entrenched in higher education. Generally student initiated, sports clubs are societal outgrowths of interest in individual activities such as fencing, the martial arts, and badminton. The team sports rugby, lacrosse, and soccer have been added to club sports programs. Club sports are generally coached and managed by students. Club teams that play other institutions are financed by the students themselves or partially from student fees which support intramural and recreational activities.

THE GREAT DEPRESSION

A drop in college athlete funds during the early 1930s was additional evidence that the country had sunk into deep economic depression. Football continued to attract spectators, but its magnetism was not as evident as some of the older established colleges and universities. A shift in campus leadership during the Depression years was revealed in a survey by *Fortune* magazine.

> The old-style campus big man no longer commands unqualified allegiance. The football star, the crew captain, ... the track manager ... these still have honor and respect. But the intellectually curious person ... is climbing past the conventional big man.[74]

Associations were formed in some sports in the wake of economic despair. The American Softball Association (ASA) organized in 1934 and in 1937 the American Badminton Association (ABA) ratified a constitution. The game which gained the largest following during the depression was softball. By 1939, there was an estimated half a million teams and over five million players of all ages and both sexes.[75] The National Recreation Association (NRA) promoted softball by emphasizing its virtues. The game was inexpensive to maintain and was enjoyed by those possessing varying levels of skill. Football, after reaching its lowest attendance level in the early 1930s, began to show signs of revitalization with the South and Far West gaining many converts to the game. Smaller high schools were still forced to economize which led to the development of six-man football and was adopted by many states.

By the 1930s, it was evident that more people than ever were participating in athletics and recreational pursuits which began to dispel the claims of critics that Americans were destined to become a nation of onlookers. One important development which contributed to more active leisure-time par-

Figure 12.5. Intramurals, University of Florida, Gainesville, Florida.

ticipation was the tremendous growth of public recreational facilities which were constructed during the Depression years by the government mobilized work force.

SPORT AND THE MEDIA

Since the turn of the century, large sections of newspapers have been devoted to sports. The telegraph and later the radio more rapidly transmitted the coverage of competitive events to a nation that seemed nearly obsessed with sports. The first collegiate sports telecast began in 1940 when the University of Pennsylvania's football games were televised. One year of Pennsylvania's telecasts was interrupted during World War II.[76] Since the pioneering University of Pennsylvania television coverage, live visual transmissions of collegiate sports have experienced unprecedented growth in both their variety and the number of hours devoted to them. Revenue from television has been an important addition to athletic budgets.

THE NCAA CONTINUES REFORM MEASURES

War veterans swelled the ranks of collegiate athletic teams and post-World War II NCAA growth was phenomenal. Athletic programs of the 1940s and early 1950s were not without problems. Many of the disputed practices evident in earlier decades were still being condemned in the 1940s. Pressure to win caused coaches to ignore NCAA standards and engage in illegal practices. In 1946 the "Conference of Conferences," or meeting of representatives from the major conferences was held. In general, the representatives called for improved institutional control with sound academic standards. Enforcement of NCAA regulations was crucial in an atmosphere of intense competition in which winning was strongly emphasized.

In 1948, the NCAA approved five governing principles:

Principle of Amateurism: An amateur sportsman is one who engages in sports for the physical, mental, or social benefits he derives therefrom, and to whom the sport is an avocation. Any college athlete who takes or is promised pay in any form for participation in athletics does not meet this definition of an amateur.

Principle of Institutional Control and Responsibility. The control and responsibility for the conduct of both intercollegiate and intramural athletics shall in the last analysis be exercised by the institution itself.

Principle of Sound Academic Standards. Athletes shall be admitted to the institution on the same basis as any other students and shall be required to observe and maintain the same academic standards.

Principle Governing Financial Aids to Students. Financial aids in the form of scholarships, fellowships or otherwise, even though originating from sources other than persons on whom the recipient may be naturally or legally dependent for support, shall be permitted without loss of eligibility.

Principle Governing Recruiting. No member of an athletic staff or other official representative of athletic interest shall solicit the attendance of his institution of any prospective student with the offer of financial aid or equivalent inducements. This, however, shall not be deemed to prohibit such staff member of (sic) other representative from giving information regarding aids. . . . [77]

Despite the NCAA's endeavors to maintain high standards of conduct, a major basketball scandal erupted and shocked the collegiate athletic world. The college game was immensely popular and the exposé severely damaged the reputation of the game. Over 30 from Bradley University, City College of New York, Long Island University, Manhattan College, New York University, University of Kentucky, and the University of Toledo were discovered to have fixed game scores during the 1949 and 1950 seasons. Coaches at the schools claimed no knowledge of the conspiracy. Some players and bribers were sentenced to prison terms, and the careers of several respected coaches were ruined. Big-time basketball was especially hurt in New York for several years.

Much to the chagrin of collegiate sports officials, basketball "point shaving" occurred in 1961 and 1965. On the positive side, soccer and skiing were added to the NCAA championships during the 1950s. In the next decade, water polo and volleyball championships were included in NCAA championships. During the early 1960s, while higher education institutions were experiencing a construction boom, baseball became more visible. Football and basketball continued to dominate collegiate sports. The latter two collegiate sports had long provided a "feeder system" for professional leagues, and during the 1970s, college basketball teams were supplying more talent for the professional game.

During the 1970s, many of the perennial problems in athletics still existed. There were recruiting violations, academic record falsifications, and charges of illegal aid being offered to athletes. Because of illegal uses of drugs in an attempt to enhance athletic performance, drug education became more important. The ramification of Title IX of the Education Amendments kindled heated debate among men and women sports leaders. In its annual report issued in January 1975, the NCAA's Long Range Planning Committee concluded that five major problems confronted intercollegiate athletics:

1. The problem of integrating women's athletic programs fairly and equitably into intercollegiate athletics.
2. Inflation and increasing costs of varsity and intercollegiate athletic competition.
3. The strengthening of the image of intercollegiate athletics and of the support of intercollegiate athletic programs on the campuses by students and faculty members.
4. Providing a strong commitment to comply with rules and regulations by all institutional members and the willingness to take strong action against violators.
5. The ability of the NCAA to remain flexible as an organization and adapt to the changing needs of varsity competition. . . . [78]

The NCAA approved reorganizational changes in 1973 and formed division I, II, and III schools. Each division has separate national championships in many sports. Despite rising costs of athletic programs the membership roster increased during 1974 for the 25th consecutive year and included over 800 membership institutions. Soccer was the fastest growing sport and reflected the nations' at large sporting interest. On the other hand, the largest reduction in sponsorship of sports was in track and bowling.[79] During 1973–1974 the NCAA championships produced record participation, and paid attendance. A record 10,131 student-athletes vied for honors in the Association's 33 championship events. Paid attendance for the 1973–1974 championship totaled 604,044 surpassing the previous year's record by nearly 50,000.

While athletic programs of the 1970's experienced growth in attendance, use of sophisticated sports medicine data, psychological input from specialists, routine travel across the continent, and schedules arranged years in advance; the end of the decade brought the realization that financial stability was imperative to survival. Some institutions were forced to respond to the financial crisis with the elimination of sports which included wrestling and football. In the wake of financial disaster, the importance of producing winning teams, especially in revenue producing sports, is considered of paramount importance. In the public's opinion, a primary factor in assessing an institution's value, regardless of its academic assets, is its ability to produce winning teams. The production of championship teams offers many contrasts to the main purposes of a university, which are teaching, research, and service.

During the 1980s, intercollegiate athletic programs became even more visible. The revenue producing sports, football and basketball, continued to lead the way, producing higher television ratings, larger crowds, and enthusiastic support from alumni and booster organizations. Emerging from the facade of popularity was a growing negative perception expressed by the general public. Many large institutions with highly successful teams were viewed with skepticism. Recruiting violations, grade improprieties, the lack of academic progress of student-athletes, and lavish gifts to athletes from alumni tainted the image of many institutions. Furthermore, the rising costs of intercollegiate athletic programs and gender equity added to the challenges encountered by administrators.

On October 19, 1989, the Trustees of the Miami-based Knight Foundation, instituted the Knight Foundation Commission on Intercollegiate Athletics to advance a reform plan for intercollegiate athletics. The reform plan was issued in March, 1991. The Knight Foundation report, *Keeping Faith with the Student-Athlete, A New Model for Intercollegiate Athletics,* presented a positive approach which called upon " . . . academic administrators [to] define the terms under which athletics will be conducted in the university's name."[80]

The Commission's reform plan focused on "the one-plus-three" model. The "one" refers to presidential control which is " . . . directed toward the 'three'—academic integrity, financial integrity and accountability through certification."[81] The Knight Commission recommended that the president of the university be involved in all aspects of athletic governance, exercise voting in athletic conferences, control the NCAA, insure equity in intercollegiate athletics, and control their institution's association with commercial television.

Academic integrity, according to the Commission, must be based on the premise that athletes are students. Furthermore, they should not be admitted to an institution unless they show reasonable promise of completing an academic degree. Monitoring academic progress and basing eligibility on making progress toward a degree were some of the other recommendations regarding academic integrity.

Financial integrity was deemed an essential to avoid financial scandals that plagued a number of institutions in the past. The reduction in operating costs of athletic programs, monitoring of all funds raised for athletics, and reviews of coaches' income were among the Commission's recommendations.

The certification or assessment of a program by an outside agency can insure the integrity of the overall program.[82] Leaders in intercollegiate sport have insisted on accountability. If athletic programs are to survive in the next century, assessments of operations, expenditures, and the role of intercollegiate sports in higher education must be reviewed on a regular basis.

SUMMARY

The Young Men's Christian Association (YMCA), private clubs, and educational institutions contributed to the organization of men's sports in the United States. The first YMCA in America was founded in 1852 in New York City to promote religion among young men. In 1869, a gymnasium was opened which eventually led to the establishment of physical training departments nationwide. Dr. Luther Gulick was instrumental in developing the physical training program of the YMCA for 16 years. The first private club in the United States was the New York Athletic Club founded in 1868. In colleges, intracampus sports contests and eventually more organized intercollegiate athletic programs helped to control disruptive student behavior. Rowing, baseball, cricket, football, and track and field were the first intercollegiate sports. In 1852, Yale and Harvard competed in the first intercollegiate rowing event. Rowing events were conducted at a number of colleges throughout the eastern part of the country. The Rowing Association of American Colleges (RAAC), established in 1871, was short-lived because of frequent disputes brought about by intense rivalry.

The first intercollegiate baseball contest took place in 1859 between Amherst and Williams. An intercollegiate game of cricket occurred in 1864 between Haverford College and the University of Pennsylvania. Unlike baseball, the sport never achieved widespread recognition. Most institutions of higher learning had a baseball team which generated much interest and served as a rallying point for the student body. By the late 1860s athletic programs had attained a recognized position on college campuses. Football was first played in 1869 between Princeton and Rutgers. Track events were initially established as an appendage of crew regattas. Some authorities identify the first intercollegiate track event as being held at Saratoga, New York, in 1873. Efforts to formally govern college sport were undertaken in 1876 with the formation of the Intercollegiate Association of Amateur Athletes of America.

Prior to 1880, athletic programs were generally organized and administered by undergraduate students. In spite of poor continuity brought about when student sports leaders graduated, athletic programs garnered support from alumni, students, and townspeople. College faculty members, concerned about undue student interest in sports, took action to regulate and even eliminate athletics on campus. However, colleges did not assume a great deal of responsibility for the conduct of their athletic programs which became plagued with abuses. Programs lacked a national parent organization with general regulations governing competition. Three types of athletic governments were in operation at the end of the century. There were programs conducted solely by students, and those of a cooperative nature involving students, faculty, and alumni, or students and faculty.

In 1905, representatives from colleges and universities convened to discuss intercollegiate athletics with football being a primary target for reform. The meeting resulted in the formation of the Intercollegiate Athletic Association (IAA) which was renamed the National Collegiate Athletic Association (NCAA) in 1910. The purpose of the newly formed organization was to regulate and supervise college athletics in the United States. The call for reforms in football continued and the NCAA responded by implementing new rules to make the game safer. Regulations were implemented in an attempt to control such abuses as falsifying academic records.

Early in the 20th century, college officials began to realize that they, rather than students, must assume responsibility for athletic program management. Programs had become increasingly complex and required a staff which could devote more time to organization and administration. Monetary assistance was solicited from alumni who began to use their financial clout as a means of influencing athletic policies.

The game of basketball, developed in 1891, was added to intercollegiate programs during the 1890s by James Naismith who was a YMCA instructor at Springfield, Massachusetts. Athletic organizations sponsored basketball tournaments whereby encouraging its growth throughout colleges and universities. Other collegiate competitive opportunities were provided with the organization of fencing in 1894 and swimming two years later. Volleyball, developed in 1895 by William G. Morgan, was adopted by colleges and universities and played in athletic programs. Collegiate gymnastics competition progressed slowly with college leagues in the early 1920s staging gymnastic meets. The first NCAA national gymnastics meet was held in 1938. In the same year, the National Association for Intercollegiate Athletics (NAIA) was founded to govern athletics in small colleges.

Intramural sports became a part of educational institutions prior to World War I. Intramurals developed from a need not met in physical education or athletic programs. The first intramural sports building was constructed at the University of Michigan in 1928. Programs initially consisted of organized competitive sports but have expanded to include informal physical activities. Since the 1950s there has been a resurgence of the sports club concept which was prevalent in the mid-nineteenth century.

The Great Depression brought about a drop in college athletic funds. In the years of President Roosevelt's New Deal, basketball had become a common attraction, and by 1939, the NCAA had sponsored an annual tournament. Economy measures forced the development of six-man football which spread to other states. During the Depression years there was a large increase in the growth of public recreational facilities which were constructed by the government mobilized work force.

Post World War II NCAA growth was phenomenal, but athletic programs were still faced with many of the problems reminiscent of earlier decades. In 1946, a conference was held to identify principles applicable to the conduct of Intercollegiate Athletics. Despite the NCAA's efforts to maintain ethical standards of conduct, a major basketball scandal was discovered during the 1949 and 1950 seasons. Perennial problems remained in athletics during the 1970s, such as recruiting violations and academic record falsifications. A new controversy surrounded the inclusion of women in intercollegiate sports. Nevertheless, the membership roster increased during 1974 for the 25th consecutive year and NCAA championships have produced record participation and paid attendance.

During the 1980s, intercollegiate athletic programs became even more visible. Revenue producing sports such as football and basketball continued to lead the way in producing higher television ratings, larger crowds, and enthusiastic support from alumni and booster organizations. Emerging from the facade of popularity was a growing negative perception expressed by the general public. Many large institutions with highly successful teams were viewed with skepticism. Recruiting violations, grade improprieties, the lack of academic progress of student-athletes, and lavish gifts to athletes from alumni tainted the image of many institutions.

In 1991, the Knight Foundation Commission issued a reform plan for intercollegiate athletics. The Commission's reform plan focused on "the one-plus-three" model which called for presidential control, academic integrity, financial integrity, and accountability. If athletic programs are to survive in the next century, assessments of operations, expenditures, and the role of intercollegiate sports in higher education must be reviewed on regular basis.

REFERENCES

1. L.L. Doggett. *Life of Robert R. McBurney.* New York: Association Press, 1912, p. 24.
2. Doggett. *ibid. Life of Robert R. McBurney.* p. 26.
3. Doggett. *ibid.* p. 26.
4. Cleveland E. Dodge. *Y.M.C.A. A Century at New York, 1852–1952.* New York: Newcomen Society in North America, 1953, p. 11.
5. C. Howard Hopkins. *History of the Y.M.C.A. in North America.* New York: Association Press, 1951, pp. 37, 221.
6. Doggett. *op. cit.* pp. 95–96.
7. Hopkins. *History of the Y.M.C.A. in North America.* pp. 247–248, 253, 256, 258.
8. Charles P. Sawyer. "Amateur Track and Field Athletics," *Scribner's Magazine.* 7 (June, 1890), p. 775.
9. Duncan Edwards. "Life at the Athletic Clubs," *Scribner's Magazine.* 18 (July, 1895), p. 19.

10. Sawyer. "Amateur Track and Field Athletics," p. 776.

11. Edwards. "Life at the Athletic Clubs," *op. cit.* p. 14.

12. Sawyer. "Amateur Track and Field Athletics," *op. cit.* p. 775.

13. James H. Worman. "The Manhattan Athletic Club," *Outing.* 16 (June, 1890), p. 166.

14. Edward Mussey Hartwell. "Physical Training in American Colleges and Universities." *Circulars of Information of the Bureau of Education.* Washington, D.C.: Government Printing Office, 1886, pp. 610, 613.

15. Will Grimsley. *Tennis, Its History, People and Events.* Englewood Cliffs: Prentice-Hall, Inc., 1971, p. 33.

16. Diane M. Hales. "A History of Badminton in the United States from 1878 to 1939," Unpublished master's thesis, California State Polytechnic University, Pomona, 1979, pp. 28, 29, 32.

17. H.B. Martin. *Fifty Years of American Golf.* New York: Dodd, Mead and Co., 1936, pp. 1–2, 20, 28.

18. Will Grimsley. *Golf, Its History, People and Events.* Englewood Cliffs: Prentice-Hall, 1966, p. 35.

19. Grimsley. *ibid.* pp. 35, 189, 190.

20. "Ouimet World's Golf Champion," *The New York Times,* September 21, 1913, p. 1.

21. Grimsley. *op. cit.* pp. 201–203.

22. Eugene L. Richards. "College Athletics," *Popular Science Monthly* 24 (March, 1884), pp. 593–594.

23. Richard M. Hurd. "American College Athletics," *Outing.* 13 (February, 1889), pp. 404, 406.

24. W.S. Quigley. "Aquatics," *Athletic Sports of America, England and Australia.* Philadelphia: Hubbard Brothers, Publishers, 1889, pp. 627, 629.

25. "The Regatta at Worcester," *The New York Times,* July 28, 1859, p. 1.

26. W.S. Quigley, "Aquatics," pp. 627, 629–630.

27. Henry Davidson Sheldon. *The History and Pedagogy of American Student Societies.* New York: D. Appleton & Co., 1901, p. 193.

28. Brander Matthews (ed.). *A History of Columbia University 1754–1904.* New York: Columbia University Press, 1904, p. 173.

29. Sheldon. *The History and Pedagogy of American Student Societies. op. cit.* pp. 230–231.

30. Albert G. Spalding. *America's National Game.* New York: American Sports Publishing Co., 1911, pp. 345–347.

31. J.C. Morse. "College Baseball" *Athletic Sports of America, England and Australia.* Philadelphia: Hubbard Brothers, Publishers, 1889, p. 560.

32. William H.S. Demarest. *A History of Rutgers College 1766–1924.* Princeton: Princeton University Press, 1924, pp. 428–429.

33. Parke H. Davis. *Football the American Intercollegiate Game.* New York: Charles Scribner's Sons, 1914, p. 48.

34. Demarest. *A History of Rutgers College 1766–1924. op. cit.,* p. 429.

35. Parke H. Davis. *Football the American Intercollegiate Game. op. cit.* p. 48.

36. Davis. *ibid.* pp. 49–50.

37. "The Foot-Race," *The New York Times,* July 18, 1873, p. 1.

38. J. Mott Hallowell. "American College Athletics I Harvard University," *The Outing Magazine.* 13 (December, 1888), p. 234.

39. Davis. *op. cit.* pp. 52, 62–67.
40. George Wilson Pierson. *Yale College An Educational History 1871–1921.* New Haven: Yale University Press, 1952, pp. 38–39.
41. Morse. *op. cit.* pp. 567–568.
42. Howard J. Savage. *American College Athletics.* New York: The Carnegie Foundation for the Advancement of Teaching. 1929, p. 21.
43. D.A. Sargent. "History of the Administration of Intercollegiate Athletics in the United States," *American Physical Education Review.* 15 (March, 1910), pp. 252–253.
44. Edward Mussey Hartwell. *Circulars of Information of the Bureau of Education Number 15, 1885, Physical Training in America.* Washington, D.C.: Government Printing Office, 1886, pp. 656–658.
45. J.H. McCurdy. "The Essential Factors in the Control of Intercollegiate Athletics," *American Physical Education Review.* 15 (February, 1910), pp. 114–115.
46. Wilbur P. Bowen. "The Evolution of Athletic Evils," *American Physical Education Review.* 14 (March, 1909), pp. 152–154.
47. Hartwell. *Circulars of Information of the Bureau of Education Number 15, 1885, Physical Training in America.* pp. 644–649.
48. Ray Taylor. "Lacrosse, the Original American Game," *School Athletics in Modern Education Wingate Memorial Lectures.* New York: Wingate Memorial Foundation, 1931, pp. 469–470.
49. Arthur B. Reeve. "The World's Greatest Athletic Organization," *Outing.* 57 (October, 1910), pp. 109, 113.
50. Savage. *op. cit.* p. 24.
51. Clark W. Hetherington. "Analysis of Problems in College Athletics," *American Physical Education Review.* 12 (June, 1907), p. 177.
52. Dudley A. Sargent. "Competition in College Athletics," *American Physical Education Review.* 15 (February, 1910), pp. 101–102.
53. Palmer E. Pierce. "The Intercollegiate Athletic Association of the United States," *American Physical Education Review.* 13 (February, 1908), pp. 85–87.
54. Pierce. "The Intercollegiate Athletic Association of the United States," *ibid.,* pp. 87–88.
55. Palmer E. Pierce. "The Intercollegiate Athletic Association of the United States," *American Physical Education Review.* 14 (January, 1909), pp. 79–80.
56. James Roscoe Day. "The Function of College Athletics," Intercollegiate Athletic Association Proceedings, New York, New York, December 28, 1909, p. 40.
57. H.L. Williams. "Report of the Football Rules Committee," National Collegiate Athletic Association Proceedings, New York, New York, December 29, 1910, pp. 27–28.
58. Thomas Le Duc. *Piety and Intellect at Amherst College 1865–1912.* New York: Columbia University Press, 1946, p. 133.
59. "Editorial Note and Comment," *American Physical Education Review.* 11 (June, 1906), p. 135.
60. James Naismith. *Basketball Its Origin and Development.* New York: Association Press, 1941, pp. 35–36, 52–53.
61. Naismith. *ibid.* pp. 53–55.
62. Naismith. *ibid.* p. 59.
63. Hopkins. *History of the Y.M.C.A. in North America. op. cit.* p. 263.

64. Richard Edd Laptad. "A History of the Development of the United States Gymnastics Federation," unpublished dissertation, University of Oregon, 1971, pp. 6–7.
65. "Indoor Tourney On," *The Chicago Tribune,* March 5, 1898, p. 7.
66. "Mr. Stagg's Circus," *The Chicago Tribune,* March 6, 1898, p. 7.
67. "Mr. Stagg's Circus," *The Chicago Tribune, ibid.,* p. 7.
68. Laptad. *op. cit.,* pp. 6–7.
69. "Penn State Drops Boxing from Athletic Program," *The New York Times,* May. 30, 1954, sec. V, p. 3.
70. R. Tait McKenzie. "Boxing Rules Committee," *National Collegiate Athletic Association Proceedings.* New York City, December 30, 1924, p. 61.
71. Carlton R. Meyers. "The Status of Boxing in Institutions of Higher Learning," *Research Quarterly,* 21 (October, 1950), pp. 292–293.
72. "Penn State Drops Boxing from Athletic Program," *The New York Times, op. cit.,* p. 3.
73. "Varsity Boxing Dropped from Maryland State," *The New York Times,* March 22, 1955, p. 24.
74. "Youth in College," *Fortune,* 13 (June, 1936), pp. 99–100.
75. Ted Shane. "The American Magazine," 127 (June, 1939), pp. 36–37.
76. *The National Collegiate Athletic Association 1949 Yearbook.* NCAA Publication, 1950, p. 106.
77. "Report on Constitutional Revisions," *The National Collegiate Athletic Association The Nineteen-Forty-Seven Yearbook,* 1948, pp. 188–191.
78. William H. Baughn. "Long Range Planning Committee," *1973–74 Annual Reports of the National Collegiate Athletic Association.* Shawnee Mission: Kansas, 1975, p. 43.
79. "1973–74 Statistical Review," *1973–74 Annual Reports of the National Collegiate Athletic Association,* Shawnee Mission: Kansas, 1975, p. 12.
80. *Keeping Faith with the Student-Athlete, A New Model of Intercollegiate Athletics,* Report of the Knight Foundation, Commission on Intercollegiate Athletics, 1991, p. 11.
81. Ibid., p. 11.
82. Ibid., pp. 12–21.

Chapter 13

WOMEN'S SPORTS PROGRAMS

Participation in sports by women, until late in the nineteenth century, was regarded as a pastime or a mild form of exercise. A few pioneer educators saw the value of physical activity and encouraged women to engage in exercise. Emma Willard, Catherine Beecher, Mary Lyon, and Dio Lewis were early advocators of education and exercise for women. In 1821, Emma Willard introduced dancing in her school at Troy, New York. Willard thought dancing was a beneficial activity for girls. Later in 1823, Catherine Beecher, who favored calisthenics, included this form of exercise to cure distortions and promote graceful movement.[1] Mary Lyon of Mount Holyoke required calisthenics as part of her students' course of studies in 1835. Liva Baker, from *The Autobiography and Letters of Matthew Vassar* wrote:

> Miss Lyon required her earliest students to carry wood and coal, to wash, iron, cook, sweep, do dishes, and clean, as much for their value as physical exercise as for institutional economy ... The girls also did simple calisthenics based on dance steps of the time, (and) were required to walk a mile every day ... [2]

In 1861, Dr. Dio Lewis succeeded in establishing the Normal Institute for Physical Education. Lewis promoted gymnastics for men, women, and children in his Boston School.[3] Dr. Lewis' system of light gymnastics was adopted by other colleges including Vassar College for women shortly after it opened in 1865. Lewis also emphasized proper dress which allowed freedom of movement while women exercised.

THE YOUNG WOMEN'S CHRISTIAN ASSOCIATION

The distinction of being called the first Young Women's Christian Association (YWCA) goes to the Boston YWCA, formed in 1866 because the women in Boston were the first to use the name "Young Women's Christian Association." In the late 1850s, there was an organization in New York City having purposes similar to those of the Boston Association. Both groups provided religious activities for self-supporting young women who had moved to the cities.[4] Like the YMCA, their male counterpart, the YWCA was established in an atmosphere of intense religious interest, but ties to England are not as clearly linked as are those of the YMCA. There were a few religious-oriented women's groups in England prior to the beginning of the YWCA movement in the United States. Both in England and America there

224

was a need to offer assistance to young women who had moved to urban areas.

The Young Women's Christian Association (YWCA), recognizing the lack of recreational facilities, extended its services beyond the spiritual development of its members and initiated a summer camp program in 1874 at Asbury Park, New Jersey. Resting, reading, walking, and swimming at "Sea Rest" provided working women with a pleasant respite from their jobs. Furthermore, many women were undernourished and ill-prepared physically to withstand the rigors of factory and shop work. The YWCA recognized the need to improve the physical health of women. The Boston YWCA introduced calisthenics in 1877 and other associations soon followed suit. The first gymnasium was constructed at the Boston YWCA's Berkeley Street building in 1884. Physical education became an integral part of the YWCA's program. By 1916 some 65,000 women were enrolled in gymnasium classes and more than 32,000 entered swimming programs.[5]

RESTRAINTS ON PHYSICAL ACTIVITY

Having few exercise programs of which they could avail themselves, the pursuit of high levels of physical fitness and sports participation by the female members of society progressed at a snail-like pace. Nearly two decades into the twentieth century, society still expected women to adhere to a subdued demeanor hidden by yards of fabric. In addition, the emancipation of waistlines and feet stuffed into "fashion" shoes took several decades. The medical profession cautioned women against vigorous physical activity. Restrained by clothing, medical restrictions, and social customs, women slowly engaged in exercise and even more slowly pursued highly competitive sports opportunities.

The fashionable corset constricted the waist and probably hindered physical activity on the part of many women. Some women expressed disapproval of the corset. In 1861, Helen Lewis, in Lewis's *New Gymnastics and Boston Journal of Physical Culture* decried the woes of the corset and called it a "sad mistake."[6] The corset was often the subject of heated debate among members of the medical profession. Dr. Robert L. Dickinson, in 1887, reported the results of a study in which he examined waist restriction of females. Dickinson measured the amount of pressure exerted by the corset and the distribution of pressure. In studying 52 corseted women who, with corsets on, measured on the average, two and one half inches smaller in the waist, Dickinson found the total pressure ranged from 30 to 80 pounds. He observed that the abdominal wall was thinned and weakened by the corset and that the liver suffered more direct pressure and was more frequently displaced than any other organ.[7] Fashion not only hindered exercise but contributed to the preservation of the weaker sex concept.

During the 1870s, women encountered controversy over their ability to withstand the rigors of a college education. Influenced by the medical profession and parental concern a number of women's colleges in the East guided their charges with "motherly pampering and overprotectiveness."[8] The Seven College Conference comprised of seven women's colleges in the east and popularly called the Seven Sisters, offered women an early opportunity to pursue higher education. Careful attention was directed toward the health status of Seven Sister students. Exercise and good health habits were required.

THE SEVEN SISTER INSTITUTIONS

Mount Holyoke was the first of the Seven Sister Institutions, founded in 1837. Barnard College was established in 1889, the last to join the Seven College Conference.

Mount Holyoke Female Seminary	1837
later Mount Holyoke College	1888
Vassar College	1865
Smith College	1875
Wellesley College	1875
Society for the Private Collegiate Instruction of Women (chartered as Radcliffe College, 1894)	1879
Barnard College	1889

Physical training at Vassar was accorded early special consideration. Although the gymnasium was not completed when Vassar opened, Elizabeth M. Powell conducted physical training classes in the corridors of the college. Harriet Ballintine in compiling a *History of Physical Training at Vassar College 1865-1915,* depicted the playing areas as ample and secluded. Ballintine, in her search of early Vassar catalogs found college supplied apparatus for calisthenics and for "feminine" sports such as archery, croquet, and shuttlecock. Horseback riding was also a prominent phase of physical training during the early years of Vassar. The "Calisthenium" was ready for use the year after the college opened and housed the riding school, gymnasium, and bowling alley.[9] By the remaining decade of the nineteenth century, most women's colleges offered physical training programs and had erected gymnasiums.

Festivals and pageants on land and sometimes on lakes were customary at women's colleges in the 1890s. Flowers, long dresses, candles and lanterns accentuated the processionals. Leisure hours were often filled with preparations for holiday pageants. Unlike their male counterparts who spent many of their leisure hours engaged in athletics, this form of exercise wrote Susan Walker of Bryn Mawr in 1895 had "not yet acquired the importance for women that they have for men, and social pleasures far outweigh..." athletics.[10]

By the turn of the century, women had proven that they were the intellectual equals of men and debate over their frailties gradually showed evidence of subsiding. Urban women demonstrated they were capable of learning and performing numerous tasks. The Seven Sister colleges, through high academic standards, helped to elevate the status of women. Discrimination against women in their economic, social, and political pursuits persisted and stifled their productivity in the larger social milieu.

WOMEN'S SPORTS BECOME MORE VISIBLE

Sports participation eventually became part of the college woman's activities. The popularity of basketball and other sports resulted in some degree of intercollegiate competition. During the first decade of the twentieth century, the level of competition varied. Some colleges offered intercollegiate sports, while others limited participation to interclass contests. Money from gate receipts was practically nonexistent, and in some instances audiences were admitted by invitation.[11] Later in the early 1920s, intercollegiate sport was curtailed. Playdays, sportsdays, and interclass games became the mode of competition throughout the United States.

SPORTS WITHOUT EDUCATIONAL AFFILIATION

Meanwhile in the late 1870s, the advent of organizations without educational affiliation provided the sportswoman with a chance to compete. Tennis, bowling, archery, and golf were among the first sports which initiated championships for women. These sports were generally accepted as appropriate activities for women partly because early competition was not vigorous and participants could appear dressed like "ladies."

By the 1890s, many newspapers included society columns. Newspaper accounts of luncheons, dinners, travel, club activities, holiday festivities, fashionable attire, and golf and tennis tournaments were of special interest to America's prosperous citizens. Country clubs highlighted many of these events with golf and tennis tournaments. The acceptance of women's participation in golf and tennis can be partially attributed to their involvement in these sports at country clubs which played a prominent role in the lives of wealthy people. Furthermore, the descriptions of women's sports participation by society columnists gave added credibility to women's involvement in golf and tennis.

In February 1874, Mary E. Outerbridge of Staten Island New York observed British army officers playing tennis while vacationing in Bermuda. She purchased the equipment and introduced tennis to America at the Staten Island Cricket and Base Ball Club. Lawn tennis was so well received that club membership nearly doubled three years after its introduction.[12] In 1887, the Philadelphia Cricket Club hosted the women's tournament and Ellen Hansell won the first national title.[12]

In 1875, the National Bowling Association also referred to as the National Bowling League (NBL) was organized. The American Bowling Congress was

Figure 13.1. Archery, a mild form of exercise.

founded in 1895. Bowling in the 1870s was an amusement in which upper-class men and women participated. By 1890, there were numerous bowling clubs for women in New York City and other large cities. In 1890, New York's Ladies' Berkeley Athletic Club "that temple of feminine sport and gymnastics ... (contained) a most complete and well furnished alley for women's use exclusively."[13]

The purpose of the club was to provide women with an opportunity to benefit from exercise. A club house, adjoining the Berkeley Lyceum, housed a gymnasium. In addition there was a reception room and parlor, library, swimming pool, three bowling alleys, baths, dressing and toilet facilities.[14] Athletic clubs were not solely a facet of men's sports participation. As women's physical activities transformed from a recreational to a more organized endeavor athletic clubs offered women a place to take part in sports and opportunities to enter organized competition.

In 1879, the National Archery Association (NAA) was organized. The NAA inaugurated its first tournament, open to men and women, in Chicago's White Stocking Park. Mrs. M.C. Howell of Norwood, Ohio, was one of the most successful archers, having won the women's championship seventeen times between 1883 and 1907.[15] It was not surprising that Mrs. Howell was among the first American women to represent the United States in Olympic archery at St. Louis.

Golf, another of the socially approved sports for women, under the

Figure 13.2. Members of the Staten Island Cricket and Baseball Club, 1887.

auspices of the Amateur Golf Association, later known as the United States Golf Association, provided America's pioneer women golfers with a chance to participate in a national tournament. Mrs. C.S. Brown became the first national champion in 1895.[16]

The Delineator, a magazine appealing to the interests of women, featured fashion, culture, and fine arts articles. In 1902, a series of nine articles on sports for women was published. The underlying theme of the articles was appropriate attire, proper execution of the skills in the various sports, and the benefits of sports participation. Fencing, basketball, swimming, bowling, rowing, golf, tennis, track and field, and horse back riding were included in the series. The publication of the sports series indicated that there was an interest in a variety of sports and that women were being accepted as sports participants.

By the end of the first decade of this century fashion gave way to comfort and became less restricting. Readers of the July 23, 1911 edition of *The New York Times* were made aware that because a woman swam, walked, played golf or tennis, and worked for a living, she could no longer pose as "wasp-waisted and tiny-footed."[17] Women were so concerned about their larger shoe sizes that manufacturers obliged them by adopting a coding system. The increasing stature of women and their visibility in society as workers and to some degree as sportswomen caused them to be pictured in more than the singular domestic role which encompassed only household responsibilities.

THE WOMEN'S SWIMMING ASSOCIATION OF NEW YORK

The Women's Swimming Association of New York (WSA) provided American women with their first opportunity to train for national and international competition under the auspices of an organization founded and developed by women. Charlotte Epstein called together key swimming enthusiasts and on October 20, 1917, the Association was officially organized. The founding members agreed to promote interest in swimming, provide instruction in all phases of aquatics, and offer opportunities for competition.

The "golden years" of the WSA were from 1920 to 1940, and during these years the organization that used a winged foot as a symbol launched America into national and international swimming prominence. At the helm was Louis de Brada Handley, the renowned swimming authority. Handley coached the club from its inception until his death in 1956. He, like other Association workers, received no compensation for coaching the team. Expert coaching and talented swimmers enabled the WSA to enter international competition in 1920. American women, competing in the Antwerp Olympic Games of 1920, primarily because of performances by WSA swimmers and divers, achieved unprecedented success. During the 20 "golden years" of the WSA, 25 Olympic team berths were claimed by the New York based club. In some instances the same swimmer competed in multiple events. The WSA launched America into Olympic prominence by clearly dominating the 1920, 1924, and 1928 Games. From 1920 to 1936 WSA swimmers and divers accounted for seven individual gold medals and had at least one swimmer on three championship 400 meter relay teams. From 1920 to 1940, WSA swimmers held all national outdoor records and 64 national indoor records. They established 17 world records between 1920 and 1936. From 1925 to 1940, the WSA was the power to be challenged at the AAU's national Swimming and Diving Championships. Nine outdoor and indoor championships were claimed in this 15 year span.

By the late 1920s, the production of Olympic caliber swimmers and divers began shifting to other parts of the country. In 1944, the WSA shared the domination of women's swimming with the Riviera Swimming Club of Indianapolis and the Multnomah Club of Portland, Oregon. No longer did the WSA enjoy the status associated with being America's number one swimming power. The advent of AAU age-group swimming competition in 1951 and its national implementation in 1952 furthered women's competitive swimming in the United States.

On September 30, 1974, the Women's Swimming Association of New York officially disbanded after 57 years of existence. The closing was due to four factors:

1. The declining membership meant less financial support
2. Property taxes were continually increasing and the swimming pool became too costly to operate

Figure 13.3. Courtesy Aileen Riggin Soule, 1920, 1924 Olympics.

3. Parents, concerned for their children's safety, were reluctant to permit travel to the city for practice
4. Growth of other clubs in the region, staffed by an increasing number of qualified coaches, offered easier access for increasing numbers of swimmers.

A prominent era in the development of women's swimming in the United States had come to a close. However, the purpose of the Women's Swimming Association was a very functional one in that, aside from encouraging participation in a socially acceptable competitive outlet for women in the 1920s, the level of women's competitive swimming was elevated to a new level of public consciousness through the production of Olympic caliber swimmers.[18]

FENCING

Organized fencing championships for American women were inaugurated in 1912. The competition was sponsored by the New York City based

Figure 13.4. Louis de Brada Handley.

Amateur Fencers' League of America. Adelaide Baylis of New York City won the championship for women.[19] When fencing was added to the women's events in the 1924 Olympic Games, the AFLA provided a channel for Olympic fencing preparation and selection.

WOMEN SEEK THEIR OWN MODEL FOR SPORTS PROGRAMS

Early in the development of collegiate sport programs, women opposed the adoption of a male model for their competitive activities. Frances A. Kellor, writing in the *American Physical Education Review* listed three essential considerations for women's programs:

1. Women's sports should be conducted for large numbers of participants rather than training a few athletes for championship teams.
2. The joy of playing rather than determination to win at any cost should be the most important aspect of women's sports programs.
3. Women's contests should be conducted for the benefit of the players and not for spectators who pay admission fees.[20]

Women physical educators cautioned their peers about the overemphasis on winning, gate receipts, illegal recruiting practices, and other "evils" that were already deeply rooted in men's intercollegiate sports programs.

A stigma to sportswomen grew out of the belief that participation in

Figure 13.5. Former home of the WSA. Courtesy of Dan Donelin, University of Florida.

sports brought out unladylike behavior and masculine appearance in women. Dudley Sargent contributed to the antiathletic sentiment for women by suggesting that women who excelled in sports "either inherited or acquired masculine characteristics." Because Sargent believed women were unable "to bear prolonged mental and physical strain . . . " he thought games and sports should be modified for women. Furthermore, the former president of the American Physical Education Association advocated the cultivation of good form by women rather than the establishment of records. Athletic programs at that time were designed to meet male needs and were not suitable for the more delicate female. Women should:

> know enough about (sports) to be the sympathetic admirer of men and boys . . . This kind of devotion has made heroes of men in the past, and it will continue to make heroes of them in the future.[21]

Another article in the *American Physical Education Review* condemned athletics for excluding those who needed an "upbuilding of health." It was believed that the health of both boys and girls could be "better conserved by having no relation to athletics." The writer called for "teamwork to train toward cooperation, but it should be team against time, rather than against another team."[22] The value, as well as detrimental aspects, of interscholastic and intercollegiate sports programs for females became a frequent topic for debate among physical educators.

BASKETBALL REFLECTS THE STATE OF WOMEN'S COMPETITION

Basketball, the first team sport played extensively by women, reflects the state of women's competition in higher education from prior to the turn of the century through the 1970s. Early in 1892, Senda Berenson read about a new game called basketball and in the spring of 1892, introduced the sport to her students at Smith College. During the winter of 1893, the first interclass game at Smith was played.

In the March 23, 1893, edition of the *Daily Hampshire Gazette* a recount of the inaugural interclass game is described under the caption "Ethics, Esthetics and Ball." The sophomores were pitted against the freshman — the classes of 1895 and 1896. A capacity crowd packed the gymnasium and the excitement of the contest reached a high pitch. Class colors, green for the sophomores and lavender for the freshmen, were displayed on scarfs, flags and clothing. The players, 12 on a side, which included three substitutes, donned blue gymnasium costumes, and each woman wore an arm band exhibiting the color of her class. Readers of the *Gazette* were informed that the 30-minute spectacle produced sore throats from the constant shouting and that "The friends of '96 sang appropriate and encouraging words to the tune of "Long, Long Ago" while "Hold the Fort" was the tune for '95.[23] During the opening tip-off the captain of '95 dislocated her shoulder. According to Miss Berenson's account of the game the already excited onlookers became more excited. The injured player was taken into the office, the joint was pulled into place, a substitute entered the contest, and the game resumed.[24] The final score was 5 to 4 in favor of the sophomores.

Basketball was not only played by women in educational settings but by women who belonged to athletic clubs. Early in 1895, *The National Police Gazette* reported that the Berkeley Ladies' Club in New York City was playing basketball. In a description of the game *The Gazette* depicted the women's version as "skillful depositing of a ball in a basket at opposite ends of the gymnasium.... Light, swift exercise and coolness..."[25] was displayed by the Berkeley ladies. Ill-manners were not condoned because any display of unacceptable behavior resulted in the awarding of 3 points to the opposite team, whereas a goal counted 1 point.

The success of the game went beyond the expectations of the directors of gymnasia for women. Physical training schools adopted basketball and their women graduates helped to introduce the game in many parts of the country.

It supplemented physical training programs and provided an opportunity to teach sportsmanship. Early in April 1896, the University of California at Berkeley and Stanford University agreed to play a basketball game which may have been the first women's intercollegiate basketball contest on the west coast. Like their male counterparts who had relied on the train to travel to their first intercollegiate competition 44 years earlier, the women of Berkeley traveled by rail to San Francisco. The game was played in an Armory, the admission price was 50 cents and ladies only were admitted. Stella McCray, captain of the Stanford nine, summarized in part the state of women's athletics in 1896.

A reporter for the *San Francisco Examiner* quoted Captain McCray's views and aspirations:

> We shall take great satisfaction in having introduced the game and made women's athletics recognized. We have derived great benefit from our training and in what we have learned in a business way. The uniforms will be a cardinal toboggan cap, red sweaters and dark blue bloomers. We are denied cardinal sweaters by the athletic board. . . .
>
> We are not at all discouraged by the little support we have been given in a financial way. There may not be a large attendance, but this is the first game and we could hardly expect a crowd. This was so with football when it started. We hope to make our game as popular as football some day.[26]

The game was played on April 4, 1896 just two days before James Connolly became the first American Olympic champion and the first Olympic victor of the modern era. Women were four years away from participation in the Olympic Games and 80 years away from Olympic basketball. Nevertheless, much excitement accompanied the contest between the Berkeley and Stanford nines. Hardly had the game commenced when a goal sagged and wrote the reporter for the *San Francisco Examiner:*

> interfered with the scientific precision of the game. The aid of men—mere men—would have to be invoked. Two laborers marched in. With a series of muffled screams, Berkeley fled to corners . . . and huddled. . . . Stanford, on the contrary, strutted manfully and indifferently to a convenient area, where the girls threw themselves down in various becoming postures. . . . The job was completed . . . and (the) . . . laborers marched out, . . . the most embarassed beings in the building.

Another incident occurred:

> A man looked in at one of the windows. Instantly, the spectators broke forth in hisses so loud and vehement that he fled in terror. The hissing of an assemblage of women (was) a formidable affair.[27]

The game ended 2 to 1; Stanford defeated Berkeley. A crowd of several hundred men and women students met the victorious team at the train station. The players and their followers returned to the university to celebrate. The houses on "'Faculty row' were illuminated . . . in honor of the team."[28]

Figure 13.6. Stanford vs. University of California, 1896.

As early as 1903, there was a women's basketball team and mascot at the East Florida Seminary now known as the University of Florida. Women had been exposed to basketball for barely a decade; it had reached diverse sections of the country. There was limited intercollegiate competition but apparently no championships among first generation players. The rules varied from region to region probably because women in physical education had not established a network of communication. Teams differed in size from five to nine players and forwards were sometimes referred to as "homes."

COLLEGIATE PHYSICAL EDUCATORS LAUNCH
A RESTORATION CAMPAIGN

Figure 13.7. Woman's basketball team and mascot. East Florida Seminary, 1903. Courtesy of the University of Florida Archives, Gainesville, Florida.

Not long after women began playing basketball rule changes were introduced to curb the roughness of basketball and thereby adapt the game to the more delicate demeanor expected of the female. It was thought that the game's "fighting" features developed aggressive characteristics that were not in harmony with female behavior. Perpetual rule changes also confirm the persistence of women physical educators to regulate the physical demands of the game. The belief that basketball, as played by men, was too vigorous for women prevailed for several decades. Additionally, regulations curtailing competition were continually approved. By 1899, rule modifications were so diverse that few institutions used the same rules. Dissatisfaction with numerous sets of rules led to the appointment of a basketball committee at the Physical Training Conference held at Springfield, Massachusetts in June, 1899. A Basketball Committee was appointed at the Conference and included Dr. Alice B. Foster, All Saints School; Elizabeth A. Wright, Radcliffe College;

Ethel Perrin, Boston Normal School of Gymnastics; Dr. Alice G. Snyder, University of Michigan and Senda Berenson, Smith College.[29] Thus the organization of women's sports within the context of educational institutions was initiated. Although only one sport was of primary concern to the early leaders in physical education, their efforts to offer good experiences for sportswomen provided the foundation for the organization of future women's sports.

CONSTANCE M.K. APPLEBEE INTRODUCES FIELD HOCKEY

While basketball was receiving a great deal of attention from physical educators, another team sport was presented to women. Constance Applebee of England introduced field hockey to the United States during the summer of 1901, and she probably had no thoughts of the game becoming an Olympic sport for women 79 years later. But then, who would have imagined that the first American field hockey match played on a crude field outside the Harvard gymnasium and witnessed by less than two dozen people would have led to the establishment of the sport?

Constance Applebee, known affectionately to American field hockey players as "The Apple," introduced the sport at seven eastern schools in America and thereby established the game in the East. Players from Vassar, Bryn Mawr, Wellesley, Smith, Mt. Holyoke, Radcliffe, and the Boston Normal School of Gymnastics (merged with Wellesley in 1909) helped to spread the game. In 1904, "The Apple" joined the Bryn Mawr faculty and remained at that institution until her retirement in 1928. She contributed to the formulation of a national organization when she helped to organize the United States Field Hockey Association (USFHA) in 1922. In that year she opened her Mt. Pocono Hockey Camp in Pennsylvania and coached there for several years after her retirement.

Women's field hockey continued to grow and numerous clubs were organized, usually in large cities and in proximity to colleges and universities. In addition, summer hockey camps provided women with still another opportunity to pursue their interests in the game. In 1924, Constance Applebee became the editor of *The Sportswoman*, a magazine "published by women, for women, in the interests of women's sports and general physical activities."[30] A variety of sports including winter sports were featured in the magazine. With the help of advisory editors Anne Townsend and Mrs. Edward B. Krumbharr, Constance Applebee kept field hockey enthusiasts informed of the latest hockey events. *The Sportswoman* survived the early depression years but ceased publication in 1936. *The Eagle*, official publication of the USFHA, was first published in 1937 and continues to keep hockey players, coaches, and officials appraised of current developments.[31]

In 1973, Constance Applebee celebrated her 100th birthday and many field hockey enthusiasts from all over the world sent greetings. It was a nice tribute to a woman who spent many years promoting women's field hockey.

Current and former players identify "The Apple" as being synonymous with field hockey.

INTERNATIONAL FIELD HOCKEY

In 1924 and 1933, a team representing the United States toured several European countries. In 1936, teams from Great Britain, Australia, and South Africa toured America. Women's field hockey apparently escaped the criticism from physical educators which was directed at basketball and track and field. Teams which toured Europe seemingly went without disapproval from women leaders in physical education. Most of the competition according to Norma M. Leavitt, who played on Long Island in the 1930s, was centered in clubs. The absence of unfavorable commentary in the physical education literature was due in part to the fact that few men were playing the game and male-female comparisons were not made regarding the style of play. Furthermore, women organized, coached, officiated, and controlled teams, unlike many interscholastic basketball programs which were coached and officiated by men. Women also wore tunics rather than the more abbreviated basketball costumes.

The United States Women's Lacrosse Association was organized in 1931 and developed slowly until after World War II. In 1935, a touring team was selected to compete in the British Isles. Thus American women had embarked on another opportunity to compete at the international level.

AN INDICTMENT AGAINST COMPETITION

In her book, *The Conduct of Physical Education,* Mabel Lee reiterated the criticisms levied against highly organized athletic programs. In the late 1930s, the majority of women physical educators still opposed the male model for intercollegiate sports programs which focused attention on star performers, neglected the unskilled, and emphasized winning at all costs.[32] Leaders in physical education continued to censure athletic programs in the 1930s by speaking against athletics at conferences, criticizing athletics in the literature, and educating faculty and students in the doctrine that depicted intercollegiate sport as an inappropriate experience for women. Women physical educators still had a reputation for disapproval of competition. Mabel Lee clarified the position on competition taken by her peers when she wrote:

> (women physical educators) do believe in the competitive spirit of the true sportsman and they desire for all girls and women an opportunity to experience, in their educational process, the kind of competitive athletics which foster that kind of spirit. Instead of too much competition for a favored few they ask for a moderate amount for all. They merely advocate a democracy rather than an aristocracy of sports.[33]

STANDARDS AND OFFICIALS FOR SPORTS PROGRAMS

The 1899 basketball committee recommended the publication of modified rules for women.[34] The first *Basketball Guide* was published in 1901, but it was not until 1905 that a permanent basketball committee, chaired by Senda Berenson of Smith College, was organized. In 1917, the American Physical Education Association created the Committee on Women's Athletics to accommodate the expansion of women's sports interests. Sports committees of the Committee on Women's Athletics reflected the growing interest in women's involvement in numerous sports. The sports committees composed, revised, and interpreted rules.

THE RULES AND EDITORIAL COMMITTEE

In 1917, William Burdick, President of the American Physical Education Association, appointed Elizabeth Burchenal as the first chairman of the Rules and Editorial Committee of the Committee on Women's Athletics. Originally the Rules and Editorial Committee was established to study problems in women's athletics. The Committee on Women's Athletics formulated programs but did not serve as a legislative body nor did it have the clout to direct women's sports programs on a national basis. A basketball subcommittee was established in 1917 and additional sports committees were added. The Rules and Editorial Committee made, approved, and edited rules. When the Women's Athletic Section reorganized in 1932, the Rules and Editorial Committee became a standing committee of the Section and continued to make and edit rules.[35]

Preliminary plans for dealing with the increasing demand for qualified officials began in 1922 when the National Committee on Women's Basketball (NCWB) discussed the possibility of establishing a national board of officials. Timing for the new board was poor. Because of the varied sets of basketball rules it was thought a standardized examination formulated by a central office was inappropriate. Steps toward the establishment of a national board to develop examinations and set up ratings for officials began in 1925 with the NCWB's appointment of Anita Preston of Temple University as head of an officials' committee for basketball. Standards varied among the new boards, and in 1927 a plan to adopt uniform standards and examinations was initiated by Grace Jones, Chairman of the NCWB and Elise Nelson, 1927–1928 Chairman of the Officials Committee of the NCWB. A favorable poll of the existing boards of officials and a meeting of their chairmen in New York City, April, 1928, resulted in the establishment of a national officials' organization. The new organization, chaired by Helen Shedden of the Seiler School in Harrisburg, Pennsylvania was called the Women's National Officials Rating Committee (WNORC). In that same year, the WNORC was made a subcommittee of the Committee on Women's Athletics. In 1932, the WNORC became a subcommittee of the Women's Rules and Editorial Committee of the National Section on Women's Athletics. By 1942, the WNORC's importance warranted it standing committee status in the NSWA. WNORC standards became more stringent and an expansion of ratings in other sports materialized in 1939 when a volleyball examination was developed. In 1940, the WNORC added softball and tennis ratings. Field hockey umpire's ratings were under the aegis of the USFHA. During World War II the increase in the number of boards nearly came to a standstill. In some instances boards became inactive. Renewed interest in the establishment of additional boards occurred after the war.

Like other organizations affiliated with the AAHPER, the WNORC promoted sports programs for all rather than interscholastic or intercollegiate competition. Furthermore, the WNORC believed girls' and women's sports programs were best served when taught, coached, and officiated by qualified women.[36]

THE ATHLETIC FEDERATION OF COLLEGE WOMEN

In 1916, the criticisms directed toward organized athletic programs and basketball in particular were similar to those voiced in the previous decade. Concern over neglecting the majority, the inappropriateness of some sports for women, and winning at any cost still lingered. Unlike men's sport programs, women's programs, in 1916, still lacked a national organization that set policies for women's sports. Florence Somers called for a national control of women's programs by women.[37]

The need for college athletic associations to meet and discuss organizational procedures for the developing sports programs for women resulted in the formation of the Athletic Conference of American College Women (ACACW), March 9–11, 1917.[38] In 1933 the ACACW became the Athletic Federation of College women (AFCW). Blanche M. Trilling, Director of Physical Education for Women, University of Wisconsin, was responsible for the initial meeting which was held on campus. Trilling suggested that student representatives of Women's Athletic Associations gather to encourage sports participation by college women. The AFCW promoted a close relationship of Women's Athletic Associations with departments of physical education for women. Triannual conventions, a quarterly *Newsletter,* and a series of bulletins kept AFCW members informed of sportsdays, playdays, and special projects to encourage sports participation among college women.[39]

Because of the close alignment of the student-faculty campus organization, it was natural for the AFCW, like other educational affiliated organizations, to oppose interscholastic and intercollegiate competition for women. From its inception, the AFCW contributed to the elimination of highly organized competition for women in the nation's colleges and universities.

Between 1924 and 1940, eleven additional sports committees were established. The Section on Women's Athletics was officially organized at the 1927 American Physical Education Association Convention in Des Moines,

Iowa. In 1932, the organization became the National Section of Women's Athletics.

ELEVATION OF THE COMMITTEE ON WOMEN'S ATHLETICS TO SECTION STATUS AND THE FORMATION OF THE WOMEN'S DIVISION OF THE NATIONAL AMATEUR ATHLETIC FEDERATION

Although problems associated with basketball received a great deal of attention from women physical educators, track and field also played a prominent role in the organization of women's sports. The formation of the Women's Division of the National Amateur Athletic Federation occurred in 1923. The elevation of the Committee on Women's Athletics to section status took place at the 1927 American Physical Education Association Convention in Des Moines, Iowa. The Section on Women's Athletics became known as the National Section of Women's Athletics in 1932. The founding of the former and the change in status of the latter organization came about in part as a result of the entry of an American track and field team of high school girls and college women in the 1922 Women's Olympic Games held in Paris.[40] Participation by the American team in what was regarded as an intensely competitive atmosphere was condemned by many women physical educators. Furthermore, they ranked girls' interscholastic basketball as a nationwide problem.

TRACK AND FIELD

As well as being concerned about high school basketball, the ire of women physical educators was provoked when American women first entered international track and field competition at the 1922 Women's Olympic Games. The Women's Olympics were renamed the Women's World Games because of objections raised by the International Amateur Athletic Federation and the International Olympic Committee. The meet became a focal point for citing problems emerging on the American women's sports scene.

Dr. Harry E. Stewart, a physiotherapist from New Haven, was responsible for gathering the American team that competed in Paris. Stewart, President of the National Women's Track Athletic Association,[41] was a leading proponent of women's track and field in this country. He viewed the growing interest in women's sports from the turn of the century to 1922 as indicating society's acceptance of physical activity. He compared the growth of track and field in the United States from 1916 to 1922 as being on a par with the remarkable expansion of the sport in Europe.[42] Stewart was convinced that American women were ready for international track and field competition. However, interest in track and field among colleges and universities was primarily expressed through participation in telegraphic competition.

Although women participated in track and field they were not trained for vigorous physical efforts and their experiences were not highly competitive.

Stewart's track and field team had sailed without the approval of most women physical educators in the United States. The Committee on Women's Athletics of the American Physical Education Association disapproved of the Paris meet because track and field for women was new and loosely organized. The committee did not believe that track and field in America warranted international exposure because a national team could not be properly chosen from the existing programs.[43] Criticism was also directed against the recruitment of high school girls for the Paris meet. Formal objections by women physical educators were voiced through the American Physical Education Association, the Playground and Recreation Association, and the Women's Division of the National Amateur Athletic Federation.[44] Opposition to highly organized sport revolved around four factors: overexertion during competition, neglect of the masses, overemphasis on winning, and exploitation of athletes in order to win.

THE AAU OFFERS WOMEN OPPORTUNITIES TO COMPETE

Numerous requests for the inclusion of AAU-sponsored swimming competition for women had resulted in special AAU legislation which brought women's swimming under the jurisdiction of the Union on November 17, 1914.[45] Although outside the supervision of educational institutions, highly skilled women were afforded an opportunity to pursue competitive swimming. AAU sponsored swimming has contributed largely to the successful performances of American women in the Olympic Games and other international swimming events.

Early in 1922, the Amateur Athletic Union of the United States expressed interest in supervision of women's track and field in America.[46] The Committee on Women's Athletics of the American Physical Education Association opposed affiliation of women's sports with the AAU. The Committee on Women's Athletics believed that the American Physical Education Association was the only appropriate organization to direct sports programs for women. An AAU Committee on Women's Athletics was appointed as a direct sequel to the women's participation in France. A portion of the November, 1922, AAU meeting was devoted to reviewing reactions that took place as a result of the AAU's interest in controlling women's track and field in the United States. Opposition to AAU control of women's track and field was declared by women physical educators in at least two conferences held prior to the Paris meet.

The AAU was not anxious to increase its responsibilities by accepting jurisdiction over women's track and field. Prior to the AAU involvement no other organization had sought to organize women's track and field on a truly national basis. The Union was concerned over the lack of supervision and direction given to women's track and field in the United States.[47] Despite objections from women in physical education the AAU unanimously decided to assume jurisdiction over women's track and field.[48] Participation by the American team in the 1922 track and field meet also contributed to the curtailment of intercollegiate competition among colleges and universities.

THE WOMEN'S DIVISION OF THE NATIONAL AMATEUR ATHLETIC FEDERATION

The large number of draft rejections during World War I prompted an evaluation of physical training in the armed services and physical activities of the nation's youth. Dissatisfaction with the misconduct of men's athletic programs and a similar trend surfacing in women's sports programs led to the establishment of the Women's Division. National Amateur Athletic Federation. Early in 1922, Secretary of War, John W. Weeks, and Secretary of the Navy, Edwin Denby, met with Mrs. Herbert Hoover to discuss the formation of an organization that would set standards for girls' and women's sports programs. During the early stages of organization, it was suggested that athletic programs for both males and females adhere to the same regulations. Mrs. Hoover, after consulting a number of physical educators, opted for separate organizations.

Mrs. Hoover called a meeting of interested physical educators for April 6–7, 1923. The Washington, D.C. Conference resulted in the establishment of the Women's Division of the National Amateur Athletic Federation.[49] About 200 men and women leaders in education, physical education, and health attended the meeting.[50]

The Women's Division, NAAF, from its beginning promoted opportunities for sports participation by all regardless of skill level. Central to its function was the platform of the Women's Division, NAAF, which aimed to

> promote competition that (stressed) enjoyment of sport and the development of good sportsmanship and character rather than those types that (emphasized) the making and breaking of records and the winning of championships for the enjoyment of spectators or for the athletic reputation or commercial advantage of institutions or organizations.[51]

ORIGINAL RESOLUTIONS

As adopted by the Conference on Athletics and Physical Recreation for Women and Girls in April, 1923

1. Resolved, that it be noted that the term 'athletics' as used in this Conference has often included the problems connected with all types of non-competitive as well as competitive physical activities for girls and women.

2. WHEREAS, the period of childhood and youth is the period of growth in all bodily structures, and

WHEREAS, a satisfactory growth during this period depends upon a large amount of vigorous physical exercise, and

WHEREAS, the strength, endurance, efficiency, and vitality of maturity will depend in very large degree upon the amount of vigorous physical exercise in childhood and youth, and

WHEREAS, normal, wholesome, happy, mental and emotional maturity depends in large part upon joyous, natural, safeguarded big muscle activity in childhood and in youth.

BE IT THEREFORE RESOLVED, (a) That vigorous, active, happy, big muscle activity be liberally provided and maintained and carefully guided for every girl and boy, and (b) That all governments—village, county, state, and national—establish and support adequate opportunities for a universal physical education that will assist in the preparation of our boys and girls for the duties, opportunities and joys of citizenship and of life as a whole.

3. RESOLVED, that there be greater concentration and study on the problems and program of physical activities for the prepubescent as well as for the adolescent girl.

4. RESOLVED, in order to develop those qualities which shall fit girls and women to perform their functions as citizens, (a) That their athletics be conducted with that end definitely in view and be protected from exploitation for the enjoyment of the spectator or for the athletic reputation or commercial advantage of any school or other organization. (b) That schools and other organizations shall stress enjoyment of the sport and development of sportsmanship and minimize the emphasis which is at present laid upon individual accomplishment and the winning of championships.

5. RESOLVED, that for any given group we approve and recommend such selection and administration of athletic activities as makes participation possible for all, and strongly condemn the sacrifice of this object for intensive training (even though physiologically sound) of the few.

6. RESOLVED, (a) That competent women be put in immediate charge of women and girls in their athletic activities even where the administrative supervision may be under the direction of men. (b) That we look toward the establishment of a future policy that shall place the administration as well as teaching and coaching of girls and women in the hands of carefully trained and properly qualified women.

7. WHEREAS, a rugged, national vitality and a high level of public health are the most important resources of a people BE IT THEREFORE RESOLVED, that the teacher training schools, the colleges, the professional schools, and the universities of the United States make curricular and administrative provisions that will emphasize:

1. Knowledge of the basic facts of cause and effect in hygiene that will lead to the formation of discriminating judgements in matters of health.

2. Habits of periodical examination and a demand for scientific health
   service, and
3. Habits of vigorous developmental recreation.
   To this end we recommend:
   (a) That adequate instruction in physical and health education be
       included in the professional preparation of all elementary and
       secondary school teachers.
   (b) That suitable instruction in physical and health education be
       included in the training of volunteer leaders in organized recrea-
       tion programs.
   (c) Definite formulation of the highest modern standards of profes-
       sional education for teachers and supervisors of physical educa-
       tion and recreation, and the provision of adequate opportunity
       for the securing of such education.[52]

With the founding of the Women's Division of the National Amateur
Athletic Federation in 1923 came the nationwide curtailment of intercollegiate competition. Additionally, collegiate sports were controlled through
widespread adherence to rules and standards formulated by the National
Section on Women's Athletics of the American Association for Health,
Physical Education and Recreation. Women's sports programs developed
within Departments of Physical Education for Women whose members
generally adhered to the standards set by these sports organizations.

The Women's Division, NAAF, also was criticized for disapproving of
competition. Agnes Wayman of Barnard College explained that the Women's
Division opposed highly organized competition which included city, state,
and national tournaments at both the interscholastic and intercollegiate
levels in addition to the Olympic Games and other international championships. The Women's Division favored occasional competitive opportunities
that emphasized social and recreational experiences.

During its 17 years of operation, the Women's Division acquired nearly
2,000 individual and group memberships. Indicative of the interest in girls'
and women's sports was the widespread geographical distribution of the
membership. Not only did the Division attract memberships from schools,
colleges, and universities throughout the country, it garnered support from
YWCAs, Girl Scouts, women's clubs, parent-teacher associations, church
organizations, and recreation departments.

The Women's Division was a recognized source of counsel and information in women's sports. Numerous Division publications were distributed
across the country, annual conventions and special meetings provided opportunities for women to discuss problems and program development in athletics,
research studies requested by the membership or in response to a special
need were conducted, and use of the radio and press contributed to the
Division's influence on girls' and women's sports.[53]

The Women's Division developed a close association with the Women's

Athletic Section through an exchange of members on the respective Executive Committees.[54] Before the organizations expanded their services and eventually merged, the Women's Athletic Section complimented the standard-setting Women's Division by establishing and adapting rules for girls' and women's sports.[55] The two groups had an impact on girls' and women's sports as shown by their control of sports programs throughout the country.

GIRLS' INTERSCHOLASTIC BASKETBALL, BANE OF WOMEN PHYSICAL EDUCATORS

Figure 13.08. Courtesy of University of Kentucky Photographic Archives, Margaret I. King Library. The 1921–1922 Oliver High School basketball team from Winchester, Kentucky.

The campaign to improve basketball and the conduct of sports programs involved four generations of collegiate physical educators and spanned nearly two-thirds of a century. Interscholastic basketball spread like an epidemic. By 1926, the same year the AAU held the first national tournament for women, it was considered an acute problem of national significance.[56]

Figure 13.9. Gainesville High School State champions, 1920. Gainesville, Florida.

BASKETBALL: THE SUBJECT OF
ARTICLES, CONVENTION TOPICS

In addition to discussing basketball problems at numerous meetings, collegiate physical educators wrote countless articles depicting the evils of basketball for girls and women. They were particularly concerned with the widespread popularity of girls' interscholastic basketball. Dramatic descriptions of games accented the literature. Marjorie Bateman, Director of Physical Education for Women, Teacher College, Keene, New Hampshire gave the following account of a girls' basketball game:

> The players . . . crouch, . . . bodies tense, ready to leap in any direction. Their eyes shift quickly from ball to opponent. A rush after the ball—two bodies crash in mid-air and tumble to the floor. The radiance in their eyes has changed to an almost insane glitter. The good natured smiles are gone; faces are strained; sweat runs down into the players' eyes; mouths are half open, gasping for breath. It is a fight, and from the faces of the combatants, one would judge it to be a desperate fight. . . . [57]

Bateman referred to basketball as "the sacrifice of the maidens, the slaughter of the innocents, one of the most atrocious crimes committed in the name of education."[58]

Blanche Trilling of the University of Wisconsin, in a speech at the annual meeting of the National Association of Deans of Women in 1927, cited unacceptable practices prevalent in interscholastic basketball. She condemned long trips to contests and travel on school nights, use of male coaches, the practice of sending injured players back into games, lack of physical examinations, general disregard of participants' well-being, play during menstrual periods, championship tournaments which brought on nervous strain and excitement, overemphasis on winning and rivalry, derogatory comments from spectators, lengthy seasons, the involvement of only a small portion of the student body, and, finally, the neglect of other sports and school activities by basketball players.[59] Trilling's arguments against interscholastic basketball were in accord with the consensus of most other women physical educators. Although Trilling did not mention the use of boys' rules by girls' teams, the practice provoked considerable debate.[60] Physical educators believed that modified rules were the remedy for excluding physical contact that could result in serious injury.

A FEW WOMEN FAVORED HIGHLY ORGANIZED COMPETITION

Early in 1929, Helen Bunting, of Stanford University led a small group of women who favored the involvement of the Women's Division of the NAAF with preparations for the 1932 Los Angeles Olympics. It was unclear if Bunting gave her consent to American women entering the Olympic Games. Her comments printed in *The New York Times*, did, however, indicate her approval of the Women's Division conducting women's Olympic competition.[61]

Ina Gittings of the University of Arizona, dared to publicize her views in an article entitled "Why Cramp Competition?" which appeared in the January 1931 issue of *The Journal of Health and Physical Education*. Gittings called for a reestablishment of intercollegiate competition and predicted its return. Remembering her intercollegiate experiences Gittings explained:

> I ... was ... a member of a varsity basketball team which conducted ... two contests a year under almost ideal conditions. Our activity was ... coached by two highly cultured and intelligent women ... I ... felt (no) physical harm from the contests ... The opportunities (to) travel and the contacts made in neighboring states stand out for me as supreme experiences. This would be the testimony of all the girls who were fortunate enough to play on teams during this regime.[62]

A rebuttal appeared in the March 1931 issue of the *Journal*. Varsity competition was condemned because it did not involve the majority of students. Fear of the abuses observed in men's athletics, reasoned the authors, was sufficient cause to continue on course rather than abandon the goal—"a game for every girl—competition for all."[63]

Ten years later, in 1941, Gladys Palmer initiated a women's intercollegiate golf tournament at the Ohio State University. Palmer was criticized by a number of women physical educators. The Ohio State tournament was the first of its kind for college women.

THE MABEL LEE STUDY

The College Women's Section of the Middle West Society of Physical Education asked Mabel Lee in the Spring of 1923 to study intercollegiate sports for women. Twenty-two percent of the 50 colleges and universities reported intercollegiate athletic competition in the 1923 study. In 1930, the Women's Division of the National Amateur Athletic Federation asked Lee to replicate the 1923 study. Women physical educators of the mid-1920s incorporated their "physical activity for all" by modifying rules to suit the ability of the average participant. The thrust of women's sports programs was moving toward participation for all without specialization for the fewer highly skilled athletes. The decline in intercollegiate competition was evident when results of the 1930 study showed that only 12 percent of 98 colleges and universities engaged in intercollegiate competition.[64] Intercollegiate basketball, played in several states before the landmark decision by the Women's Division of the NAAF to eradicate highly competitive sport, had declined by 1930. The Lee study did not represent a large sampling of colleges and universities, nor was it a truly nationwide indicator of the status of intercollegiate sport. The study did reveal that women physical educators were gaining control of sports programs. On the contrary, there were some physical educators who admitted many years after the Lee study that they conducted intercollegiate sports programs under the guise of sportsdays and playdays.

By 1940, nearly all colleges utilized women officials, women coaches and required participants to have medical examinations. Women in colleges and universities engaged in playday, sportsday, and interclass competition. Ina Gittings predicted the playday would "evolve into actual varsity competition or die from pure . . . boredom."[65] Nevertheless collegiate physical educators, through basketball rule changes and standards, bred a game that was nearly immune to highly competitive play, socially oriented, and far less vigorous than the game played by men. They limited the dribble, playing time, travel, and confined players to three, then two, areas of the court. "The goal of athletes (was) not to find the 'best' team or player but to give opportunity . . . to all participating."[66] In essence they opposed competition that was a facsimile of men's athletics and designed their own model for competitive sport. The model was born in a conservative political climate and was complemented by John Dewey's education for all. Furthermore, there were four important considerations which influenced the decisions of these sportswomen: first, the goals of education; second, the well-being of the participants; third, women's role in society; and fourth, the medical knowledge of the day. Physicians in the 1920s and 1930s cautioned women about the dangers of vigorous physical activity.

Communication among physical educators had been established through the physical education literature, through convention gatherings with themes such as "Competition for Girls and Women — More Rather than Less, but of the Right Kind," and through newspapers, radio, and numerous organizations. Women physical educators had banded together in perhaps one of the most unified campaigns in the history of the profession. Unification gave way to specialization and diversification.

TUSKEGEE INSTITUTE PIONEERS COMPETITION FOR HIGHLY SKILLED ATHLETES

While controversy regarding intercollegiate sport for women in white institutions eventually declined, some black institutions provided competition for highly skilled athletes. By 1930, women at Tuskegee Institute, now Tuskegee University, participated in varsity tennis, basketball, and track and field. From 1937 to 1951, Tuskegee's "Tigerettes" dominated the National AAU competition, winning 14 of 15 outdoor championships and five of six indoor championships. Many of the athletes at this coed institution were able to pursue an education and compete in intercollegiate sports because of work-study programs. Dedicated coaches, a supportive physical education department, membership in the Southern Intercollegiate Athletic Conference (SIAC), and good facilities contributed to the success of the intercollegiate program.[67]

MERGER

The decline in interscholastic basketball during the 1940s was in part attributed to a lack of coaches. Physical educators left coaching positions to join the war effort. Furthermore, resources for athletic programs were limited during the war years.

The physical fitness and recreational needs of America's youth in an atmosphere of war prompted a concerted effort on the part of physical educators to contribute to the national preparedness program. The Women's Division, National Amateur Athletic Federation, merged with the National Section of Women's Athletics in June, 1940. Members of the two sports groups believed the maintenance of sound program standards as well as an expansion of services was essential to the war effort. The challenge brought on by the war was thought to be best met by the merger of the Women's Division and the National Section.[68] In June, 1953, the NSWA extended its services and became the National Section for Girls and Women's Sports.

The NSGWS reiterated its position on competition in 1956. Providing equal opportunity for all participants rather than determining the outstanding team or player remained the primary goal of the NSGWS. Most women physical educators still believed the development of physical fitness, leisure time pursuits, and acceptable physical, mental, and social qualities could

best be achieved through a varied sports program that deemphasized a
highly competitive atmosphere.[69]

In 1947, two decades after Blanche Trilling's speech, Norma Leavitt,
while at the University of Missouri, outlined the undesirable as well as
desirable aspects of interschool basketball; it still persisted in some parts of
the country in the late 1940s. Essentially Leavitt's summary of objections was
similar to Trilling's. However, she added four objectionable practices: the
use of male officials, the wearing of abbreviated uniforms, commercialization of the sport, and double-header games in which girls' teams played
before boys' games.[70] In essence, the conduct of the game generated the
concern of four generations of collegiate teachers.

A national decline in interscholastic basketball was evident in the late
1940s. As the disciples of collegiate physical educators entered the public
school systems they spread their doctrine of socially oriented competition.
Their mentors had convinced them "that the evils of interscholastics far
outweighed the values, and no good could ever come from girls participating in interscholastic basketball."[71] Continuance of the competition was
attributed to the prevalence of male coaches and officials. Men who had
been associated with interscholastic programs promoted similar activities
for girls and frequently used boys' rules for girls' games. Additionally, in
some small towns, where there were few other diversions, townspeople
continued to support teams.

During the 1950s, collegiate physical educators persisted with their promotion of social-recreational activities. By this time the problems were
thought to exist primarily in rural secondary schools and in recreation
departments. In November, 1953, Josephine Fiske, Chairman of the National
Section for Girls and Women's Sports reported that qualified women physical educators were rarely hired in small schools. Principals were more
inclined to hire men who, because of their athletic orientation favored
interscholastic competition.[72] Eventually most girls' high school physical
education programs reflected the beliefs of conservative physical educators
in colleges and universities. High school physical educators, schooled in the
collegiate doctrine of sports, stressed social interaction rather than aggressive competition. However, in some states such as Oklahoma, Georgia, Iowa,
and Tennessee, where men were traditionally hired to coach and officiate
girls' basketball, highly competitive programs continued.

Sportsdays in which school groups participated as a unit, Playdays consisting
of organized teams based on representatives from each school, and Telegraphic Meets involving the comparison of results by wire or mail were
highly recommended by the NSGWS in the fall of 1957. Although the
National Section was now being referred to as the Division for Girls and
Women's Sports of the American Association for Health, Physical Education
and Recreation, the elevation to division status did not become official until
January, 1958. Extramural forms of competition were considered acceptable
when scheduled within a limited geographic area and were supplemental to

the intramural program. Lengthy schedules and championships were not thought to benefit participants. However, a softening toward interscholastic and intercollegiate competition was indicated when provisions for these programs were made for girls and women whose needs were not being met through more conservative sports programs such as intramurals. Conditions for interscholastic participation stipulated that:

1. The health of the players is carefully supervised.
2. Girls and women are not exploited for the purpose of promotion.
3. The salary, retention, or promotion of an instructor is not dependent upon the outcome of the games.
4. Qualified women teach, coach, and officiate wherever and whenever possible, and in any case the professional training and experience of the leader meets established standards.
5. The approved, published DGWS rules are used.
6. Schedules are limited, not to exceed maximums set in DGWS standards for specific sports as defined in DGWS Guides.
7. Games, where possible, are scheduled separately from the boys' games.
8. The program, including insurance for players, is financed by school funds and/or allocations of budget rather than gate receipts.
9. Provision is made by the school for safe transportation by bonded carriers with a chaperone responsible to the school accompanying each group.

Additionally, colleges and universities were expected to assume:

1. Sponsorship of women participants as individuals or as members of teams who represent the institution and for whom part or all expenses may be paid.
   a. Colleges or universities organize and promote competitive events.
   b. Outside agencies use college or university facilities. Furthermore, if an institution does assume responsibility for any type of sponsorship the following principles should govern these intercollegiate events:
1. They should be conducted in conformance with DGWS standards of health, participation, leadership, and publicity.
2. They should not curtail the intramural and other extramural programs of the sponsoring institutions or the institutions entering participants.
3. They should not include events in which women participate:

    a. As members of men's intercollegiate athletic teams.

    b. In touch football exhibition games, or any other activities of similar type.

    c. Either with or against men in activities not suitable to competition between men and women, such as basketball, touch football, speedball, soccer, hockey, or lacrosse.[73]

RECOGNITION OF THE HIGHLY SKILLED ATHLETE

In the summer of 1958, a committee comprised of representatives of the National Association for Physical Education of College Women and the Division for Girls and Women's Sports of the AAHPER reported that sports programs did not meet the needs and interests of highly skilled college women. The committee proposed that these organizations expand competitive opportunities by offering extramural sports to college women.[74] For the first time in 25 years women physical educators formally recognized the need to provide sports competition for the highly skilled under the supervision of educational institutions.

In 1958, a Tripartite Committee composed of representatives from the Division for Girls and Women's Sports, the National Association for Physical Education for College Women, and the Athletic Federation of College Women joined to study the women's Intercollegiate Golf Tournament which began in 1941. The Tripartite Committee became the National Joint Committee on Extramural Sports for College Women (NJCESCW) and by 1962 was developing standards for the conduct of state and national events. The NJCESCW did not serve as a promotional agency for intercollegiate sport. Its primary function was to maintain standards of conduct for intercollegiate events.[75] The Joint Committee's scope of activities included the socially sanctioned sports: golf, tennis, skiing, badminton, competitive swimming, synchronized swimming, and fencing. Women were ready to embark on more competitive sports programs but few women were qualified to coach highly skilled athletes. It was also recognized that the demand for officials would exceed the supply of rated officials. In 1963 the DGWS took a stronger stand in favor of interscholastic competition by outlining standards for these programs. Continuation of intramural activities that would compliment athletic programs was strongly emphasized.

THE NATIONAL INSTITUTES

Representatives of the DGWS and the Women's Board of the United States Olympic Development Committee met in March, 1963, to discuss plans for a National Institute on Girls' Sports. The Institute, cosponsored by the Women's Board and the DGWS, was designed: (1) to increase the experiences and offer more opportunities for girls' and women to participate in sport and, (2) to resolve the nationwide needs of girls' and women's sports programs.

Each state was invited to send representatives to the Institute. The representatives were obligated to conduct sports workshops in their respective states for physical educators and recreation personnel.[76] Five institutes were conducted from 1963 to 1969. Diving, fencing, gymnastics, canoeing, kayaking, track and field, skiing, figure skating,[77] basketball, and volleyball.[78] The Institutes provided both men and women with opportunities to learn the latest techniques used to teach basic skills as well as to prepare themselves to coach highly skilled girls and women. Many women experienced coaching preparation for the first time. Never before had women gathered on the basis of nationwide representation to learn and disseminate information for the purpose of coaching highly skilled athletes.

Further impetus to the girls' and women's sports movement came in the spring of 1964 when the Committee on the Medical Aspects of Sports of the American Medical Association issued a statement which strongly favored sports participation by females.[79] Their statement was in sharp contrast to the more conservative opinion voiced three decades earlier.

Because of the national interest in developing competitive sports programs for highly skilled girls and women the DGWS held a Study Conference on Competition for Girls and Women in February, 1965. Twenty men and women educators from high schools and colleges established guidelines for the conduct of interscholastic and intercollegiate sports programs. Emphasis was again placed on the importance of athletic programs to serve as an extension of intramural activities.[80]

COMMISSION ON INTERCOLLEGIATE SPORTS FOR WOMEN

Implementation of guidelines for interscholastic programs was facilitated because in most states athletics for boys and girls were already controlled by high school athletic or activities associations. The previously established National Joint Committee on Extramural Sports for College Women was not an effective agent for national implementation of women's intercollegiate sports programs. In 1965 the NJCESCW, upon agreement by its founding organizations, disbanded. DGWS assumed the Committee's functions and in 1966 decided to develop a Commission on Intercollegiate Sports for Women.[81]

On December 7, 1967, Katherine Ley, chairperson of the new Commission which became the Commission on Intercollegiate Athletics for Women (CIAW), announced the new intercollegiate championships. The CIAW voted to continue the National Golf Tournament which began at Ohio State in 1941 and to cooperate with the USLTA Women's National Collegiate Tennis Championship. In 1969, the CIAW added gymnastics and track and field to its schedule of national championships.[82] A milestone in women's sports occurred when the CIAW assumed the responsibility for designing, sponsoring, and sanctioning women's intercollegiate sport opportunities.

Because of the exploding growth of women's sports and the need for reorganization, the CIAW was terminated in 1971 and the DGWS established the Association for Intercollegiate Athletics for Women (AIAW). In 1974, the DGWS became the National Association for Girls and Women in Sport (NAGWS) of the American Alliance for Health, Physical Education, and Recreation. In 1976, sports leaders recognized that the AIAW, a multisport governing body comprised of collegiate member institutions had needs that differed from those of the other alliances, which were largely made up of individual members. The AIAW, as of June, 1979, separated from the NAGWS and became an autonomous body. Both organizations shared a common yet challenging commitment to promote equality for girls and women in sport.

THE END OF AN ERA

Recognizing that women's sports were growing, attracting greater visibility, and becoming a financial asset, NCAA officials waged a campaign to gain control of women's sports. Lacking financial resources to combat the powerful NCAA, it was inevitable that the AIAW would eventually cease to function. Furthermore, many athletic directors overseeing men's programs and university presidents believed one governing body should control men's and women's athletic programs. In January, 1982, AIAW leaders charged that the NCAA had "... siphoned off members, reduced the number of teams competing in AIAW championships, and caused the organization to lose sites for championships."[83]

The end of a brief era of highly competitive collegiate sport controlled by women ended in an atmosphere charged with emotion and disappointment. The AIAW ceased functioning by the end of the 1981–1982 academic year. A decade later, women's intercollegiate sports programs had gained greater visibility; however, gender equity, the declining number of women coaches, and financial backing are lingering challenges. Women athletes of the 1990s have benefitted from legislation and from the pioneering efforts of AIAW members who sought to provide intercollegiate competition in an atmosphere which stressed the welfare of the participant.

SUMMARY

Women's participation in sports was considered a pastime until late in the nineteenth century. A few pioneer educators believed in the value of physical activity and encouraged women to exercise. Catherine Beecher favored calisthenics to cure distortions and promote graceful movement. In 1861, Dio Lewis established the Normal Institute for Physical Education in Boston where he promoted gymnastics for men, women, and children. The first Young Women's Christian Association was organized in Boston which offered assistance to young women living in urban areas. Extending its services beyond spiritual development, it initiated a summer camp program in 1874 and introduced calisthenics in 1877. During the 1870s, controversy existed concerning a woman's ability to withstand the rigors of a college education. The seven women's colleges located in the east required exercise and good health habits as part of college life. At Vassar College calisthenics and "feminine" sports such as archery, croquet, and shuttlecock were all part of physical training. By the 1890s, most women's colleges offered physical education programs.

By the turn of the century, sports participation became a part of the college women's activities. The level of competition varied in that some colleges offered intercollegiate sports while others engaged in interclass contests. However, in the early 1920s, intercollegiate sport was curtailed throughout the United States with playdays, sportsdays, and interclass games becoming the accepted form of competition. Meanwhile, the formation of organizations without educational affiliation provided the sportswoman an opportunity for open competition. Among the first sports initiating championships for women were tennis, bowling, archery, and golf because they were considered "appropriate" activities. At the turn of the twentieth century, women were developing a growing interest in a variety of sports such as fencing, basketball, swimming, bowling, rowing, and horseback riding. The Women's Swimming Association of New York offered American women their first opportunity to train for national and international competition under the auspices of an organization founded and developed by women.

Basketball was the first team sport played by women in higher education, and it reflected the state of women's competition from prior to the turn of the century through the 1970s. The first interclass game was played in 1893 at Smith College under the direction of Senda Berenson. The game was adopted by physical training schools and their women graduates helped to introduce it to other parts of the country. Soon after women began playing basketball rule changes were introduced to curb roughness and the physical demands of the game. Female physical educators believed that it was too vigorous for women. Because rule modifications were so diverse, a basketball committee was organized in 1899 which initiated the organizing of women's sports in educational institutions.

Another team sport for women was introduced by Constance Applebee in 1901. Field hockey was played at seven eastern schools and became well established. In 1922, Applebee helped to organize a national organization, the United States Field Hockey Association. Women's field hockey in America did not suffer criticism by physical educators, because male-female comparisons were not made regarding the style of play. Furthermore, women were directly involved in the organization and administration of the sport. The majority of women physical educators still objected to highly organized athletic programs in the 1930s. Rather than being opposed to competition they favored a moderate amount for all rather than too much for a favored few.

Unlike men's sports programs, women's programs lacked a national organization. The Athletic Conference of American College Women (ACACW) was formed in 1917 which became the Athletic Federation of College Women (AFCW) in 1933. The AFCW promoted a close relationship of Women's Athletic Associations with women's departments of physical education. From its inception, the AFCW opposed interscholastic and intercollegiate competition for women. The formation of the Women's Division of the National Amateur Athletic Federation occurred in 1923. The Committee on Women's Athletics was elevated to section status at the 1927 American Physical Education Association Convention. The founding of the Athletic Federation and the change in status of the Committee on Women's Athletics was partly due to an American track and field team entry in the 1922 Women's World Games. The team participated in what was considered to be an intensely competitive atmosphere. Objections voiced by concerned groups were based upon overexertion during competition, neglect of the masses, and an overemphasis on winning. The Amateur Athletic Union offered opportunities for competition when they brought women's swimming under their jurisdiction in 1914 and track and field in 1922.

Dissatisfaction with the misconduct of men's athletic programs and a similar trend surfacing in women's programs led to the establishment of the Women's Division, National Amateur Athletic Federation in 1923. It promoted opportunities for sports participation by all regardless of skill level. The Women's Division, NAAF opposed highly organized competition in addition to the Olympic Games and other international contests. During its 17 years of existence, the Women's Division attracted memberships from schools, colleges, and universities throughout the country. A few women favored highly organized competition and the involvement of the Women's Division, NAAF with preparation for the 1932 Los Angeles Olympic Games. By 1940, women in colleges and universities engaged in playday, sportsday, and interclass competition. In 1940, the Women's Division, NAAF merged with the National Section on Women's Athletics. In 1953, the NSWA became the National Section for Girls and Women's Sports and reiterated its position on competition by providing equal opportunity for all. A national decline in interscholastic basketball was evident in the late 1940s.

In 1958, representatives from two organizations reported that sports programs did not meet the needs of highly skilled college women. For the first time in 25 years, women physical educators formally recognized the need to provide sports competition for women with special abilities. By 1962, the National Joint Committee on Extramural Sports for College Women was developing standards for the conduct of state and national events. A National Institute on Girls Sports was developed with five Institutes conducted from 1963 to 1969 in diving, fencing, gymnastics, canoeing, kayaking, track and field, skiing, figure skating, basketball, and volleyball. The Institutes provided men and women with opportunities to coach highly skilled girls and women. It was the first national effort to offer women information for the purpose of helping them to coach gifted athletes. In 1965, the NJCESCW disbanded and a new organization was formed eventually called the Commission on Intercollegiate Athletics for Women. A milestone in women's sports occurred when the CIAW assumed organizational and administrative responsibility for women's intercollegiate sports. Because of the need for reorganization, the CIAW was terminated in 1971 and the Association for Intercollegiate Athletics for Women was established. In 1979, the Association for Intercollegiate Athletics for Women became an autonomous body. By the 1981–1982 academic year, the AIAW ceased operations as a result of the NCAA's desire to control women's sports.

REFERENCES

1. Dorothy S. Ainsworth. *The History of Physical Education in Colleges for Women.* New York: A.S. Barnes and Co., 1930, p. 4.
2. Liva Baker. *I'm Radcliffe! Fly Me!* New York: Macmillan Publishing Co., 1976, pp. 74–75.
3. Edward Mussey Hartwell. "Physical Training in American Colleges." *Circulars of Information of the Bureau of Education.* Washington, D.C.: Government Printing Office, 1885, p. 27.
4. Mary S. Sims. *The Natural History of A Social Institution—The Y.W.C.A.* New York: The Woman's Press, 1936, pp. 5–6.
5. Mary-Stuart Garden. "The YWCA's First 100 Years." *Journal of Health, Physical Education, and Recreation.* 26(February, 1955), pp. 16–17.
6. Helen C. Lewis. "Women's Dress," *Lewis New Gymnastics and Boston Journal of Physical Culture,* 1(March, 1861), p. 77.
7. Robert L. Dickinson. "The Corset," *New York Medical Journal.* (November 5, 1887), p. 14, 28.
8. Liva Baker. *I'm Radcliffe! Fly Me!, op. cit.,* p. 67.
9. Harriet Isabel Ballintine. *History of Physical Training at Vassar 1865–1915.* Poughkeepsie, New York: Lansing and Bros., n.d., pp. 5–8.
10. "Festivals in American Colleges for Women," *The Century Magazine* 49 (January, 1895), pp. 429, 431.
11. Gertrude Dudley and Frances A. Kellor. *Athletic Games in the Education of Women.* New York: Henry Holt and Co., 1909, p. 99.
12. Charles E. Clay. "The Staten Island Cricket and Baseball Club," *Outing,* 11(November, 1887), pp. 104–105.
13. Margaret Bisland. "Bowling for Women," *Outing.* 16(April, 1890), p. 36.
14. Eleanor Waddle. "The Berkeley Ladies' Athletic Club," *Outing.* 15(October, 1889), p. 57.
15. Louis C. Smith. "Our Best Women Archers," *The Sportswoman,* 4 (January, 1927), p. 8.
16. Grantland Rice (ed.). *Spalding Golf Guide 1931.* New York: American Sports Publishing, 1931, p. 79.
17. "Sure Sign of Woman's Emancipation in the Increased Size of Her Shoes," *The New York Times,* July 23, 1911, sec. V, p. 14.
18. Harold A. Lerch and Paula D. Welch, "The Woman's Swimming Association

of New York: The Golden Years 1920–1940," New Orleans: AAHPER Convention, History Academy, March 17, 1979.

19. "Amateur Fencers' League of America," *The Sportswoman,* 3(September, 1923), p. 25.

20. Frances A. Kellor. "Ethical Value of Sports for Women," *American Physical Education Review,* 11(September, 1906), pp. 161–163.

21. Dudley Allen Sargent. "What Athletic Games, If Any, Are Injurious for Women in the Form in Which They are Played by Men?" *American Physical Education Review,* 11(September, 1909), pp. 176, 179, 181.

22. Katherine D. Blake. "General Health of Girls in Relation to Athletics," *American Physical Education Review,* 11(September, 1906), pp. 171, 173.

23. "Ethics, Esthetics and Ball," *Daily Hampshire Gazette,* March 23, 1893, p. 4.

24. Edith Naomi Hill. "Senda Berenson," *Supplement to the Research Quarterly.* 12(October, 1941), p. 662.

25. "Strong Gotham Girls," *The National Police Gazette.* 66(January 26, 1895), p. 7.

26. "Captain McCray's Views," *The Examiner, San Francisco.* April 4, 1896, p. 16.

27. "Waterloo for Berkeley Girls," *The Examiner, San Francisco.* April 5, 1896, p. 11.

28. "Stanford Boys and Girls Wild," *The Examiner, San Francisco.* April 5, 1896, p. 12.

29. Senda Berenson (ed.). *Basket Ball for Women.* New York: American Sports Publishing Co., 1903, pp. 6, 9.

30. Constance M.K. Applebee. "Milestone," *The Sportswoman.* 11(October, 1934), p. 5.

31. Paula Welch. "Field Hockey—A New Olympic Sport," *Coaching: Women's Athletics* 4(September–October, 1978), p. 89.

32. Mabel Lee. *The Conduct of Physical Education.* New York: A.S. Barnes Co., 1937, p. 432.

33. Lee. *Conduct of Physical Education, ibid.,* p. 432.

34. Berenson. *Basket Ball for Women, op. cit.,* p. 9.

35. Helen W. Hazelton. "Seventeen Years of Progress—of the Women's Rules and Editorial Committee of the Women's Athletic Section of the A.P.E.A.," *Journal of Health and Physical Education.* 5(April, 1934), pp. 11, 60.

36. Josephine Fiske. "Twenty Years with WNORC." *Journal of Health, Physical Education and Recreation.* 20(March, 1949), pp. 170–171, 213–215.

37. Florence A. Somers. "The Right Kind of Athletics for Girls." *American Physical Education Review.* 21(June, 1916), pp. 369–375.

38. Marie D. Hartwig. "AFCW Celebrates Its Founding," *Journal of Health and Physical Education.* 13(April, 1942), p. 243.

39. Marguerite Schwarz. "The Athletic Federation of College Women," *Journal of Health and Physical Education.* 7(May, 1936), pp. 345–346.

40. Eline Von Borries. "The History and Functions of the National Section on Women's Athletics," Washington, D.C.: National Section on Women's Athletics of the AAHPER, 1941, pp. 7–12.

41. "Women to Compete in Athletic Games," *The New York Times,* May 8, 1922, p. 22.

42. Harry Eaton Stewart. "Track Athletics for Women," *American Physical Education Review* 27(May, 1922), p. 207.

43. "Report of the Business Meeting of the American Physical Education Association," *American Physical Education Review,* 27(September, 1922), p. 334.

44. Sara Addington. "The Athletic Limitations of Women," *The Ladies Home Journal,* 40(June, 1923), p. 38.

45. Paula D. Welch. "The Emergence of American Women in the Summer Olympic Games 1900–1972." Unpublished dissertation, University of North Carolina at Greensboro, 1975, p. 20.

46. "Women's Track Sports May Come Under AAU Direction," *The New York Times,* March 19, 1922, p. 22.

47. Amateur Athletic Union of the United States, Minutes of the November 20–21, 1922 Meeting (New York: Hotel McAlpin), pp. 25, 34.

48. "Prout Again Chosen As Head of AAU," *The New York Times,* November 22, 1922, p. 25.

49. Alice Allene Sefton. *The Women's Division National Amateur Athletic Federation.* Stanford: Stanford University Press, 1941, pp. 1–9.

50. Agnes Wayman. "Women's Division of the National Amateur Athletic Federation," *Journal of Health and Physical Education* 3(March, 1932), p. 3.

51. Agnes Wayman. *ibid.,* pp. 7, 53.

52. Sefton. *The Women's Division National Amateur Athletic Federation, op. cit.,* pp. 77–79.

53. Wayman. *op. cit.,* p. 6.

54. *American Physical Education Review, op. cit.,* p. 31.

55. Grace B. Daviess. "Women's Athletic Section," *Journal of Health and Physical Education,* 4(December, 1933), p. 41.

56. Helen L. Coops. "Sports for Women," *American Physical Education Review,* (November, 1926), p. 1086, and Blanche Trilling, "Safeguarding Girls Athletics," *Women and Athletics.* New York: A.S. Barnes Co., 1930, p. 11.

57. Marjorie Bateman. "Health Aspects of Girls' Basketball," *Basketball Official Guide.* New York: American Sports Publishing Co., 1936, p. 27.

58. Bateman. *ibid.,* p. 27.

59. Blanche M. Trilling. "Safeguarding Girls Athletics," *Women and Athletics,* New York: A.S. Barnes Co., 1930, pp. 11–12.

60. J. Anna Norris. "Basket Ball—Girls' Rules," (reprint) *Child Health* Magazine, (December, 1924), pp. 1–4.

61. "Non-Olympic Rule Adopted by Women," *The New York Times.* January 6, 1929, sec. XII, p. 1.

62. Ina E. Gittings. "Why Cramp Competition?" *Journal of Health and Physical Education.* 2(January, 1931), p. 12.

63. Grace B. Daviess and Anne F. Hodgkins. "In Answer to 'Why Cramp Competition?'" *Journal of Health and Physical Education.* 2(March, 1931), pp. 29–30.

64. Mabel Lee. "The Case For and Against Intercollegiate Athletics for Women and the Situation Since 1923," *Research Quarterly,* 2(May, 1931), pp. 93–127.

65. Gittings, "Why Cramp Competition?" *op. cit.,* p. 54.

66. Gittings, *ibid.,* p. 54.

67. Paula Welch. "Tuskegee Institute Pioneer in Women's Olympic Track and Field," *The Foil,* Spring, 1988, pp. 10–13.

68. Emma F. Waterman and Ruth H. Atwell. "A Merger the Women's Division,

N.A.A.F.," *Journal of Health and Physical Education.* 12(January, 1941), pp. 36–37.

69. Doris Soliday. "Functions and Purposes of NSGWS" *Journal of Health, Physical Education, and Recreation* 27(October, 1956), p. 51.

70. Norma Leavitt. "Pro's and Con's of Interscholastic Basketball for High School Girls," *Sports Bulletin for Girls and Women,* March, 1947, pp. 7–8.

71. Nora Page Hall. "The Swing of the Pendulum," *Official Basketball Guide — 1941-1942* New York: A.S. Barnes and Co., 1941, p. 27.

72. Josephine Fiske. "The Athletic Federation of College Women and the National Section for Girls and Women's Sports," *AFCW Sportlight,* November, 1953, pp. 1, 3.

73. "Statement of Policies and Procedures for Competition in Girls' and Women's Sports," *Journal of Health, Physical Education, and Recreation,* 28(September, 1957), pp. 57–58.

74. Sara Staff Jernigan. "Women and the Olympics," *Journal of Health, Physical Education, and Recreation,* 33 (April, 1962), p. 26.

75. Katherine Ley and Sara Staff Jernigan. "The Roots and the Tree," *Journal of Health, Physical Education, and Recreation,* 33 (September, 1962), pp. 36, 57.

76. Sara Staff Jernigan. "Two New Institutes on Girls' Sports," *Journal of Health, Physical Education, and Recreation,* 36 (September, 1965), p. 40.

77. Sara Staff Jernigan. "Fresh Winds Are Stirring," *Journal of Health, Physical Education, and Recreation,* 38 (March, 1967), p. 27.

78. Sara Staff Jernigan. "Highlights of the Fifth National Institute on Girls' Sports," *Journal of Health, Physical Education, and Recreation,* 40 (April, 1969), p. 81.

79. "Sports Opportunities for Girls and Women," *Journal of Health, Physical Education, and Recreation,* 35 (November–December, 1964), p. 46.

80. "DGWS Statement of Competition for Girls and Women," *Journal of Health, Physical Education, and Recreation,* 36 (September, 1965), pp. 34–37.

81. Phebe M. Scott and Celeste Ulrich, "Commission on Intercollegiate Sports for Women," *Journal of Health, Physical Education, and Recreation,* 37 (October, 1966), p. 10.

82. "DGWS National Collegiate Tennis Championship for Women," *Journal of Health, Physical Education, and Recreation,* 39 (February, 1968), pp. 24–27.

83. Cheryl M. Fields. "Women's Sports Group Plans for Possible Dissolution," *The Chronicle of Higher Education,* 23 (January 20, 1982), p. 5.

Chapter 14

ATHLETIC WEAR LTD. GROWS TO
A MULTIMILLION DOLLAR INDUSTRY

Because men became extensively involved in sports activities before women, they were first to wear attire that was specifically designed for sport. Hunting, calisthenics, and gymnastics were the earliest activities which provided manufacturers with a market for their mass production of sportswear. In addition to riding and swimming, calisthenics and gymnastics were among the first sports in which women appeared wearing specially designed attire. The general public as well as members of athletic clubs, intercollegiate, and interscholastic teams have provided a steadily growing market for sportswear manufacturers. Attire for sportsmen and women became readily available through mail order houses. Initially, a shirt designed for an athlete was recommended for several sports and only a few types of athletic shoes were available. Uniforms and active sportswear designed for the average American have grown into a multimillion dollar industry.

Wearing apparel is produced from natural or man-made fibers. Early active sportswear was made with natural fibers similar to their form observed in nature. Man-made fibers, some combined with natural fibers, replaced the earliest athletic wear which was cotton or wool. Improvements in fabrics have resulted in more durable, comfortable, and easy-care garments.

Sports attire, though functional and attractive, may also provide protection such as for football. In addition, team unity is fostered by uniforms and traditions such as style and color are observed in uniforms. The tunic in various colors has been a tradition of women's field hockey teams whereas the bold horizontally striped shirt is standard for rugby players. White is traditionally worn by tennis players. Attempts to gain a psychological edge sometimes prompts designers to alter sports attire. A two-piece women's racing swimsuit appeared in the 1979 National AIAW Swimming and Diving Championships. The scanty two-piece suits were connected by a stringlike line in order to meet the "one piece" requirement. The drastic reduction in fabric had an impact on competitors who wondered if the times of the wearers would be drastically reduced. Deception sometimes prompts color selection. Athletes wearing black shoes appear to be moving slower than those wearing white shoes.

Figure 14.1. Ladies riding habit, 1878. Courtesy of Butterick Company, Inc.

Figure 14.2. Left: Gymnastic suit for girls from 8–10 years old. Middle: gymnastic suit for boys from 10–12 years old. Right: gymnastic suit for boys from 6–8 years old.

ATHLETIC FOOTWEAR

Footwear for sports activities has expanded from boots and all-purpose gymnasium shoes to specialized sports shoes with a variety of styles for almost every sport. Since the early 1840s, rubber woven into cloth had been used as inserts in men's and women's shoes. During the 1860s a method for attaching rubber soles was perfected. In 1864, James H. Smart was convinced that women should wear buttoned boots for gymnastic and dumb bell exercises.[1]

In an 1888 publication, Alfred M.A. Beale advised calisthenic participants to wear broad-soled, low-heeled shoes. He advised women not to "attempt any exercises with the feet perched on the top of French heels."[2] As late as 1889, the rubber-soled shoe was a controversial item of sports attire because it heated the foot. Nevertheless, rubber-soled shoes were advocated because they were safe.[3]

Figure 14.3. Costumes of the physical education class, East Florida Seminary, 1902.

By the spring of 1896, the Sears, Roebuck and Company catalog offered a variety of shoes to meet the demands of specialization. The catalog pictured shoes for baseball, tennis, football, cricket, jumping, running, and shoes for the gymnasium. Bicycle and clogging shoes were advertised for both men and women. Tennis shoes were also available for women.

In 1903, suction sole basketball shoes were advertised by the Spalding Company. A special feature of the shoes was nonslip soles. Teams wearing the shoes were said to have had an advantage over non-wearers of the basketball shoe.[4]

Hunting and camping during the first decade of the twentieth century were pursued by men and women. Edward Breck, author of *Way of the Woods* apologetically informed his readers that, "there is unfortunately a very large class of male sportsmen who absolutely refuse to be 'bothered by women-folks in camp.'"[5] Nonetheless, Breck recommended that women wear high waterproof lace-boots for tramping, moccasins for canoeing, and felt slippers for the campsite. Camping and hunting footwear for men included moccasins, hunting boots, larrigan or ankle moccasins, and "sneakers" for the camp.[6] Presumably, because men were thought to have tougher feet, they could choose from two styles of moccasins which could be worn while walking in the woods. Borrowed from American Indians, moccasins were light and soft and pliable. They were supposed to fit like gloves in order to grip sticks and stones.

Sports specification and diverse interests have created an immense market for athletic footwear. Coaches and athletes continually seeking ways to improve performances, experiment with numerous styles of shoes. Sports participants can select from a variety of shoes for nearly every sport. The 1979 October issue of *Runner's World* published test results on 85 shoes for men and 60 shoes for women. Specialized athletic shoes have made the industry more competitive and have improved quality. Participants benefit from quality through injury reduction and performance improvement.

During the late 1970s and early 1980s, shoe manufacturers concentrated on durability and traction according to Dave Kuehls' October, 1993 article in *Runner's World.* Kuehls also wrote that shoe buyers selected from waffle designs, flared heels, blown-rubber soles, and many variations. In the 1980s, midsoles were given more attention with features such as gel and air cushioning. By the 1990s, manufacturers offered fewer varieties and had shifted to emphasizing fitting improvements on the upper part of the shoe.

FROM COSTUME TO UNIFORM

The second half of the nineteenth century gave rise to the clothing and textile industry's ready-made apparel. Elias Howe perfected his second sewing machine and was granted a patent in 1846. With the introduction of the sewing machine into factories came the birth of the ready-to-wear industry in 1849. Isaac Singer patented his improved sewing machine in 1851. In that same year, New York's Knickerbocker Base Ball Club appeared in a game wearing similar outfits consisting of blue trousers, white shirts, and straw hats. It was not until the Civil War that uniformity in clothing sizes occurred. Standardization of size for military uniforms occurred during the Civil War.[7] Later daily wear and sportswear were available in standard sizes.

In 1864, J. Madison Watson described the requisites for men's and women's calisthenic and gymnastics costumes. He maintained that the primary object of costumes for men was:

> not to exhibit rounded and shapely limbs and well-developed muscles, but to give ease and comfort to the student in all of his positions and movements. The military jacket, without unnecessary padding . . . has no useless skirt, and the collar is neither high or stiff. The trowsers . . . are gathered in and buttoned at the ankle, or fastened with an elastic band or a small strap.[8]

Watson described the costume for women:

> Both limbs and trunk are amply draped; and yet how plainly it is seen that the wearer is well developed and untortured. The waist, girdled in at the proper place, is of its natural size.
>
> The dress opens in front, and is both more convenient and more beautiful than one that opens behind. It is so constructed that the wearer's limbs are as free as air; that she can even clap her hands, with arms vertical, above her head without the slightest discomfort. The gown is short, and the skirt is full,

Figure 14.4. 1864 exercise costumes described by Watson.

reaching only to about the middle of the calf. . . . The trowsers, . . . also full, are gathered in at the ankle by a plain band. . . . The material, at all seasons of the year, both for male and female, should be flannel.[9]

Descriptions of women's gymnastics outfits requiring voluminous amounts of fabric continued. In 1864 the *Manual of Free Gymnastic and Dumb-Bell Exercises* advocated the Garibaldi waist, short skirt, and trousers. Warm material lined with flannel was considered necessary to prevent chilling when exercises ceased. The loosely fitting garment had long sleeves that snugged the wrist while the pants were drawn in at the ankle by an elastic band.[10] Women's bathing outfits of the 1860s incorporated the bloomer look. As the sportswomen's participation became more diverse, the bloomer style garment was adapted numerous times for many activities.

Football uniforms were first worn in 1876. Princeton and the University of Pennsylvania, in a rugby football game on November 11, 1876, appeared in unpadded regalia. The Princetonians exhibited a large orange "P" on black shirts, complimented by orange trimming around the neck and wrists. Black knee pants, black stockings, and baseball shoes completed the uniform. The Pennsylvanians wore a less elaborate outfit, a white flannel cricket suit.

Two uniform innovations were attributed to the Princeton football team in 1877. The inventive Princetonians met Harvard wearing laced canvas jackets, called "smocks." The jackets were named smocks after their originator, Ledru P. Smock, of the Princeton team. They added color to their uniforms by donning orange and black jerseys.[11]

Figure 14.5. Ladies flannel bathing costume, 1877. Courtesy of Butterick Fashion Marketing Company.

CHANGES IN FASHION

Changes in fashion have evolved slowly, dependent upon shifts in the economy and societal factors that influenced society as a whole. Urbanization of the population produced a substantial increase in white collar workers, employed in banks, stores, and offices. Consequently, demand for clothing appropriate for city living increased. Reduction of the work week resulted in more leisure time and city dwellers turned to sports participation and spectator sports to fill their leisure hours. Clothing which was functional for active sports participation or proper for spectator use grew in demand.

Ellen Hansell won the first national United States Lawn Tennis Association championship in 1887. By this time the "short" tennis dress reaching the ankles and petticoats and corset were in vogue. Hansell accented her outfit with a felt hat which was not mandatory but considered to be in good taste.

The belted Norfolk jacket, usually plaid, was widely worn by men during the 1880s. In addition, matching knickers along with heavy shoes, leggings, and a deerstalker hat made a suitable hunting outfit. A variation provided by oxfords or laced shoes and hose enabled the wearer to enjoy walking, golf, or other forms of light exercise.[12]

Figure 14.6. Nose guards, padding, and helmets, East Florida Seminary football team, 1903. Courtesy of the University of Florida Archives, Gainesville, Florida.

As the last decade of the nineteenth century approached, boys in gymnasium classes wore sailor or tennis shirts, knickerbockers, and rubber soled shoes in mixed classes. Cotton or worsted tights were seen when females were not present. The corset, a bane of physical activity, was worn even while women exercised. William G. Anderson who with Dr. Jay Seaver began the Chautaugua Summer School for Physical Education in 1886 encouraged women to wear appropriate apparel for gymnasium activities. He observed the adverse effects of the corset when women attempted to raise their arms upward. Anderson conceded that "the corset can not be abolished — it has come to stay; but it can be modified." He contended that some waists "gave form and figure." In addition to rubber-soled shoes, Anderson suggested that girls wear a loose waist or blouse, skirt, and flannel trousers while exercising in mixed classes. The divided skirt was recommended when males were not present.[13]

The Norfolk jacket and its diversity was seen in the 1890s. It was worn for hunting, golfing, fishing, and bicycling often with knickers. Mountaineering shorts were added to the sportsman's wardrobe in the 1890s. A flannel shirt and white knickers were frequently seen on tennis courts. Availability and greater variety of sports garments were evident in the 1890s as participants wore specific outfits for polo, hockey, baseball, track, rowing, tennis, bathing, and bicycling.[14]

Thousands of wheelmen and women took to the nation's roadways in the 1890s when bicycling was a national fad. By 1890, more than one million bicycles were produced. Bicycle clubs, excursions, and special clothing were the order of the day. Women especially benefitted from the cycling craze. It gave them a practical reason for wearing the once scorned bloomer. Bicycling did more to liberate women from voluminous clothing than any other activity. Women of the 1890s could choose from the midcalf skirt which revealed leggings, the floor length skirt or the bifurcated skirt for walking or cycling.

Men who chose to spend their time hunting could choose from numerous outfits in the 1890s. The 1894 Sears, Roebuck and Company catalog featured a complete array of wearing apparel for hunters. Everything from grass suits, which could be used for inclement weather or as a substitute for a blind, to canvas leggings could be purchased or for a few extra cents could be ordered and delivered by mail. The Sears, Roebuck and Company sporting goods department offered functional as well as quality hunting wear. The catalog claimed, "Our canvas goods are the best in the market. We do not handle the cheap stuff." In addition to a variety of sports equipment, the 1894 catalog included tights, shirts, sweaters, and caps which could be used for several sports. A complete line of bicycle clothing to meet the needs of numerous wheelmen, was featured in Sears, Roebuck and Company's spring catalog of 1896. Sears had 10,000 bicycles in stock and encouraged its purchasers to order early to insure prompt shipment.

Outdoor sports have influenced changes in wearing apparel since about the mid-nineteenth century. Increases in the amount of active sportswear paralleled the interest in the growing variety of sports. Specialized sports attire followed the additional demand for active sportswear. Clothing manufacturers expanded their sportswear market by designing special athletic wear which replaced the all-purpose line of products.

In an article entitled "Prevailing Fashions" published in the July 1900 edition of *American Golf,* style-setting women golfers of the day wore piqué skirts. Their shirtwaists were worn with neckties. They accentuated their hats with matching scarves.

Faculty members of women's colleges tried to avoid the masculine influence in their sports programs. They took great pride in the feminine appearance of their sportswomen. In the mid 1890s, baseball at Smith College revealed the attire for the sport and the ideals of femininity. Harriet C. Seelye suggested, "A glance at the young women playing after supper in train-dresses, the batter forgetting to drop the bat as she ran for her base, would convince any doubter of the feminine character of the game."[15]

The June 1898 issue of *The Delineator* featured several sports' costumes which clearly indicated that the women's clothing industry was meeting the demands of large numbers of sportswomen. Specific outfits in a variety of fabrics were designed for cycling, golfing, yachting, bathing, mountain climbing, tennis, and croquet.

Figure 14.7. An early effort at uniformity.

Functional as well as attractive the season's sports apparel depicted the sportswoman in less voluminous and more active outfits. Turn of the century golfers could select long skirts "though not long enough to impede the progress of the player." Jackets were recommended with "trimness being expressed emphatically in suits worn afield." Mountain climbing women could discard petticoats and opt for tights or knickerbockers worn under a skirt which reached nearly to the ankles.[16]

FASHION AND FITNESS, DELICACY AND DIGNITY

Women had been encouraged to engage in physical activity for "healthful and symmetrical development" long before the United States entered the twentieth century. However, they were cautioned to avoid extremes in demeanor and dress as they became more adept sportswomen. Because a woman was on the golf course or tennis court she was not to roll her sleeves to her shoulders or discard her collar or hat. Bathers were encouraged to enjoy the ocean during the summer months but were discouraged from lounging about the shore. Society insisted that "delicacy, dignity, and true womanliness should never be disregarded" in the pursuit of physical fitness through sports.[17]

Men who first played basketball wore almost any style of gymnasium suit or long trousers and short-sleeved jerseys. Some wore track outfits and some used football clothes. The Spalding Company first advertised basketball attire in 1901. Players could select from knee-length padded pants similar to football pants, short padded pants or knee-length jersey tights. Shirts had quarter sleeves and some were sleeveless.[18]

Properly attired female hunters and campers of the early 1900s were cautioned against wearing "those things called bloomers, great formless baggy balloons, that are as ugly as they are awkward." A list of suitable clothing for outdoor women included:

Outer dress: Khaki suit with fairly short skirt; extra cloth skirt; brown or dark grey knickerbockers. Silk neckerchief. Canvas leggings.

Underwear: Two or three sets medium weight combination flannels.

Shirts: Grey flannel shirt, similar to men's, with watchpocket in breast.

Stockings: Cotton for boots, wool for moccasins.

Headgear: Felt hat with stiff brim (to keep veil from face) or straw sailor-hat. Dark chiffon veil. Black silk head-net.

Gloves: Thick chamois. Rubber gloves for washing or other campwork.

Waterproofs: Yachting oilskin jacket. Light-weight rubber poncho. Rubber hood with cape.[19]

Men had to contend with less cumbersome hunting and camping attire but were encouraged to travel with an ample supply of clothes. Wool under-clothing was suggested for the winter and cotton for the summer months. Wool stockings were considered the best; however, cashmere socks next to the skin were to be worn by those with tender feet. A grey flannel shirt with a pocket for a watch was recommended. A strong silk handkerchief served as protection from the sun and cold and also as a bandage or sling. Outer garments consisted of a khaki coat, duxbak trousers or wool knickerbockers, a sweater, a suit of oilskins for rainwear, and a poncho. A widebrimmed felt hat, and a silk or knit wool skull cap were musts for camp wear and nightcaps. Leggings were especially comfortable with knickers when hunters encountered briars and sharp sticks.[20]

As the end of the first decade of the twentieth century approached, the demand for baseball uniforms was so enormous, that the Sears, Roebuck and Company issued a special catalog with illustrations of a variety of baseball uniforms. Sears was proud of the quality of its uniforms and boasted that they "would wear like leather."

In 1916, the Football Rules Committee rejected a rule making it manda-tory for players to wear numerals on uniforms. After a lengthy debate the committee defeated the proposed rule by a 7 to 5 vote. Nearly all committee members agreed that numbers on jerseys would aid spectators in identifying players. On the other hand, coaches maintained that numbered jerseys would enable opposing players and coaches to easily identify each other.[21]

The beginning of the 1920s was an era of prosperity. The knee length skirt was a boon to hosiery manufacturers while the Charleston aided the shoe industry. The corset became a casualty of a more care-free America. College men wore polo coats and raccoon coats. Demand for active sportswear and spectator sports apparel was a natural byproduct of an activity-oriented society that was acknowledging sports heroes and heroines.

Thomas M. Broderick, who was founder of the Broderick Company, Incorporated, introduced girls' gymnasium wear at sporting goods stores in 1929. Broderick was the first to produce competitive sports attire designed specifically for females.

A census report issued in 1935 revealed dramatic increases in men's sport clothing during a four-year period beginning in 1927. Two items, hunting coats and riding breeches, however, declined in production between 1927 and 1931. Shifts in style, sports interests and unstable economic conditions were probable causes for the reduction of these items. In 1927 baseball, basketball, and polo suits were included in "other sport clothing" and in 1931 the three were listed as a separate category with a production quantity of over 300,000. Track or running pants, also excluded as a separate category in 1927, reached a production number of over 3 million in 1931. A category listed as "other sport clothing," showed an increase in quantity of nearly 700,000 during the four-year interval.[22] While the census report did not itemize all sports attire, the specific sports categories of baseball, basketball, polo, and track indicated the major sporting interests of men just prior to the depression and two years into the depression years.

Sport clothing for women was excluded from the 1935 census report because the number of manufacturers of sports attire was not large enough to be included in a specific category. Since the 1850s, women's magazines featured patterns for sports clothes enabling many women to make their own clothes cheaper than ready-made apparel.

An important advancement in easy-care apparel occurred when nylon was introduced in 1938. However, during World War II, government regulations curtailed the amount of fabric for civilian use. Nylon was needed for parachutes and cotton was in demand for military uniforms. Fabric reduction altered clothing styles for both men and women. Ruffles and pockets were limited and men's suits were sold with one rather than two pairs of pants. Cuffs disappeared from men's trousers. Active women benefitted from changing styles of the war years as clothing designers complied with government regulations. With less fabric women's sportswear became more functional.

In 1959, spandex was available for commercial production. The fabric, lightweight and durable, was used in swimming suits, golf jackets, and ski pants. Repeated stretchings did not alter the length of the fabric.[23] In the late 1950s, bonding and laminating with polyurethane foam improved sports attire by imparting warmth and body to the fabric.

The 1960, United States Olympic team appeared in wash-and-wear dress uniforms made of acrylic blended with acetate and rayon. During the early 1960s, sweatshirts were made of a new cloth which resisted rain, snow, moisture and water-borne dirt.[24]

ACTION FASHION

By the end of the 1970s, active sportswear became the fastest growing apparel category. In 1979, Americans spent nearly $200 billion on leisure-related activities. The textile industry, aided by the Olympic movement and America's enthrallment of physical fitness and sports, has ushered in new colors and textures in active and nonactive attire. Participant sportswear of the 1980s reflected visual appeal and versatile styling. Action sportswear in knits and wovens produced from natural and manmade fibers was engineered for comfort, stretch, and absorbency.[25] Sports participation has long been the clothing industry's catalyst for design in the mainstream of fashion. Americans like the active sportswear look whether they are active or not. Although much of the population is overweight, "the lean look" is preferred.

Body awareness of appearance and action is seen in trendy athletic wear. Body clinging swimming suits and gymnastics attire reveals the esthetics of sports through the functional give and take fabric. Cotton next to the body with a satin outer finish allows for comfort and visual appeal in uniforms. Raglan sleeves in sweatshirts and uniforms permit a fuller range of arm movement. Manufacturers have also inserted knit fabrics at yokes and shoulders to allow for more unrestricted motion. What was once dull athletic wear is now available in numerous color combinations. Americans are concerned about their physical fitness status and how they appear while exercising.

Swimwear companies have continued to improve competition, fitness, and fashion suits. Variations in color, design, and fabric have increased markedly since the 1980s. By the 1990s, more sophisticated fabrics with even faster movement through the water were available and endorsed by Olympic swimmers. Arena®, the company that introduced Strush, a high-tech micro fiber, emphasized the low drag coefficient of this "breathable" fabric. Strush suits are made of a tightly woven fabric consisting of polyester filaments and specially produced lycra. The extremely sheer fabric conforms to the shape of the body for a precision fit.[26] Speedo®, another swimwear company, introduced a full torso suit for men and women combining polyester and polyurethane. The full torso suit with a high neck line reduces resistance. High cut shoulders and leg openings allow for freedom of movement.[27] Manufacturers that supply fitness attire and performance wear are constantly testing fabrics and styles to improve performance, comfort, and freedom of movement.

SUMMARY

Men became involved in sports activities before women and were first to wear sporting attire. The earliest activities providing a sporting wear market for manufacturers were hunting, calisthenics, and gymnastics. Among the first activities in which women wore special clothing were riding, swimming, calisthenics and gymnastics. Early sportswear was made of fabrics derived from cotton and wool fibers.

Aside from being functional and attractive, sports attire fosters team unity and tradition. The selection of design or color is sometimes motivated by a desire to gain a psychological advantage over an opponent. Uniforms and sportswear designed for the average American has grown into a multimillion dollar industry.

Athletic footwear has progressed in development from all-purpose shoes to specialized sports shoes having a variety of styles. In the 1860s rubber soles were attached to shoes and calisthenic participants were advised to wear broad-soled, low heeled shoes. In 1896, the Sears, Roebuck and Company catalogue contained a variety of specialized shoes for such activities as baseball, football, cricket, and shoes for the gymnasium. Tennis, bicycle, and clogging shoes were available for both men and women. Hunting and camping was pursued by both sexes in the first decade of the twentieth century with footwear consisting of such items as high waterproof lace boots, moccasins, and hunting boots. Sport specialization and diverse interests have created a large demand for athletic footwear.

The invention of the sewing machine gave rise to the ready-to-wear industry in 1849. Costumes for physically active men and women were fashioned to permit relative freedom of movement while maintaining an acceptable degree of modesty, especially for women. Fashion changes have evolved dependent upon the economy and living conditions brought about by urbanization. Appropriate clothing for city living increased and casual clothing for sports participation or viewing grew in demand.

Sporting manufacturers, even in the early 1900s, designed their apparel for fashion as well as fitness. The Spalding Company advertised basketball attire in 1901 and players could select from three different types of pants and two shirt styles. As the year 1910 approached, a great demand for baseball uniforms prompted Sears, Roebuck and Company to issue a special catalogue illustrating a variety of baseball uniforms. The 1920s was a prosperous era in which sports apparel became a natural part of an activity-oriented society. The women's corset was "cast off" which signaled a more care-free America. The Broderick Company acknowledged this trend and was the first to display competitive sports attire designed specifically for females. Prior to the depression, sports clothing production figures indicated that baseball, basketball, polo, and track dominated men's interests. The number of manufacturers' interest in sport clothing for women was still limited. During the War years the government regulated the amount of fabric for civilian use which altered clothing styles for both men and women. Women profited from federal regulations because sportswear became more functional due to less fabric. In 1959 spandex was used in such items as swimming suits, golf jackets, and ski pants. In the 1960s other synthetic fibers were being commercially used which resisted wrinkling and withstood moisture.

By the end of the 1970s, active sportswear was the fastest growing apparel category. The textile industry has responded to America's fitness and sports consciousness of the 1980s with new sportswear colors and textures enhancing visual appeal and styling. Contemporary knit and woven sportswear is designed to provide maximum comfort, stretch, and absorbency.

REFERENCES

1. James H. Smart. *Manual of Free Gymnastic and Dumb-Bell Exercises.* Cincinnati: Wilson, Hinkle and Co., 1864, p. 37.
2. Alfred M.A. Beale. *Beale's Calisthenics and Light Gymnastics for Young Folks.* New York: Excelsior Publishing House, 1888, p. 114.
3. William G. Anderson. *Light Gymnastics.* New York: Charles E. Merrill Co., 1889, p. 231.
4. James Naismith. *Basketball Its Origin and Development.* New York: Association Press, 1941, p. 90.
5. Edward Breck. *Way of the Woods.* New York: G.P. Putnam's Sons, 1908, pp. 59–60.
6. Breck. *ibid.* pp. 21–25, 61.
7. "Bicentennial of American Textiles," *American Fabrics and Fashions.* No. 106, Winter-Spring 1976, pp. 66–67.
8. J. Madison Watson. *Watson's Manual of Calisthenics: A Systematic Drill-Book Without Apparatus, for Schools, Families and Gymnasiums.* New York: Schermerhorn, Bancroft and Co., 1864, p. 25.
9. Watson. *ibid.* pp. 24–25.
10. Smart. *Manual of Free Gymnastic and Dumb-Bell Exercises. op. cit.* pp. 36–37.
11. Parke H. Davis. *Football the American Intercollegiate Game.* New York: Charles Scribner's Sons, 1912, pp. 67–68, 71.
12. Blanche Payne. *History of Costume from the Ancient Egyptians to the Twentieth Century.* New York: Harper and Row Publishers, 1965, p. 470.
13. Anderson. *Light Gymnastics. op. cit.* pp. 230–231.
14. Payne. *op. cit.* p. 473.
15. Harriet C. Seelye. "Festivals in American Colleges for Women." *The Century Magazine.* 49 (January, 1895), p. 433.
16. "Dress for Outdoor Sports," *The Delineator* 51 (June, 1898), pp. 716–717, 719.
17. "Outdoor Sports," *The Delineator* 54 (July, 1899), p. 105.
18. Naismith. *Basketball Its Origin and Development. op. cit.*, p. 89.
19. Breck. *Way of the Woods. op. cit.* p. 61.
20. Breck. *Way of the Woods. ibid.* pp. 15–21.
21. "Athletic Notes," *Mind and Body* 23 (April, 1916), p. 88.

22. "Wearing Apparel," *Biennial Census of Manufactures 1931.* Washington, D.C.: Government Printing Office, 1935, p. 315.
23. "Man-Made Fibers Fact Book," Man-Made Fiber Producers Association, Inc., 1978. Washington, D.C., 1150 Seventeenth Street, N.W., pp. 23–24.
24. "Bicentennial of American Textiles," *American Fabrics and Fashions,* No. 107, Summer, 1976, pp. 53–54.
25. "Directions," *American Fabrics/Fashions,* No. 116, Summer, 1979, p. 12.
26. "Arena Swimwear Fast Facts," 1995, pp. 1–2.
27. *Speedo Performance Swimwear Spring 1995,* Catalog, p. 41.

Chapter 15

THE ANCIENT OLYMPIC GAMES
PROTOTYPE FOR THE MODERN ERA
776 B.C.–393 A.D.
1896–1912

ANCIENT GREEK ATHLETIC FESTIVALS

The Olympic Games are an unrivaled sports legacy left by the ancient Greeks. Held in honor of the Greek god Zeus, the Olympic Games were conducted every four years at Olympia for nearly 1200 years. Origins of the Olympics have been lost and original accounts of the early contests have not been found. Most authorities designate the beginning of the ancient Games in 776 B.C., the year of the earliest recorded victor, Coroebus of Elis. The Games ended in 393 A.D. when the Emperor Theodosius I banned them.

Although the Olympic Games were the most prestigious of the Panhellenic festival, other notable athletic contests included the Pythian Games honoring Apollo at Delphi; the Isthmian Games held in honor of Poseidon at Corinth; and the Nemean Games at Nemea paying homage to Zeus. The Pythian Games were celebrated at four-year intervals and the Isthmian and Nemean Games were biennial events.

THE ANCIENT OLYMPIC PROGRAM

The Olympic program consisted of four running events: the stade, 200 yards; the diaulos, 400 yards or two stades in length; the race in armor also two stades in length; and a long distance race, the dolichos. The dolichos varied between seven and twenty-four stades. Twenty stades was the most likely distance at Olympia.

The pentathlon was comprised of five events: the long jump, discus, javelin, wrestling, and a foot race which was probably one stade in length. The number of attempts permitted for the field events is unknown. The long jump was a triple or perhaps a double jump because of the great distances that were recorded. The Greeks used weights or halteres to aid them in jumping. The discus and javelin throws used in warfare were among the ancient athletic events. Little is known about the achievements of the Greeks in these contests.

Figure 15.1. The ancient Olympic Stadium, Olympia, Greece.

Boxing was classified according to age-group rather than by weight divisions. A bout continued without interruption until a competitor was knocked out or signaled defeat by raising his hand. Leather straps were worn around the hands presumably to protect the boxer's fingers.

Wrestling was the most popular Greek sport. There were numerous wrestling schools in Greek cities. A match consisted of the best of three falls. There was no interval after a throw; the wrestlers immediately resumed the match. Wrestlers and other Greek athletes rubbed their bodies with olive oil to keep sand and dust out of the pores. Wrestlers also dusted their bodies with a fine powder. After training or competition, the oil was scraped off with a curved instrument known as a strigil.

The pancration was a combination of boxing and wrestling. The object of the event was to cause the opponent to admit defeat. Kicking and hitting were permitted, however, biting and gouging were illegal. Umpires holding rods stood ready to flog an athlete when a rule was broken.[1]

PRIZES FOR THE VICTORS

The Olympic victor received a wild olive wreath while a pine wreath was awarded at the Isthmian Games. Laurel acknowledged the victor at the Pythian Games and wild celery was offered at the Nemean contests.[2] It was an extraordinary honor for one to achieve an Olympic victory. Although a wreath was a revered symbol, many ancient athletes profited from their sports participation. Dr. David Young's book, *The Olympic Myth of Greek Amateur Athletics,* offers significant insight into the amateur versus professional status of ancient Olympic athletes. Young's meticulous investigation of primary sources determined that the ancient Greeks used neither the word nor concept for amateur. While many people believed the modern Olympic Games were founded on the premise of amateurism derived from the ancient Olympics, Dr. Young reveals that, "Ancient athletes regularly competed for valuable prizes in other games before they reached the Olympics, and they openly profited from athletics whenever they could."[3]

WOMEN IN ANCIENT GREEK ATHLETICS

The priestess of Demeter was the only woman permitted at Olympia. The penalty for women who trespassed was the threat of death. Women were to be cast down from Mount Typaeum if discovered at the Olympic Games. Greek women did participate in athletic events but little is known about the origin of these athletic contests or how long they lasted. Historian Rachel Sargent Robinson, through Pausanias, an ancient Greek writer describes one fragment of evidence:

> Every fourth year there is woven for Hera a robe by the Sixteen women, and the same also hold games called Heraea. The games consist of footraces for maidens. These are not all of the same age. The first to run are the youngest; after them come the next in age, and the last to run are the oldest of the maidens. They run in the following way: Their hair hangs down, a tunic reaches to a little above the knee, and they bare the right shoulder as far as the breast. These too have the Olympic stadium reserved for their games, but the course of the stadium is shortened for them by about one-sixth of its length. To the winning maidens they give crowns of olive and a portion of the cow sacrificed to Hera. They may also dedicate statues with their names inscribed upon them.[4]

Although the athletic contests in the women's festival were limited by comparison to the men's contests, their importance was evident as indicated by the ritual associated with participation and victory.

THE DEMISE OF THE ANCIENT OLYMPIC GAMES

The demise of the ancient Greek Olympics was the result of three major factors. First, the Greek States lost their independence under the growth of Roman power. The true spirit of the Greek Games no longer existed with Roman rulers using them for self-aggrandizement. Secondly, in time the Games became too commercialized and professionalism was widespread. Contests were "fixed" with victories being sold for a price. Finally, as the roots of Christianity took firmer hold, the Games were viewed as pagan festivals and therefore abolished.

REVIVAL OF THE OLYMPIC GAMES

For over a century, Baron Pierre de Coubertin had been credited with conceiving the idea of initiating the modern Olympic Games. Dr. David Young's contrasting version of reviving the ancient Olympics surprised followers of the Olympic movement. While Young recognizes that Coubertin played a vital role in restoring the Olympics, he was not the first to propose a plan to resume the ancient contests. Dr. Young's scholarly research uncovered the seeds for the Greek Olympic rejuvenation which began nearly three-quarters of a century prior to Coubertin's Olympic involvement. In 1833, the Greek poet, Panagiotis Soutsos, wrote of the Olympics in his first poem and eventually received financial support from Evangelis Zappas.

A medical doctor, William Penny Brookes, began sponsoring annual athletic events in 1850. A decade earlier, Brookes organized a reading society for the men in Much Wenlock, England. Brookes referred to the athletes who competed in his Much Wenlock athletic events, as the "Olympian class" of his reading society. While Brookes' events were continuing, the Greeks were planning the first modern Olympiad for 1859. Brookes heard about the Greeks' plans, and sent an inquiry about the Games to Sir Thomas Wyse, British ambassador in Athens. Wyse wrote back to Dr. Brookes who responded with advice for the Athens program and prize money for one of the events, the 1500 meters. The 1859 Olympics in Athens were surpassed by a more organized Olympics in 1870. The Greek revival of the modern Olympics faded after another unsuccessful Olympics in 1875. Financial wrangling, political turmoil, and the professional versus amateur issue ended the Greek Olympic revival in the nineteenth century.

In England, Dr. Brookes had become enthralled by the 1859 Olympics in Athens and began calling his contests Olympic Games. His annual Olympics flourished for several years until class conscious elitists began to inject the movement with a call to include "gentlemen" rather than working men or professionals in sports. In 1866, the Amateur Athletic Club (AAC) was formed and defined professional as one who was a mechanic, artisan, or laborer. Brookes eventually met Baron Pierre de Coubertin and shared his Olympic ideas and ideals with the Frenchman.[5]

The Frenchman, Baron Pierre de Coubertin, (1863–1937) was the architect of the modern Olympic Games. Coubertin was enthralled with the idea of bringing together the youth of the world to compete in sport. His dream reached fruition when the first international quadrennial sports festival of the modern era was revived on Easter Sunday, 1896.

Coubertin endeavored to keep sport on a "lofty plane." On the fortieth anniversary of the revival of the Olympic Games, he appealed to the American youth through the Associated Press:

To take up and make fruitful the inheritance I pass on . . . In doing so I evoke the memory of Theodore Roosevelt, of William Sloane and of Andrew D. White and so many of my American friends who have worked willingly with me, understood me and sustained me throughout that long period in which I have had to struggle throughout the world—and particularly in France, my own country—against the lack of understanding of public opinion ill-prepared to appreciate the value of the Olympic revival.[6]

Coubertin served as President of the International Olympic Committee (IOC) from 1896 to 1925. After leaving office he was made Honorary President of the International Olympic Committee for life.

Upon his death September 2, 1937, *The New York Times* referred to Coubertin as "a strong champion of sport for sport's sake." He considered the development of a strong and vigorous manhood as essential to the world, but the "paid gladiator" never appealed to him.[7]

THE INTERNATIONAL OLYMPIC COMMITTEE

Organized in 1894, the IOC is responsible for the control and development of the Olympic Games. The IOC selects and elects its own members from those it deems qualified. Although nearly 200 National Olympic Committees (NOC) exist, not all countries have representatives from the IOC. One IOC member for each country is permitted, however, the IOC may elect a second member if the Summer or Olympic Winter Games have been hosted in a country. Members elected prior to 1966 serve for life, while all others must retire in their 80th year. The IOC elects a president, from its members, for an eight-year term and may re-elect the president for successive four-year terms. The IOC representatives from the United States are Anita DeFrantz and James D. Easton.

THE UNITED STATES OLYMPIC COMMITTEE

By an Act of Congress on September 21, 1950, the United States Olympic Association, now known as the United States Olympic Committee (USOC), was incorporated.[8] On November 8, 1978, The Amateur Sports Act named the USOC" . . . as the coordinating body for amateur athletic activity in the United States directly relating to international amateur athletic competition.[9] USOC jurisdiction includes Olympic and Pan American Games sports. The Amateur Sports Act also charged the USOC with promoting physical fitness and public sports participation through developmental sports programs. Furthermore, the Amateur Sports Act called for recognition of National Governing Bodies (NGB) for Olympic and Pan American Sports.

THE OLYMPIC CALENDAR

The Olympic Games are comprised of the Games of the Olympiad and the Olympic Winter Games. An Olympiad is a period of four successive years which begins with the opening of the Games of the Olympiad and ends with the opening of the following Games. The Games of the Olympiad are held during the first year of the Olympiad which they celebrate. Olympiads are numbered consecutively, beginning with the first Olympic Games of the modern era celebrated in Athens in 1896. Although the Olympics were canceled because of World Wars I and II, the Olympiads of those years are recognized in the numbering system. The first Olympic Winter Games were held in 1924. Beginning with the Chamonix Olympic Winter Games in 1924, the Games are numbered in the order in which they are held. The length of the competitions of the Games of the Olympiad and Olympic Winter Games is now 16 days.

THE OLYMPIC MOTTO, SYMBOL, AND FLAG

"Citius, Altius, Fortius," were the words of a Dominican monk, Father Henri Didon. Translated, the words mean "faster, higher, braver." The modern version is "swifter, higher, stronger." The Olympic symbol is comprised of five rings which are blue, yellow, black, green, and red. The five rings appear on the Olympic flag which has a white background. At least one of these colors appears in the flag of every nation. The flag was introduced at the Antwerp Olympics in 1920. The five rings are symbolic of the union of five continents and the gathering of athletes from all over the world at the Olympic Games.

THE OPENING CEREMONY

The opening ceremony reflects the ideals of the Olympic movement and the cultural displays selected by the Organizing Committee. The President of the International Olympic Committee and the President of the Organizing Committee greet the Sovereign or Head of State who has been invited to open the Olympic Games. After the greeting, which occurs at the entrance to the stadium, the two Presidents, the Sovereign or Head of State, proceed to the tribune of honor. The parade of participants dressed in official uniforms often representing the dress code of their country then follows. The delegations parade in alphabetical order according to the language of the host country, with the exception of the Greek contingent, which leads the parade and the host country which marches last.

After opening remarks by the President of the Organizing Committee and the President of the IOC, the Sovereign or Head of State says: "I declare open the Olympic Games of city celebrating the number Olympiad of the modern era." The Olympic anthem is played and the Olympic flag is raised.

A three-gun salute is fired, followed by the release of pigeons. The Olympic flame, ignited at the altar of Hera at Ancient Olympia, and carried by a relay of runners, is brought into the stadium by the last runner. After circling the track, the runner ignites the Olympic flame, which is not extinguished until the close of the Games.

The Olympic Oath, on behalf of all the athletes, is expressed by an athlete of the host country. A judge from the host country recites the oath of the judges and officials. The national anthem of the host country is played or sung and the artistic program commences.

THE VICTORY CEREMONY

Medals are awarded by the IOC President or an IOC member selected by the IOC President. The president or deputy of the International Federation (IF) involved accompanies the IOC President. The first, second, and third place finishers stand on a platform. The winner is slightly elevated above the second place competitor and stands to the right, while the third athlete stands to the left. The flag of the winner's delegation is raised on the center flagpole, while flags of the second and third finishers are displayed on either side of the center flagpole. An abbreviated anthem of the winner's delegation is played.

THE CLOSING CEREMONY

The athletes march without distinction of nationality. While the Greek national anthem is played, the Greek flag is raised on the right of three flagpoles, then the flag of the country organizing the Games is raised on the center flagpole as its national anthem is played. Finally, the flag of the country organizing the next Olympic Games is raised on the left flagpole while its national anthem is played. After speeches by the President of the Organizing Committee and the IOC President, a fanfare sounds. The Olympic flame is extinguished, the Olympic anthem is played, and the Olympic flag is lowered and carried horizontally out of the stadium.

THE OLYMPIC PROGRAM

To be included in the Olympic Games program, an Olympic sport approved by the IOC must meet these criteria:

1. sports widely practiced by men in at least 75 countries and on four continents, and by women in at least 40 countries and on three continents, may be included in the Games of the Olympiad;
2. sports widely practiced in at least 25 countries and on three continents may be included in the Olympic Winter Games.

Sports are admitted to the Olympic program at least seven years before specific Olympic Games. Events and disciplines are subject to the approval of the IOC in consultation with the recognized international federation. For example, a new event, the women's triple jump, was added to the 1996 Olympic Games, while the discipline of beach volleyball was also added to the 1996 Olympic program.

The IOC recognizes the expertise of each IF and therefore allows the federations, with IOC approval, to set regulations for competition. There are no age restrictions for competitors unless an agreement between the IOC and an IF has been established and is usually based on safety precautions. The IOC reviews the Olympic program after each Olympic Games.[10]

THE INTERNATIONAL OLYMPIC ACADEMY

Although Baron Pierre de Coubertin had intended to establish an institute where young people from all over the world could gather to study the Olympic Games, he never succeeded. John Ketseas of Greece and Dr. Carl Diem of Germany carried out the plan to establish an International Olympic Academy (IOA). Final approval for the IOA was granted by the IOC in 1949. The First Session of the IOA was held June 16–23, 1961, in Ancient Olympia, Greece, 200 miles west of Athens. The first IOA participants met in tents. Permanent facilities were constructed and young people gather each summer to learn about and to help perpetuate the Olympic movement. Located a short distance from the ancient Olympic stadium, the Academy provides a unique atmosphere conducive to the study of the Olympic movement. National Olympic Committees select the participants for the annual session.[11]

ATHENS, 1896, THE FIRST MODERN OLYMPIC GAMES

The 1896 Athens Olympic Games drew competitors from 13 nations. A reporter for *The San Francisco Examiner* estimated that a crowd of 80,000 inside and outside the stadium was present for the opening ceremonies. Nine sports for men were approved for the inaugural Olympics. The selection of the American representatives to Athens did not represent a nationwide effort to formulate a team. Ability to meet travel expenses rather than athletic prowess, was an important consideration for team membership.[12] James B. Connolly was among the first Americans to announce his intentions to participate in the 1896 Games.[13] Connolly, a Harvard University student and avid reader of the classics, was enthralled with the opportunity to travel to Athens where he might encounter the ancient Greek spirit.

When Harvard officials denied Connolly's request for a leave of absence from classes, the Amateur Athletic Union triple jump champion left the university.[14] Connolly, who was affiliated with the Suffolk Athletic Club of Boston, joined nine other members of the 1896 American Olympic contingent. Connolly's teammates were Princeton University students and Boston Athletic Association members. James E. Sullivan of the AAU organized the all-male 1896 team.

On March 20, 1896, America's first Olympians sailed for Naples, the first leg of their journey to Athens. Training on board the steamer consisted of jumping up and down on the steamer's small deck. After 12 days onboard ship, the athletes arrived in Naples where Connolly lost his wallet. Naples police delayed Connolly in an attempt to recover his wallet and nearly cost him the opportunity to compete in the Olympic Games.[15] Writing for *Collier's* in the summer of 1936, Connolly recalled his race to catch the train to Brindisi, the second leg of the journey to Athens:

> The train was moving out. I sprinted down the platform with chaps in uniform yelling and gesturing wildly at me not to try to leap on the running board of the coach from which most of the team . . . were yelling for me to come on. . . . I finished my sprint with a running long step for the running board. (Three teammates) . . . grabbed me and hauled me through the compartment window.[16]

From Brindisi, the athletes took another steamer to Patras and finally arrived in Athens after a 10-hour journey. The Americans had planned to practice for 12 days prior to the beginning of Olympic competition but first sought some much needed sleep soon after arriving in Athens. Their planned 12-day training regime was considerably shortened when they discovered the morning of their first day in Athens that the Games of the first modern Olympiad were to begin that very day! The Games were scheduled according to the Hellenic calendar which was a startling fact previously unknown to the Americans.

On the first day of Olympic competition, James Connolly entered the trials and reached the finals of the triple jump.[17] Ten competitors were in the triple jump. Connolly's jump of 12 meters, seventy centimeters brought wild college cheers from his countrymen, " . . . the peculiarity of which excited much amusement"[18] among the spectators who were unaccustomed to college cheers. On April 6, 1896, James Connolly became the first American Olympic champion and the first Olympic victor of the modern era. Connolly and his teammates won nine of the 12 championships in track and field.[19]

PARIS, 1900, AMERICA'S FIRST WOMAN OLYMPIC CHAMPION

Marion and Georgina Jones were the first American women to compete in the Olympic Games. Shortly after the Jones sisters entered the Olympic tennis tournament, Margaret Abbott, of the Chicago Golf Club, won the women's golf event at Compiegne, France. She was awarded a porcelain bowl trimmed in gold and became the first American woman Olympic champion.[20] There were ten entries in the championship round, including Mary Abbott, mother of Margaret. Americans Polly Whittier and Daria Pratt finished second and third. Ellen Ridgway also of the United States brought the number of American golfers to five. The American tennis players could afford to travel to tournaments and devote the time necessary to excel in their sport. The golfers also represented elite sport in that they could afford to belong to country clubs where golf was the center of social life. The somewhat disorganized Olympics of 1900 dragged on for four months and were confused with the World's Fair. Until recent years, the first generation of American women Olympians have received limited acknowledgment. Nonetheless, they represent a milestone in Olympic history. Twenty years later, swimmer Ethelda Bleibtrey became the first American woman Olympic gold medalist.

American men began a winning tradition in 1896 and again dominated the track and field events in Paris, claiming 17 of the 22 events. Intercollegiate sports and athletic clubs in the United States provided men with opportunities to train and compete, thus enabling them to succeed in international competition. The athletic club movement and intercollegiate sports provided a strong competitive foundation in America.

The Paris Olympics were a disappointment and were attended by few spectators. In some instances officials and athletes failed to appear for some scheduled events.[21] The Olympics were a sideshow of the World's Fair and therefore received little recognition.

Nevertheless, a commemoration of the tenth anniversary of the revival of the ancient Greek festivals was held in Athens in 1906. By 1906, the more organized American Olympic Committee (AOC), led by the influential James E. Sullivan, sent a team which was representative of a national attempt to select competitors. Because the contests occurred only two years after the previous Olympics, they are considered unofficial by the IOC. Some scholars believe the successful 1906 competition saved the Olympic movement.

ST. LOUIS, 1904—NO COMPETITION FOR AMERICAN WOMEN

The Third Olympiad, coinciding with the Democratic National Convention and the World's Fair in St. Louis, included archery for women.[22] Archery, the only sport open to women, was declared by Olympic dignitaries an unofficial exhibition event. No foreign female competitors entered the St. Louis Games of 1904 in which ten nations competed. Leading archers of the 1904 competition were from Cincinnati and included Lydia Scott Howell, Double National, Double Columia, and Team Round Champion. The remaining members of the Team Round were Mrs. H.C. Pollock, Miss L. Taylor, and Mrs. C.S. Woodruff.[23] No coverage was given the archers because news of the day highlighted the Democratic National Convention, the World's Fair, and official Olympic events for men.

Lydia Howell was later judged as one of the truly outstanding archers in America. She won the United States women's archery championship 17 times between 1883 and 1907.[24] It is unfortunate that Lydia Howell was unable to test her skill in official Olympic competition. James E. Sullivan, organizer of America's all-male 1896 Olympic team and of the American Olympic Committee, did not encourage women to compete in the Olympics. Sullivan, chairman of the 1904 Olympic organizing committee, apparently succeeded in curtailing women's events at the St. Louis Games.

The American women's participation in two of the first three Olympiads was not backed by a nationwide effort to select athletes to represent the United States. Early Olympians did not enjoy support from the American Olympic Committee and a national sport organization directed by women for the purpose of training athletes did not exist. Women's competition was not truly international in scope because few women from other countries competed in the early Olympic Games. Records documenting the American woman's involvement in early Olympic competition are scarce.

The St. Louis Olympics were conspicuously dominated by American athletic clubs. All of the track and field championships were won by Americans. The New York Athletic Club, Chicago Athletic Association, Milwaukee Athletic Club, and the Greater New York Irish Athletic Association earned most of the awards.[25] Because of the distance and travel expense, few foreign athletes journeyed to St. Louis. Rivalry between athletic clubs and the partisan spectators made the Games an American sports festival. Basketball, barely a decade old, was introduced as a demonstration sport. Only five teams from the United States participated. The popularity of the sport had not spread to other countries.

Thousands of spectators witnessed the start of the 1904 Olympic marathon, while others cheered the runners as they raced through the country roads. Fred Lorz of New York City was the first to cross the finish line but was quickly disqualified for having accepted a ride in an automobile. He admitted to having ridden for nearly three miles. Thomas Hicks of Cambridge, Massachusetts, was declared the winner of the race in which 31 athletes participated. Although the runners represented six countries, most of them were from the United States.[26]

LONDON, 1908—A DRAMATIC MARATHON

Rain prior to the opening ceremonies of the fourth Olympiad reduced spectator attendance. King Edward VII of Great Britain and Ireland opened the Games before the representatives of 21 countries. The Olympic spirit was gradually spreading and certainly the Games were more accessible to Europeans. Many of the Americans were members of athletic clubs but more collegiate athletes were beginning to represent the United States in the Olympics.[27] During the opening ceremony the American team was greeted "with shouts of general applause, punctuated by the college yells . . . " which, remarked a *London Times* writer, were now familiar because of the presence of Harvard and Yale athletes.[28]

The tug-of-war, in its first of three appearances, marred the competition for the Americans because of what they believed were unfair advantages taken by the British. Americans, in compliance with tug-of-war rules, did not attach anything to their shoes to give them better stance. They charged the British with wearing improper shoes of great weight which enabled them to dig into the ground prior to a pull and thereby gain an unfair advantage. After one half-hearted pull against the British the American tuggers dropped out of the event.[29]

Attendance at the 1908 Olympic Games was disappointing. Most of those attending the Games in the morning were responsible for some part of the conduct of the contests. The crowds increased when ticket prices were reduced.[30]

The marathon especially drew a large number of spectators and according to *The London Times* not a single seat was vacant. While waiting for the marathon finish which had attracted 58 entrants, the spectators viewed pole vaulting, hurdling, wrestling, and swimming.[31] However, the crowd grew silent when they learned that runners were approaching the stadium, heralding the end of their grueling effort. For the second consecutive time in modern Olympic history, the first man to cross the finish line was disqualified. An Italian named Pietro Dorando entered the stadium in a state of utter exhaustion. Staggering and tottering down the final stretch, he fell to the ground three times and was aided by officials each time. He was finally pushed across the finish line. John Hayes, an American, reached the stadium during the Italian's struggle, crossed the finish line of his own accord and was declared the winner of the marathon. Another American, Joseph Forshaw, finished third.[32]

The excitement of the marathon victory seemed to nullify the resentment expressed by Americans in the conduct of the tug-of-war and some of the track events. A rivalry between English and American athletes had developed and the marathon championship was especially pleasing to Americans because the English athletes prided themselves on their successes in distance races. American athletes had now dominated the track and field events for four Olympic Games.

Although no women from the United States journeyed to London to compete in the Olympic Games of 1908, women from Great Britain, Sweden, Hungary, and France took part in tennis. Great Britain was the only country to compete in archery. Unofficial events included displays of foils and mass exercise.[33] American women showed no interest in Olympic Games participation and the all-male AAU and AOC were not advocating their admission to international competition.

When the 1908 Olympic Games concluded there were feelings of exhilaration as well as disappointment. Improved performances were exciting and indicated a rise in the level of competition. Small crowds and disputes over judges' decisions marred the spirit of the Games. A dramatic marathon finish produced an Italian hero who, though assisted by officials, was lauded for completing the race. The marathon was considered by some to be too physically exhausting, but elimination of the event was never achieved.

The Olympians of 1908 were welcomed back to America by an estimated quarter of a million New Yorkers who cheered as the athletes paraded nearly five miles to City Hall. *The New York Times* declared the celebration as "the greatest ovation in the history of athletics . . ."[34] By 1908 more Americans were aware of the Olympic Games and basked in the victories of their countrymen. Because newspapers were aware of the growing appeal of the international sports event, increased space was devoted to coverage of the Games.

OLYMPIC SWIMMING AND DIVING FOR WOMEN

In June, 1910, at the Congress of the International Swimming Federation in Brussels and again in May, 1911, at the International Olympic Committee meeting in Budapest, Great Britain requested the IOC to open swimming and diving competition to women. The IOC voted in favor of Great Britain's proposal and included aquatic events for women in the 1912 Stockholm Olympics.[35] The United States and France were the only countries that opposed women's swimming. Everett C. Brown of the Amateur Athletic Union of the United States suggested that James E. Sullivan was responsible for the negative vote cast by the United States at the international meetings.[36] Although women from other countries gained entry into Olympic swimming and diving, Sullivan continued to squelch efforts by women in this country to enter the realm of Olympic sport. Women from 11 countries participated in tennis, swimming, and diving at the Stockholm Olympic Games. Representatives from Sweden, Denmark, Norway, and Finland took part in the noncompetitive team gymnastic demonstrations.

Ida Schnall, captain of the New York Female Giants baseball club, wrote to *The New York Times* in 1913 and suggested that some women in the United States were interested in the diving events at the Stockholm Olympics. James E. Sullivan's attitude toward women's swimming was also reported in *The New York Times* during 1913. In a letter to E.C. Brennan of the American Life Saving Society, published in *The Times,* Sullivan, President of the AAU wrote:

> ...I notice in the papers that you are conducting schoolboy races in connection with women's events.
>
> Of course you know that the Amateur Athletic Union of the United States does not permit women or girls to be registered in any of its associations, and does not sanction open races for women in connection with Amateur Athletic Union events.[37]

Apparently Sullivan believed that sport was morally a questionable experience for women. Sullivan, reflecting the views of society at large, was unswayed by women's attempts to enter sport. Ida Schnall countered in *The New York Times,* attacking Sullivan's opposition to women's athletic competition.

> ...he is always objecting, and never doing anything to help the cause along for a girls' AAU. He objects to a mild game of ball or any kind of athletics for girls. He objects to girls wearing a comfortable bathing suit. He objects to so many things that it gives me cause to think he must be very narrow minded and that we are in the last century.[38]

STOCKHOLM, 1912—AMERICANS DOMINATE TRACK AND FIELD

One hundred fifty enthusiastic athletes sailed for Stockholm onboard the steamer *Finland* in June 1912. A cork track measuring an eighth of a mile and having a 100-yard straightaway was available for training on board ship.[39] With the exception of the cyclists, the Stockholm bound United States Olympic team trained with two-a-day workouts enroute to the Games. The discus and hammer throwers "hurled" and "put" their implements, attached to lines. They sent them out into the ocean and then hauled them in like fish and repeated their throws. The pistol marksman practiced at a range of 25 yards and the swimmers worked out in two canvas water tanks.[40]

The representation of college athletes on the 1912 Olympic team had increased from previous years. By the fifth Olympiad, intercollegiate athletic programs were more organized with a greater number of athletes from which to select Olympic team members. The team selection process in the United States and the well-trained American athletes who dominated the track and field events were the envy of British partisans and competitors. American officials had improved organizational procedures a great deal since the 1896 Olympics.

The Stars and Stripes were raised on all three flag poles during the victory ceremony for the 100-meter dash. Americans finished first, second, and third in the event. An American sweep also occurred at Stockholm in the 800-meter race. Another notable event occurred when Jim Thorpe of the Carlisle Indian School won the pentathlon and the decathlon.[41]

Stockholm, in contrast to a solemn Fourth Olympiad in London, was the scene of a carnival-like atmosphere. The athletes were loudly cheered by their respective fans. The successful American athletes were enthusiastically received. The Stockholm public heartily applauded the victorious Americans during the parade of winners. One of the most extraordinary accomplishments was Jim Thorpe's victory in the decathlon. Many proclaimed him the greatest all-around athlete. The women tennis champions were also very popular. The close of the Games ended on a tragic note when a Portuguese marathon runner who had collapsed about the 17-mile mark died without regaining consciousness.[42] Again there were objections to the marathon and discussions as to whether it should be continued. Some even predicted the elimination of the marathon from the Olympic program.

Once again New Yorkers turned out in great numbers to welcome the American athletic delegation returning from Stockholm. The most picturesque portion of the parade route was the Swedish-American delegation who cheered as the athletes rode by in automobiles. Several Swedish societies including the Swedish-American Athletic Club were attired in their national costumes.[43] Ethnic athletic clubs had contributed members to America's Olympic team. The contributions of ethnic groups in sport as well as in society was a distinctly American trait. Foreign athletes often spoke of the advantage America had in team selection because of the numerous competitors who were sons of parents from many countries.

THE AAU ASSUMES CONTROL OF WOMEN'S SWIMMING

In March, 1914, Sullivan was present at a meeting of the American Olympic Committee that recorded opposition "to women taking part in any event in which they could not wear long skirts."[44] The American Olympic Committee obviously ruled out vigorous sport and certainly swimming and diving competition for women. Rejection of appropriate sport attire for women and lack of competition sponsored by the AOC left women virtually without opportunities to pursue Olympic competition.

An incident at Rye Beach in August, 1914, again brought the women's swimming issue under attack by Sullivan. The Rye Beach Swimming Club endangered its membership in New York's Metropolitan Association of the AAU when it conducted an exhibition 50-yard swim for women. In discussing the Rye Beach incident Sullivan softened his adament opposition to the women's swimming issue.

> ... if those daring to have swimming races for females in connection with a sanctioned A.A.U. swimming meet will come to the annual meeting of the A.A.U. next November and have the rules changed to allow girls in, all is well and good. But so long as the rules are on our A.A.U. books I will insist that they be lived up to.[45]

Other than the Rye Beach incident no further indication supports the notion that Sullivan would have voted in favor of promoting AAU swimming for women. James E. Sullivan died September 16, 1914. On November 17, 1914, the AAU voted to assume control of women's swimming, thereby becoming the first group to regulate women's swimming in America. Everett Brown, representing the Central AAU Association, presented a positive report of women's aquatic activities after investigating AAU programs in a number of states. At the November meeting Brown appealed for special Union legislation that brought women's swimming under the jurisdiction of the AAU. A major obstacle to women's Olympic competition crumpled with the death of James E. Sullivan. Few women except for mavericks such as Ida Schnall had dared to openly defy the powerful Sullivan. Furthermore, there was no organized attempt by women to officially control highly competitive sports for women in this country before the AAU entered the women's sport scene. The AAU continued to organize national swimming competition for women.

World War I brought an abrupt halt to the Olympic Games and the sixth Olympiad was never celebrated. Berlin had been awarded the 1916 Games. Baron Pierre de Coubertin was deeply disturbed by the cancellation of the Olympic Games.

SUMMARY

The ancient Greek Olympic games were conducted every four years at Olympia for nearly 1200 years. Although other athletic festivals were held to pay homage to various gods, the Olympic festival was the most prestigious. The ancient Olympic program included four running events, the pentathlon, boxing, wrestling, and pancration. Greek women participated in the Heraean Games which were staged every four years and consisted of footraces for maidens. Although limited by comparison to the men's contests, their importance was evident as shown by ritual associated with participation and victory. The demise of the ancient Greek Olympics was attributed to a loss of political independence to the Romans, the waning of the true spirit of the Games, and the spread of Christianity.

The Modern Olympic Games were initiated by Baron Pierre de Coubertin who wished to bring the youth of the world together for sports competition. The first Games of the modern era were held on Easter Sunday, 1896 in Athens. The International Olympic Committee is responsible for controlling and developing the Olympic Games. The IOC selects its own members consisting of one person from each country with a maximum of two members from the larger countries. The Committees' headquarters are located in Lausanne, Switzerland.

The United States Olympic Committee was incorporated by an act of Congress on September 21, 1950. A primary function of the USOC is to coordinate and develop amateur athletics in the United States in relation to international amateur athletic competition. The USOC is a nonpolitical organization with headquarters in Colorado Springs, Colorado.

An Olympiad is a period of four successive years and each Olympiad since 1896 is numbered consecutively. The Games were canceled because of World War I and II. The term "Olympiad" is not used when referring to the Winter Games.

The aims of the Olympic Movement focus upon physical and moral qualities, peace, and goodwill. The Olympic motto, "citius, altius, fortius" was formulated by a Dominican monk.

The Olympic flag recognizes the symbolic union of the five continents and the gathering of athletes throughout the world. The opening and closing ceremonies follow an established format with a featured event being the parade of participants with the Greek contingent leading and the organizing country last. The Olympic flame which is ignited from the alter of Hera at Olympia and carried by a relay of runners to the stadium, is not extinguished until the Games are closed.

The Summer and Winter Olympic program consists of a variety of sports which are common to participating countries. Certain criteria must be met before a sport can be added to the program. The criteria are based upon the extensiveness of participation.

The International Olympic Academy was envisioned by Coubertin but established by John Ketseas of Greece and Dr. Carl Diem from Germany. Final approval for the Academy was granted by the IOC in 1949. The first session of the IOA was held June 16–23, 1961 in Olympia, Greece. Each summer participants gather to study the Olympic Movement at a site a short distance from the ancient Olympic stadium.

The first modern Olympiad celebrated in 1896 drew competitors from Denmark, England, France, Germany, Greece, Hungary, Switzerland, and the United States. The American team was composed of 10 young men affiliated with the Suffolk Athletic club of Boston, the Boston Athletic Association, and Princeton University. The all-male team won nine of the 12 championships in track and field with James Connolly becoming the first American Olympic champion and Olympic victor of the modern era.

At the 1900 Games in Paris, Margaret Abbott became the first American woman to win an Olympic championship. She won the ladies singles golf tournament at Compiegne. American men dominated track and field by winning 17 of the 22 events. The Paris Games were a disappointment in that athletes and officials failed to appear for scheduled events in some instances, and few spectators attended. The AOC issued no official report of the quadrennial event.

The Third Olympiad was held in St. Louis and coincided with the Democratic National Convention and World's Fair. Archery, the only sport for women, was declared by officials as an unofficial or exhibition event. No foreign female competitors entered the Games of 1904 in which ten nations competed. Early female Olympians were not supported by the AOC and they did not have a national sport organization to train athletes. In the early Games women's competition was not truly international in scope because few women from other countries competed. American athletic clubs dominated the St. Louis Olympics with all of the track and field championships being won by Americans. Because of the distance and expense, few foreign athletes participated in St. Louis thereby making the Games largely an American sports festival.

The Fourth Olympiad in London was attended by representatives from twenty-one countries. American women did not compete in 1908 because the all-male dominated AAU and AOC did not support their admission to international competition. Great Britain requested the IOC to open swimming and diving competition to women. The IOC voted in favor of the proposal and scheduled aquatic events for women in the 1912 Stockholm Games. The United States and France opposed the proposal, however, and efforts of American women to enter Olympic sport continued to be thwarted.

The 1912 festival was held in Stockholm with an increased number of college athletes representing the United States. The successful American athletes were very popular with the spectators with many proclaiming Jim Thorpe as the greatest all-around athlete. In 1914, the AOC reaffirmed its stand prohibiting women taking part in any event in which they could not wear long skirts. James E. Sullivan was president of the AAU who also favored this rule. After Sullivan's death in 1914 the AAU voted to assume control of women's swimming in the United States, the first group to do so. The outbreak of World War I brought an abrupt halt to plans for the 1916 Games which had been awarded to Berlin.

REFERENCES

1. H.A. Harris. *Greek Athletes and Athletics.* London: Hutchison, 1964, pp. 65, 77, 80–82, 85, 92, 97–98, 102–103, 106.
2. Harris. *Greek Athletes and Athletics.* ibid. p. 36.
3. David C. Young. *The Olympic Myth of Greek Amateur Athletics,* Chicago: Ares Publishers, Inc., p. 7.
4. Rachel Sargent Robinson. *Sources for the History of Greek Athletics.* Cincinnati: published by the author, 1955, p. 109.
5. David C. Young. "Sorry Baron—But It Wasn't All Your Idea," Unpublished manuscript, pp. 1, 3–7, 9–10, 12, and 15.
6. "De Coubertin Dies; Olympic Leader," *The New York Times.* September 3, 1937, p. 17.
7. Ibid.
8. "Constitution and By-Laws, United States Olympic Committee," Colorado Springs: United States Olympic Committee, 1979, pp. 1–3, 5–6, 11, 20–21.
9. Public Law 95-606, November 8, 1978.
10. Olympic Charter of the International Olympic Committee.
11. Nina K. Pappas. "The Greek Concept Realized in the Founding of the International Olympic Academy," *Perspectives of the Olympic Games Proceedings of the First United States Olympic Academy,* University of Illinois, Chicago Circle, June 19–23, 1977.

12. Arthur Daley. "Sports of the Times," *The New York Times,* April 4, 1951, p. 37.

13. James B. Connolly. "Fifteen Hundred Years Later," *Colliers,* 98(August 1, 1936), pp. 24, 28.

14. Daley. "Sports of the Times," op. cit. p. 37.

15. Connolly. "Fifteen Hundred Years Later," op. cit. pp. 24, 28.

16. *Ibid.*

17. *Ibid.*

18. Spyr P. Lambros and N.G. Polites. *The Olympic Games B.C. 776–A.D. 1896.* New York: American Olympic Committee, 1896, p. 85.

19. James B. Connolly. "They Also Ran," *Collier's.* 82(July 14, 1928) pp. 8, 41.

20. "Chicago Woman Wins at Paris," *The Chicago Record,* October 5, 1900, p. 6.

21. John Kieran. "On Your Mark for the Olympic Games," *The New York Times,* July 26, 1936 sec. VII, p. 10.

22. E.G. Heath. *The Grey Goose Wing A History of Archery.* Greenwich: New York Graphic Society, 1972, p. 207.

23. "Cincinnati Woman Won the Olympic Archery Contest at World's Fair," *The Cincinnati Enquirer,* September 23, 1904, p. 4.

24. Louis C. Smith. "Our Best Women Archers," The Sportswoman, 4(January, 1927), p. 8.

25. "New York Athletes Victory Protested," *The New York Times,* September 4, 1904, p. 10.

26. "American Runner Wins," *The New York Times.* August 31, 1904, p. 5.

27. "Two Americans Win at London," *The New York Times,* July 14, 1908, p. 6.

28. "The King and the Olympic Games," *The London Times,* July 14, 1908, p. 10.

29. "English Unfair in Olympic Games," *The New York Times,* July 18, 1908, p. 5.

30. "The Olympic Games," *The London Times,* July 21, 1908, p. 13.

31. "The Games," *The London Times,* July 25, 1908, p. 8.

32. "Hayes, American, Marathon Winner," *The New York Times,* July 25, 1908, p. 1.

33. Theodore Andrea Cook, (ed.). "Foil Display," *Games of the Fourth Olympiad Official Report of Organizing Committee.* London: The British Olympic Association, 1908, pp. 170, 209, 412, 487.

34. "Thousands Cheer Victors of the Olympic Games," *The New York Times,* August 30, 1908, sec. IV, p. 1.

35. Erik Bergvall, (ed.) "General Programme," *The Fifth Olympiad the Official Report of the Olympic Games Stockholm.* Stockholm: Wahstrom and Widstrand, 1912, p. 713.

36. Amateur Athletic Union of the United States, *Minutes of the November 17, 1914 Meeting.* New York: Waldorf-Astoria Hotel, p. 3.

37. "Bar Mixed Athletics," *The New York Times,* July 13, 1913, sec. VI, p. 2.

38. "Hot Shot for 'Jim' Sullivan," *The New York Times,* July 19, 1913, p. 5.

39. "American Athletes Sail for Stockholm," *The New York Times,* June 15, 1912, p. 9.

40. "Training Aboard Ship," *The New York Times,* June 17, 1912, p. 10.

41. "Americans Capture First Olympic Race," *The New York Times,* July 8, 1912, p. 1.

42. "America First As Olympics End," *The New York Times,* July 16, 1912, pp. 1–2.

43. "Olympic Champions Cheered and Dined," *The New York Times,* August 25, 1912, p. 4.
44. "No Women Athletes for American Team," *The New York Times,* March 31, 1914, p. 9.
45. "Rye Beach Club in Bad," *The New York Times,* August 12, 1914, p. 7.

Chapter 16

THE SUMMER OLYMPIC GAMES 1920-1936

ANTWERP, 1920—AQUATIC DEBUT FOR AMERICAN WOMEN

The flames of World War I extinguished the celebration of the sixth modern Olympiad. The 1916 Olympic Games, awarded to Berlin, unlike their ancient counterparts had no effect on halting the devastation of war. When the war ended, Antwerp was granted the honor of hosting the 1920 Olympics. Servicemen from both the United States Army and Navy, a reminder of America's deep involvement in World War I, comprised a large proportion of the American delegation to Antwerp.

In their Olympic aquatic debut, American women won four of the five swimming and diving events. The amazing naiads not only won the two individual swimming events but in addition, claimed the bronze and silver medals in the 100- and 300-meter freestyle races. The United States' first distaff swimming gold medalist was Ethelda Bleibtrey. She placed first in both the 100-meter freestyle and the 300-meter freestyle events. Bleibtrey was also a member of the championship four hundred meter relay team.[1]

Foreign entrants withdrew from the fancy diving competition after seeing the Americans practice.[2] It was obvious to them that the Americans had progressed beyond their skill levels. In addition to the required fancy dives, competitors had to execute any dive drawn from a hat by Olympic judges. Preliminary competition was omitted and there were only four Americans in the finals. Olympic officials scheduled the diving competition early in the morning to avoid criticism for continuing international competition in which only one nation participated.

Helen Wainwright returned to the Hostess Hotel, having earned the Olympic fancy diving championship, and had lunch with 14-year-old Aileen Riggin who was the youngest member on the team. An error was discovered in the diving computations and Olympic officials declared Riggin the champion with Wainwright as the silver medal recipient.[3]

Much of the swimmers and divers success at Antwerp can be attributed to the Women's Swimming Association of New York (WSA). The combination of skilled athletes and WSA instruction produced the nucleus of the 1920 Olympic Team. Six of the 15 team members were from the WSA with club members winning four gold medals.

The American men, in an outstanding display of aquatic prowess, won five of the seven swimming events and two of the three Olympic diving titles. Hawaiian Duke Kahanamoko captured the 100-meter freestyle event and was a member of the championship 100-meter relay team. Norman Ross earned three gold medals. Ross placed first in the 400- and 1500-meter freestyle events. He also swam in the 800-meter relay race.

American men entered 15 of the 20 Olympic sports. In addition to outstanding performances in swimming, the United States won more championships than any other country in boxing, shooting, and rowing. The track and field team finished first, second, or third in 20 of the 28 events. Charles Paddock, the leading American track man, took the gold medal in the 100-meter dash and the silver medal in the 200-meter race. He was also a member of the winning 400-meter relay team. Only two countries finished one-two-three in a single event. The United States swept the first three places in the 400-meter hurdles while Finland took the top four places in the javelin throw.[4]

THE UNITED STATES LAWN TENNIS ASSOCIATION AND OLYMPIC TENNIS

The 1920 Olympics involved dissension between the United States Lawn Tennis Association (USLTA) and Olympic officials. In November 1919, the USLTA accepted the American Olympic Committee's invitation to participate in the Antwerp Games. Not long after the USLTA accepted the Olympic invitation the dates for the Antwerp competition were announced. Because the Olympic competition coincided with the United States National Tennis Championships, the USLTA requested that Olympic authorities change the dates of the Antwerp matches. A change was impossible because the tennis courts were not scheduled for completion until mid-August 1920 and later dates did not coincide with the Olympics. The USLTA withdrew from the Antwerp Olympics because the Olympic tennis schedule was not altered. Thirteen nations entered Olympic tennis open to men and women in Antwerp.[5]

The USLTA's withdrawal from the Antwerp Games was unfortunate as it prevented both men and women from representing the United States in Olympic tennis. The USLTA was in a better position to change an annual national tournament rather than expecting Olympic officials to change quadrennial competition involving 13 countries.

PARIS, 1924—THE END OF OLYMPIC TENNIS

The second swimming and diving appearance by American women at the Paris Olympics established America as a swimming and diving power. Five out of six first places in swimming events and both diving crowns were won by American women. Gertrude Ederle, who was to conquer the English Channel in 1926, led the United States team by acquiring a gold medal in

Figure 16.1. The 1920 Olympic team parades in New York City. Courtesy of Alice Lord Landon.

Figure 16.2. Mayor John Hylan receives the 1920 Olympic team. Courtesy of Alice Lord Landon.

the 400-meter relay and bronze medals in the 100- and 400-meter freestyle events.[6]

John Weissmuller, who was later to star as one of Hollywood's Tarzans, secured two individual gold medals in the 100- and 200-meter freestyle events and was a member of the championship 800-meter freestyle relay team.[7] The American men contributed to the United States domination of the aquatic competition with five out of six swimming victories and Albert White's first place finishes in two of the three diving events.[8]

OLYMPIC TENNIS

As with the 1920 Games the USLTA received an invitation to participate in the 1924 Olympics. A scheduling conflict was avoided this time and Helen Wills entered and won the women's singles event, and teamed with Hazel Wightman to claim the doubles championship. Recalling the excitement of her appointment to the Olympic team, Helen Wills reflected:

> ... in May, just before the final examination at college, I had word from the United States Lawn Tennis Association that I had been chosen to be a member of the Olympic tennis team. . . . It would have been difficult for me to keep my mind on the college examinations, had I not been so concerned about them. I worried about all of them, but especially about zoology. When I heard I had an "A" on my zoology paper, I felt I could face Olympic tennis with a clear conscience.[9]

The United States was clearly in command of the Olympic tennis courts. Both mixed doubles teams met in the finals. Hazel Wightman and R. Norris Williams II defeated Marion Jessup and Vincent Richards.[10] Vincent Richards won the men's singles championship and teamed with Francis T. Hunter for the doubles victory.[11]

Tennis was excluded from the Olympic program following the Paris Games. The International Lawn Tennis Federation (ILTF) criticized the conduct of the tennis events in Paris and demanded more Olympic representation by tennis officials. The International Olympic Committee refused to comply with the ILTF's demands and the International Lawn Tennis Federation withdrew from the 1928 Olympics.[12]

Women's fencing was added to the 1924 Olympic program. The Amateur Fencer's League of America served as the Olympic selection organization for America's entry into the international contests.[13] Adeline Gehrig and Irma Hopper were eliminated in the first round of the individual foils competition.[14]

The success of American women in Olympic tennis and swimming was due in part to the competition available to women. The USLTA had included women in its championship since 1887. The Women's Swimming Association of New York and the Amateur Athletic Union of the United States promoted aquatic competition for women prior to the 1920s. Fencing, on the other hand, was popular only in major cities in the United States and competitive opportunities were not as extensive as those in tennis and swimming.

Previous superiority in track and field by American men, as well as the popularity of the sport, stimulated more intense preparations among foreign athletes. Outstanding performances were exhibited by athletes representing a variety of nations. In 1924, American men shared track and field superiority with the Finns. Each country won 12 events out of a possible 29. Finland's Paavo Nurmi dominated the running events by winning the 1,500-meter, 5,000-meter, and 10,000-meter races.

The United States excelled in baseball, gymnastics, and wrestling. Baseball gained recognition in the 1924 Olympics during an exhibition played at Colombes Stadium. The Ranelagh Club of Paris lost by a score of 5–0 to the American nine who were from several different states.[15] For the first time since 1904 an American claimed an Olympic gymnastics title when Frank Kriz won the long horse event. The United States reigned over catch-as-catch-can wrestling by winning four of the seven weight classifications.[16]

AMSTERDAM, 1928—OLYMPIC TRACK AND FIELD, A FIRST FOR WOMEN

Track and field was first included in the women's Olympic program in 1928. While the American women were making their first appearance in Olympic track and field their male counterparts, in an eighth trip to the Olympic Games, managed to win only three of the 13 track events. On the other hand, the superiority of the American men in the field events was evident; when the competition was over they had won five of the nine gold medals. No other country claimed more than one of the remaining four gold medals. Despite outstanding accomplishments in the field events Americans found difficulty in accepting the track results at Amsterdam. Explanations for the disappointing track performances ranged from criticism of team selection to superior competition from foreign athletes. Some critics thought the American selection process involving lengthy eliminations kept athletes "keyed up" for too long and caused them to reach their peak before the Olympic Games. Another explanation for poor performances at Amsterdam was "overcoaching and overmanaging." It was reported that some athletes admitted, "they (got) orders from so many sources that they (didn't) know which to take."[17]

Track coach Jack Ryder suggested that conceit and formidable competition beat the Americans. Ryder's impression of the team was printed in *The New York Times:*

> We in the United States have swelled heads. The managers, the coaches, the athletes, and the public. We think we are the best, but it has been proved that we are not the best. We are one nation and there are . . . other nations in the world.[18]

Figure 16.3. Johnny Weismuller and Betty Robinson in 1928. Courtesy of Betty Robinson Schwartz.

In swimming, American men won three of the six events, and because of Peter Desjardins' outstanding performances, the United States claimed both Olympic diving titles. John Weissmuller successfully defended his 1924 100-meters freestyle swimming title and was a member of the championship 800 meters relay team. Weissmuller, during ten years of amateur swimming, accomplished the amazing feat of having never lost a race in distances from 50 yards to one-half mile. He won 52 national championship events,[19] broke two dozen world records, and is credited with influencing the development of the American crawl throughout the world. His chest high crawl stroke, independent head turning for breathing, and deep flutter kick were radically innovative.

Four factors which contributed to the admission of women's track and field to the 1928 Olympics were: (1) the success of international competition which began in 1922, (2) influential women leaders, (3) a world governing body, the Federation Sportive Feminine Internationale and (4) medical research presented by the Germans which clearly identified the benefits of exercise to the health of women. American women had received encouragement from Harry E. Stewart, Chairman of the Women's National Track Committee and the AAU since 1922 but female track and field athletes were often ridiculed by the public at large. Track and field events, unlike such sports as swimming, golf, and tennis, were thought to be unladylike. Ridicule did not keep American women from entering the first Olympic track and field events open to women. Betty Robinson became America's first woman gold medalist in track and field with her victory in the 100-meter dash. American women also won silver medals in the discus throw and 400-meter relay and a bronze medal in the high jump. They entered all events open to their sex with the exception of team gymnastics. Daniel Ferris, long-time Secretary to the AAU, reported that Americans did not enter gymnastics because they were not prepared for team gymnastics.[20] The American aquatic entry, in another display of strength, collected five gold laurels out of seven. The fencing team was unsuccessful in reaching the final rounds of competition.

THE CONTROVERSIAL 800-METER RUN

Sportswriter John R. Tunis' adamant opposition to the participation of women in the Olympics intensified when he attended the finals of the 800-meter run. Tunis, a strong supporter of the Women's Division. National Amateur Athletic Federation, gave the following account of the race:

> ...below us on the cinder path were eleven wretched women five of whom dropped out before the finish, while five collapsed after reaching the tape. I was informed later that the remaining starter fainted in the dressing room shortly afterward.[21]

The race was deleted from the Olympic program following the 1928 Games and was not reinstated until 1960. Women physical educators were greatly disturbed by the results of the 800 meter run. In contrast, Gustavus T. Kirby, American Olympic Association official, did "not believe that any contestant was physically injured, mentally upset, or morally offended by her presence in competition"[22] at the Olympics. Frederick W. Rubien, Secretary of the American Olympic Association, and Murray Hulbert, AAU President, also approved of women participating in the Olympics. On the other hand, Fred Steers, Chairman of the Women's Athletic Committee of the AAU, reported that the Union had not received evidence of physical detriment to its 800-meter runners but summed up the opinion of a lot of people regarding female track and field participation when he stated:

> ...the effort and fatigue of competitors does not conform to the American ideals of womanly dignity and conduct. It does not lead to the promotion of the sport, but on the contrary, because of its effect upon the spectators, is detrimental.[23]

Even though there were no problems encountered in preliminary rounds of the 800-meter run, the final event triggered a furor among women physical educators in the United States. In January of 1929, the Women's Division, National Amateur Athletic Federation, inaugurated a campaign to oppose the participation of women in track and field at Los Angeles in 1932. Women physical educators' opposition to highly competitive sport and the attendant "evils" of athletics such as the exploitation of athletes for the purpose of winning, the unknown effects of vigorous physical activity on females, and the participation of girls and women in the 1922 Paris track and field meet were other factors besides the final run of the 800-meter race which instigated the Olympic protest.

In summary, the January 1929 meeting of the Women's Division resulted in resolutions to:

1. disapprove Olympic competition for women
2. host and entertain foreign women participants at the Los Angeles Olympics
3. promote play day types of competition
4. substitute for Olympic competition a festival of singing, dancing, music, mass sports and games, and banquets
5. campaign extensively for properly conducted sports programs emphasizing participation rather than winning.[24]

The Women's Division, in April 1930, requested that the International Olympic Committee and the Amateur Athletic Federation eliminate track and field events for women in the 1932 Olympic Games.[25] Several organizations supported the Division's Olympic protest.

The Olympic Congress of May 1930 devoted nearly a day to deliberating the effects of highly competitive experiences on feminine participants. The International Olympic Congress resolved the women's participation issue by unanimously rejecting a motion to limit women to gymnastics, tennis, swimming, and skating.[26] A *New York Times* writer credited the efforts of the American delegates, led by Gustavus T. Kirby, with the outcome of the vote.[27]

Although the Women's Division was unsuccessful in preventing women from entering Olympic track and field, efforts to reduce highly competitive sport continued. The panacea for problems produced by Olympic competition and other forms of highly competitive athletics was the play day. The play day exemplified the reigning ideal of the Women's Division—"a game for every girl and every girl in a game."

LOS ANGELES, 1932—AN OLYMPIAD DURING THE DEPRESSION

Following "the collapse of the stock market in the autumn of 1929 . . . came the Great Depression which lasted, with varying severity, for ten years."[28]

For the second time, a city in the United States was awarded the honor of hosting the Olympic Games. Los Angeles was the site of the tenth Olympiad. Advance preparations prior to 1929 enabled the organizers of the 1932 Games to present an exciting panorama of sport.

President Herbert Hoover refused the honor of opening the Games of the tenth Olympiad because of a lengthy Congressional session and the domestic situation. Preoccupied with his own nomination ceremony, the President appointed Vice President Charles Curtis to represent him at the Los Angeles Olympics.[29] A lengthy train trip to and from California would have caused President Hoover to be away from the nation's capital at a time of national economic crisis.

Citizens of Los Angeles as well as visitors to the city had an opportunity to forget the effects of the Depression during the Games. Interest was not evident a month before the Games but suddenly the city rose to the occasion. Los Angeles became vibrant with enthusiasm for the Olympics.

> ... Contestants began to arrive; the Olympic village filled with its international residents; streets bulged with automobiles bearing licenses from every State and many distant possessions; ... stores and hotels looked like old times; ticket demands perked up. Los Angeles was finally Olympic conscious.[30]

THE OLYMPIC STADIUM WAS SOLD OUT FOR THE OPENING CEREMONIES

Because of the distance and the worldwide financial crisis fewer athletes traveled to the Olympics in 1932. In the previous Games, 46 nations were represented in Amsterdam while only 37 countries sent athletes to Los Angeles. There were nearly 1500 fewer competitors present for the tenth Olympiad.

American men excelled in track and field, wrestling, diving, and for the first time won five of the nine gymnastics events. Two gymnastics events won by Americans, club swinging and rope climbing, were excluded from the Olympic program following the tenth Olympiad.

Qualification standards were instituted for semi-final trials to remedy the problem of lengthy try-outs.[31] The 1932 selection process for track and field was far different than in earlier years when athletic clubs formed the basis for Olympic team representation. Americans participating in well-organized intercollegiate programs in addition to athletic club members offered a good foundation for international competition.

American women again entered Olympic fencing, track and field, and swimming. Women's gymnastics was not included in the 1932 Olympic program. The Americans made an unsuccessful bid for fencing medals. However, they won five of the six track and field events.

THE REMARKABLE BABE DIDRIKSON

Mildred "Babe" Didrikson qualified for the Olympic team by winning the National AAU Track and Field Championship as a one-woman team from Texas. While enroute to Los Angeles, she continued training for the Olympics by jogging the length of the train several times a day.[32] Didrikson won gold medals in the javelin and 80-meter hurdles, and placed second in the high jump.

Preceding the high jump finals Didrikson broke four world's records in the javelin, two in the 80-meter hurdles, and one in the high jump. The high jump finals were between Babe Didrikson and fellow American Jean Shiley. Both contestants cleared the bar at five feet five inches and set a new world record. Shiley and Didrikson missed clearing the bar at the new height of five feet five and three fourths inches. The bar was moved back to five feet and one fourth inch. Shiley cleared the bar followed by Didrikson. But the presiding judge ruled that Didrikson dived across the bar and thereby violated a rule:

> The rule demands that the head follow the hands and feet across the bar. Miss Didrikson had been jumping with a whirl and a flip that sent her head downward after clearing the bar. Up to this point no warning had been issued, as far as anyone could see she had not changed her style in the slightest.[33]

Reacting to the outcome of her final Olympic event Didrikson said, "I have kept the same style through an AAU Championship. I know I never changed today, but I have no kick to make. It is okeh (sic) with me. Miss Shiley is a great high jumper."[34]

Women's aquatic competition included four individual events, one relay race, and two diving events. The list of American Olympic championships was extended when the 1932 naiads won six of the seven titles. Helene Madison led the Americans by acquiring gold medals in the 100-meter freestyle, 400-meter freestyle, and 400-meter relay races.[35]

The United States dominated the diving events by winning all six Olympic medals. Georgia Coleman and Dorothy Poynton won the high diving titles, but not without first being delayed by chaste Olympic officials. They ruled that the American girls were wearing suits which exposed too much of the back:

> ... It made no difference to the officials that the back exposed was pleasing to the eye. Anyhow, Georgia, (Coleman) Katherine (Rawls) and Jane (Fauntz) had to rustle up some new suits. Miss Coleman didn't have a spare suit, so (she) borrowed one from Margaret Hoffman, the 200-meter breast-stroke swimmer. Miss Hoffman is rather slim and tall, while Georgia is inclined toward huskiness, so the suit wasn't exactly a perfect fit, but Miss Coleman didn't let a little thing like that hamper her diving. . . . [36]

Skeptics who had thought the 1932 Olympics were doomed to failure because of the world-wide economic depression were proven wrong. "Record weather, record crowds, record performances in all fields of sport and records in the treasury . . . "[37] surely offered a respite from the gloom brought forth by economic disaster.

BERLIN, 1936—THE CONTROVERSIAL GAMES, CALL FOR A BOYCOTT

Much of the excitement of the eleventh modern Olympiad was dampened by Adolph Hitler's discrimination against Jews. In January, 1936, Chancellor Hitler issued an internal party order to remove all anti-Jewish boycott posters and banners presumably to shroud the unjust treatment of Jews by Nazis.[38] Opposition to the Berlin Olympics "gathered momentum in this country scarcely a year after the 1932 Olympics."[39] The world of sport in particular was shocked by the barring of Jewish athletes from participation in German sports clubs. Assaults by Nazi supporters on Jewish women and orphanages, in addition to the intolerance of Jewish athletes, brought a gloomy atmosphere to the 1936 Olympics.

The American Jewish Congress played a prominent role in gathering support for a United States Olympic boycott. As might be expected, groups such as the Jewish War Veterans and B'nai B'rith opposed American participation in the Berlin Olympics. Other endorsements to boycott or change the location of the 1936 Olympics came from organizations, individuals, and publications. *Christian Century,* a Protestant periodical; *Commonweal,* a Catholic publication; Friends of Democracy, a German-American organization; former Assistant Secretary of the Navy, Ernest L. Jahncke; and *The New York Times* were either opposed to the participation of American athletes in Germany or favored a change of venue for the Olympics.

Late in January, 1936, over 2,500 delegates to the Federation of Jewish Women's Organization (FJWO), representing 250 groups, adopted a resolution opposing the sending of American athletes to the 1936 Olympics. In its sixteenth annual meeting, the FJWO also called for a boycott of German products.[40]

Some unbeaten basketball teams and other teams considered contenders for the championship of the NCAA, YMCA, and AAU tournament declined to enter the competition because it would lead to the selection of representatives for the Berlin Olympics. Among teams declining to enter the tri-sponsored tournament were the largely Jewish New York University and Long Island University basketball teams. Purdue and City College of New York refused to enter the Olympic trials. Notre Dame did not enter the try-outs because players would be absent from classes for too long and Adolph Rupp of the University of Kentucky opposed the tournament because of the expense and conflict with spring football.[41]

Jewish athletes were urged not to try out for the American Olympic team. In a March 11, 1936, letter to a Jewish contender for the United States canoe team, Dr. Stephen S. Wise, president of the American Jewish Congress, wrote:

> No . . . self-respecting Jew has the right to go to Nazi Germany. If you go to Nazi Germany, your presence as an American Jew signifies your approval of the Nazi attitude toward all the groups and peoples whom Nazi Germany is oppressing and wronging day after day.[42]

The American Good-Will Athletic Union to Preserve the Olympic Ideal was approved for incorporation by Supreme Court Justice William Black. Incorporated in January 1936, the Union was established to move the Olympics from Berlin and to organize athletic contests which would rival the Olympic Games.[43] The New York based Union assumed a monumental task when it sought to change the location of the Olympic Games.

Count Henri Baillet-Latour of Belgium, International Olympic Committee president announced in March 1936 that the summer Olympic Games would not be moved from Berlin. In an adamant statement he declared that only war could stop the Games.[44]

The AAU and the American Olympic Association battled fiercely over the discrimination issue and a proposed boycott of the Games. In spite of opposition from various groups and individuals the AAU and the American Olympic Association voted to prepare a team for the 1936 Olympics.[45] The discrimination issue as well as the Depression hindered the Olympic fund-raising campaign. Some athletes did not know until the last minute if there would be adequate resources available for all competitors to sail to Germany. Team morale was jeopardized by the uncertain atmosphere.

Arrangements were made for athletes to train while on board the ship *Manhattan.* The "floating gymnasium" was equipped with a 200 yard track, a designated practice area for boxers, weightlifters and wrestlers, rowing and cycling machines, fencing strips, gymnastics equipment, and a shooting range. No baskets were installed but basketball team members were assigned an area on the sun deck where they could work on passing drills. Swimmers were fastened to harnesses so that distance swims could be simulated in the small pool.[46]

The German version of Olympic Village, a contrast from the austere accommodations in Los Angeles, was elaborately designed to provide housing and training facilities for 3,500 athletes and coaches. The German Army acting as hosts to the athletes cast a military atmosphere over the 159 building encampment. The village, built by the army, was constructed for use as a military training school and hospital upon conclusion of the Games.[47]

THE CONTROVERSIAL ELEANOR HOLM JARRETT

Backstroker Eleanor Holm Jarrett had competed in the 1928 Olympics, won a gold medal in Los Angeles, and was a leading contender for a backstroke victory in Berlin. The fun-loving swimmer, however, got into difficulty with Olympic officials for drinking champagne at an all-night party aboard ship while enroute to the 1936 Games. American Olympic officials placed Jarrett on probation.[48] Another party and promenade along the deck with a male companion, where she was greeted by chaperone Ada Taylor Sackett, brought the champion backstroker more trouble.[49] Avery Brundage, President of the American Olympic Association (AOA), issued a succinct statement: "Mrs. Jarrett has been dropped from the American Olympic team for violation of training rules and her entry in the Olympic Games has been canceled."[50] Jarrett's appeal to the American Olympic Association and a petition requesting her reinstatement signed by 220 coaches and athletes failed to alter the AOA's decision to dismiss the star performer.

The New York Times carried a running commentary on the events surrounding the controversial swimmer's dismissal and printed Jarrett's rebuttal:

> I've never made any secret of the fact that I like a good time, particularly champagne. Everyone knows that, including the (American Olympic) committee. The newspapers published my statements on that subject during the final tryouts at New York. Why then, if they felt so strongly on the subject, didn't all the American Olympic Committee keep me off the team right away? Why did they have to wait until we were in the middle of the Atlantic Ocean before suddenly deciding that my conduct was too unbearable to permit my remaining on the team . . . ?[51]

Mrs. Jarrett pointed out that at least 100 other athletes stayed up after the curfew. She explained that she was not condemning other athletes but considered them as innocent as she.[52]

Circumstances which contributed to Jarrett's expulsion from the Olympic team included the swimmer's relationship with chaperone Ada Taylor Sackett, the athlete's accommodations on board ship, the change in Olympic coaching personnel, and the manner in which Olympic officials dealt with the highly publicized backstroker. Ada Sackett and Alice Lord Landon accompanied the swimming team to the Amsterdam Olympics as chaperones. According to Landon, the backstroker and Sackett did not get along. Hints of jealousy and resentment on the part of Mrs. Sackett toward Eleanor Jarrett surfaced in 1936. Additionally, Olympic officials were given first class accommodations on board ship while the athletes were assigned to third class. Mrs. Jarrett objected to the athletes' lodgings which did not place her in good standing with officials. The alteration in coaching personnel was probably the most influential event which altered the career of America's often photographed swimmer. Initially, the 1936 Olympic Games Women's Swimming Committee selected Alice Lord Landon head chaperone and Lewis de Brada Handley swimming coach. Avery Brundage notified Handley that Ray Daughters was replacing him as the Olympic coach because the AOC was given $10,000 to change personnel. Landon resigned her position in protest and contended that, "Had Mr. Handley been the coach and had I been the chaperone I doubt that Eleanor would have jeopardized her opportunity to swim in Berlin." Jarrett had discussed her drinking habit with Handley and Landon while they were still part of the 1936 Olympic delegation. Handley suggested that Jarrett modify her drinking and she accepted the advice of the WSA mentor. Finally, Mrs. Jarrett resented being treated as a first-time Olympian even though she had made her third Olympic team. She claimed Olympic officials informed athletes to continue their own training routines. On the other hand, the Olympic team handbook inaugurated in 1936 precisely explained the behavior expected of athletes, which prohibited drinking. Eleanor Holm, having caused a furor unknown to American Olympic officials and much to their chagrin, decided to remain in Berlin at her own expense. She amused herself by touring Berlin and visiting dignataries. In a meeting with Hitler, she was informed that if she were a German her behavior on board ship would have been dealt with after she swam in the Olympics.

Not a single gold medal was won in the swimming events; moreover, American naiads lost the 400-meter relay for the first time since they began competing in Olympic swimming at the 1920 Antwerp Games. Americans did manage three third-place finishes in swimming events and were kept from being shut-out of aquatic titles with Dorothy Poynton Hill's victory in platform diving.[53] In addition, thirteen-year-old Marjorie Gestring became the youngest springboard gold medalist with her championship performance in Berlin.[54]

Although American women failed to win a field event, they finished first in the one hundred meter dash and the four hundred meter relay. Helen Stephens placed first in the one hundred meter dash. Harriet Bland, Annette Rogers, Betty Robinson, and Helen Stephens, the anchor, represented the United States in a relay. The highly rated German relay team dropped the baton on the last exchange and the United States won the event in an eight yard margin over Great Britain.[55]

For the fourth consecutive Olympiad, Americans failed to win a medal in fencing. The first entry in team gymnastics resulted in a fifth place finish out of eight teams. America's first women gymnasts were required to pay their own expenses, and because some qualifiers were unable to meet these costs, less qualified gymnasts took their places. The team was further handicapped because the final team was not assembled for training until 10 days before the sailing date.[56]

THE REMARKABLE JESSE OWENS

The United States continued its dominance of the Olympic track and field events by compiling five of the nine field championships including the decathlon. Half of the fourteen track events were won by the American team. Amid racial strife and in front of capacity crowds, the remarkable Jesse Owens shattered Olympic and world records in his efforts to claim three Olympic championships. His record-breaking performances in the

100-meter race were disallowed because of an aiding wind. In addition to winning the 100-meter event, Owens won the running long jump, the 200-meter race, and ran the first leg of the championship 400-meter relay team.

In the running long jump Owens experienced difficulty in reaching the qualifying standard of 23 feet, 5½ inches. Owens, unaware that the competition had started, took a warm-up run through the pit and was charged with his first of three trials. He qualified on his last attempt. Lutz Long of Germany equaled Owens' best jump, however; on his last effort Owen won with a jump of 26 feet, 5 5/16 inches.[57] The competition was outstanding during the long jump finals. The Olympic record was equaled once and surpassed five times. After the event ended Owens and Long the runner-up walked arm in arm about the area.

The American men won six of the 14 track events, while Great Britain and Finland were a distant second with two Olympic championships each. The Americans won five of the nine field events including the decathlon. No other country won more than one of the remaining field events. The best performances ever in gymnastics were realized when Americans accumulated half of the 10 gold medals in gymnastics. Gymnastics victories by Americans included the horizontal bar, flying rings, rope climb, club swinging, and tumbling.

A Japanese shut-out in all six swimming events was avoided with Clarence "Buster" Crabbe's victory in the 400-meter freestyle race. Americans again dominated the diving events by claiming the springboard and high diving titles. In other competition the first yachting gold medals were won in the Eight meter and Star classes.[58]

AN EXPANDED SCHEDULE OF EVENTS

After a hiatus of 32 years, basketball returned to the Olympic program. The game was first included in Olympic competition at the St. Louis Games in 1904. Through the efforts of the Amateur Athletic Union of the United States, the Young Men's Christian Association, the National Collegiate Athletic Association, and the International Amateur Basketball Federation the sport was approved for the 1936 Olympics.[59]

Dr. James Naismith, inventor of basketball, opened the tournament. Twenty-two nations were represented in the revival of Olympic basketball. Games were played out-of-doors on clay courts. Because of its civil war, Spain withdrew and thereby forfeited its opening round game to the United States. The Americans advanced to the quarter-finals by defeating Estonia 52 to 28 and drawing a bye in the third round. Prior to the championship game the United States defeated the Philippines 56 to 23 and Mexico 25 to 10. The final contest, played in the rain, resulted in the Americans defeating the Canadians 19 to 8.[60] Basketball, once a YMCA game, was now approaching worldwide popularity.

Canoeing and team or field handball were admitted to the Olympics for the first time in 1936. The United States' entries gained valuable experience but did not fare well against the more experienced Europeans. The United States had no experienced international competitors in these sports because team handball and canoeing were not widely done.

Baseball was a demonstration sport at the 1936 Olympics. The two American baseball teams, comprised of players from several colleges and Philadelphia's Penn Athletic Club, played before the largest European crowd ever gathered for the sport. The teams were given an ovation when they gave the Nazi salute before the first inning. The game was explained in three languages. The crowd cheered each time a batter hit the ball. Even the Americans were unsure of some aspects of the game. The German interpreter translated third base into "third location," center field as "middle outside" and "thrower in" for the pitcher. Poor lighting made it impossible for spectators to see the ball at all times.[61] An enthusiastic crowd of 100,000 watched the two American teams. The game was well received[62] but never gained status on the official Olympic program. Timing was probably against the sport. The 1940 and 1944 Olympic Games were cancelled because of World War II and when the Games resumed in 1948 an expanded program was rejected. In planning the program for the fourteenth modern Olympiad, members of the International Olympic Committee reasoned that the idea was to resume the Olympics rather than overexpand the program.[63]

The Berlin Olympics drew a record 49 nations. Three countries, the United States, Germany, and Hungary entered all of the 23 Olympic events. Forty-five nations entered the men's track and field competition while women athletes represented 19 countries. Swimming was second in representation with 40 countries for the men's events and 22 for women's swimming.[64]

When it became obvious that the summer Olympics would remain in Berlin, the Committee on Fair Play in Sports, as a symbolic protest, sent an American team to Barcelona, Spain, to participate in a People's Olympics July 19–25, 1936, but on the eve of the contests the Spanish Civil War began. A Jewish Olympics was held on Randall's Island, New York City on August 15–16, 1936. The mid-August contests, under the aegis of the Jewish Labor Committee, honored athletes who did not compete in Germany.[65]

SUMMARY

At the 1920 Antwerp Games, American women made their Olympic debut in aquatics by winning four of the five swimming and diving events. Ethelda Bleibtrey became the United States' first distaff swimming gold medalist. Fourteen-year-old Aileen Riggin was the youngest member of the team and winner of the fancy diving championship. The Women's Swimming Association of New York (WSA) was instrumental in producing the nucleus of the successful 1920 team. American men entered 15 of the 20 Olympic sports and recorded outstanding performances in swimming, track and field, boxing, shooting, and rowing. Leading swimmers were Hawaiian Duke Kahanamoko and Norman Ross. Track dashman, Charles Paddock earned two gold medals and one silver medal.

Dissention occurred between the United States Lawn Tennis Association and Olympic officials. Because Olympic competition dates coincided with the United States Tennis Championships, the USLTA withdrew from the Games. As a result, American men and women did not represent the United States in Olympic tennis.

The 1924 Paris Games established America's naiads as a swimming and diving power. They were led by Gertrude Ederle, future conqueror of the English Channel. The men's swimming team also dominated their competition with John Weissmuller establishing himself as a champion in the freestyle events.

As in the 1920 Games, the USLTA was again invited to participate in Paris. American men and women took command of the Olympic tennis courts by winning in mixed doubles, men's and women's singles and doubles. Following the Paris Games, tennis was dropped from the program because of a dispute between the International Lawn Tennis Federation and the International Olympic Committee.

One addition to the Olympic program was women's fencing. Baseball was also recognized at the Olympics with an exhibition contest held between an American team and a club from Paris.

Track and field for women was first included in the Amsterdam Olympics in 1928. Factors contributing to this were successful international competition, the influence of women leaders, support of a world governing body, and medical research evidence which identified the benefits of exercise for women. American women entered the 1928 competition with Betty Robinson becoming America's first gold medalist by winning the 100-meter dash. Opposition to women's track and field intensified when in the finals of the 800-meter run the competitors either dropped out or collapsed after reaching the tape. The race was deleted from the Olympic program and not reinstated until 1960. In 1929 the Women's Division of the National Amateur Athletic Federation officially opposed the participation of women in the upcoming 1932 Olympiad. Although they were unsuccessful, efforts continued to reduce highly competitive sport for women.

Nearly 1,500 fewer competitors came to Los Angeles in 1932 for the tenth Olympiad because of the world-wide financial crisis. American men excelled in track and field, wrestling, diving, and for the first time in the gymnastic events. Mildred "Babe" Didrikson dominated the women's competition by breaking the world records in the javelin, hurdles, and high jump.

The Berlin Olympics in 1936 were marred by Hitler's discrimination against the Jews. The American Jewish Congress gathered support for a United States Olympic boycott and Jewish athletes were urged not to try out for the American team. The American Good-Will Athletic Union to Preserve the Olympic Ideal sought to change the location of the Games but their efforts were unsuccessful. In spite of opposition by various groups, the Amateur Athletic Union and American Olympic Association voted to send a team to Berlin. Eleanor Holm Jarrett was a controversial American swimmer dropped from the team for violating training rules aboard ship enroute to the Games. Jesse Owens led the men's domination of track and field by shattering Olympic and world records.

An expanded schedule of events were conducted at the Berlin Games. After an absence of 32 years basketball was included in the program with 22 participating nations. Canoeing and team handball were also played for the first time with the more experienced Europeans dominating these events. Baseball was played as a demonstration sport between two American teams.

A record 49 nations competed at the Berlin Olympics with the United States, Germany, and Hungary entering all of the 23 official events. The Committee on Fair Play in Sports sent an American team to Barcelona, Spain, as a symbolic protest to participate in a People's Olympics. On the eve of the July, 1936, contests, the Spanish Civil War broke out and they were cancelled. A Jewish Olympics was held August, 1936, in New York City to honor athletes who declined to compete in Germany.

REFERENCES

1. "Swimming Women," *Report of the American Olympic Committee.* Greenwich, Connecticut: Conde Nast Press, 1920, pp. 320–321.
2. "Will American Girls Decide the 1924 Olympics?" *The Literary Digest,* 81(April, 1924), p. 62.
3. Alice Lord Landon, Personal Interview, New York, New York, July 15, 1975.
4. "A Summary of the Performances," *Report of the American Olympic Committee,* 1920, pp. 214, 279–345.
5. S. Wallis Merrihew, ed., "Lawn Tennis at the Olympic Games." *American Lawn Tennis.* 14(October 15, 1920), p. 480.
6. Asa S. Bushnell (ed). "All Time U.S. Olympic Team Personnel," *United States 1956 Olympic Book.* New York: United States Olympic Association, Inc. 1957, p. 419.
7. "Olympic Champions," *United States Olympic Team.* New York: United States Olympic Team, 1976, pp. 79–80.
8. "Complete Record of Olympic Champions 1896–1936," *Report of the American Olympic Committee,* New York: American Olympic Committee, 1936, p. 385.
9. Helen Wills. *Fifteen-Thirty.* New York: Charles Scribner's Sons, 1937, p. 30.
10. Julian S. Myrick. "Report of Manager of Olympic Tennis Team." *Report of the American Olympic Association 1924.* Paris: Comite Olympique Francais, 1925, p. 95.
11. "Complete Record of Olympic Champions 1896–1936," *op. cit.,* p. 385.
12. "Tennis Bodies Withdraw from Olympic Competition." *The Olympic.* 1(June, 1927), p. 17.
13. "Fencing in Philadelphia," *The Sportswoman,* 6(February, 1930), p. 9.
14. Bushnell (ed). "All Time U.S. Olympic Team Personnel," 1957, *op. cit.,* p. 417.

15. "U.S. Nine Defeats Ranelagh Club, 5–0." *The New York Times.* July 19, 1924, p. 5.
16. "Complete Record of Olympic Champions 1896–1936," pp. 379–380, 383, 386.
17. Wythe Williams. "U.S. Captures Two Olympic Events: Williams Wins 200 Meters," *The New York Times,* August 2, 1928, p. 17.
18. "Conceit Is Blamed for U.S. Defeats," *The New York Times,* August 16, 1928, p. 17.
19. "Johnny Weissmuller," *Swimming Hall of Fame Pool Dedication Souvenir Program.* Fort Lauderdale: International Swimming Hall of Fame, 1965, p. 23.
20. Daniel Ferris. Personal Letter. Secretary Emeritus, Amateur Athletic Union, July 9, 1974.
21. John R. Tunis. "Women and the Sport Business," *Harper's Monthly Magazine,* 159(July, 1929), p. 213.
22. Gustavus T. Kirby. "The 1928 Olympics," *The Playground,* 22(March, 1929), p. 718.
23. Amateur Athletic Union of the United States, Minutes of the November 18–20, 1928 Meeting. New York, Waldorf Astoria Hotel.
24. Agnes Wayman. "Women's Division of the National Amateur Athletic Federation," *Journal of Health and Physical Education.* 3(March, 1932), pp. 4–5.
25. Alice Allene Sefton. *The Women's Division National Amateur Athletic Federation.* Stanford: Stanford University Press, 1941, p. 55.
26. "Women to Compete in Olympic Track," *The New York Times,* June 29, 1931, p. 25.
27. "Women to Remain in Olympic Games," *The New York Times,* May 25, 1930, sec. XI, p. 9.
28. John Kenneth Galbraith. *The Great Crash 1929.* Boston: Houghton Mifflin Co., pp. 173–174.
29. "Hoover and Snell Plan Notification," *The New York Times,* July 20, 1932, p. 3.
30. Chapin Hall. "Los Angeles Rises Above Depression," *The New York Times,* August 7, 1932, sec. II, p. 7.
31. Arthur J. Daley. "Path to Olympics Offers New Trials," *The New York Times,* April 10, 1932, sec. V, p. 6.
32. Babe Didrikson Zaharias. *This Life I've Led.* New York: A.S. Barnes and Co., 1955, pp. 28–29.
33. Grantland Rice. "Sudden Rule Defeats Babe," *Los Angeles Times,* August 8, 1932, sec. I, p. 13.
34. Rice, "Sudden Rule Defeats Babe," *ibid.*
35. Frank W. Blankley. "Report of the Manager of the American Olympic Swimming Team," *The Games of the Xth Olympiad, Los Angeles, 1932.* Los Angeles: Wolfer Printing Co., Inc., 1932, pp. 192–194.
36. Bob Ray. "Crabbe Annexes Swim Thriller By Inches," *Los Angeles Times,* August 11, 1932, sec. I, p. 14.
37. John Kieran and Arthur Daley. *The Story of the Olympic Games 776 B.C. to 1972.* Philadelphia: J.B. Lippincott, 1973, p. 129.
38. Otto D. Tolischus. "Nazi Cloak Anti-Semitism," *The New York Times,* January 12, 1936, sec. IV, p. 7.
39. "Olympic Fund Problems," *The Literary Digest,* 121(April 18, 1936), p. 44.

40. "Fight to End War Urged on Women," *The New York Times,* January 31, 1936, p. 20.
41. "L.I.U. and Notre Dame Refuse to Play in Olympic Basketball Trials," *The New York Times,* March 4, 1936, p. 29.
42. Letter from Dr. Stephen S. Wise to Alexander S. Gottlieb, March 11, 1936, courtesy of the American Jewish Historical Society.
43. "Sports Unit Approved," *The New York Times,* January 4, 1936, p. 18.
44. "Baillet-Latour Sees No Shift in Olympics," *The New York Times,* March 11, 1936, p. 25.
45. "Olympic Problems," *The Literary Digest,* 121(April 18, 1936), p. 44.
46. Joseph M. Sheehan. "Liner Manhattan to be Converted Into Floating Gym for U.S. Team," *The New York Times,* June 18, 1936, p. 30.
47. Albion Ross. "Olympic Village Now Finished, Is A Model City in Miniature," *The New York Times,* May 24, 1936, sec. V, p. 4.
48. "Eleanor Holm Jarrett Dropped from Olympic Team for Breaking Training." *The New York Times,* July 24, 1936, p. 21.
49. "Mrs. Jarrett's Plea Denied, But She Is In Berlin Hopeful of Another Chance," *The New York Times,* July 25, 1936, p. 7.
50. "Eleanor Holm Jarrett Dropped from Olympic Team For Breaking Training," *op. cit.,* p. 21.
51. "Text of Mrs. Jarrett's Statement," *The New York Times,* July 26, 1936, sec. V, p. 2.
52. "Text of Mrs. Jarrett's Statement," *ibid.* sec. V, p. 2.
53. Herbert D. Holm, "Report of Manager of Women's Swimming Committee," *Report of the American Olympic Committee.* New York: American Olympic Committee, 1936, pp. 278–279, 281, 283, 285.
54. Pat Besford. *Encyclopedia of Swimming.* New York: St. Martin's Press, 1971, p. 140.
55. George Pallett. *Women's Athletics.* London: Normal Press, 1955, p. 54.
56. Roy E. Moore. "Gymnastics-Women," *Report of the American Olympic Committee,* 1936, p. 227.
57. James F. Simms. "The Olympic Track and Field Championships," *Report of the American Olympic Committee,* 1936, pp. 125–149.
58. "Complete Record of Olympic Champions 1896–1936," *op. cit.,* pp. 379–380, 383, 385.
59. J. Lyman Bingham. "Olympic Games Basketball Committee," *Report of the American Olympic Committee,* 1936, pp. 165–170.
60. "Olympic Basketball Championships," *Report of the American Olympic Committee,* 1936, p. 171.
61. "Baseball Planned to Enlighten Berlin Puts 100,000 in the Dark," *The New York Times,* August 13, 1936, p. 14.
62. Leslie Mann. "Demonstration Events Report of Manager of Baseball Team," *Report of the American Olympic Committee,* 1936, pp. 302–303.
63. "Baseball Refused in Olympics," *The New York Times,* September 7, 1946, p. 10.
64. "53 Nations Enter Berlin Olympics," *The New York Times,* June 23, 1936, p. 31.
65. Moshe Gottlieb. "The American Controversy Over the Olympic Games," *American Jewish Historical Quarterly.* 61(March, 1972), pp. 181–213.

Chapter 17

THE SUMMER OLYMPIC GAMES 1948–2000

LONDON, 1948, A CONSERVATIVE POST-WAR
RESUMPTION OF THE OLYMPICS

The Olympic Games of 1944, though never held, were technically awarded to London. Therefore, the British were in an advantageous position to host the celebration of the Games of the Thirteenth Olympiad in 1948. "Hardly had the last shot gone echoing down the halls of time before the International Olympic Committee met in London in August of 1945 . . ."[1] and officially awarded the 1948 Olympics to London.

The ravages of war imposed financial difficulties on British Olympic officials but they admirably coped with this troublesome situation. In January, 1948, austerity medals for 17 sports became an alternative which eased their financial burden. The London Organizing Committee regretfully announced plans to use austerity medals which resembled gold but were actually silver plated.[2] British Olympic organizers also had to contend with the lack of refrigeration for food and arranging transportation to and from Olympic Village, which was located 10 miles from Wembley stadium.

The ruins of bombed buildings were a stark reminder of the devastating effects of war, yet the resumption of the Olympic Games offered spectators and participants the opportunity to forget for at least a while its lingering effects. Long-time American Olympic officials were eventually to describe the London Games as the most harmonious in the history of the modern Games. Readers of the official Olympic souvenir publication were given a feeling of the prevailing mood: "London is proud to welcome the visitor even before she has had time to put on her best dress again. The old lady wears her scars as medals, and her indomitable spirit is not crushed."[3]

Most of the American Olympic team sailed to London on the *America*, but a few were flown on chartered planes. While on board ship, some of the teams were able to continue partial training programs. Long distance swims were simulated by attaching belts to swimmers which held them in place while in the pool.[4] A small outdoor gymnasium and good weather enabled the track and field team to practice.

Upon arrival in London most of the athletes were housed at the Royal Air Force depot which had been converted into an Olympic Village. The athletes overlooked the inconvenient location of the stadium and concentrated on proceeding with their competition. After an absence of twelve years the resumption of the Games brought together a new generation of Olympians.

The Soviet Union sent a delegation to the Sixteenth Congress of the International Amateur Athletic Federation. Presumably the Soviets, who had not been represented at the Olympic Games since 1912, were in attendance to learn the necessary procedures for entry into the quadrennial athletic contests. Their observations of the 1948 Olympics provided them with essential information for future team preparation. The Soviets were aware that many male athletes were adequately trained for international competition, whereas female athletes had not experienced adequate preparation. American women would later find themselves at a disadvantage when competing against the superbly trained Soviets.

American women staged a comeback in their collection of gold medals in swimming by capturing three swimming events and both diving events. A one-two-three sweep occurred in springboard diving while the first two positions were claimed by the American women in platform diving. Victoria Manalo Draves made Olympic history by winning both the springboard and platform diving championships.[5]

The women's track and field program was increased by three events when the International Amateur Athletic Federation (IAAF) added the 200-meter dash, the shotput, and the long jump. Two medals were won by Americans: a bronze laurel in the 200-meter dash and a gold medal in the high jump. Thousands watched the high jump duel between Alice Coachman of the United States and Dorothy Tyler of Great Britain. Coachman won the event with a western roll on her first attempt at five feet six and one-eighth inches.[6] Coachman became America's first black female gold medalist. She attended Tuskeegee Institute where athletic director Cleve Abbott provided women with an opportunity to compete in track and field. Coachman completed her senior year at Albany State College in Georgia. Her teammate, Nell Jackson, later named the 1972 women's Olympic track and field coach, became the first black woman named to an Olympic coaching position.

In 1948, Olympic fencing for women was still limited to individual foil competition. Maria Cerra placed fourth which was the highest place ever achieved by an American woman. Few American women were participating in fencing and those who did compete in the sport could not match the skill level of the more experienced Europeans. In sports such as swimming and track and field the United States has contributed to improved training regimens, coaching, and equipment which have benefited countries throughout the world. However, in fencing, Americans have gained from the expertise of Europeans.

After 12 years without Olympic competition, the United States was remarkably consistent. Nine of the American men's 11 Olympic victories were in the same events as those they had won in Berlin in 1936. The United States defended the 100-, 200-, and 800-meter races, the 110-meter high hurdles, the 400-meter hurdles, and the 400-meter relay, as well as the long jump,

Figure 17.1. Mabel Walker, Theresa Manuel, Alice Coachman, Nell Jackson (from left to right). Courtesy of the late Nell Jackson.

pole vault, and decathlon. Victories in the 1,600 meter relay and the shot put enabled the United States to claim supremacy in Olympic track and field. Sweden was the next most successful in track and field with five first place finishes.[7] Seventeen-year-old Bob Mathias won the decathlon and became the fourth American to achieve this feat since its inclusion in 1912.

Films played an important part in the eventual outcome of the 400-meter relay. In unprecedented action the Olympic Jury of the International Amateur Athletic Federation reversed a decision which had disqualified the American 400-meter relay team for passing the baton out of the zone. The British team was declared the winner of the event, but after a review of films the American team was awarded the championship and another victory ceremony had to be scheduled. The decision reversal was especially good news for Barney Ewell and Lorenzo Wright who were thought to have exchanged the baton outside the specified zone.[8]

The United States successfully defended its 1936 basketball title. Olympic officials were so certain the American basketball team would win the championship game that they brought only one flag to the arena. At halftime the Americans led France 28 to 9 and won the game 65 to 21.[9] By 1948, the United States had an exceptionally strong pool of players who were members of college or AAU teams. European players could not contend with the highly organized basketball programs and skillful players who characterized the American system of basketball.

AVERY BRUNDAGE ATTEMPTS TO REDUCE
THE OLYMPIC PROGRAM

Avery Brundage, President of the United States Olympic Association, in mid-April of 1949, approached the International Olympic Committee with a plan to reduce the Olympic program. Brundage contended that it was almost impossible to complete the Olympic competition within the prescribed two-week period. Brundage proposed reductions in women's track and field, rowing, race walking, gymnastics, and basketball. He anticipated that representatives of affected sports would meet him at the IOC meeting in Rome "with blood in their eyes."[10] Opposing Brundage's views, the IOC rejected the elimination of events from the 1952 Olympic program.

The United States Field Hockey Association (USFHA), governing body of women's field hockey, also voiced disapproval of a possible move to include women's field hockey in the 1952 Olympics. The USFHA believed their international triannual tournament should not be discarded for Olympic competition.[11] Moreover, the International Federation of Women's Hockey Association (IFWHA) thought it hopeless to pursue the admission of women's Olympic hockey because of continued efforts to reduce the Olympic program.[12]

Meanwhile, in men's field hockey there was a dispute between the USOC and players regarding their ability to compete at the international level. The 1952 field hockey team withdrew before the Helsinki competition because the USOC did not think the team would do well against teams consisting of more experienced players. The 1948 team had lost all three of its matches to Britain, Switzerland, and Afghanistan.[13] Men's field hockey did not gain widespread participation in the United States. A few clubs were established along the Atlantic Seaboard.

HELSINKI, 1952, THE ENTIRE AMERICAN
OLYMPIC TEAM FLIES FOR THE FIRST TIME

Helsinki, scene of the 1952 Olympics, was the smallest city ever awarded the Games. It was also the site of the first meeting of athletes from two powerful countries, the United States and the Soviet Union. Although Czarist Russia was represented at the 1912 Stockholm Games, only a small delegation of athletes competed. Upon reentering the Olympics in 1952, a large Soviet contingent was sent.[14] In June, 1952, the Soviet Union announced that USSR athletes would enter all Olympic events with the exception of field hockey.[15]

For the first time, the United States Olympic team traveled exclusively by air, thus eliminating the inconveniences of make-shift training facilities on board ship. The concerned Avery Brundage observed that air travel did not afford the Olympic team's various units an opportunity to develop rapport.[16] Flying drastically reduced travel time, enabling athletes to quickly resume their training schedules. However, upon arrival in Helsinki the men's and women's swimming team learned that they were allotted just one hour of pool time each day. Ten Swimmers were assigned to each of the four lanes in Helsinki's 50-meter pool.[17]

Although the American women failed to win an Olympic swimming championship, they swept the platform diving finals. Pat McCormick distinguished the American team by winning both the platform and springboard championships.[18] American men won both diving events with David Browning winning the springboard title and Dr. Samuel Lee successfully defending his 1948 platform diving championship. The United States team also won four out of six swimming events.

A 20-year victory drought for American boxers ended in Helsinki when they won five gold medals. The last American boxing victories had occurred in 1932 when two gold medals were won. All five boxers were black. American Norvel Lee who won the light-heavyweight title was named the outstanding boxer of the tournament. The remaining gold medals were won by Nate Brooks, Charley Adkins, Floyd Patterson, and Eddie Sanders.[19]

American women won only one medal in the Helsinki track and field competition. The favored Australians led in the finals until they dropped the baton during the last exchange in the relay. Catherine Hardy of the United States raced to a victory by inches over Germany's Marge Peterson in the 400-meter relay.[20] Lucile Wilson, Manager-Coach of the 1952 women's track and field team was disappointed because of the Americans' performances and criticized the lack of competitive opportunities for girls and women in high schools and colleges.[21]

AMERICAN WOMEN ENTER THE EQUESTRIAN EVENTS

Army equestrian teams represented the United States in the Olympic Games from 1912 to 1948. Elimination of Army cavalry units after 1948 resulted in the formation of the United States Equestrian Team in 1950. The organization began selecting and training teams for Olympic and other competitions.[22] The withdrawal of Army control of Olympic equestrian representation provided American women with another opportunity to try out for the Olympics.

The entry of American women into Olympic equestrian events was marred in 1951 by the announcement that Carol Durand was barred from the Helsinki competition.[23] She was named to the Prix de Nations event, but the International Equestrian rules barred women from that phase of Olympic competition at that time. In April, 1952, costume designer Marjorie Haines was named to the Olympic dressage team. Haines became the first woman to represent the United States in an Olympic equestrian event.[24] She placed seventeenth out of 27 contestants.[25]

Figure 17.2. Emil Zatopek of Czechoslovakia runs past Coca Cola signs on his way to a victory in the 1952 Olympic marathon. Zatopek had already won gold medals in the 5,000 nd 10,000 meters. Coca Cola has been involved in ther Olympic movement since 1928. Courtesy Phil Mooney, Manager, Archives Department, The Coca Cola Company.

AN AMERICAN BECOMES PRESIDENT OF THE IOC

Avery Brundage, president of the United States Olympic Committee since 1929, was elected president of the International Olympic Committee in July, 1952. The Chicagoan was the first American ever elected president of the international sport organization. He considered nationalism, the progressively growing size of the Games, and the threat of professionalism the major problems of the Olympic movement. Brundage, a very wealthy man, had been a member of the IOC since 1936 and was president of the AAU for four terms. A graduate of the University of Illinois in 1909, Brundage participated in track and basketball. He was an AAU all-around champion and placed fifth in the pentathlon at the Stockholm Olympics.[26]

1952 United States Women's Olympic Gymnastic Team

Left to Right—RUTH GRULKOWSKI, CLARA SCHROTH LOMADY, META ELSTE, DORIS KIRKMAN, DOROTHY DALTON, MARIAN BARONE, RUTH TOPALIAN, MARIE HOESLY

United States Representative to International Women's Division

Figure 17.3. 1952 United States women's Olympic gymnastic team. Souvenir Gymnastics Program, Courtesy of Don Holder.

MELBOURNE, 1956—FIRST CITY IN THE SOUTHERN HEMISPHERE TO HOST THE GAMES

Before the Melbourne Games began, the IOC struck from the athlete's pledge the requirement that the participants would remain amateurs after the Games were over. The IOC decision was an indicator that pragmatism was becoming a part of the Olympic movement. Labor disputes held up construction of athletic venues and there were doubts as to whether the Melbourne Organizing Committee could get the Games underway on schedule. The Games did begin on time and few problems were encountered. The United States Olympic team traveled farther than ever before to participate in the Games of the Sixteenth Olympiad. The flight from Los Angeles to Melbourne, site of the Games, was approximately 11,000 miles.

American women won three aquatic titles at Melbourne and finished one-two-three in two of the three events in which they won titles. Pat

Figure 17.4. 1952 United States Olympian Don Holder. Courtesy of Dr. Joe Regna.

McCormick led the platform diving sweep, while Shelley Mann finished first in the butterfly event. McCormick also won the springboard title. Silver medals were received by Americans in the Springboard competition, the 400-meter relay, and the 100-meter backstroke. A bronze medal was won by an American in the 400-meter freestyle event.[27]

Pat McCormick's double diving titles in the 1952 and 1956 Olympic Games distinguished her as the first person in diving history ever to score a "double-double" in Olympic competition. She received the James E. Sullivan trophy in 1956 and in 1965 became the first woman diver to be honored by the submission of her name for inclusion in the International Swimming Hall of Fame in Fort Lauderdale, Florida.[28]

J. Lyman Bingham, Executive Director of the United States Olympic Association, in May, 1956, called attention to the fact that the status of women's track and field in this country had improved little since the 1952 Olympics. Bingham favored teams sponsored by factories and industrial plants as a source for Olympic team preparation since schools and colleges were still not providing highly competitive track and field competition.[29] Bingham's comments may have stimulated subsequent developments. The women's track and field team gathered for the first time to take part in pro-Olympic training the following fall. It met in Los Angeles on October 15, 1956, and had access to facilities at the University of Southern California and the Los Angeles Memorial Coliseum. The services of trainer Celeste Hayden were available for the training sessions in Los Angeles and the Melbourne competition.[30] Hayden was the first female Olympic trainer. Previous Olympic teams had competed without the assistance of a trainer or were assigned a male trainer.

The Americans improved their track and field performances. The 400-meter relay team placed third. Wilma Rudolph, making her first Olympic appearance in 1956, was a member of the relay team which won the bronze medal. Willye White placed second in the running long jump. Mildred McDaniel produced a world and Olympic record in the high jump with a 5 feet 9¼ inches effort. Over 100,000 people cheered the world's best female high jumper.[31]

Because of an Australian law requiring a quarantine period of six months for horses entering the country,[32] Stockholm, Sweden, was chosen as the site for the equestrian events.[33] One American, Shirley Watt, made the equestrian team but did not win a medal in her event, the Grand Prix de Dressage.[34] It was unfortunate that the equestrian teams could not enjoy the spirit of Olympic competition in Melbourne.

Bobby Morrow of San Benito, Texas, became the first athlete since Jesse Owens to win both the 100- and 200-meter championships in the same Olympics. Again the American men exhibited superior track and field performances. They were products of collegiate and AAU programs.

Enroute to the Olympic basketball championship and eventual victory the United States team encountered some opposition from the officials when Bill Russell's "stuff shot" was disallowed. In an easy 85 to 44 victory over Bulgaria, the American shooting techniques caused quite a controversy. Coach Gerald Tucker protested the questionable call during half-time and convinced officials that the shot was legal.[35]

The inevitable USSR–USA comparison which began four years earlier revealed that the Soviets won 37 gold medals while the United States placed second with an accumulation of 32 championship medals. Americans, unwilling to accept second place, wanted explanations for disappointing Olympic performances. The results of the 1956 Games also gave rise to discussions on what course of action the United States should take to improve America's chances of regaining supremacy in the Olympics.

WOMEN'S ADVISORY BOARD

Following the 1956 Olympics, another opportunity for women to gain increased involvement in the United States Olympic Association occurred. Dr. Rachel Bryant of the Division of Girls and Women's Sports (DGWS) met with Olympic officials in 1957. Dr. Bryant and Dr. Carl A. Troester, Jr., American Association for Health, Physical Education, and Recreation (AAHPER) representative to the USOA, attended the Olympic Association's meeting early in December 1957. Bryant and Troester requested that the USOA include DGWS representatives on Olympic Sports Committees governing women's activities.[36] The joint DGWS–AAHPER request was unanimously accepted by the United States Olympic Association.

In September, 1958, the USOA formulated the Women's Advisory Board for the United States Olympic Development Committee. The latter committee was established "to expand, improve, and coordinate programs involving Olympic activities"[37] in an effort to enrich women's Olympic ventures. The word "Advisory" was dropped from the Women's Board title, and in 1963 the group was placed under the auspices of the United States Olympic Development Committee.[38]

ROME, 1960, WILMA RUDOLPH IMPROVES THE IMAGE OF TRACK AND FIELD

By 1960, most American women, with a few exceptions, had entered Olympic competition through sources existing outside educational institutions. The Amateur Athletic Union of the United States had provided the majority of opportunities for women to train for Olympic competition. The Women's Swimming Association of New York provided early national and international aquatic training for women but was an exception because few organizations sponsored competitive training solely for women. Some specialized sport organizations such as the American Canoe Association and the Amateur Fencers League of America sponsored competition for women during their fledgling years of Olympic competition.

On the other hand, men received early impetus to their preparation for international sport from athletic clubs. Furthermore, having had a long history of intercollegiate competition in a variety of sports they benefitted from educational sports programs long before women. In addition to specialized sport organizations such as the United States Yacht Racing Union (USYRU) and the numerous AAU sponsored sports, the armed services offered Olympic training time for athletes in equestrian and shooting events.

In 1960, Barbara Nullmeyer and Mary Ruddy, in an unsuccessful attempt, became the last WSA members to try out for an Olympic team. In that same year, the powerful Santa Clara Swim Club, under the tutelage of George Haines, resumed the production of Olympians. Five out of nine aquatic titles were claimed by American women at the Rome Olympics. Leading female swimmer of the 1960 Games was Christine Von Saltza, who anchored the gold medal 400-meter medley relay and 400-meter freestyle teams. She won the 400-meter freestyle and placed second in the 100-meter freestyle.[39] Lynn Burke won the 100-meter backstroke in world record time while Carolyn Schuler won the 100-meter butterfly title. Both relay teams set world records. The 400-meter freestyle relay victory was an especially happy occasion for the Americans and for Carolyn Wood. Fourteen-year-old Wood made up for her disappointing 100-meter butterfly race, when on the turn she swallowed water, dropped out of the event, and ran from the pool in tears.[40] The triumph of the aquatic team was credited largely to the AAU's age-group swimming program. Christine Von Saltza was the first female Olympic champion to emerge from the AAU's age-group program.[41]

Ingrid Kramer of Germany interrupted America's Olympic springboard diving monopoly which began with the 1920 Games in Antwerp. Kramer also halted the United States domination of platform diving which dated back to the 1924 Paris Olympics. The American divers were not completely shut out of the diving competition. Three-time Olympian Paula Meyers Pope placed second in both diving events.[42]

America's female runners, throwers, and jumpers of the Games of the Seventeenth Olympiad were coached by Edward Temple and Francis Welch. Earlene Brown won the bronze medal with her final heave of the shotput. The popular Wilma Rudolph was victorious in both the 100- and 200-meter dashes and anchored the gold medal 400-meter relay team. She set an Olympic record in the 200-meter dash; however, an Olympic record was disallowed in the 100-meter dash because the wind speed exceeded the allowable maximum. Rudolph was the first American woman to win the 200-meter dash. Wilma Rudolph's success in Rome helped to stimulate the popularity of track and field among girls and women in the United States. The 400-meter relay team had set a world record during a preliminary heat.[43]

Americans did not win a medal in the once controversial 800-meter run which appeared in the 1960 program after a lapse of five celebrated Olympiads. A medal in the 80-meter hurdles eluded Americans and not a single American participated in the awards ceremonies in the field events.

The gymnasts competed:

> ... in the historic Caracalla Baths, constructed in 217 A.D. by Antonius Caracalla. An arena seating 5,000 was built within the centuries-old arches, vaults, and columns of the huge monument in the heart of Rome.[44]

The Americans placed ninth among 17 nations in team competition and did not win any medals in the individual events.[45] Olympic gymnastics was indeed a highly competitive event and finishing in the top 10 was a remarkable accomplishment for the Americans.

The first appearance of American women in Olympic canoeing took place at the Rome Games. Organized kayak programs for women in the United States began in 1957 and by 1960 women were ready to embark on another Olympic challenge. Fund-raising campaigns were successful and Olympic expenses for both men and women were provided.[46] Two kayaking events were open to women at the Rome Olympics: the 500-meter kayak pairs and the 500-meter kayak singles. The three American entries were eliminated early in the competition.[47]

A 24-year-old Olympic record was rewritten when American Ralph Boston jumped 26 feet, 7¾ inches and eclipsed Jesse Owen's 1936 running long-jump record. Boston had set a world record of 26 feet, 11¼ inches in the American trials. Of the 24 events on the men's program nine were won by the United States. The Soviet athletes were a distant second having won only four championships. In an amazing display of consistency three Americans successfully defended their 1956 Olympic titles. For the second consecutive time Lee Calhoun won the 110-meter hurdles, while Glenn Davis and Al Oerter, respectively, won the 400-meter hurdles and the discus.

American Rafer Johnson, and his University of California at Los Angeles teammate C.K. Yang of the (Taiwan) Republic of China had carried the flag of their respective countries during the opening ceremonies. The two friends finished one-two in the decathlon. Rafer Johnson had lost 15 pounds when the grueling two-day competition ended. Although Johnson had won only one of the 10 events, he scored enough points to place first even though Yang had won seven of the events. The decathletes concluded their efforts late at night and the victory ceremony was held the next day.

American men won four of the eight men's swimming races. Americans also won both the platform and springboard diving events. The United States, a long-time power in swimming and diving, reaped the benefits of aquatic programs that prepared young men to enter Olympic competition on a par with world class performers. In addition to the AAU's age-group swimming, the YMCA, club teams, interscholastic programs, and intercollegiate competition have established a sound foundation for producing outstanding swimmers.

The Italians defeated the American boxers and took team honors at the Games in Rome by winning three gold medals, three silver laurels, and one bronze award. The American team also won three gold medals but managed to claim only one other Olympic boxing medal, a bronze. Later to rise as one of the most outstanding professional boxers of all time was Cassius Clay. He won the Olympic light heavyweight championship. Clay, who later preferred to be called Muhammad Ali, became known throughout the world.

Referred to as an impressive technical achievement, taped television coverage of the Rome Olympics was flown to the United States and aired the same day the event occurred. Athletes such as Wilma Rudolph and Rafer

Johnson brought the excitement of competition into American homes. Wilma Rudolph is also credited with contributing to greater societal acceptance of track and field for females.

TRAGEDY

Two Danish cyclists competing in a preliminary race collapsed and one died a few hours after fainting. Olympic officials disclosed that the cyclist died as a result of a drug injection. It was the first drug related Olympic death.[48] Drug usage was common practice among professional European cyclists who received lucrative pay-offs for their endorsements and appearances. The monetary rewards were enticing to amateur cyclists who looked forward to professional careers. Some experimented with drugs in an attempt to better their performances. The United States did not win a cycling medal, because it could not compete on a par with countries having fewer express highways and cars and more velodromes and numerous cycling races.

TOKYO, 1964, VOLLEYBALL BECOMES AN OLYMPIC SPORT

In 1959, the International Olympic Committee declared Tokyo, largest city in the world, as the site of the 1964 summer Olympic Games. Japanese organizers presented a proposal to drop canoeing and the modern pentathlon, replacing them with judo and volleyball. European and South American countries opposed the proposal. IOC members were given the opportunity to vote against any of the recognized Olympic sports which they did not favor for the Tokyo Games. A majority of the IOC voted to delete archery and handball. Canoeing and the modern pentathlon remained in the Olympic program and judo and volleyball were added to the 1964 events.[49] When the Tokyo Olympic facilities were completed, an entire area of the metropolis was transformed into a marvelous park for sports. The Olympic Village was within a 15-minute walk from the competition venues.

In the fall of 1963, *Sports Illustrated* reiterated the woes of women's track and field in the United States. There were very few coaches to teach or encourage girls and women to participate in track and field. The 1928 Olympics were again blamed for causing women physical educators to oppose interscholastic and intercollegiate track and field. In addition, the dismal performances of the American women in the 1962 USA–USSR track and field meet may have shrouded the impetus Wilma Rudolph had given to the sport. Interest in track and field was declining, according to *Sports Illustrated.*

There were some coaches, such as Tennessee State University's Edward Temple and Roxanne Andersen of San Francisco's Laurel Club, who were doing a great deal to further the sport. The National Institutes on Girls' Sports were a positive attempt to improve the skill of females and offer coaching techniques.[50] A number of women launched successful interscholastic and intercollegiate coaching careers as a result of their participation in the National Institutes. Previous to the institutes there were few opportunities for women to learn the skills of coaching.

Concern for the rapid improvement of Soviet athletes in a variety of sports and a failure of the American athletes to dominate the Olympic Games led to the initiation of plans to refine the structure of American sport. A program designed to restore American superiority in the Olympic games began in December 1963. The program, under the auspices of the United States Olympic Committee, was endorsed by President Lyndon Johnson. Background information included a survey of facilities, coaching methods, and financing for all sports in the Olympic program. The survey was intended to determine the procedures for producing international caliber athletes. A cooperative effort by corporations, individuals, municipalities, counties, and the federal government[51] was requested to aid programs that could prepare Olympic athletes who could successfully compete against athletes whose prowess was refined by advanced research and technology.

The 1964 women Olympians representing the United States won seven out of ten swimming and diving championships in Tokyo. Sharon Stouder's three gold medals in the 400-meter relay, 400-meter medley relay, and the 100-meter breaststroke, and her silver medal in the 100-meter freestyle events were unprecedented. No other woman swimmer had achieved so much in a single Olympic appearance. After the Tokyo Olympic Games Sharon Stouder was named World Woman Swimmer of the year by *Sports Illustrated, Swimming World,* and the American Broadcasting Company. In 1973, Stouder was inducted into the International Swimming Hall of Fame.[52]

Claudia Kolb, by winning the silver medal in the 200-meter breaststroke, became the first American to finish in the top three places in that event. The event was first included in the 1924 Olympic program[53] and then dropped until the Tokyo Games.

Donna de Varona won the 400-meter individual medley and swam a leg on the world record 400-meter freestyle relay team. Her most outstanding swimming achievements extended over a five-year period beginning with the 1960 Olympics and ending after the Tokyo Games. She won thirty-seven individual national championship medals and three national high point awards. Donna de Varona dominated the individual medley and set world record times in three of the four strokes in the event. She repeatedly lowered times in the backstroke, butterfly, and freestyle.

Following the Tokyo Olympics, Donna de Varona was voted America's Outstanding Woman Athlete, Outstanding American Female Swimmer, San Francisco's Outstanding American Female Swimmer, and was presented with the National Academy Sports Award. She was one of the most photographed woman athletes, appearing on the covers of *Sports Illustrated, Saturday Evening Post, Life Magazine,* and *Time Magazine.*[54]

Edward Temple of Tennessee State University, coach of the 1964 women's Olympic track team, was no doubt disappointed when the female delegation received only four medals. Americans finished second in the 400-meter relay. Wyomia Tyus won the 100-meter dash and Edith McGuire established an Olympic record in the 200-meter event. McGuire won the silver medal in the 100-meter dash. Americans were unsuccessful in their attempts to win medals in either of the two new events, the 400-meter run or the pentathlon. The 800-meter run, high jump, long jump, discus throw, javelin throw, and shotput awards all went to foreign competitors.[55]

In 1948, women from Tennessee Agricultural and Industrial State University, since renamed Tennessee State University, a predominantly black institution in Nashville, Tennessee, began representing the United States in the Olympics. Between 1948 and 1964, 29 Olympic track and field medals were won by American women. Nineteen of the medals were won by Tennessee State University women. Names like Wilma Rudolph, Willye White, Edith McGuire, and Wyomia Tyus made lasting impressions in the sport of track and field. Long before women's national collegiate track and field championships were in existence Edward Temple attracted top black track and field performers and provided competitive opportunities through the AAU.

Americans were successful in the 1964 Olympic canoeing competition. Marcia Jones became the first American woman to win a medal in Olympic kayaking when she finished third in women's singles. In the kayak doubles competition Francine Fox and Gloriane Perrier finished second, barely two seconds behind the victorious Germans.[56]

In Tokyo, American women entered volleyball, the first team sport open to women in Olympic competition. The United States entry came about when Brazil withdrew because of financial difficulties. Substitution by the United States was made upon the recommendation of the International Volleyball Federation.[57] Brazil had qualified for the Olympics by winning the 1963 Pan American volleyball title and the United States team was runner-up.[58] Six teams entered women's Olympic volleyball. The United States won only one match.[59]

Al Oerter, the 1956 and 1960 Olympic discus champion, with a heavily taped side because of torn rib cartilage, won the 1964 championship. Another American, Dave Weill, won the bronze medal. Regarding his injury, Oerter said, "I was thinking of dropping out. Then the competition came and the adrenalin started flowing and everything worked."[60]

Eddie Hurt of Morgan State College in Baltimore served as an assistant Olympic track and field coach, the first black named to the men's coaching staff. Hurt had been at Morgan State for 35 years and coached many outstanding sprinters.[61] It was a fitting honor for one who had dedicated a career to the advancement of track and field.

When the Olympic flame was extinguished in Tokyo, American athletes had won more championships than foreign competitors for the first time in the 12 years. The basketball title was included in the championship won by Americans. The United States defeated the Soviet Union in the final game

73 to 59 and maintained its unbeaten Olympic basketball record. By 1964 the unbeaten record was extended to 47 games and 6 consecutive championships. Although the United States was usually strong in boxing, Joe Frazier was the only American to win a gold medal. Frazier, an outstanding black boxer, later won the heavyweight boxing title as a professional.

The IOC has always vigorously opposed an overall medal count, but members of the news media have continually publicized the number of championships, second, and third place finishes won by each respective country. The Soviet Union-United States comparison of performances has added to the interest in the medal count.

MEXICO CITY, 1968, TURMOIL BLENDS INTO FESTIVITY

Harry Edwards, a sociology teacher at San Jose State College, tried to organize a boycott movement preceding the Mexico City Olympics. The boycott proposal was initiated at the 1967 Black Power Conference in Newark, New Jersey. Edwards believed a boycott "would dramatize to the world the inequities faced by American (blacks) in everyday life." Boycott opponents believed the Olympic Games provided black athletes with an equal opportunity to compete. Ralph Boston, the 1960 Olympic long jump champion, and Stan Wright, one of the four assistant coaches of the Olympic track team and the only black coach on the staff, opposed the boycott.[62] For a long time black athletes were torn between supporting the boycott and entering competition for which they had spent years preparing. The boycott was abandoned in the fall of 1968 when many leading contenders for Olympic team membership failed to offer their support. Instead black athletes decided to participate in symbolic gestures such as the wearing of black arm bands.

Other threats of boycotts ensued when the IOC readmitted South Africa to the Olympic movement despite the country's racial policies against blacks. The Soviet invasion of Czechoslovakia generated other proposals for a boycott. University students in conflict with the Mexican government staged riots. Forty-nine students were killed in gun battles.

The International Olympic Committee adopted femininity testing for women athletes to insure equality in competition. Beginning with the winter and summer Olympics of 1968 women were required to take a test to substantiate their femininity. A saliva test approved by the International Sports Medicine Federation was chosen for the chromosome determination and thus indicate the athlete's sex.[63] The test was administered on a selective basis only in 1968.

The American Broadcasting Company paid $4.5 million for the television rights to cover the 1968 Olympic Games. ABC termed the 44 hours of Olympic coverage, much of it live and in primetime viewing, the "biggest challenge" in the history of television. The record number of television hours surpassed the 14½ hours transmitted from Tokyo. The network included 15 commentators, the most ever used to cover a sports event.[64]

For the first time in the history of the Olympic Games the young people of the world gathered to compete in a Latin American city as Mexico City hosted the Games of the Nineteenth Olympiad. Janice-Lee York Romary, in her sixth consecutive Olympic fencing appearance, was the first woman to carry the American flag and lead the United States contingent for the opening ceremony. American Olympic officials had considered giving hammer thrower Harold Connolly the honor of carrying the flag but Connolly indicated that he would dip the flag before the Tribune of Honor where Mexican and Olympic dignitaries sat, thereby breaking the American tradition which according to *The New York Times* was established at the 1908 Olympic Games. Some of America's athletic delegation to the London Games of 1908 consisted of a group of Irish-born Americans nicknamed "The Whales" because of their enormous size. The night before the opening ceremonies they gathered for a beer drinking festival:

> The more they drank the deeper grew their indignation at the perfidies that the English had perpetrated on the Irish over the centuries. The prospect of dipping the American flag before His Majesty King George V, was even more than they could bear.
>
> "Our flag bows to no earthly king," growled Martin Sheridan. They issued orders to Ralph Rose, the flag bearer. As the Americans paraded past the King the flag did not dip.[65]

For the first time in the Summer Olympic Games, a woman, 20-year-old Norma Enriqueta Basilio, brought the Olympic torch into the stadium, circled the track, climbed the steps and then ignited the flame. She was a member of the Mexican Olympic team, a hurdler, a 400-meter relay participant and 400-meter runner.

The festive atmosphere and Mexican hospitality were shrouded by the actions of two angry young Americans. Sprinters Tommie Smith and John Carlos, wearing black gloves and with fists clinched held overhead in the black power symbol, demonstrated their discontent with the status of black Americans during the Olympic awards ceremony. Smith, the 200-meter dash victor, and Carlos, the third place finisher defiantly refused to look at the flag as "The Star-Spangled Banner" was played. The runners were expelled from the United States Olympic team and sent home.

During a press conference, Wyomia Tyus, spokeswoman for the 400-meter relay team, dedicated the American 400-meter relay championship to John Carlos and Tommie Smith.[66] Reactions to the Carlos-Smith incident were mixed, but members of the USOC were embarrassed by the behavior of these outstanding track athletes. American athletes, amid social pressures resulting from racial problems, performed exceptionally well. Lee Evans led an American sweep in the 400-meter race, the first accomplishment of its kind in track since 1960. In an incredible long jump performance, Bob Beamon set a world record by jumping 29 feet, 2½ inches.[67] Beamon's jump was probably the most astonishing accomplishment of the Mexico City

Games. He jumped nearly three feet farther than the champion long jumper in the previous Olympics. For the fourth consecutive time Al Oerter won the Olympic discus title. His throw of 212 feet 6½ inches was nearly 115 feet farther than the winning throw in the First Olympiad of the modern era.

American women dominated the aquatic events in Mexico City by claiming an astonishing 12 out of 16 swimming and diving diadems. The United States swept the 100- and 200-meter freestyle events and the 200-meter individual medley. Deborah Meyer led the American collection of gold medals by setting Olympic records in the 200-, 400-, and 800-meter freestyle events. Sue Gossick and Keala O'Sullivan placed first and second in springboard diving.[68]

The 1968 women's Olympic track and field team, coached by Conrad Ford and Alex Ferenzy, encountered stiff opposition in Mexico City. Nine of the women's Olympic track and field records were broken. The United States won three titles.[69] Wyomia Tyus made Olympic history and added another first to the achievements of American women in Olympic competition by successfully defending her 100-meter dash championship. She anchored the 400-meter relay team, sprinting to a five-yard margin of victory. Madeline Manning broke the world record in the 800-meter run. She raced down the final stretch nearly 20 meters in front of her nearest rival.[70] Manning, one of America's premier black runners, was the first woman from the United States to win the 800-meter run, the once controversial event for women.

Previous American basketball teams were composed of well-known players having exceptional talent. The 1968 Olympic team was different for its individual players were unknown. A number of America's outstanding players had bypassed the tryouts for one reason or another. After pre-Olympic preparation basketball officials were in general agreement that the team was truly representative of the usual high caliber of basketball skill so representative of the United States.

Coach Henry Iba of Oklahoma State University was selected as the Olympic basketball coach. Spencer Haywood, according to the Yugoslavian coach, was the "best amateur player in the world." The United States led by only a 32 to 29 margin at half-time in the gold medal contest and ended the game by defeating Yugoslavia 65 to 50.[71]

Dick Fosbury won the Olympic high jump championship and introduced a new style of jumping. He went over the bar while executing a backward flip-like motion. Numerous male and female jumpers adopted the "Fosbury Flop" after the 1968 Olympics.

Payton Jordan, head coach of the American men's track and field team, offered three reasons for the numerous outstanding performances at Mexico City. First, there were more world class athletes from more countries than ever before. Second, the high altitude and thin air provided less body resistance and had adverse effects only on distance runners. Third, the Tartan or synthetic track had a consistent surface which produced uniform balance among performers and enabled them to run faster and jump higher.[72]

Embarrassed because of mediocre performances at the 1968 Olympics, the Soviet Union reorganized its vast sports program and established a position equivalent to a Minister of Sports having membership on the Soviet Cabinet. The Council of Ministers reported the formation of the Union Republican Committee on Physical Culture and Sports.[73]

MUNICH, 1972, THE GAMES ARE SUSPENDED

The splendor of the opening ceremony and the excitement of competition were dealt a near disastrous jolt by an incomprehensible attack on the living quarters of the Israeli athletes. Palestinian terrorists broke into the Olympic Village and introduced murder and massacre to the arena of Olympic sport.[74] Two Israelis were murdered during the predawn attack. Within 24 hours nine Israeli hostages and a West German policeman were killed in a shootout at an airport 20 miles from where the attack began. Five of the terrorists were killed and three were captured. The Olympic Games were turned into a ceremony of mourning. Eighty thousand persons gathered in the Olympic stadium to mourn the deaths of 11 Israelis. Harshly criticized by some, the IOC voted to continue the Games and end one day late at the request of Premier Golda Meir of Israel. For the first time in modern history the Olympic Games were suspended.

The American women's swimming team won seven of the 16 aquatic events compared to 12 in Mexico City. Results of the women's track and field competition were far more disappointing. American women failed to win a single gold medal for the first time since the sport was admitted to the women's Olympic program in 1928. C. Robert Paul, Jr., Senior Editor of *The Olympian,* interpreted the American women's performances at Munich:

> No excuses can be made for the lack of success of the USA in track and field. A comparison of performances in the Olympic Trials indicates, for the most part, the athletes performed up to their potential but they are not in the same class with the Europeans who captured most of the medals.[75]

Archery was readmitted to the Olympics in 1972. Archery had not been in the Olympics since 1920. Americans John Williams and Doreen Wilbur won both gold medals in Munich. In Olympic competition, an average shooting day lasts five hours and there are two days of competition for men and women.

In an intensely disputed basketball game accompanied by a vociferous protest from the United States, the Soviet Union ended America's 63-game Olympic winning streak. Veteran Olympic coach Henry Iba had coached the 1964 and 1968 championship Olympic teams but lost the 1972 protest. The final score ended 51 to 50 in favor of the Soviet team. In a unanimous decision the United States team refused to accept the silver medal.[76]

Another display of racially incited behavior occurred at Munich. Two United States sprinters, Vince Matthews and Wayne Collett, were banned from Olympic competition for life because of disrespectful behavior during the victory ceremony for the 400-meter run. Matthews put his hands on his hips and then stroked his goatee. Both runners were barefooted and talked during the playing of "The Star Spangled Banner."[77]

Frank Shorter, an American born in Munich, became the first United States runner to win the marathon since 1908. For the third time in Olympic history, the second man to enter the Olympic stadium as the end of the marathon approached was declared the winner. A mysterious runner entered the track as the crowd awaited Shorter's reappearance for the final two laps. At first the crowd seemed confused and then began whistling and taunting the runner as he left the stadium. Later it was learned that the bogus marathoner was a sixteen-year-old German youth who was protesting the resumption of the Olympic Games in the wake of the murders of the Israelis. Another American, Ken Moore, of Eugene, Oregon, finished fourth. Shorter's Florida Track Club teammate, Jack Bacheler, finished ninth.

The most heralded swimmer at the Munich Games was American Mark Spitz. Spitz won an unprecedented seven gold medals. The events in which he won gold medals were the 100- and 200-meter freestyle, 100- and 200-meter butterfly, 400- and 800-meter freestyle relay, and 400-meter medley relay. Spitz, a Jewish athlete, left Munich the day after the Israeli massacre because of fear for his safety.

After 20 years as president of the IOC, Avery Brundage was still concerned about the vast size of the Olympic Games. Brundage also believed the Games had become too expensive. He opposed team sports such as soccer, basketball, and ice hockey saying, "All the better players in these sports are ineligible for the Olympic Games. So the Olympic Games, which are supposed to attract the best in sport, have only secondary people." His suggestions for the Olympics included limiting gold medal recipients to a single appearance and imposing an age limit on competitors as well as restricting competitors to two appearances.[78]

MONTREAL, 1976, BASKETBALL IS ADDED TO THE WOMEN'S OLYMPIC PROGRAM

On July 17, 1976, Queen Elizabeth II declared the Games of the Twenty-First Olympiad opened before 7,300 athletes, over 72,000 spectators and a world television audience of an estimated billion.[79] Excitement of the festivities was dampened when Taiwan withdrew from the Olympics on the eve of the opening ceremonies. The Taiwanese team withdrew after agreeing to a compromise and after the IOC voted to allow them to use their flag and national anthem, but not the name "Republic of China." IOC president Lord Killanin had criticized the Canadian government for their refusal to recognize the "Republic of China." The Taiwanese government declined to be recognized under any name other than Republic of China.[80] Other

Figure 17.5.

withdrawals marred the opening celebrations because of the IOC's refusal to expel New Zealand for allowing a rugby team to tour South Africa while "the authorities there were committing wanton massacres of defenseless African women and children in Soweto, Johannesburg, and other cities."[81]

The Montreal Olympics did, however, open in a joyful, festive atmosphere. Queen Elizabeth II appeared at a variety of events and frequently drew the attention from the athletes as spectators acknowledged her presence. The boycott of African countries seemed to go unnoticed by the spectators who obviously enjoyed the pageantry of the parade of athletes. In addition to the absence of Taiwan were Iraq and 28 African nations which withdrew to protest New Zealand's sporting involvement with South Africa.

> The entry of the Greek team, by tradition the first to march in the procession, triggered an enormous eruption of applause that almost drowned out gladiatorial music pouring from 40 loudspeakers around the stadium.[82]

The Queen remained standing for over eighty minutes, resting only thirty seconds. The parading teams numbered as many as 522 in the Soviet contingent to as few as one representing Fiji, a woman pentathlete.

The United States team received a volcanic applause as the 470 red, white and blue-attired athletes poured into the stadium. In an ironic aside, ABC television, which paid $25 million for the U.S. rights to the Games, was showing two minutes of commercial at the time the American team made its rousing entry.[83]

"United States girls averted a whitewash at the hands of East Germany's wonder women on the very last event of the Olympic swimming program . . . "[84] American women, by winning only the 400-meter freestyle relay were referred to as the "number two female swim power" by the Canadian press. In the 400-meter freestyle relay "the Germans started their ace—and possibly the world's greatest ever woman swimmer, Kornelia Ender . . . As expected, Ender took a lead but not of any particular significance."[85] American, Shirley Babashoff, who had won three silver medals behind the dominant East Germans, swam the anchor leg and out-touched the East German swimmer.

For the third consecutive Olympic Games, American men dominated the swimming competition. Twelve of the 13 men's swimming championships were won by Americans. John Naber won four gold medals with first place finishes in two backstroke events and two relays. At the conclusion of the 1976 Olympics, swimmers from the United States had won 52 gold medals, more than any other country in the world. American men had also won more diving championships than any other nation, a total of 13.

American archers Luann Ryon and Darrell Pace won the Olympic championship. Ryon, in her first international competition, won her event with a score of 2,499, establishing a new Olympic record. She outshot her nearest rival, a Soviet, by 39 points. In the men's division, Darrell Pace dominated from the first day of competition. His 2,571 total for the four days of shooting was 69 points higher that the second place finisher from Japan. Pace also set a new Olympic record.[86]

EQUAL COMPETITION

In the Olympics, men and women compete on an equal basis and can be on the same team in yachting, and the equestrian events. Through the 1980 Olympics women competed equally with men in shooting. American shooters Lanny Bassham and Margaret Murdock were tied for first place in the three-position small bore rifle event at Montreal. Bassham was declared the champion. While "The Star Spangled Banner" was being played during the victory ceremony, "Bassham turned to Murdock, helped her onto the winner's stand and held her tightly around the waist until the music stopped."[87] In general, American representatives have performed well in Olympic shooting, yachting, and equestrian competition but have not dominated the sports.

Figure 17.6. Olympic village, Montreal, 1976.

More men than women from the United States have participated in these sports.

For the first time, women's basketball was admitted to the Olympic Games in 1976. Six teams were included in the competition. The United States qualified as one of the five entries. The host automatically qualifies a team or competitor in every Olympic sport if that country fields a team. The American women won the silver medal by defeating Czechoslovakia 83–67. The world-dominating Soviet women defeated the remaining entries: Bulgaria, Japan, and Canada. Billie Jean Moore, who was named women's basketball coach at the University of California at Los Angeles, was the Olympic mentor.

A much anticipated rematch of the Soviet Union-United States men's basketball game did not materialize. In an unexpected turn of events, the Soviet team did not advance to the final round of the tournament and the

United States went on to win the gold medal against another traditional European foe, Yugoslavia.

THE U.S. OLYMPIC FESTIVAL

In 1963, Robert J. Kane envisioned a gathering of amateur athletes for national competition. Kane's idea did not reach fruition until 15 years later. The USOC embarked on a National Sports Festival in July, 1978, at Colorado Springs, Colorado. Over 2,000 athletes participated in 22 sports. The USOC conducts the Festival in the summer months between the Olympic Games.[88] After the 1985 Festival in Baton Rouge, the name was changed to the U.S. Olympic Festival to identify its with the Olympic movement and to add prestige. By 1994, the U.S. Olympic Festival included 37 winter and summer sports.

BOYCOTT OF THE 1980 OLYMPIC GAMES

The Olympic Games of the Twenty-second Olympiad were awarded to Moscow. For the first time in modern Olympic history, the United States was not represented. Because of the Soviet Union's invasion of Afghanistan and subsequent refusal to withdraw its military troops by February 20, 1980, the United States, at the insistence of President Jimmy Carter, did not send an Olympic team to Moscow. Furthermore, the President was concerned over the threat to national security if a team went to Moscow. Without consulting the USOC or IOC officials, President Carter announced boycott plans. He proposed three alternatives which were rejected by the IOC: postponement of the 1980 Games, selection of a new host city, and cancellation of the Games. President Carter took other action against the Soviet Union when he ordered cutbacks in the sale of technical equipment and a grain embargo.

The boycott issue was constantly covered by the media. Both the House of Representatives and the United States Senate voted against sending a team to Moscow. Polls conducted by Roper, Harris, and Gallup revealed that the majority of Americans opposed sending a team to the Moscow Olympic Games. Still there was hope among some athletes, leaders in the Olympic Movement, and staunch followers of the Olympic Games that the USOC would resist pressure from the United States government and vote to send a team. Hope for participation of American athletes in Moscow was abandoned when the USOC House of Delegates voted in favor of the boycott in April, 1980.[89]

LOS ANGELES, 1984—RONALD REAGAN, THE FIRST AMERICAN PRESIDENT TO OPEN THE OLYMPIC GAMES HELD IN THE UNITED STATES

When the 1904 St. Louis Olympic Games opened, Alice Roosevelt, daughter of President Theodore Roosevelt was present for the opening ceremonies. Governor Franklin D. Roosevelt of New York made a plea for world peace when he opened the 1932 Olympic Winter Games in Lake Placid.[90] Vice President Charles Curtis was sent to Los Angeles by President Herbert Hoover in 1932, while Vice President Richard Nixon opened the 1960 Olympic Winter Games in Squaw Valley. Vice President Walter Mondale opened the 1980 Olympic Winter Games in Lake Placid. After five Olympic Games were held in the United States, President Ronald Reagan became the first American President in office to participate in the opening ceremonies of the Olympic Games.

During an IOC ceremony, in mid-January 1983, a long overdue error was corrected when IOC President Juan Antonio Samaranch presented Jim Thorpe's children with gold medals for his championship performances in the decathlon and pentathlon. Thorpe's 1912 Olympic victories were deleted from the record books after it was learned that he had received money while playing in two seasons of minor league baseball prior to the Stockholm Olympics.[91] The once uncompromising protectors of the amateur code which did not permit athletes to receive payment for sport involvement had given way to the more pragmatic needs of athletes in the 1980s.

An ironic coincidence put a damper on the start of the 1984 torch relay. The Soviet Union had announced a decision to boycott the Los Angeles Olympics on the same day runners in New York City began the Olympic torch relay. Although the Soviets had cited insufficient security and were aware that some athletes might be encouraged to defect, they more likely had remained piqued that President Jimmy Carter's administration had initiated a boycott of the 1980 Olympics. Nevertheless, the 82-day torch relay proceeded with participants that included Bill Thorpe, Jr., the grandson of Jim Thorpe and Gina Hemphill, the granddaughter of Jesse Owens.

When the Games of the XXIII Olympiad in Los Angeles were opened by President Ronald Reagan, almost 7,000 athletes representing 140 delegations had assembled for the largest sporting event in the world. Just 80 National Olympic Committees had sent 5,200 athletes to the American led boycott four years earlier. Despite the absence of athletes from the Soviet Union and most of its allies, there were extraordinary athletic performances and an attendance record that reached nearly six million.

The Greco-Roman wrestler, Jeff Blatnick, who had overcome Hodgkin's disease and radiation treatments advanced to the final match. He defeated

Thomas Johansson of Sweden who was 30 pounds heavier. The first Olympic women's marathon was won by another American, Joan Benoit. Benoit had undergone arthroscopic knee surgery two and half weeks prior to the United States Olympic trials. Benoit pulled ahead early in the race and defeated 49 other competitors in 2:24:52.[92]

Carl Lewis matched the legendary Jesse Owens' record when he collected gold medals in the 100 and 200 meters, the long jump, and anchored the four by 100 meter relay team. In gymnastics, Tim Daggett's horizontal bar performance, Mitch Gaylord's effort on the rings, and Bart Connor's routine on the parallel bars earned scores of 10. Daggett, Gaylord, and Connor, along with James Hartung and Scott Johnson, upset the favored Chinese and won the team gold medal. Another gymnast, 16-year-old Mary Lou Retton won more medals than any other competitor in Los Angeles. She won the all-around event, finished second in the vault and team event, and was third in the floor exercise and uneven bars.

Edwin Moses won his 105th 400-meter hurdles race and the gold medal. Valerie Brisco-Hooks became the first woman to win the 200- and 400-meter races. She ran the third leg of the four by 400-meter relay and collected her third gold medal. Twenty-four years earlier, in 1960, Wilma Rudolph had become the first American woman triple gold medalist.

Bobby Knight of Indiana University coached the men's gold medal winning basketball team. Pat Summitt of the University of Tennessee coached the American women to their first gold medal in Olympic basketball.

Because Peter Ueberroth, President of the Los Angeles Olympic Organizing Committee (LAOOC), elected to use existing venues and corporate sponsors who were willing to contribute millions of dollars, an astonishing $225 million income over expenses remained at the conclusion of the Los Angeles Olympics. One of the Olympic benefactors, Levi Strauss and Company, had contributed $10 million inkind and supplied uniforms for the United States team and 60,000 employees and volunteers.[93]

Beneficiaries of LAOOC funds have included young people in southern California, National Governing Bodies, and the Olympic Foundation. The Amateur Athletic Foundation of Los Angeles (AAFLA) is a legacy of the 1984 Olympics which provides young people with opportunities to learn sports skills and to participate in sports events. Eighty percent of the LAOOC money was equally divided between the AAFLA and the NGBs while the remaining 20 percent of the funds was used to establish the Olympic Foundation. The Olympic Foundation is a not-for-profit corporation created by LAOOC's surplus income over expenses and from money generated by the Olympic coin program. Grants from the Olympic Foundation's endowment are used to promote amateur sports in the United States.[94] The 1984 Olympic Games marked a turning point in the Olympic movement resulting from Peter Ueberroth's successful marketing of the Games. Ueberroth was forced into a marketing strategy to sell the Games because the citizens of Los Angeles had refused years of future taxation in order to host the Olympics. Because of debts incurred by some past Olympic Organizing Committees, few cities expressed a desire to host the Games. As the 1990s approached, numerous cities had expressed an interest in hosting the Summer or Olympic Winter Games.

SEOUL, 1988, HARMONY AND PROGRESS

The Seoul Olympic Organizing Committee (SLOOC) chose "Harmony and Progress" as the motto for the 1988 Seoul Olympic Games. The lofty goal of the SLOOC was to provide all people with an opportunity to progress toward worldwide harmony. The SLOOC had selected September 17–October 2, 1988, to hold the Games. Weather statistics for the previous 30 years had shown mild temperatures and limited precipitation during those dates. Three weekends and two Korean national holidays allowed many citizens to attend the Games.[95]

Tennis returned as an official sport after a hiatus of 64 years. It had been an demonstration sport in Los Angeles. Table tennis appeared as a new sport on the program while badminton was also a demonstration sport.

Some had misgivings regarding the selection of Seoul as the site of the XXIV Olympiad when students and the South Korean government clashed over political differences and threats of disruption came from North Korea. The SLOOC and the Korean people charmed the world with their culture and beautiful venues. Florence Griffith-Joyner won gold medals in the 100- and 200-meter dashes and the four by 100-meter relay, and a silver medal in the four by 400-meter relay. Her sister-in-law, Jackie Joyner-Kersee, won gold medals in the heptathlon and the long jump. Canadian sprinter, Ben Johnson, stunned the world with his record-breaking time of 9.79 in the 100 meter dash and then shocked the sports world when he tested positive for a banned anabolic steroid. Carl Lewis was later awarded the gold medal for the 100-meter event. Lewis also won the long jump title and a silver medal in the 200-meter sprint.

Diver Greg Louganis became the second "double-double" Olympic champion when he collected two more gold medals in springboard and platform diving. Prior to his final Olympic dive on the springboard, Louganis had hit the board and sustained a head injury that required several stitches. The first "double-double" diver was Patricia McCormick who had won gold medals in 1952 and 1956.

Kay Yow of North Carolina State University coached the American women to a gold medal in basketball while the American men, coached by John Thompson, finished a disappointing third. In another team sport, Karch Kiraly, voted Most Valuable Player of the Olympic Volleyball Tournament, led the American team to an undefeated record in Seoul.

Figure 17.7. Courtesy Dr. LeRoy T. Walker, 22nd President of the United States Olympic Committee.

1992, BARCELONA, "FRIENDS FOR LIFE"

Barcelona, the beautiful city on the Mediterranean Sea, extended the motto, "Friends for Life," to all peoples. "Friends" referred to an invitation to everyone to participate and "for Life" meant the loyalty and constancy of friendship. Over 9,000 athletes from an unprecedented 162 delegations assembled in Barcelona for the 1992 Olympic Games. Apartheid practices in South Africa had ended and athletes from that African country competed in the Olympics for the first time in over 30 years. Competitors from former republics of the Soviet Union competed as the Unified Team at the direction of President Samaranch. The action was taken because new NOCs were in formation. Meanwhile, athletes from Croatia, Estonia, Latvia, Lithuania, and Slovenia, once forced to compete for the Soviet Union, entered as separate delegations. Those who watched the opening ceremonies were captivated by Spain's archer, Antonio Rebollo, when he touched an arrow to the Olympic flame, and shot it toward the cauldron awaiting to be ignited. The flame burned in the Olympic Stadium, the customary 16 days, in the homeland of IOC President Juan Antonio Samaranch.

Chef de mission of the 1992 Olympic Team was Dr. LeRoy Walker, first African-American President of the USOC and highly regarded educator, coach, and contributor to the Olympic movement. In 1977–1978 he served as the first African-American President of AAHPERD. After teaching and coaching at North Carolina Central University, he became its chancellor.

Figure 17.8. Doug Gjertsen, Dara Torres-Gowen, Nicole Haislett, and Christine Ahmann-Leighton relax in Barcelona. Courtesy of Erika Hansen.

Although the IOC does not recognize a country as an official winner of the Olympic Games, members of the media have traditionally "counted" the number of medals won. The Unified Team claimed 112 medals while the United States won 108. For the first time since 1968, a united German team collected the next highest number of medals with 82.

Among the many outstanding performances was Jackie Joyner-Kersee who successfully defended her heptathlon title and finished third in the

Figure 17.9. Kristen Babb-Sprague and Erika Hansen on their way to the 1992 closing ceremonies. Courtesy of Erika Hansen.

long jump. Evelyn Ashford became the oldest American woman to win a gold medal in track. The 35-year-old sprinter ran the first leg of the United States four by 100-meter relay which won in 42.11. Gymnast Trent Dimas won the individual high bar event, the only gold medal in gymnastics claimed by a man. Dimas' championship performance produced the first American gold medal in gymnastics in a nonboycotted Games since 1932.

American swimmers set three world records and tied another. Mike Barrowman set a world record in the 200 meter breaststroke while the women's four by 100-meter medley relay team and four by 100-meter freestyle relay established world marks. The women's medley relay team was composed of Lea Loveless, Anita Nall, Crissy Ahmann-Leighton, and Jenny Thompson. The other women's relay team was made up of Nicole Haislett, Dara Torres-Gowen, Angel Martino, and Jenny Thompson. The men's four by 100-meter team which equaled the world record included Jeff Rouse, Nelson Diebel, Pablo Morales, and Jon Olsen. Synchronized swimmers from the United States won both gold medals. Kristen Babb-Sprague won the solo event while twins Karen and Sarah Josephson won the duet event.[96]

The "Dream Team," the basketball squad dominated by National Basketball Association (NBA) players and one collegiate player, was chosen to reclaim American supremacy in basketball. A team time-out was never called by the United States in the Olympic basketball tournament, and in the gold medal game against Croatia, the Americans easily won by a score of 117–85. For over a decade, the "amateur code" had been absent from the Olympic movement. President Samaranch's request for the best Olympic athletes in the world whether amateur or professional had been answered. For decades, athletes from the United States had known that "state athletes" supported by their governments had competed as "amateurs." While the IOC Charter specifies that International Federations establish the eligibility of athletes, the ideology of the Olympic movement is open to amateurs and professionals. Athletes from the United States have benefitted from financial support through endorsements by sponsors and from National Governing Bodies.

The year 1992 marked the last time the Games of the Olympiad and the Olympic Winter Games were to be held in the same year. The numbering order of the Games of the Olympiad remained the same while the Olympic Winter Games were held just two years later in 1994. Thereafter, the Olympic Winter Games, which were scheduled for Nagano in 1998, continue with four year intervals. Peoples of the world can now follow Olympic competition every two years. The decision to change the Olympic calendar was made in order to generate additional revenue from increased exposure every two years. Furthermore, those National Olympic Committees that send athletes to compete in both Summer and Olympic Winter Games are now able to concentrate fund raising and preparation for one team every two years.

THE CENTENNIAL OLYMPIC GAMES

Atlanta's quest for hosting the 1996 Olympic Games began less than four years before the IOC's designation of the Centennial Olympic city. Some thought this was a late start to host the quadrennial event. Many followers of the Olympic movement believed that Athens, the sentimental favorite to host the 100th anniversary of the modern Olympics was the favored site of the IOC. Nevertheless, a visionary Atlanta attorney, Billy Payne, invited Peter Candler, senior vice president of an insurance company, to become his partner in the Georgia Amateur Athletics Foundation (GAAF) and the new sports organization was founded in February 1987. Payne convinced then Atlanta Mayor Andrew Young to offer support in a bid to host the 1996 Games. The following September, Atlanta submitted a formal request to the USOC to become the American bid city. In April, 1988, the USOC Executive Board based on a recommendation from its Site Selection Committee, chose Atlanta as the American bid city.[97]

In addition to Atlanta and Athens, four other cities that had expressed an interest in hosting the 1996 Summer Olympics included Belgrade, Manchester, Melbourne, and Toronto. On September 18, 1990, *The Atlanta Journal's* headline seemed to leap from the front page with bold letters, "IT'S ATLANTA!" On the morning of September 17, 1990, thousands of Atlantans watched their televisions while an enthusiastic crowd had gathered in downtown Atlanta anxiously awaiting the announcement that was carried live from Tokyo, Japan, site of the IOC's 96th General Session. When IOC President Samaranch announced that Atlanta had been awarded the honor of hosting the Centennial Olympics, the city seemed to erupt with jubilation.

2000, SYDNEY OPENS THE NEW CENTURY

Sound financial backing, cultural diversity, ample hotel accommodations, and excellent transportation were among the reasons that persuaded the IOC to select Sydney to lead the Olympic Games into the new century. Moreover, free travel for athletes and officials were included in the budget proposed by the Organizing Committee. Unlike the United States, most countries can offer government financial support for cities to host the Olympic Games. Sydney offered the necessary financial plan and also emphasized the diversity of the city with 140 ethnic groups residing there. Construction of a single Olympic Village from which athletes will be able to walk to 14 venues revealed convenience for athletes.[98]

SUMMARY

London was awarded the Olympic Games of 1948. The ruins of bombed buildings served as a stark reminder of the devastating effects of war. The Soviet Union, who had not been represented at the Games since 1912, sent observers to the London Games. Three events were added to women's track and field—the 200-meter dash, the shot put, and the long jump. Alice Coachman became America's first black female gold medalist by winning the high jump. The United States claimed supremacy in men's track and field with seventeen-year-old Bob Mathias winning the decathlon. Other American victories were in the sprints, relays, and field events.

Helsinki was the scene of the 1952 Olympics and site of the first meeting of athletes from the United States and Soviet Union. American boxers ended a 20-year drought when they won five gold medals. All five pugilists were black and led by Norvel Lee who was named the outstanding boxer of the tournament. Army equestrian teams had previously represented the United States in Olympic competition, but they were replaced by the United States Equestrian Team which was formed in 1950. American women were provided with another opportunity to try out for the Olympic team.

Avery Brundage became the first American to be elected president of the International Olympic Committee in July, 1952. He considered major problems of the Olympic movement to be nationalism, the increasing size of the Games, and the threat of professionalism. Brundage was past president of the United States Olympic Committee and had been a member of the IOC since 1936.

Melbourne became the first city in the Southern Hemisphere to host the 1956 Games. American women won three aquatic titles with Pat McCormick winning the platform diving and springboard title. Double diving titles in the 1952 and 1956 Games distinguished her as the only person in diving history ever to score a "double-double" in Olympic competition. Concern was voiced about the low status of women's track and field in the United States and some initial efforts were taken to improve performances in international competition. American men again displayed superior track and field performances with athletes coming from collegiate and AAU programs. When comparing USSR and USA Olympic performances, the United States was behind the Soviet Union which prompted discussions concerning how United States supremacy could be regained in Olympic competition.

Following the 1956 Games, women gained another opportunity for increased involvement in affairs of the United States Olympic Association (USOA). Dr. Rachel Bryant and Dr. Carl Troester requested that the USOA include representatives from the Division of Girls and Womens Sports (DGWS) on Olympic Sports Committees. The request was accepted by the USOA.

When the Rome Olympics were held in 1960, most American women had entered Olympic competition through sources existing outside educational institutions. In contrast, men had received early impetus to their preparation for international sport from athletic clubs. At Rome, five of nine aquatic titles were won by American women and credited largely to the efforts of the AAU's age-group swimming program. The winning efforts of Wilma Rudolph helped to enhance the appeal of track and field among girls and women in the United States. Of the 24 track events on the men's program nine were won by the United States with the Soviet athletes winning four. The Italians defeated the American boxers for team honors, but one American light heavyweight named Cassius Clay won the gold medal and went on to become one of the most outstanding professional boxers of all time. He later changed his name to Muhammad Ali.

Tokyo, the largest city in the world, was chosen as the site of the 1964 Olympic Games. Upon conclusion of the Games, American athletes had won more championships than foreign competitors for the first time in 12 years. A program designed to restore American superiority in the Games began in December, 1963, under the auspices of the USOC and endorsed by President Lyndon Johnson. A cooperative effort was requested of corporations, individuals, municipalities, counties, and the federal government to aid programs for the preparation of United States Olympic caliber athletes.

Mexico City was the scene of the 1968 Olympiad which was held in a Latin American city for the first time. Harry Edwards, a sociology teacher at San Jose State College, proposed a boycott of black American athletes which he believed would call attention to the inequities facing black people in daily life. The boycott did not take place however, and black athletes decided to participate wearing black arm bands instead. Amid the racial unrest, Americans did well. Bob Beamon set a world record in the long jump and the amazing Al Oerter won the discus title for the fourth consecutive time. American women dominated the aquatic events by winning 12 of 16 swimming and diving diadems. Reasons for numerous outstanding performances were attributed to the involvement of world class athletes from more countries than in the past, the high altitude and thin air offered less body resistance adversely affecting only the distance runners, and the synthetic track had a consistent surface.

The 1972 Games in Munich were marred when Palestinian terrorists broke into the Olympic Village and murdered two Israelis in a pre-dawn attack. Within 24 hours nine Israeli hostages and a West German policeman were killed in a shootout 20 miles from where the attack began. The IOC voted to continue the Games and end one day late.

In track and field, American women failed to win any event which was the first such occurrence since the sport was admitted to the program in 1928. In basketball the Soviet Union ended America's 63-game Olympic winning streak. The game was protested by the United States but the score remained final in favor of the Soviets. Frank Shorter became the first American runner to win the marathon since 1908. American swimmer, Mark Spitz won an unprecedented seven gold medals.

The Games of the Twenty-First Olympiad opened in Montreal before 7,300 athletes, over 72,000 spectators, and a world-wide television audience. For the third consecutive Games, American men dominated the swimming competition with John Naber winning four gold medals. Women's basketball was admitted to the program for the first time with six teams entering the competition. The Soviet team captured the gold medal with the United States women earning the silver medal.

The 1980 Olympic Games were awarded to Moscow, but for the first time in modern Olympic history the United States was not represented because of the Soviet Union's invasion of Afghanistan. President Carter proposed three alternatives which the IOC rejected: postpone the 1980 Games, select a new host city, or cancel the Games. Both the House of Representatives and the United States Senate voted against sending a team to Moscow. The majority of Americans were also opposed to sending a team to the Games. The USOC House of Delegates also voted in favor of the American boycott.

President Ronald Reagan became the first American President in office to participate in the opening ceremonies of the Olympic Games. When the Games of the XXIII Olympiad in Los Angeles were opened by President Reagan, almost 7,000 athletes representing 140 delegations were present. Because Peter Ueberroth, President of the Los Angeles Olympic Organizing Committee elected to use existing venues and corporate sponsors who were willing to contribute millions of dollars, an astonishing $225 million income over expenses remained at the conclusion of the Los Angeles Olympics.

The Seoul Olympic Organizing Committee chose "Harmony and Progress" as the motto for the 1988 Seoul Olympic Games. The goal of the Organizing Committee was to provide all people with an opportunity to progress toward worldwide harmony. Tennis returned as an official sport after a hiatus of 64 years. Table tennis appeared as a new sport on the program while badminton was a demonstration sport. The Games were held September 17–October 2, 1988 because weather statistics for the previous 30 years had shown mild temperatures and limited precipitation during those dates.

Over 9,000 athletes from an unprecedented 162 delegations assembled in Barcelona for the 1992 Olympic Games. Chef de mission of the 1992 Olympic team was Dr. LeRoy Walker, first African American President of the USOC. The year 1992 marked the last time the Games of the Olympiad and the Olympic Winter Games were to be held in the same year. The numbering order of the Games of the Olympiad remained the same while the Olympic Winter Games were held just two years later in 1994. Thereafter, the Olympic Winter Games which were scheduled for Nagano in 1998 continue with four-year intervals. The decision to change the Olympic calendar was made in order to generate additional revenue from increased exposure every two years.

Atlanta was awarded the honor of hosting the Centennial Olympics. Many followers of the Olympic movement believed that Athens, the sentimental favorite to host the one hundredth anniversary of the modern Olympics was the favored site of the IOC. Sydney was selected to lead the Olympic Games into the next century. Sydney, like Atlanta, was selected because of sound financial backing, cultural diversity, ample hotel accommodations, and excellent transportation.

REFERENCES

1. John Kieran and Arthur Daley. *The Story of the Olympic Games 776 B.C. to 1972.* Philadelphia: J.B. Lippincott, 1973, p. 184.
2. "'Austerity' Medals Cast for Olympic Champions," *The New York Times,* January 17, 1948, p. 12.
3. Elsie V. Jennings. "Women's Swimming Report of Committee Chairman and Team Manager," *Report of the United States Olympic Committee 1948 Games,* New Haven: Walker-Rackliff Co., 1948, pp. 132–133.

4. "Wembley and Other Olympic Arenas." *Olympic Games London 1948 Official Souvenir.* London: Sun Printers Ltd., 1948, p. 22.
5. "Testing Conditions for Olympic Athletes," *The London Times,* August 7, 1948, p. 2.
6. George Pallet. *Women's Athletics.* London: Normal Press, Ltd., 1955, pp. 66–67.
7. Allison Danzig. "Olympic Track and Field True to Form With 10 American Triumphs," *The New York Times,* August 9, 1948, p. 14.
8. Allison Danzig. "Olympic Jury Voids Disqualification and Awards Sprint Relay to Americans," *The New York Times,* August 11, 1948, p. 25.
9. Benjamin Welles. "U.S. Basketball Squad Scores Easy Victory Over France for Olympic Title," *The New York Times,* August 14, 1948, p. 8.
10. "Brundage Leaves for Rome Talks, Ready for Battle on Olympic Cuts," *The New York Times,* April 15, 1949, p. 35.
11. "Olympic Field Hockey Hit," *The New York Times,* April 17, 1950, p. 28.
12. Letter from Betty Shellenberger, Executive Secretary, United States Field Hockey Association, July 24, 1974.
13. "U.S. Field Hockey Team Out of Games at Helsinki," *The New York Times,* July 2, 1952, p. 32.
14. "Rivalry Between U.S. and Russia to Enliven Helsinki Competition," *The New York Times.* July 6, 1952, Sec. V, p. 5.
15. "Russia Enters All Olympic Sports at Helsinki Except Field Hockey," *The New York Times,* June 4, 1952, p. 34.
16. Charles L. Ornstein. "Food and Housing Report of Committee Chairman," *United States 1952 Olympic Book,* New Haven: Walker-Rackliff Co., 1952, pp. 267–268.
17. Edwin J. Aspinall. "Women's Swimming Report of Committee Chairman and Team Co-Manager," *United States 1952 Olympic Book,* New Haven: Walker-Rackliff Co., 1952, pp. 139, 141.
18. Allison Danzig. "Miss McCormick Wins Dive, but U.S. Suffers First Swim Loss in 2 Olympics," *The New York Times,* July 31, 1952, p. 15.
19. "U.S. Fighters Take Five Gold Medals," *The New York Times,* August 3, 1952, sec. V, pp. 1, 3.
20. Pallett. *Women's Athletics.* op. cit. pp. 89–90.
21. Lucile Wilson. "Women's Track and Field Report of Team Manager-Coach," *United States 1952 Olympic Book,* New Haven: Walker-Rackliff Co., p. 113.
22. John W. Wofford. "Equestrian Report of Team Manager," *United States 1952 Olympic Book,* New Haven: Walker-Rackliff Co., 1952, p. 178.
23. "Mrs. Durand Ineligible," *The New York Times,* December 5, 1951, p. 50.
24. "Women Will Ride for First Time With American Team in Olympics," *The New York Times,* April 2, 1952, p. 46.
25. John W. Wofford. "Equestrian Report of Team Manager," *United States 1952 Olympic Book,* New Haven: Walker-Rackliff Co., 1952, p. 179.
26. "Brundage Is Chosen Over Briton as Head of International Olympic Committee," *The New York Times,* July 17, 1952, p. 28.
27. Mrs. Arthur Toner. "Report by Manager-Chaperone," *United States 1956 Olympic Book,* New Haven: Walker-Rackliff Co., 1957, p. 188.
28. Buck Dawson, (ed). "Pat McCormick," *Swimming Hall of Fame Pool Dedication Souvenir Program.* Fort Lauderdale: Swimming Hall of Fame, 1965, p. 26.

29. "Factories Are Held Title Team Source," *The New York Times*, May 11, 1956, p. 31.

30. Roxanne Andersen. "Report by the Manager-Chaperone," *United States 1956 Olympic Book.* New Haven: Walker-Rackliff Co., 1957, p. 88.

31. Andersen. "Report by the Manager-Chaperone," *op. cit.,* p. 89.

32. "Equestrian Tests Out of '56 Olympics," *The New York Times*, August 2, 1953, sec. V, p. 4.

33. "Olympic Group Picks Stockholm to Stage 1956 Equestrian Events," *The New York Times*, May 14, 1954, p. 28.

34. "Personnel 1956 United States Equestrian Olympic Team at Stockholm, Sweden," *United States 1956 Olympic Book, op. cit.,* p. 449.

35. "U.S. 'Stuff Shot' Is Called Legal," *The New York Times,* November 28, 1956, p. 42.

36. Sara Staff Jernigan. "Women and the Olympics," *Journal of Health, Physical Education and Recreation.* 33 (April, 1962), p. 26.

37. Jernigan. *ibid.* pp. 25–26.

38. Sara Staff Jernigan and Marguerite A. Clifton, "Introduction," *Proceedings First National Institute on Girls Sports.* Washington, D.C.: AAHPER, 1965.

39. Arthur G. Lentz, (ed). "American Girls' Performance Sensational in Swimming Triumph; 3 Golds for von Saltza," *1960 United States Olympic Book.* New Haven: Walker-Rackliff Co., 1961, p. 162.

40. Kenneth Rudeen. "Dangerous When Wet," *Sports Illustrated* 13 (September 12, 1960), p. 71.

41. Lentz, (ed). "American Girls' Performance Sensational in Swimming Triumph; 3 Golds for Von Saltza," *op. cit.,* p. 162.

42. Buck Dawson, (ed). "Chris Von Saltza-Honor Swimmer," *International Swimming Hall of Fame Fifth Anniversary Yearbook 1965-1970.* Fort Lauderdale: International Swimming Hall of Fame, 1971, p. 108.

43. Arthur G. Lentz, (ed). "Triple Gold Medal Triumph by U.S.A.'s Wilma Rudolph Rated Best Ever in Women's Track," *1960 United States Olympic Book.* New Haven: Walker-Rackliff Co., 1961, pp. 86–87, 89–90.

44. Arthur G. Lentz, (ed). "All But One of 16 Medals Awarded Russia in Women's Gymnastics: Improved U.S.A. Ninth," *1960 United States Olympic Book.* New Haven: Walker-Rackliff Co., 1961, p. 132.

45. Lentz. "All But One of the 16 Medals Awarded Russia in Women's Gymnastics; Improved U.S.A. Ninth," *ibid.*

46. Letter from L.M. Schindel, Executive Secretary, American Canoe Association, July 15, 1974.

47. Arthur G. Lentz, (ed). "All Canoeing Records Broken, U.S.A. Entries Unplaced But Improved Over 1956 Showing," *1960 United States Olympic Book.* New Haven: Walker-Rackliff Co., 1961, p. 101.

48. "Italy Opens Investigation Into Death of Danish Cyclist Who Received Drug." *The New York Times,* August 30, 1960, p. 33.

49. "Olympic Amateur Code Altered; Judo, Volleyball Join Program," *The New York Times,* June 22, 1961, p. 38.

50. "Why Can't We Beat This Girl?" *Sports Illustrated.* 19 (September 30, 1963), p. 54.

51. Allison Danzig. "Olympic Group Opens a Drive to Restore Supremacy of U.S." *The New York Times,* May 5, 1964, pp. 1, 58.

52. Buck Dawson, (ed). "Sharon Stouder—Honor Swimmer," *International Swimming Hall of Fame 1973 Yearbook.* Fort Lauderdale: Press Time, Inc., 1972, p. 19.

53. Harald Lechenperg, (ed). "Women's Swimming," *Olympic Games 1964.* New York: A.S. Barnes, 1964, p. 172.

54. Buck Dawson, (ed). "Donna de Varona," *International Swimming Hall of Fame 1970 Yearbook.* Fort Lauderdale: International Swimming Hall of Fame, 1970, p. 8.

55. Harald Lechenperg, (ed). "The Track and Field Sports," *Olympic Games 1964.* New York: A.S. Barnes Co., 1964, p. 239.

56. Asa S. Bushnell, (ed). "Canoeing," *United States Olympic Book Games of the XVIII Olympiad, Tokyo.* Providence: Riverhouse Publishing Co., 1964, p. 147.

57. "U.S. in Volleyball Event," *The New York Times,* May 7, 1964, p. 48.

58. Asa S. Bushnell, (ed). "Pan American Games," *1964 United States Olympic Book.* Providence: Riverhouse Publishing Co., 1964, p. 301.

59. Asa S. Bushnell, (ed). "Official Summaries-Volleyball-Men and Women-1964 Olympic Games," *1964 United States Olympic Book.* Providence: Riverhouse Publishing Co., 1964, p. 106.

60. Emerson Chapin. "Oerter, Despite Painful Injury, Wins Third Discus Title in Row," *The New York Times,* October 16, 1964, p. 46.

61. Frank Litsky. "Eddie Hurt: Builder of Athletes," *The New York Times,* July 19, 1964, sec. V, p. 6.

62. "U.S. Olympic Boycott Leaders Remain Undecided on Course," *The New York Times,* June 23, 1968, sec. V, p. 1.

63. "Olympics Require Sex Test," *The New York Times,* January 30, 1968, p. 48.

64. Steve Cody. "Stay-at-Homes Can Watch 44 Hours of Olympics, Much of It Live and in Color," *The New York Times,* October 6, 1968, sec. V, p. 18.

65. Arthur Daley. "With Matchless Pageantry," *The New York Times,* August 27, 1972, sec. V, p. 2.

66. "U.S. Women Dedicate Victory to Smith, Carlos," *The New York Times,* October 21, 1968, p. 60.

67. Neil Amdur. "Beamon's 29-2½ Long Jump and Evan's 43.8-Second 400 Set World Marks," *The New York Times,* October 19, 1968, p. 44.

68. Frederick Fliegner, (pub). "Swimming and Diving-Women," *1968 United States Olympic Book.* Stuttgart: International Olympic Editions, 1969, pp. 294–296.

69. Frederick Fliegner, (pub). "Athletics (Track and Field) Women," *1968 United States Olympic Book.* Stuttgart: International Olympic Editions, 1969, pp. 183–184.

70. Frederick Fliegner, (pub). "Results," *1968 United States Olympic Book.* Stuttgart: International Olympic Editions, 1968, pp. 355–357.

71. Arthur Daley. "Sports of the Times," *The New York Times,* October 27, 1968, sec. V, p. 2.

72. Arthur Daley. "Sports of the Times," *The New York Times,* October 22, 1968, p. 5.

73. "Soviet Council Names A Minister of Sports," *The New York Times,* November 10, 1968, sec. V, p. 15.

74. Rudolf Hagelstange. "Black September 5," *1972 United States Olympic Book.* Stuttgart: International Olympic Editions, 1972, p. 231.

75. C. Robert Paul, Jr. "East Germany Dominates Women's Track Meet: U.S.A. Wins 1 Silver and 2 Bronze Medals," *U.S.O.C. Newsletter,* October, 1972, p. 12.

76. Neil Amdur. "Disputed Basket Halts Streak," *The New York Times,* September 10, 1972, sec. V, p. 1.

77. Neil Amdur. "Matthews and Collett Banned from Olympics," *The New York Times,* September 9, 1972, p. 17.

78. "Brundage: Games Getting Too Big for Ideals," *The New York Times,* July 23, 1972, sec. V, p. 6.

79. Claude Adams. "The Great Day's Really Here," *The Montreal Star,* July 17, 1976, p. A1.

80. Richard Low. "Taiwan Quits Games," *The Montreal Star,* July 17, 1976, p. A1.

81. Mike Boone. "Africans Withdraw," *The Montreal Star,* July 17, 1976, pp. A1, A2.

82. Claude Adams and Claude Arpin. "Opening's Pageantry Dazzles," *The Montreal Star,* July 19, 1976, p. A8.

83. Adams and Arpin. "Opening's Pageantry Dazzles," *ibid.*

84. Ian MacDonald. "Canada's Girls: 4 More Medals," *The Gazette,* July 26, 1976, p. 1.

85. McDonald. "Canada's Girls: 4 More Medals," *ibid.*

86. "Archery," *Daily Summary,* August 1, 1976, p. 43.

87. George Gruenefeld. "American Shooters Battle Procedure After Finishing One–Two in Small Bore," *The Gazette,* July 23, 1976, sec. 0, p. 5.

88. C. Robert Paul, Jr. and R. Michael Moran. (eds). "The National Sports Festival," *The Olympic Games.* Colorado Springs United States Olympic Committee, 1979, p. 9.

89. C. Robert Paul, Jr. "The USOC Position for the 1980 Olympic Games," Symposium, Tennessee State University, May 19, 1980.

90. "Roosevelt Invokes an 'Olympic Peace,'" *The New York Times,* February 5, 1932, p. 21.

91. Robert Lindsey. "Thorpe's Medals Returned," *The New York Times,* January 19, 1983, p. B13.

92. "Women/Marathon," *Olympic Record,* Published by the Los Angeles Olympic Organizing Committee, 1984, pp. 10–11.

93. Thomas C. Hayes. "Shortfall Likely in Olympic Income," *The New York Times,* May 9, 1984, p. A17.

94. "Olympic Foundation," *1995 Fact Book United States Olympic Committee,* Colorado Springs: USOC, 1995, p. 61.

95. "Harmony and Progress," *Seoul 1988,* Seoul: Seoul Olympic Organizing Committee, 1988, pp. 20, 22.

96. Gayle Plant. "Muchas Gracias Barcelona," *Olympian,* 19(September/October, 1992), pp. 12, 15, 17.

97. "Chronology," *Press Guide January 1995,* Atlanta Committee for the Olympic Games, pp. 4–6.

98. "Sydney Gets Highest Praise from IOC for 2000 Olympics," *The Irish Times,* July 13, 1993, p. 17.

Chapter 18

THE OLYMPIC WINTER GAMES
1924–2002

ANTWERP, 1920 AMERICANS BECOME INTERESTED IN THE WINTER OLYMPICS

There was no provision for winter sports when the modern Olympics began in 1896. Having no precedent and no ancient history, winter sports were slow to gain entry in the prestigious Olympic movement. The popularity of winter activities, particularly in European countries, and the organization of winter sports federations eventually established a basis for international competition. The appearance of a winter sport in 1908 at the London Games was subdued by the then more established Summer Olympics.

Figure skating for men and women was included in the 1908 Summer Olympic Games at London, but the United States was not represented. After one celebrated summer Olympiad, figure skating and ice hockey were scheduled in 1920 at Antwerp. In January 1920, the American Olympic Committee was informed that an ice hockey team from the United States could participate in Antwerp. Cornelius Fellowes, President of the International Figure Skating Union of America, organized the team. Teams in the Boston and Pittsburgh areas played. An all-star team was selected from the winners who were the Boston Athletic Association and the Pittsburgh Athletic Club.[1]

The emergence of American women in Winter Olympic competition began in February, 1920 when Theresa Weld of Boston learned of the figure skating competition scheduled in connection with the Antwerp Olympics of 1920. Winter sports were not an official part of the Antwerp Olympic Games and took place in April, three months prior to the summer competition.[2] Cornelius Fellowes requested that American Olympic officials send a figure skating delegation to the Antwerp Olympics. The American Olympic Committee appointed Fellowes manager of America's first Olympic figure skating team, and he selected Theresa Weld and Nathaniel Niles for both the pairs and individual events.[3] Olympic funds were not provided for the skaters and aside from a formal request granted by the American Olympic Committee, Niles and Blanchard competed as private individuals. Theresa Weld qualified for the Antwerp competition by winning the United States senior figure skating title at the national championships March 20, 1920. *The New York Times* proclaimed her title-winning performance superior to those of the male contestants.[4] Pairing with Nathaniel Niles, Weld won the waltzing championship and placed second in the 10-step competition.

On April 7, 1920, America's winter sport competitors, comprised of 11 hockey players and two figure skaters, sailed for Antwerp on board the *Finland*. Because of the lengthy 13-day voyage, Belgian Olympic officials postponed the competition to allow the Americans time to practice.[5]

Ladies singles competition began April 24, 1920, and Theresa Weld became the first American woman figure skater to compete in Europe. Considerable attention was focused on the American skaters, first to compete against Europeans since Irving Brokow who visited Europe several years prior to the Antwerp competition.

America's premier woman skater placed third among six contestants from Sweden, England, and Norway. Nathaniel Niles finished sixth out of 11 skaters. In the pairs event, Weld and Niles placed fourth among eight entries representing Finland, Norway, England, Belgium, and France.[6]

The Americans were pleased with the overall conduct of the skating competition although much discussion was generated by the decisions of the judges. Competitors as well as officials suggested that the Americans were at a disadvantage for not having brought a judge. It was intimated that some judges thought Theresa Weld, the only woman to perform jumps beyond simple toehops, included loops and other moves inappropriate for a "lady's program."

While on board the *Finland*, the ice hockey team, comprised of seven team members and four alternates, continued training by practicing with the puck and performing sit-ups. Most of the team came from Pittsburgh.[7] The American ice hockey team scored impressive victories over Switzerland, Sweden, and Czechoslovakia. They lost to the powerful Canadian team by a score of 2–0 and received the silver medal. The style of hockey played by the two North American teams made a favorable impression on the Europeans. Spectators were turned away at every game because the rink could not accommodate the large crowds.[8]

CHAMONIX, 1924, THE FIRST OLYMPIC WINTER GAMES

During the Olympic Congress of Prague in 1925, an official decision was made to institute a program of winter sports held in the same year but distinct from the Summer Olympics. In a retroactive decision, members of the Prague Congress voted to call the 1924 competition at Chamonix the first Winter Olympic Games.[9] There were five sports for men and one for women. Both men and women participated in singles figure skating and the pairs event. The remainder of the men's program included speed skating, bobsledding, skiing, and ice hockey. Two hundred ninety-three athletes representing 16 countries participated in the First Olympic Winter Games.

Speed skating became an Olympic sport in 1924. Charles Jewtraw, the first American gold medalist in Winter Olympic competitions, won the 500-meter speed skating event at Chamonix. In 1891, the United States was among the first countries to initiate national skating championships. In 1921, speed skating championships were included for women.[10]

ST. MORITZ, 1928, A GOLD MEDAL FOR THE BOBSLED TEAM

Nearly 500 men and women from 25 countries entered the 1928 Winter Olympics. *The New York Times* reported 50 inches of snow for the opening ceremonies at St. Moritz. A 21-gun salute honored the winter teams as they entered the Olympic stadium during a blinding snow storm.[11]

Nathaniel Niles and Theresa Weld Blanchard, having won the American national pairs championship for the tenth consecutive season, represented the United States for the third time in Winter Olympic competition. They finished a disappointing ninth. American skaters were not skating on a par with the Europeans who improved year after year in style and technique.

Theresa Weld Blanchard recalled a frightening experience at St. Moritz:

> Mr. Niles and I brought a thermos of tea to the stadium and I gave him a cup of it which we drank hastily just before we were to skate. To my horror on pouring out my cup I discovered that the thermos was broken and glass was floating around in the tea! I rushed for Mr. Badger, who being a doctor's son, I felt sure would know what to do. He said that probably Mr. Niles hadn't gotten much glass, to forget it and skate my best. All through the pair I was wondering if my partner were going to drop dead, but he never felt any ill effects.[12]

The American five-man bobsled team driven by 17-year-old William Fiske won the gold medal in St. Moritz. The other entry from the United States finished second. There was no American entry in the four-man competition at the 1924 Games and 1928 was the only year for the five-man event.[13]

LAKE PLACID, 1932, THE POPULARITY OF FIGURE SKATING

The United States Figure Skating Association's (USFSA) decision to host the 1930 World Championships in New York City drew attention to figure skating and helped to promote figure skating in the eastern part of the country. New Yorkers had not seen the likes of performances by the renowned European skaters Sonja Henie and Karl Schafer.[14]

Lake Placid, America's pioneer winter sport resort, was awarded the Third Olympic Winter Games. The American Olympic Association credited the Lake Placid Olympic Games with extending the interest in figure skating in the United States. Prior to the 1932 Olympics figure skating had not enjoyed widespread popularity. Aside from the fact that few communities had adequate facilities, only those who had leisure time were attracted to the skating rinks.

A number of other factors contributed to the interest in figure skating.

MRS. THERESA WELD BLANCHARD
MR. NATHANIEL W. NILES
of Boston.
Winners of the National Pairs Skating Championship, 1924.

Figure 18.1. Mrs. Theresa Weld Blanchard and Mr. Nathaniel W. Niles of Boston. Winners of the National Pairs Skating Championships, 1924.

European champions arrived in New York City to practice for the 1932 Games. Newspaper reporters and magazine writers converged on the practice sessions. Sports columns began to include predictions of America's chances of winning titles in the figure skating events. For the first time, all Olympic figure skating events were held in an indoor rink where spectators could view the competition regardless of weather conditions. Spectators crowded into the Olympic rink during practice sessions and nearly fought to see the competition. Figure skating had arrived in America or at least in the eastern part of the United States.[15]

With hopes for success in the 1932 Lake Placid Games, the USFSA postponed the 1931 championships to allow Maribel Vinson and Roger Turner sufficient time to compete in Europe and return to the United States to

Figure 18.2. Maribel Vinson, 1927.

defend their titles. The European trip offered the skaters not only competitive experience but an opportunity to observe European skating styles.[16]

The 1932 Olympic figure skating results revealed that for the first time Americans placed second in pairs skating. Beatrice Loughran and Sherwin Badger attained the highest finish ever in America's attempts at Olympic pairs skating. Maribel Vinson finished third in figure skating.[17]

The International Olympic Committee, in a move initiated by Poland, approved women's speed skating as a demonstration sport at the Third Olympic Winter Games in Lake Placid.[18] Five contestants each from Canada and the United States comprised the women's entry in the speed skating demonstration.

Theresa Weld Blanchard, Beatrice Loughran, Nathaniel Niles, and Sherwin Badger were the leading figure skaters in the United States during most of the years encompassing the first three opportunities to compete in winter Olympic sports. Theresa Weld Blanchard and Nathaniel Niles in addition to their unofficial Olympic debut in 1920, skated in the 1924 and 1928 Games. Beatrice Loughran won three of the four medals credited to American women during the first four Winter Games. Loughran placed second in singles figure skating in 1924, third in singles figure skating in 1928 and, with her partner Sherwin Badger, won the silver medal in pairs skating at the 1932 Games.

The American representatives for ski jumping, ice hockey, and figure skating were selected at national tryouts. Because of a thaw during January, 1932, the men's and women's speed skating, bobsled, and cross-country ski teams were selected on the basis of previous performances.[19]

American men made their best showing ever in speed skating by winning all four Olympic titles. John Shea won the 500- and 1,500-meter events. Irving Jaffee was another double winner in the 5,000- and 10,000-meter races. Edward Murphy won the silver medal in the 5,000-meter competition.[20]

Edward Eagan distinguished his Olympic performances by becoming the first person to win gold medals in both the summer and winter Olympic Games. In 1920, Eagan won a gold medal in the light heavyweight boxing division and was a member of the championship four-man bobsled team in the Lake Placid Olympics.[21]

GARMISCH–PARTENKIRCHEN, 1936 THREAT OF OLYMPIC BOYCOTT

Warm weather that plagued the Winter Games at Chamonix and Lake Placid threatened the Fourth Olympic Winter Games. During pre-Olympic practices, ski jumpers zoomed down several tons of snow hauled from the nearby mountains by Army trucks. The Fourth Winter Olympics were declared open by Chancellor Adolf Hitler as a light snow fell and continued throughout the ceremony. An estimated 50,000 spectators stood on high ground and jammed into the Olympic stadium to watch the parade of athletes representing 28 nations. Some 1,600 athletes took part in the competition. The presence of German military troops sent an uncomfortable tension over the 1936 Winter Games. While the Games were opening, massive German Army regiments formed a solid block near the stadium.[22]

In the official report of the 1936 Olympic Games, Dr. Joel H. Hildebrand, manager of the men's ski team, praised the Germans for their efficient conduct of the Games. Hildebrand was in favor of the United States decision to participate in the Garmisch Games. He was dismayed at the thought of an Olympic boycott. Tampering with the continuation of the Olympics, declared Hildebrand, would destroy the opportunity:

> for young people to learn that young people in other countries are mostly rather decent and not eager to go to war against them, despite any propaganda of their governments and munition makers. Let us not sacrifice this to the pleasure we could derive from making a political protest whose effect might be the reverse of that intended.[23]

The collection of gold medals plummeted from six in 1932 to one in 1936. The only gold medal performance in Garmisch by Americans occurred in the two-man bobsled race. The Norwegians took over the speed skating championships claimed by the American men in 1932.

The debut of American women skiers occurred at the Fourth Olympic Winter Games when Alpine skiing was added to the program. Alice Wolfe, manager of the women's skiing team, credited Roland Palmedo, President of the Amateur Ski Club of New York, as the primary organizer of the first women's ski team that represented America in Olympic competition.[24] German women dominated the skiing events in 1936. Elizabeth Woolsey, top finisher from the United States, placed nineteenth among 30 entries in the combined downhill and slalom race. Alice Wolfe suggested that the large crowds, noisy press, and Olympic atmosphere unnerved the inexperienced Americans.[25]

America's distaff skaters did not fare well at the Garmisch Olympics of 1936. For the first time since entering Olympic figure skating American women failed to claim a single medal. A large number of entries in women's figure skating drastically reduced practice time. American skaters, unaccustomed to outdoor competition, had to wear coats and sweaters. Some American Olympic officials thought the extra clothing and reduced practice time hindered the athletes' performances.[26]

Most of America's early women Olympians came from Boston and New York City and all learned their sport skills outside the context of educational institutions. Women physical educators in the 1920s who refused to endorse high level competition for girls and women extended their disapproval to highly competitive winter sports. Agnes Wayman, Director of Physical Education and Hygiene at Barnard College, writing in the March, 1934, *Sportswoman* summarized the prevailing attitude expressed by most women physical educators during the first four Winter Olympics. Wayman wrote:

> The spirit of skiing like the spirit of canoeing, or fishing, or climbing, should be to ski better and not to ski like the best . . . or be involved in high pressure competition.[27]

ST. MORITZ, 1948, THE FIRST GOLD MEDAL FOR AMERICAN WOMEN

Like the summer Olympics in 1940 and 1944, the Winter Olympics in those years were not celebrated because the world was embroiled in conflict. The winter Games resumed in 1948 and St. Moritz was awarded the honor of hosting the competition. The St. Moritz schedule of events for women included figure skating, Alpine skiing and a demonstration of ice dancing. A request from Great Britain and the United States led to the International Olympic Committee's approval of ice dancing as a demonstration event in the 1948 Games.[28] American women entered all three winter events and for the second consecutive time failed to place in any of the top three positions in singles or pairs skating. However, Gretchen Frazer's performance in the 1948 slalom event produced America's first gold medal in skiing.[29] Thus, Gretchen Frazer became the first American woman to win an Olympic championship in the winter Olympics. Eighteen-year-old Dick Button became the first American male to win the Olympic figure skating title in the singles event.

The 1948 ice hockey team was selected amid controversy. The Amateur Hockey Association (AHA) sent a team to Europe with hopes of entering it in the Olympics. The United States Olympic Committee also selected a team. Avery Brundage, President of the USOC, explained that the IOC required team membership in an international sport body and approval of the national Olympic organization in order for athletes to enter the Olympics. The controversy stemmed from the ineligibility of both teams. The AHA team met only the first requirement while the USOC team met only the second stipulation.[30]

The USOC voted to withdraw all American teams if the AHA team competed in the Games. The Swiss Organizing Committee had designated the AHA team as the official United States entry. The USOC team was comprised of AAU and NCAA members. The USOC was angered by the Swiss action because they considered the AHA a "commercial" group designed to develop professional hockey players.[31]

The Swiss Organizing Committee, in defiance of IOC wishes, permitted the AHA team to enter the Olympic competition. Boos from the crowd, which included 200 Americans, no doubt affected the play of the AHA team which lost to Switzerland. In a special meeting of the IOC, the international sports organization voted to declare the 1948 hockey competition unofficial.[32]

The spirit of the Olympic Games was sadly moved to the background by the internal dispute of the United States hockey teams which was extended to an international conflict. Charges by American bobsleders that their equipment was tampered with because of the ill-will created by the hockey teams further dampened the Olympic spirit. The United States, along with 10 other nations, was involved in protests of speed skating rules.

OSLO, 1952, THE OLYMPIC TEAM TRAVELS BY AIR

Long and tiresome ocean voyages were abandoned and for the first time America's Olympic Winter team traveled by air to Oslo, site of the Sixth Winter Games. A capacity crowd of 29,000 viewed the lighting of the Olympic torch. The flame was brought from Moregdal, Norway, birthplace of skiing.[33]

The presence of America's figure skaters was well known at Oslo. Dick Button successfully defended his singles championship and teammate James Grogan won the bronze medal in the singles competition. For the first time in two Olympic Games, American women won a medal in the singles event. Sixteen-year-old Tenley Albright placed second in singles. Karol and Peter Kennedy shared Tenley Albright's honor by becoming the first Americans to win an Olympic pairs skating laurel in two winter Olympics. The Kennedy's placed second among 13 competitors representing nine countries.[34]

Andrea Mead Lawrence became the first American woman to win two gold medals in one Winter Olympic celebration. She became the reigning skier in the slalom events at Oslo. Lawrence won the slalom event, placing first among 43 skiers from 14 countries. Her championship in the giant slalom represented a victory over 47 competitors from 17 countries.[35] She was heralded by *The New York Times* as the "world's greatest in her specialty."[36]

CORTINA, 1956, EXQUISITE FIGURE SKATING

Four-time United States figure skating champion, Tenley Albright, made history by becoming the first American woman to win a gold medal in figure skating competition. In spite of the severe gash sustained in her right ankle, Tenley Albright won the championship. Her teammate Carol Heiss won the silver medal.[37]

For the first time, the Americans swept an Olympic Winter sport. Hayes Alan Jenkins won the men's singles figure skating title while Ronald Robertson and David Jenkins, younger brother of Hayes Alan, won the silver and bronze medals.[38]

Although the American team won only seven medals, five of them in figure skating, the ice hockey team scored a first-ever win over the Canadians. The United States had to settle for the silver medal after losing to the Soviet Union which made its first appearance in Winter Olympic competition. The other medal won by the American delegation to Cortina was the bronze medal for a third-place finish in the four-man bobsled event.

SQUAW VALLEY, 1960, AN EXPANDED PROGRAM OF EVENTS

Squaw Valley, site of the 1960 Games, was barren of snow in early December, 1959. On December 4, 1959, Chief Harry Winnemucca led a band of Piute Indians in an ancient snow dance. After the dance, the Chief forecast snow over the valley within a two-week period.[39] A snowstorm covered Squaw Valley with eight inches of snow delaying the opening ceremonies 15 minutes. The artistry of Walt Disney provided spectators with a display of American pageantry. Andrea Mead Lawrence swooped down Little Papoose slope carrying the Olympic torch flown from Norway. She was the first woman to carry the Olympic flame in the Summer or Winter Games. She passed the torch to skater Ken Henry who held it high during a circuit of the 400-meter speed skating oval and then lit the sacred Olympic flame. Carol Heiss became the first woman to recite the Olympic oath on behalf of all the athletes.[40]

In 1960, speed skating was added to the women's Olympic program.

American women entered speed skating and all other events except Nordic skiing. Seven medals were claimed at the 1960 Games, the most ever won by American women. Carol Heiss won the figure skating title. Three silver medals were won in alpine skiing and three bronze medals won by the women in figure skating, pairs skating, and speed skating. Again the Americans claimed both individual figure skating championships with David Jenkins' superb performance. The other gold medal was secured by the best-ever American ice hockey team.[41] The Canadians had dominated ice hockey until 1956 having all but one Olympic championship.

The biathlon, added to the Olympic program in 1960, combines cross-country skiing with rifle marksmanship. In the individual competition, the biathlete skis 20 kilometers while carrying a rifle. The skier stops to shoot at four areas, five times at a target which is 150 meters downrange. At areas one and three the targets are shot from the prone position, while the second and fourth targets are shot from a standing position. Scoring is based on elapsed time over the course and on marksmanship. Penalty time is added for each shot missing the bullseye. Four team members ski a 7.5 kilometer leg in the relay event. Each racer stops to shoot once in a prone position and once standing.[42]

INNSBRUCK, 1964, SIMPLICITY—A RETURN TO REASON

Three years before the Ninth Olympic Winter Games, eighteen members of the United States figure skating team were killed in an airplane crash enroute to the world championships in Prague.[43] The loss of America's best skaters dealt a tragic setback to men's and women's figure skating in the United States. Maribel Vinson Owen, nine times the American figure skating champion and her two daughters, both of whom were skaters, died in the crash. Mrs. Owen's daughter, 16-year-old Laurence, had recently won the United States and North American individual Championships. Twenty-year-old Maribel Owen teamed with Dudley Richards, also on the ill-fated plane and won the American pairs Championships the month before the crash. As a skater and a coach, Maribel V. Owens was outstanding. Her protege, Tenley Albright, had won the 1956 Olympic championship.[44]

The motto for the preparation and conduct of the Ninth Winter Games was "Simplicity—A Return to Reason." The Austrians, determined to be economical and practical, designed the new Olympic facilities with plans to use them in the future.[45] Functional use of Olympic venues upon conclusion of the Games had become a necessity because of the expense of athletic facilities.

Tobogganing or luge was added to the 1964 Olympic Program. Men's singles, women's singles, and the men's two-seater events were approved by the IOC in June, 1961. Neither the American men nor women won medals in the luge event. Luge had not attracted the attention of a large number of athletes in America.

In 1964, the value of cross-country skiing for women was a controversial topic. In spite of divided opinion even among the European countries where the sport was a popular family activity, 35 women from 12 nations entered the 10 kilometer race. American women did not enter cross country skiing.[46] Limited participation by American women in cross country skiing provided no basis for competing in a sport dominated by the Soviet Union whose reputation is widely known for scientifically training athletes at young ages.

Tragedy marred the Innsbruck Games with the deaths of an Australian skier and a British luge racer during pre-Olympic preparations. Additional safety precautions were ordered as a result of the first Winter Olympic deaths.[47] The unfortunate mishaps cast a sad and quiet atmosphere among the athletes at Olympic Village.

There were some encouraging results for two American skaters. Terry McDermott acquired the only gold medal when he won the 500-meter speed skating event. Scott Allen won the sole medal in figure skating with a third place finish in singles.

GRENOBLE, 1968, PEGGY FLEMING EXCELS

When the figure skating competition ended at the 1968 Olympics in Grenoble, the reigning world champion skater, Peggy Fleming from the United States, became the first woman ever to be awarded a unanimous score of 5.9 out of 6.0. One of the most remarkable situations occurred when Jennifer Fish, Dianne Holum, and Mary Myers tied for second place in the 500-meter speed skating event. They were the first competitors from the same country involved in a triple tie and each received a silver medal.

For the second consecutive winter Games, the United States acquired only one gold medal. The seven medals won by Americans were all in skating. Tim Wood's silver medal performance in individual figure skating was incredibly close to the champion's score. Austrian Wolfgang Schwarz scored 1904.1 and Wood's total was 1891.6. The remaining medals were won by defending 500-meter speed skating champion Terry McDermott, who finished second, and Dianne Holum, who finished third in the 1,000-meter speed skating race.[48]

Credit for the speed skater's performances was given to the Olympic development program and the outstanding facilities at West Allis, Wisconsin, site of an Olympic-size refrigerated track in the United States.[49]

While injuries plagued the women Alpine skiers, hopes for high rankings in luge were never high for the Americans. There were no Olympic luge facilities in the United States. A pre-Olympic tour of Europe by the American squad was doomed because of the lack of time. Unseasonably warm weather in Grenoble prevented use of the Olympic run before the Games commenced. The Americans were no match for the experienced Europeans.[50]

SAPPORO, 1972, THREAT OF COMMERCIALISM

In 1972, the Winter Games drew 35 countries and more than 1,000 athletes. Over 3,000 newsmen converged on Sapporo to cover a sporting event which had grown into a major spectacle. Having a population of one million, Sapporo became the largest city ever to host the Winter Olympics.

Prior to the opening of the Eleventh Olympic Winter Games, IOC President Avery Brundage warned athletes of regulations forbidding advertising of any kind. Commercialism, associated with the Winter Games for many years, had resulted in the dismissal of an athlete, which was the first such instance since the Winter Games began. Several Alpine and Nordic skiers were thought to have broken the amateur codes because of alleged payments from sporting goods companies. Only one, Karl Schranz of Austria, was singled out by the IOC and expelled prior to the beginning of the competition.

Avery Brundage was so angered over the commercialism surrounding the skiers that he questioned the continuation of the Winter Games. Nevertheless, the Eleventh Olympic Winter Games were declared open by Emperor Hirohito. A capacity crowd of 50,000 were present for the opening festivities. The climax of the ceremony was the lighting of the torch which had been flown in from Greece. A Japanese girl skated into the speed skating rink and passed the torch to a Japanese boy who raced up the 103 steps and ignited the cauldron.[51]

The well-organized Japanese had completed all of the sports facilities a year before the Games. Enthusiastic support from the government and the people of Sapporo contributed to the successful conduct of the Games, a source of pride for Japan. The athletes and spectators were the beneficiaries of the Japanese enthusiasm.

In 1972, American women for the first time entered all Olympic events. They won seven medals while their male counterparts managed just one medal acquisition with a second place finish in ice hockey. More athletes have chosen summer Olympic events, making the selection pool for the winter sports smaller.

For the first time since 1952 an American woman, Barbara Cochran, won a gold medal in a skiing event. Not since Andrea Mead Lawrence's two championship performances had an American skied so well. By a narrow margin Cochran won the slalom event. A comprehensive development program conducted under the auspices of the United States Ski Association, aided by funds allocated by the United States Olympic Committee Development Fund, produced the first women's Nordic team.

Northbrook, Illinois, was recognized as a producer of Olympic speed skaters. Community interest along with financial support and energetic coach Ed Rudolph yielded a first-rate skating program. Northbrook boasted two outdoor rinks and one indoor rink. Northbrook's Anne Henning finished first in the 500 meter speed skating event and third in the 1,000-meter competition. Dianne Holum, also of Northbrook, won the Olympic title in the 1,500-meter speed skating race and a silver medal in the 3,000-meter event. The Northbrook skaters won half of the United States' eight medals.[52] The remaining bronze medals were won by Janet Lynn in figure skating and Susan Corrock in downhill skiing.

INNSBRUCK, 1976, A MAJOR SPORTING EVENT

Denver, Colorado, was denied financial backing by a state referendum and was forced to withdraw from hosting the Twelfth Olympic Winter Games. Innsbruck again offered to host the Games, and the IOC, led by its new President Lord Killanin of Ireland, granted the request.

Once again, military presence was evident at the Olympic Games. Nearly 5,000 Austrian military troops and policemen, more than twice the number of athletes, were assigned to protect the Games from terrorist attacks which disrupted the 1972 Summer Olympics. By 1976 the Olympic Winter Games had expanded to a representation by 37 nations and 1,054 competitors.[53]

Extravaganza was again abandoned and the Twelfth Olympic Winter Games opened amid "low-key pageantry." Two hundred school children sent up balloons; then a three-gun salute was heard; followed by the release of carrier pigeons. The scene was then set for the lighting of the Olympic flame.[54]

Although the United States team was not recognized as a strong contender for many Olympic championships, the American television audience rose from 27 percent to 35 percent of the viewing audience during the Innsbruck Games. The audience exceeded the American Broadcasting Company's expectations. The network paid over ten million dollars to air the events.[55]

Dorothy Hamill claimed the Olympic figure skating championship in an almost flawless performance. The overall collection of medals by American athletes was again dominated by skaters who won eight of the ten medals. The remaining medals included a bronze laurel in the women's downhill and a silver medal in the men's 30 kilometer cross-country by skier Bill Koch. James Millns and Colleen O'Conner finished third in ice dancing. Ice dancing was first included in the 1976 Olympic program. Speed skater Shelia Young became the first American triple medal winner in a single Olympics. She placed first in the 500-meter, third in the 1,000-meter, and second in the 1,500-meter races.

LAKE PLACID, 1980, ERIC HEIDEN WINS FIVE GOLD MEDALS

The Winter Olympics were held at Lake Placid, a pleasant little mountain town which provided a respite for Americans troubled by the capture of 53 of their countrymen by Iranian terrorists in Tehran, Iran. The occupation of Afghanistan by Soviet military troops brought fears of war but the Games supplanted overtones of conflict with shouts of joy for the incredible collection of five gold medals by Eric Heiden and an ice hockey upset.

For a time the Lake Placid Games were on the verge of a disastrous transportation snarl. Thousands who had purchased tickets to the events waited in freezing temperatures for buses which were sometimes hours late. Some would-be spectators missed events. Nevertheless, skilled athletes with their enthusiasm and eagerness to excel made the Games a splendid spectacle in a festive atmosphere.

ERIC HEIDEN WINS AT EVERY DISTANCE

Nothing in Olympic history rivals the performance of speed skater Eric Heiden. He alone won more gold medals than any American team in previous Winter Olympics since 1932, when the United States claimed six. Before Heiden's appearance in Lake Placid, no man had won more than three gold medals in the Winter Games and no woman had won more than four gold medals since 1964 when Soviet speed skater Lydia Skoblikova performed so well in Innsbruck. The record holder for gold medals is held by American swimmer Mark Spitz, who won seven in 1972, but three were for relays. Heiden's accomplishment is so awesome because he won at every distance from the sprinter's 500 meters to the endurance skater's 10,000-meter event. Foreign coaches marveled at his ability to outskate competitors who specialized at specific distances. Heiden's sister Beth Heiden won a bronze medal in the 3,000 meter event. Hampered by an ankle injury and pressured by the press to excel, Beth Heiden was disappointed in her performance at Lake Placid.

AMERICA'S THIRD OLYMPIC ALPINE MEDAL

American Phil Mahre, who had injured his ankle the year before in Lake Placid on the same Whiteface course, won a silver medal in alpine skiing. Despite skiing with four screws and a metal plate in his ankle, Mahre was just one half second behind Sweden's superb skiier Ingemar Stenmark. Mahre's second place finish made him the third American ever to win an Olympic Alpine skiing medal. His predecessors Billy Kidd and Jimmy Heuga won a silver and bronze respectively at Innsbruck in 1964. After his last descent Mahre went to Stenmark, congratulated him, and the two watched the remainder of the competition.

AN ICE HOCKEY UPSET

Enroute to a final gold medal performance, the American ice hockey team defeated the seemingly unconquerable Soviets by a score of 4 to 3. Partisans in the streets of Lake Placid, as well as the spectators in the skating arena, burst forth with shouts of "USA! USA!" When the American team, comprised of collegiate players, defeated Finland 4 to 2 and won the gold medal, the news spread rapidly across the United States. Steeped in ritual, American sports followers responded in numerous ways. A professional basketball team stopped a game and for the second time in one evening played "The Star Spangled Banner." It was the first ice hockey gold medal since the American victory at Squaw Valley twenty years earlier.

FIGURE SKATING

American Charlie Tickner won the bronze medal in the singles figure skating event while Linda Fratianne won the silver medal in the women's event. Because of an injury, Randy Gardner had to withdraw from the pairs event. Gardner and his partner Tai Babilonia represented America's best chances for a gold medal in the pairs figure skating event. Their withdrawal was a great disappointment to the American crowd and the vast television audience.

Olympic Village, constructed for use as a minimum security prison, was at first disliked by athletes, but the warmth of the Olympic spirit which brought the athletes together improved their feelings. The Games were wonderful despite disappointments such as the withdrawal of the American figure skaters and the loss of a bronze medal by skier Fabienne Serrat of France. Serrat wept when she learned of losing the Giant Slalom race by one hundredth of a second.

SARAJEVO, 1984, THE FIRST AMERICAN DOWNHILL GOLD MEDALIST

The 1984 Olympic Winter Games were awarded to the city of Sarajevo, which was surrounded by mountains and situated in the central part of Yugoslavia. February 7–19, 1984, were the dates chosen for the Olympic competition because climatic statistics had shown that the region had never been registered without snow in February. During the XIV Olympic Winter Games, Sarajevo had been the capital of the Socialist Republic of Bosnia and Herzegovina, one of six republics in the Socialist Federative Republic of Yugoslavia.[56] A decade after the XIV Olympic Winter Games, the republics were divided by a Civil War.

A record 49 National Olympic Committees sent delegations to Sarajevo. The American ice hockey team finished a disappointing seventh and failed to attract much interest from television viewers in the United States. Nevertheless, a number of athletes from the United States recorded outstanding performances and Olympic firsts.

Cocky Bill Johnson accurately predicted that he would win the downhill race in Alpine skiing. Johnson became the first American downhill gold medalist. Twins Phil and Steve Mahre finished first and second in the slalom. Phil Mahre also became the first American man to claim a gold medal in the slalom. Two other Americans won skiing medals. Debbie Armstrong won the giant slalom, while Christin Cooper finished second.

American men had not won a singles figure skating gold medal since 1960 when David Jenkins claimed the Olympic title. Scott Hamilton interrupted the British domination of the event by John Curry and Robin Cousins in the previous two Olympic Winter Games. Hamilton, who had begun skating as therapy for an intestinal disorder, claimed the gold medal in the singles figure skating event. Katarina Witt of the then East Germany won the women's event while Rosalynn Summers of the United States won the silver medal.

CALGARY, 1988, THE FIRST SMOKE-FREE OLYMPICS

During the IOC meeting in Baden-Baden, then in West Germany, the Calgary Olympic Winter Games Organizing Committee submitted a bid to host the 1988 Olympic Winter Games. On September 30, 1981, the IOC chose Calgary, as the site of the XV Olympic Winter Games. The Calgary Organizing Committee had competed against Falun, Sweden and Cortina d'Ampezzo, Italy. The Calgary Committee had submitted three previous bids.

Olympic firsts involving facilities, health, and mascots occurred in Calgary. The speed skating venue on the University of Calgary campus housed the only indoor 400 meter speed skating oval in the world. Calgary Olympic officials considered the health of athletes and spectators when they prohibited smoking in Olympic venues and on Olympic transportation. As a result of this action, Calgary became the first smoke-free Olympics. Hidy and Howdy, the Olympic bears, were the first ever double mascots designated for an Olympic Games. The bears were attired in western outfits depicting the cultural influence of the province of Alberta and the annual Calgary stampede.

Disabled skiing exhibitions were held for men and women in cross country skiing for the blind and in alpine skiing for amputees. Demonstration events included curling, short track speed skating and freestyle skiing.[57] Originally, demonstration sports represented sports indigenous to the country where the Olympics were held and as a means to introduce sports not on the Olympic program. Exhibition sports have had less clearly defined purposes and appear to be at the discretion of the IOC leadership. Olympic Organizing Committees in recent years, particularly those organizing Summer Games, have been less inclined to include sports not a part of the official program. Because of the increasing number of athletes and the added expense, Olympic Organizing Committees have been reluctant to include unofficial sports.

For a decade, Brian Boitano of the United States and Brian Orser of Canada had been figure skating rivals. Both skaters presented superb performances, but Boitano edged out Orser for the gold medal. Katarina Witt defended her Olympic championship while Elizabeth Manley of Canada claimed the silver medal. Debi Thomas of the United States won the bronze medal and became the first African American to win an Olympic

Winter Games medal. Speed skater Dan Jansen, favored to win two gold medals, began a series of disappointments when he fell in the 500 and 1,000 meters races. He skated in the 500 meter event on the day he learned that his sister, Jane had died of leukemia, but had wanted him to compete. Another speed skater and long time friend of Dan Jansen, Bonnie Blair, in her second Olympic Games, exhibited impressive Olympic performances with a gold medal in the 500 meter race and a bronze medal in the 1,000 meters. She was the only athlete from the United States who won two medals. The United States ice hockey team finished in seventh place.

In an embarrassing display of limited athletic ability, Eddie "the Eagle" Edwards of Great Britain barely went down the 70 and 90 meter ski jumps with faltering flights and shaky landings. He was very popular with the spectators and at times drew more attention than Matti Nykanen of Finland, winner of both jumping events. Later, qualifying standards were established to insure high level performances.

The total medal count for the United States was six. Before the Olympic Winter Games had ended, USOC officials knew that a definite plan to improve performances had to be instituted. Some people had overlooked the results of previous Olympic Winter Games. Americans had never dominated the winter competition and had collected the most medals, 12, in 1932 and 1980, when the Games were in Lake Placid. Limited winter sports facilities could not produce a large pool of talented athletes. However, the medal count was considered the primary means of measuring success. The Olympic Overview Commission was created to analyze the operations of the USOC. A year after the formation of the Commission, a report was presented to the USOC. Among the recommendations issued by the Commission was a call for a more efficient governance structure, improved funding, and a reduction in size.[58] As a result of the Commission's recommendations, the USOC adopted a two-tier system of governance consisting of the Board of Directors and Executive Committee. The two-tier system reduced the size of the USOC and has resulted in efficiently conducted meetings. Increased funding has been directed to the preparation of athletes while National Governing Bodies continue to have a voice in the governance structure.

ALBERTVILLE, 1992, WOMEN COLLECTED NINE OF THE ELEVEN MEDALS WON BY UNITED STATES' ATHLETES

Sixty-four delegations participated in the XVI Olympic Winter Games. A world wide television audience and 30,000 spectators awaited the 5,597th Olympic torch bearer. Michel Platini, a soccer star, took the hand of a child and led him up the steps to the cauldron. The boy took the torch and the Olympic flame burst into the night.[59]

By 1992, women were competing in cross country skiing, biathlon, Alpine skiing, luge, figure skating, speed skating, and ice dancing, a discipline of figure skating. The other official Olympic sports, ski jumping, Nordic combined, bobsled, and ice hockey, were approved for only men. The demonstration sports and events in Albertville were open to men and women and included curling, speed skiing, and the three events of moguls, ballet, and aerials in freestyle skiing. Freestyle skiing had formerly been known as "hotdog" skiing. Although some long-time Olympic sports remain open only to men, the IOC, when adding sports and events, has included women's events in order to insure greater gender equity. Women made their first appearance in the biathlon which had been in the Olympics since 1960. Neither men nor women from the United States won medals in the biathlon, however, nine medals were garnered by women in Albertville. Veteran athletes, more USOC funding, and Title IX have benefitted women athletes. Moreover, society's view of women as athletes is far more acceptable than it was two decades ago. These factors contributed to the Olympic preparation and performances of American women.

Three time Olympian, Bonnie Blair, collected two gold medals in speed skating. Another veteran, Cathy Turner, who had retired from her sport a decade before the Albertville Games, made a comeback and won gold and silver medals in short-track speed skating. World champion, Donna Weinbrecht, took first place in the moguls. For the first time since 1976, an American, Kristi Yamaguchi, won a gold medal in figure skating while Nancy Kerrigan won a bronze medal in that event. Skiers, Diann Roffe and Hilary Lindh, won silver medals in the giant slalom and the downhill events.

Paul Wylie won a silver medal in figure skating while the remaining medal claimed by American men in Albertville, was a bronze by mogul skier, Nelson Carmichael. The former Soviet Union competed as the Unified Team and defeated Canada in the finals of the ice hockey championship. The United States finished fourth in the 12 team tournament.

LILLEHAMMER, 1994, THE UNITED STATES SENDS A VETERAN TEAM

The United Nations General Assembly declared 1994, the "International Year of Sport and the Olympic Ideal." The XVII Olympic Winter Games marked the beginning of the new cycle of the Winter Games and a concerted effort on the part of the IOC to emphasize culture and the environment.[60] Norway, the birthplace of skiing, provided a rich backdrop for cultural festivities and a union with the environment. The Lillehammer Olympic Organizing Committee (LOOC) established environmental priorities early in the planning stages of the Games. The selection of sites, construction materials, transportation, and waste collection were based on the environmental impact. For example, plans for the Olympic speed skating venue at Hamar were modified to ensure that the entrance would not interfere with a bird sanctuary.

The Lillehammer Olympic Winter Games attracted 1,738 athletes from 67 countries. Thirteen medals, the most medals ever won by a United States team in Olympic Winter Games competition, were collected in Lillehammer. Just two years separated the Olympic Winter Games in Albertville and Lillehammer and many winter sports athletes decided to extend their sports careers. The 147 member United States delegation included 74 veterans, although just 3 of the 23 ice hockey players were repeat Olympians. Speed skaters, Bonnie Blair and Dan Jansen, made their fourth Olympic Winter Games appearance while 21 other athletes were three-time Olympians.[62]

Tommy Moe became the first American downhill gold medalist since Bill Johnson a decade earlier. Moe also won a silver medal in the super giant slalom. Dan Jansen slipped in the 500 meter race and in his final Olympic race, the 1,000 meter event, he finally climbed to the top of the medal podium to receive his gold medal. Bonnie Blair's Olympic championships in the 500 and 1,000 meters brought her collection of gold medals to five, more than any other American woman in summer or winter competition. Sprinter, Evelyn Ashford, diver, Patricia McCormick, and swimmer, Janet Evans each had won four gold medals.[63]

Short-track speed skating, which had appeared as an official Olympic Winter event for the first time in 1992, involved an amazing series of circumstances for American women. The 3,000 meter relay team had not even qualified for the Olympic competition. The opportunity to enter the Lillehammer competition occurred when North Korean officials withdrew a team and the Australians and Japanese chose not to enter a team. The United States' team finished fourth in the final but moved up to third place and took the bronze medal, after an appeal for interference in the exchange zone was upheld.[63]

During the women's figure skating trials, Nancy Kerrigan was attacked and sustained a leg injury. The husband of Tonya Harding was later convicted of conspiring to injure Kerrigan. Harding won the Olympic trials without competition from Kerrigan. Media throughout the world carried news of the Kerrigan attack and followed both skaters even after they arrived in Lillehammer. Kerrigan narrowly lost to Oksana Baiul of Ukraine and took her second ladies singles silver medal. Tonya Harding finished in sixth place and eventually was implicated in the plot to injure Kerrigan. She was expelled from the United States Figure Skating Association, ending her amateur career.

For the first time, two children were mascots of the Olympic Games. Kristin and Hakon, portrayed by real children, rather than an adult clad in an animal costume, delighted the crowds in Lillehammer. Named after royal children who lived when two warring kingdoms thrived in Norway, they conveyed a cultural message. Symbols and mascots have played an increasingly important role for Olympic Organizing Committees in providing valuable sources of merchandising income.

The Olympic tradition of hosting competition for the disabled was continued when the VI Paralympic Winter Games were held in Norway, following the XVII Olympic Winter Games. Summer competition for the disabled has a longer history and began at the 1960 Paralympic Games in Rome with 400 participants and 23 delegations. By the IX Barcelona Paralympic Games, 4,500 participants and 82 delegations took part in the competition.

NAGANO, 1998, EDUCATION FOR YOUNG PEOPLE

The Mayor of Nagano received the Olympic flag during the closing ceremonies of the XVII Olympic Winter Games in Lillehammer. The transferring of the Olympic flag directed attention to the site of the 1998 Olympic Winter Games. For the third time, a Japanese city had been chosen to host Olympic competition. On March 2, 1994, the Olympic flag arrived in Nagano during a gala celebration which marked the event. Children waving flags of different countries paraded through the city with the Nagano mascots, "Snowlets." The 1998 mascots are collectively called "Snowlets," and are reminiscent of an owl motif. More than 50,000 residents of Nagano welcomed the arrival of the Olympic flag.[64]

In 1992, the IOC, in conjunction with the International Ice Hockey Federation, approved women's ice hockey as a medal sport for the 1998 Nagano Olympic Winter Games.[65] In addition to insuring gender equity, the IOC is interested in promoting Olympic education. A number of National Olympic Committees have provided educators with materials designed to teach young people about the Olympic movement. In keeping with this tradition, the Japanese Ministry of Education, Science and Culture has published a textbook for young people in elementary and junior high schools. The textbook, *Winter Olympic Reader,* explains the meaning of the Olympic Games and offers a timely opportunity for the Nagano Olympic Committee to teach young people about the Olympic movement.

2002, SALT LAKE CITY, THE EIGHTH APPEARANCE OF OLYMPIC COMPETITION IN THE UNITED STATES

On June 16, 1995, the IOC, meeting in Budapest, Hungary, chose Salt Lake City to host the 2002 Olympic Winter Games. After nearly three decades, Salt Lake City Olympic promoters realized their dream and were awarded the XIX Olympic Winter Games. In January, 1995, the IOC reduced the contending cities from nine to four. In addition to Salt Lake City, the IOC voted to consider Sion, Switzerland, Ostersund, Sweden, and Quebec, Canada. The city was determined on the first round of the secret ballot when the required majority was reached. If a majority vote is not reached during the first round, the city receiving the fewest number of votes is eliminated and ballots are cast again. Voting rounds continue until a city receives the majority vote of IOC members. High quality technological capabilities, a sound infrastructure, a feasible financial plan, and a number of completed facilities were among the strengths of the Salt Lake City Organizing Committee.[66] Environmental concerns, which have become a primary consideration, were addressed and also approved by the IOC.

The United States has hosted more Olympic Games than any other country starting with the 1904 Summer Olympics in St. Louis. In 1932, the Olympic Winter Games were held in Lake Placid while the Summer Olympic Games were conducted in Los Angeles. Twenty-eight years later in 1960, the Winter Games were in Squaw Valley and in 1980, the Olympic Winter Games returned to Lake Placid. The 1984 Los Angeles Olympic Games marked the sixth appearance of the Olympic Games in the United States followed by the IOC's selection of Atlanta as the 1996 Summer Olympic site and Salt Lake City as the XIX Olympic Winter Games. The Salt Lake City Olympic Winter Games in 2002 will mark the eighth appearance of the Olympics in the United States.

OLYMPIC TRAINING CENTERS

In December, 1976, the USOC authorized the establishment of regional training centers where athletes possessing the potential to perform in international competition could develop their skills. In addition, training provisions were made for athletes of all ages and levels of ability. In 1977, two training centers were opened. One center was at Squaw Valley, California, site of the 1960 Olympic Winter Games, and the other at Colorado Springs, Colorado, on a former Air Force Base.[67] The USOC closed the Squaw Valley facility in the fall of 1980 because of its higher operational costs. In addition to the Olympic Training Center (OTC) at Colorado Springs, OTCs are at Lake Placid, New York, site of the 1932 and 1980 Olympic Winter Games, and San Diego, California. An Olympic Education Center is located at Northern Michigan University in Marquette, Michigan. The OTCs are operated by the USOC and are made available to athletes selected by their respective National Governing Bodies (NGBs). The NGBs provide transportation expenses to the OTCs for the athletes, coaches, and administrative personnel, while the USOC assumes the expenses of the athletes while they are at the OTCs. Room and board, training facilities, sports medicine, testing and analysis of sports skills, and recreational facilities are made available to athletes.

SUMMARY

When the modern Olympics began in 1896, there were no provisions for winter sports. Men and women participated in figure skating in the 1908 Summer Games in London, but the United States was not represented. In the 1920 Summer Antwerp Games, figure skating and ice hockey were scheduled events in which the United States took part. Eleven hockey players and two figure skaters comprised the American team. Theresa Weld, a figure skater, was the first American woman in Winter Olympic Sports competition.

The 1924 competition at Chamonix was recognized as the first official Olympic Winter Games. Charles Jewtraw became the first American gold medalist in Winter Olympics competition by winning the 500-meter speed skating event.

Twenty-five countries were represented at St. Moritz in the 1928 festival. American skaters Nathaniel Niles and Theresa Weld Blanchard were participating for the third time in Winter Olympic competition. The five-man bobsled team won gold medal honors and the other American entry finished second.

The third Olympic Winter Games was awarded to America's pioneer winter sport resort, Lake Placid. Prior to 1932, figure skating was not widely recognized in the United States but the Games at Lake Placid contributed to increased interest in the sport. For the first time Americans placed second in pairs skating. American men won all four speed skating titles while the women participated in speed skating for the first time as a demonstration sport.

The 1936 Games were held at Garmisch-Partenkirchen where some 1,600 athletes representing 28 nations took part. The United States rejected a call for an Olympic boycott by some individuals and groups, and took part in the competition. The only gold medal won by Americans was in the two-man bobsled race. Alpine skiing was added to the program and American women made their debut in that event.

The Winter Games resumed after the war in 1948 and were hosted by St. Moritz. Scheduled events for women were figure skating, Alpine skiing, and a demonstration of ice dancing. Gretchen Frazer's performance in the slalom event produced America's first gold medal in skiing, and 18-year-old Dick Button became the first American male to capture the singles figure-skating crown. Because of the controversy surrounding the selection of the United States' hockey team, the IOC voted to rule the hockey competition unofficial.

The 1952 Olympic team traveled for the first time by airplane to Oslo, site of the sixth Winter Games. Dick Button was successful in defending his singles championship, and 16-year-old Tenley Albright placed second in women's singles. Andrea Mead Lawrence became the first American woman to win two gold medals in one Winter Olympic festival by capturing the slalom and giant slalom events.

The 1956 Games in Cortina was the site of exquisite figure skating for Americans. Tenley Albright was the first American woman to win a gold medal in figure skating competition. For the first time Americans swept a winter event by capturing all three places in men's singles figure skating. Five of seven medals won by Americans were in figure skating.

An expanded program of events was featured at Squaw Valley, site of the

1960 Games. Speed skating was added to the women's program with the United States represented. Carol Heiss won the figure skating title with American women placing in alpine skiing, figure, pairs, and speed skating. American men captured gold medals in singles figure skating and ice-hockey. The biathlon was a new addition to the 1960 program which combines cross-country skiing and rifle marksmanship.

Three years prior to the Ninth Olympic Winter Games, 18 members of the United States figure skating team were killed in an airplane crash. It dealt a tragic blow to men's and women's figure skating in the United States. Tobogganing or luge was added to the 1964 Innsbruck Olympics program consisting of men's and women's singles, and the men's two-seater events. Tragedy marred the Games with the deaths of an Australian skier and a British luge racer during the pre-Olympic preparations.

At Grenoble in 1968, World Champion Skater Peggy Fleming from the United States became the first woman to be awarded a unanimous score of 5.9 out of a possible 6.0. Second and third place medals were won by American male and female speed skaters. The speed skaters' success was credited to the United States Olympic development program and Olympic-size facilities at West Allis, Wisconsin.

Thirty-five countries were present at the 1972 Games in Sapporo which had grown into a major spectacle. Commercialism had resulted in the dismissal of an athlete which was the first incident of its kind since the Winter Games began. Avery Brundage was angered at the commercialism element and questioned the continuation of the Games. For the first time American women entered all the events and won a total of seven medals.

Innsbruck was again awarded the 1976 Games by the IOC, now led by its new president, Lord Killanin. Because terrorist attacks had disrupted the 1972 summer festival, more than twice the number of policemen to athletes were assigned watch over the representatives from 37 nations. Although the United States team was not a strong contender, the American television audience nevertheless grew from 27 to 35 percent during the Games. Sheila Young was a speed skater who became the first American triple medal winner in a single Olympics.

Impressive American victories were achieved at the 1980 Lake Placid Games in speed skating and ice hockey. Speed skater Eric Heiden won at every distance from 500 to 10,000 meters. Enroute to a gold medal performance, the American ice hockey team defeated the Soviet Union. It was the first gold medal for the American ice hockey team in 20 years.

The 1984 Olympic Winter Games were awarded to the city of Sarajevo and a record 49 National Olympic Committees sent delegations. Bill Johnson became the first American downhill gold medalist. Twins Phil and Steve Mahre finished first and second in the slalom. Scott Hamilton had taken up figure skating as therapy for an intestinal disorder claimed the gold medal in the singles event.

In a fourth bid to host the Olympic Winter Games, Calgary was awarded the honor in 1988. The total medal count for the United States was six. Before the Olympic Winter Games had ended, USOC officials knew that a definite plan to improve performances had to be instituted. The Olympic Overview Commission was created to analyze the operations of the USOC. As a result of the Commission, the USOC adopted a streamlined governance system.

Sixty-four delegations participated in the XVI Olympic Winter Games. By 1992, women were competing in cross country skiing, biathlon, Alpine skiing, luge, figure skating, speed skating, and ice dancing, a discipline of figure skating. The other official Olympic sports, ski jumping, Nordic combined, bobsled, and ice hockey were approved for only men.

The 1994 Olympic Winter Games marked the beginning of the new cycle of the Winter Games and a concerted effort on the part of the IOC to emphasize culture and the environment. The Lillehammer Olympic Organizing Committee established environmental priorities early in the planning stages of the Games. The selection of sites, construction materials, transportation, and waste collection were based on the environmental impact.

Nagano was chosen to host the XVIII Olympic Winter Games and became the third city in Japan to host Olympic competition. In 1964, the Summer Olympic Games were in Tokyo and in 1972 the Olympic Winter Games were held in Sapporo. On June 16, 1995, the IOC chose Salt Lake City to host the 2002 Olympic Winter Games. Salt Lake City Olympic promoters had attempted to host the Olympic Winter Games for nearly three decades.

REFERENCES

1. Cornelius Fellowes. "First to Arrive-the Skaters," *Report of the American Olympic Committee.* Greenwich, Connecticut: Conde' Nast Press, 1920, p. 100.
2. Theresa Weld Blanchard. "The Olympics: 1920, 1924, and 1928," *Skating,* 25 (December, 1947), p. 9.
3. Fellowes. "First to Arrive-the Skaters," *op. cit.* p. 103.
4. "Badger New King of Figure Skaters," *The New York Times,* March 21, 1920, p. 19.
5. Theresa Weld. "The Figure Skating Team," *Report of the American Olympic Committee.* Greenwich, Connecticut: Conde' Nast Press, 1920, p. 104.
6. Weld. *ibid.* p. 104.
7. "American Skaters Sail for Belgium," *The New York Times,* April 8, 1920, p. 13.
8. "Six Hockey Stars Back From Europe," *The New York Times,* May 14, 1920, p. 14.
9. W.A. Wewitt. "Winter Sports," *Canadian Olympic Committee Report,* Hamilton, Ontario, Canada: The Canadian Olympic Committee, 1928, p. 142.
10. "Olympic Speed Skating," *Olympic Sports.* New York: United States Olympic Committee, n.d., p. 111.
11. "900 Athletes Open Olympics in Storm," *The New York Times,* February 12, 1928, sec. X, p. 1.

12. Blanchard. "The Olympics: 1920, 1924 and 1928," *op. cit.* p. 42.
13. "Olympic Bobsled and Luge," *Olympic Sports.* New York: United States Olympic Committee, n.d., p. 39.
14. Maribel Y. Vinson. "Figure Skating Glides into American Favor," *The New York Times,* February 9, 1936, sec. VII, p. 14.
15. George M. Lattimer (ed). "Figure Skating," *Official Report III Olympic Winter Games.* New York: United States Olympic Committee, 1932, p. 213.
16. Richard L. Hapgood. "National Figure Skating Championships," *Olympic News* 5 (February, 1931), p. 3.
17. Asa S. Bushnell and Arthur G. Lentz (eds). "Olympic Winter Games Champions and Medal Winners," *1964 United States Olympic Book.* Providence: Riverhouse Publishing Co., 1964, p. 122.
18. "News Bulletin," *Olympic News* 5 (July–August, 1931), p. 6.
19. "Third Olympic Winter Games Open February 4th," *Olympic News,* 6 (January–February, 1932), p. 4.
20. Bushnell and Lentz. "Olympic Winter Games Champions and Medal Winners," op. cit., pp. 125–126.
21. Frederick W. Rubien. "Complete Record of Olympic Champions 1896–1936," *Report of The American Olympic Committee Games of the XIth Olympiad.* New York: American Olympic Committee, 1936, p. 381, and Bushnell and Lentz (eds), p. 121.
22. Frederick T. Birchall. "Hitler Opens the Winter Olympics: U.S. Defeats Germany in Hockey," *The New York Times,* February 7, 1936, pp. 1, 22.
23. Joel H. Hildebrand. "Report of Manager of 1936 Olympic Ski Team," *Report of the American Olympic Committee.* New York: American Olympic Committee, 1936, p. 337.
24. Alice Damrosch Wolfe. "American Women Skiers at the Olympics," *Report of the American Olympic Committee.* New York: American Olympic Committee, 1936, pp. 345–347.
25. Alice Damrosch Wolfe. "American Skiers at the Olympics," *American Ski Annual.* Brattleboro: Stephen Daye Press, 1936, p. 11.
26. William W. Weigel. "Report of the Manager 1936 Olympic Figure Skating Team," *Report of the American Olympic Committee.* New York: American Olympic Committee, 1936, p. 325.
27. Agnes Wayman. "Let's Take it in Our Stride," *Sportswoman* 10 (March, 1934), p. 14.
28. Walter S. Powell. "1947 Congress of the I.S.U.," *Skating,* 25 (November, 1947), p. 19.
29. Alice Kiaer. "Women's Skiing Report of Team Manager," *Report of the United States Olympic Committee.* New York: United States Olympic Association, 1948, pp. 321–326.
30. James Roach. "U.S. Olympic Body Names Hockey Team," *The New York Times,* January 20, 1948, p. 31.
31. "U.S. Body Adamant in Hockey Quarrel," *The New York Times,* January 20, 1948, p. 31.
32. "Sabotage, Fist Fights and Continued Disputes Peril Winter Olympics' Future," *The New York Times,* January 31, 1948, p. 15.
33. J. Lyman Bingham. "Report of the Chef de Mission," *United States 1952 Olympic Book.* New Haven: Walker-Rackliff Co., 1953, p. 289.

34. Harry E. Radix. "Figure Skating Report of Team Manager," *United States 1952 Olympic Book*. New Haven: Walker-Rackliff Co., 1953, pp. 298, 301.

35. Gretchen Fraser. "Women's Skiing Report of Women's Team Manager," *United States 1952 Olympic Book*. New Haven: Walker-Rackliff Co., 1953, p. 315.

36. "Mrs. Lawrence First American Ever to Win Twice in A Winter Olympics Meet," *The New York Times*, February 21, 1952, p. 32.

37. Fred Tupper. "Tenley Albright and Miss Heiss Finish One, Two in Olympic Figure Skating," *The New York Times*, February 3, 1956, p. 26.

38. Henry M. Beatty. "Figure Skating Report by Chairman," *United States 1956 Olympic Book*. New Haven: Walker-Rackliff Co., 1957, p. 253.

39. "Snowless Squaw Valley Calls on Indian Dances," *The New York Times*, December 5, 1959, p. 29.

40. Gladwin Hill. "Winter Olympics Open Amid Heavy Snow," *The New York Times*, February 19, 1960, pp. 1, 30.

41. Arthur G. Lentz (ed). "United States Medal Winners in Winter Games," *United States 1960 Olympic Book*. New Haven: The Walker Rackliff Co., 1961, p. 197.

42. C. Robert Paul, Jr. "Winter Games," *The Olympian* 2 (December–January, 1975–1976), p. 16.

43. Harry Gilroy. "18 U.S. Skaters Among 73 Dead in a Jet Crash," *The New York Times*, February 16, 1961, p. 1.

44. "3 Owens, All Star Skaters, Die," *The New York Times*, February 16, 1961, p. 19.

45. Harald Lechenperg (ed). "Innsbruck," *Olympic Games 1964*. New York: A.S. Barnes and Co., 1964, p. 11.

46. Harald Lechenperg (ed). "Women's Cross-Country Skiing," *Olympic Games 1964*. New York: A.S. Barnes Co., 1964, pp. 61–62.

47. "Few Call Course Dangerous Despite the Fatality—Girls' Track Shortened," *The New York Times*. January 27, 1964, p. 27.

48. Frederick Fliegner (ed). "X Olympic Winter Games Grenoble, France, February 6–18, 1968," *1968 United States Olympic Book*. Stuttgart: International Olympic Editions, 1969, pp. 301, 302.

49. Frederick Fliegner (ed). "Speed Skating (Men and Women)," *1968 United States Olympic Book*. Stuttgart: International Olympic Editions, 1969, p. 309.

50. Frederick Fliegner, (ed). "Luge," *1968 United States Olympic Book*. Stuttgart: International Olympic Editions, 1969, p. 306.

51. John M. Lee. "Winter Olympics Open in Splendor at Sapporo," *The New York Times*, February 3, 1972, p. 39.

52. Andrew H. Malcum. "Jubilant Despite Sun, Village Salutes Ice Champions," *The New York Times*, February 15, 1972, p. 1.

53. "Games Security Guards to Outnumber Athletes, 2 to 1," *The New York Times*, January 25, 1976, sec. V, p. 3.

54. Fred Tupper. "Low-key Pageantry Marks Start of the Olympics at Innsbruck," *The New York Times*, February 5, 1976, p. 19.

55. Les Brown. "Olympic Games Average 35% of the TV Audience," *The New York Times*, February 11, 1976, p. 91.

56. "Olympic Winter Games Sarajevo 1984," Sarajevo Olympic Organizing Committee, pp. 62, 64–65.

57. "Facts and Information," *Calgary 1988 Olympic Winter Games*, Calgary, Alberta,

Canada, Olympic Winter Games Organizing Committee, 1986, pp. 2, 10, 13, 26.

58. "USOC Overview Commission, February 19, 1989, Portland, Oregon," pp. 1, 2, 21.

59. "A Magic Moment," *Olympic Review,* Mo. 294 (April, 1992), pp. 158–160.

60. Juan Antonio Samaranch. "Nature and Culture," *Olympic Message,* No. 38 (February, 1994), p. 42.

61. "Final Facts and Figures," *Olympic Beat,* 9(April, 1994), p. 6.

62. "Jansen, Blair End Olympic Careers in Glory," *Olympic Beat,* 9(April, 1994), p. 5.

63. "Medal Torch Passed to Short Track Speed Skaters," *Olympic Beat,* 9(April, 1994), pp. 5–6.

64. "The Olympic Flag Arrives," *Olympic Review,* No. 319(June, 1994), p. 231.

65. Darryl Seibel. "Breaking the Ice," *Olympian,* 21(May, June) 1994, p. 33.

66. Denis Echard. "Four Candidates for 2002," *Olympic Review,* No. 25(February, March), pp. 6–7.

67. C. Robert Paul, Jr. and R. Michael Moran (eds). "The National Training Centers," *The Olympic Games.* Colorado Springs: United States Olympic Committee, 1979, p. 8.

INDEX

A

Abbott, C., 320
Abbott, M., 288
Academic standards, 215, 217
Adkins, C., 323
Aerobics (Cooper), 13
African dance, 6, 150, 154–56, 159–60
Agricultural revolution, 70
Ahmann-Leighton, C., 347–48
Albertville, 1992 Olympics, 374–75
Albright, T., 366–67
Allen, S., 368
Amateur Athletic Club, 282
Amateur Athletic Foundation of Los Angeles, 344
Amateur Athletic Union of the United States, 94, 191, 209–10, 287, 291–94, 302, 305, 308, 310, 324, 327–30, 343–44, 365
Amateur Fencer's League of America, 232, 302, 328
Amateur Hockey Association, 365
Amateur Sports Act (1978), 283
Amateurism, 14, 215, 281
America Learns to Play, (Dulles), 172
American Alliance for Health, Physical Education, Recreation, and Dance, 132–33, 135, 146, 166, 241, 252, 256, 328, 347
American Association for the Advancement of Physical Education, 131, 172
American Association for Health, Physical Education and Recreation, 134–35, 181, 183–84
American Badminton Association, 213
American Bowling Congress, 227–28
American Broadcasting Company, 334, 370
American crawl, 304
American Equal Rights Association, 90–91

American Golf, 271
American Physical Education Association, 131, 240–43
American Physical Education Review, 131, 204, 206, 232–34
American Softball Association, 213
American Turf Register and Sporting Magazine, 40, 52, 58
American Turner Topics, 109
American Woman Suffrage Association, 91–92
Amherst College, 199, 201, 207
Amsterdam, 1928 Olympics, 303–06
Amusement parks, 74
Ancient Olympics (*see* Olympics, ancient)
Andersen, R., 331
Anderson, M., 52
Anderson, W., 131, 141–43, 270
Angling (*see* Fishing)
Animal Locomotion, (Muybridge), 77
Anthony, S., 85, 90
Anthropometric measurements, 125–27
Antwerp, 1920 Olympics, 284, 299–300, 358–59, 363
Applebee, C., 142, 238–39
Apollo, 279
Aquatic sports (*see also* Diving; Swimming)
Archery competition, 10–11, 228; in Olympics, 288–89, 291, 331, 337, 340, 347
Arena, 275
Armstrong, D., 372
Art of Gymnastics, The, (Jahn), 99
Ashe, T., 44, 62
Association for the Advancement of Physical Education, 107, 131
Association of Intercollegiate Athletics for Women, 94–95, 256, 262
Ashford, E., 348, 376
Astaire, F., 160
Athens, 1896 Olympics, 286–87